D1583602

Moving Objects Databases

The Morgan Kaufmann Series in Data Management Systems

Series Editor: Jim Gray, Microsoft Research

Moving Objects Databases
Ralf Hartmut Güting and Markus Schneider

Foundations of Multidimensional and Metric Data Structures
Hanan Samet

Joe Celko's SQL Programming Style
Joe Celko

Data Mining, Second Edition: Concepts and Techniques
Ian Witten and Eibe Frank

Fuzzy Modeling and Genetic Algorithms for Data Mining and Exploration
Earl Cox

Data Modeling Essentials, Third Edition
Graeme C. Simsion and Graham C. Witt

Location-Based Services
Jochen Schiller and Agnès Voisard

Database Modeling with Microsft® Visio for Enterprise Architects
Terry Halpin, Ken Evans, Patrick Hallock, Bill Maclean

Designing Data-Intensive Web Applications
Stephano Ceri, Piero Fraternali, Aldo Bongio, Marco Brambilla, Sara Comai, and Maristella Matera

Mining the Web: Discovering Knowledge from Hypertext Data
Soumen Chakrabarti

Advanced SQL: 1999—Understanding Object-Relational and Other Advanced Features
Jim Melton

Database Tuning: Principles, Experiments, and Troubleshooting Techniques
Dennis Shasha and Philippe Bonnet

SQL:1999—Understanding Relational Language Components
Jim Melton and Alan R. Simon

Information Visualization in Data Mining and Knowledge Discovery
Edited by Usama Fayyad, Georges G. Grinstein, and Andreas Wierse

Transactional Information Systems: Theory, Algorithms, and Practice of Concurrency Control and Recovery
Gerhard Weikum and Gottfried Vossen

Spatial Databases: With Application to GIS
Philippe Rigaux, Michel Scholl, and Agnes Voisard

Information Modeling and Relational Databases: From Conceptual Analysis to Logical Design
Terry Halpin

Component Database Systems
Edited by Klaus R. Dittrich and Andreas Geppert

Managing Reference Data in Enterprise Databases: Binding Corporate Data to the Wider World
Malcolm Chisholm

Data Mining: Concepts and Techniques
Jiawei Han and Micheline Kamber

Understanding SQL and Java Together: A Guide to SQLJ, JDBC, and Related Technologies
Jim Melton and Andrew Eisenberg

Database: Principles, Programming, and Performance, Second Edition
Patrick and Elizabeth O'Neil

The Object Data Standard: ODMG 3.0
Edited by R. G. G. Cattell and Douglas K. Barry

Data on the Web: From Relations to Semistructured Data and XML
Serge Abiteboul, Peter Buneman, and Dan Suciu

Data Mining: Practical Machine Learning Tools and Techniques with Java Implementations
Ian Witten and Eibe Frank

Joe Celko's SQL for Smarties: Advanced SQL Programming, Third Edition
Joe Celko

Joe Celko's Data and Databases: Concepts in Practice
Joe Celko

Developing Time-Oriented Database Applications in SQL
Richard T. Snodgrass

Web Farming for the Data Warehouse
Richard D. Hackathorn

Database Modeling & Design, Third Edition
Toby J. Teorey

Management of Heterogeneous and Autonomous Database Systems
Edited by Ahmed Elmagarmid, Marek Rusinkiewicz, and Amit Sheth

Object-Relational DBMSs: Tracking the Next Great Wave, Second Edition
Michael Stonebraker and Paul Brown,with Dorothy Moore

A Complete Guide to DB2 Universal Database
Don Chamberlin

Universal Database Management: A Guide to Object/Relational Technology
Cynthia Maro Saracco

Readings in Database Systems, Third Edition
Edited by Michael Stonebraker and Joseph M. Hellerstein

Understanding SQL's Stored Procedures: A Complete Guide to SQL/PSM
Jim Melton

Principles of Multimedia Database Systems
V. S. Subrahmanian

Principles of Database Query Processing for Advanced Applications
Clement T. Yu and Weiyi Meng

Advanced Database Systems
Carlo Zaniolo, Stefano Ceri, Christos Faloutsos, Richard T. Snodgrass, V. S. Subrahmanian, and Roberto Zicari

Principles of Transaction Processing
Philip A. Bernstein and Eric Newcomer

Using the New DB2: IBMs Object-Relational Database System
Don Chamberlin

Distributed Algorithms
Nancy A. Lynch

Active Database Systems: Triggers and Rules For Advanced Database Processing
Edited by Jennifer Widom and Stefano Ceri

Migrating Legacy Systems: Gateways, Interfaces, & the Incremental Approach
Michael L. Brodie and Michael Stonebraker

Atomic Transactions
Nancy Lynch, Michael Merritt, William Weihl, and Alan Fekete

Query Processing for Advanced Database Systems
Edited by Johann Christoph Freytag, David Maier, and Gottfried Vossen

Transaction Processing: Concepts and Techniques
Jim Gray and Andreas Reuter

Building an Object-Oriented Database System: The Story of O_2
Edited by François Bancilhon, Claude Delobel, and Paris Kanellakis

Database Transaction Models for Advanced Applications
Edited by Ahmed K. Elmagarmid

A Guide to Developing Client/Server SQL Applications
Setrag Khoshafian, Arvola Chan, Anna Wong, and Harry K. T. Wong

The Benchmark Handbook for Database and Transaction Processing Systems, Second Edition
Edited by Jim Gray

Camelot and Avalon: A Distributed Transaction Facility
Edited by Jeffrey L. Eppinger, Lily B. Mummert, and Alfred Z. Spector

Readings in Object-Oriented Database Systems
Edited by Stanley B. Zdonik and David Maier

Moving Objects Databases

Ralf Hartmut Güting
Hagen, Germany

Markus Schneider
Gainesville, Florida, USA

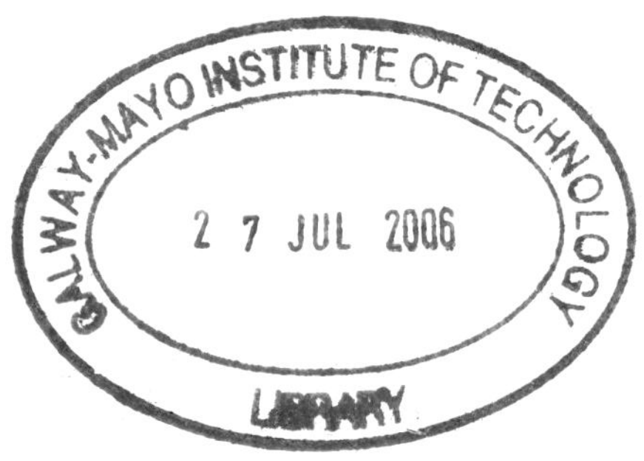

AMSTERDAM • BOSTON • HEIDELBERG • LONDON
NEW YORK • OXFORD • PARIS • SAN DIEGO
SAN FRANCISCO • SINGAPORE • SYDNEY • TOKYO
MORGAN KAUFMANN PUBLISHERS IS AN IMPRINT OF ELSEVIER

Publisher	Diane D. Cerra
Publishing Services Manager	Simon Crump
Project Manager	Andrew Therriault
Editorial Assistant	Asma Stephan
Production Assistant	Melinda Ritchie
Cover Design	Yvo Riezebos Design
Composition	Multiscience Press, Inc.
Copyeditor	Multiscience Press, Inc.
Proofreader	Multiscience Press, Inc.
Indexer	Multiscience Press, Inc.
Interior printer	The Maple-Vail Book Manufacturing Group
Cover printer	Phoenix Color Corp.

Morgan Kaufmann Publishers is an imprint of Elsevier.
500 Sansome Street, Suite 400, San Francisco, CA 94111

This book is printed on acid-free paper.

Library of Congress Cataloging-in-Publication Data
Application submitted.

ISBN-13: 978-0-12-088799-6

ISBN-10: 0-12-088799-1

To Edith, Nils David, and Helge Jonathan

R. H. G.

To Annette, Florian Markus, and Tim Christopher,
and my parents Hans and Christel Schneider

M. S.

Contents

Foreword xv

Preface xvii

Chapter 1 **Introduction 1**

1.1 **Database Management Systems 1**

1.2 **Spatial Databases 3**

1.2.1 Modeling Spatial Concepts 4

1.2.2 Extending Data Model and Query Language 6

1.2.3 Implementation Strategy 9

1.3 **Temporal Databases 9**

1.3.1 Managing Time in Standard Databases 9

1.3.2 The Time Domain 10

1.3.3 Time Dimensions 11

1.3.4 Extending the Data Model 12

1.3.5 Extending the Query Language: TSQL2 19

1.4 **Moving Objects 21**

1.4.1 The Location Management Perspective 21

1.4.2 The Spatio-Temporal Data Perspective 22

1.4.3 Moving Objects and Questions about Them 23

1.4.4 A Classification of Spatio-Temporal Data 23

1.4.5 Temporal Databases with Spatial Data Types 26

1.4.6 Spatio-Temporal Data Types 27

1.5 **Further Exercises 29**

1.6 **Bibliographic Notes 30**

Chapter 2 **Spatio-Temporal Databases in the Past 33**

2.1 **Spatio-Bitemporal Objects 33**

2.1.1 An Application Scenario 33
2.1.2 Bitemporal Elements 35
2.1.3 Spatial Objects Modeled as Simplicial Complexes 36
2.1.4 Spatio-Bitemporal Objects 39
2.1.5 Spatio-Bitemporal Operations 41
2.1.6 Querying 46

2.2 **An Event-Based Approach 48**

2.2.1 The Model 48
2.2.2 Query Processing Algorithms 51

2.3 **Further Exercises 53**

2.4 **Bibliographic Notes 54**

Chapter 3 **Modeling and Querying Current Movement 57**

3.1 **Location Management 57**

3.2 **MOST—A Data Model for Current and Future Movement 59**

3.2.1 Basic Assumptions 59
3.2.2 Dynamic Attributes 60
3.2.3 Representing Object Positions 61
3.2.4 Database Histories 61
3.2.5 Three Types of Queries 62

3.3 **FTL—A Query Language Based on Future Temporal Logic 64**

3.3.1 Some Example Queries 64
3.3.2 Syntax 66
3.3.3 Semantics 68
3.3.4 Evaluating FTL Queries 71

3.4 **Location Updates—Balancing Update Cost and Imprecision 77**

3.4.1 Background 77
3.4.2 The Information Cost of a Trip 78
3.4.3 Cost-Based Optimization for Dead-Reckoning Policies 80
3.4.4 Dead-Reckoning Location Update Policies 82

3.5 **The Uncertainty of the Trajectory of a Moving Object 84**

3.5.1 A Model of a Trajectory 85
3.5.2 Uncertainty Concepts for Trajectories 86
3.5.3 Querying Moving Objects with Uncertainty 88
3.5.4 Algorithms for Spatio-Temporal Operations and Predicates 91

3.6 **Further Exercises 95**

3.7 **Bibliographic Notes 97**

Chapter 4 **Modeling and Querying History of Movement 99**

4.1 **An Approach Based on Abstract Data Types 99**

4.1.1 Types and Operations 99
4.1.2 Abstract versus Discrete Models 102
4.1.3 Language Embedding of Abstract Data Types 104

4.2 **An Abstract Model 105**

4.2.1 Data Types 106
4.2.2 Formal Definition of Data Types 108
4.2.3 Overview of Operations 113
4.2.4 Operations on Nontemporal Types 114
4.2.5 Operations on Temporal Types 121
4.2.6 Operations on Sets of Objects 133

4.3 **A Discrete Model 136**

4.3.1 Overview 136
4.3.2 Nontemporal Types 139
4.3.3 Temporal Types 143

4.4 **Spatio-Temporal Predicates and Developments 150**

4.4.1 Motivation 151
4.4.2 Topological Predicates for Spatial Objects 152
4.4.3 The Problem of Temporally Lifting Topological Predicates 155
4.4.4 Temporal Aggregation 156
4.4.5 Basic Spatio-Temporal Predicates 157
4.4.6 Developments: Sequences of Spatio-Temporal Predicates 159
4.4.7 A Concise Syntax for Developments 162
4.4.8 An Algebra of Spatio-Temporal Predicates 165
4.4.9 Examples 172
4.4.10 A Canonical Collection of Spatio-Temporal Predicates 174
4.4.11 Querying Developments in STQL 177

4.5 **Further Exercises 181**

4.6 **Bibliographic Notes 184**

Chapter 5 **Data Structures and Algorithms for Moving Objects Types 187**

5.1 **Data Structures 187**

5.1.1 General Requirements and Strategy 187
5.1.2 Nontemporal Data Types 188
5.1.3 Temporal Data Types 190

5.2 **Algorithms for Operations on Temporal Data Types 192**

5.2.1 Common Considerations 192
5.2.2 Projection to Domain and Range 195
5.2.3 Interaction with Domain/Range 197
5.2.4 Rate of Change 202

5.3 **Algorithms for Lifted Operations 204**

5.3.1 Predicates 205
5.3.2 Set Operations 208
5.3.3 Aggregation 210
5.3.4 Numeric Properties 211
5.3.5 Distance and Direction 212
5.3.6 Boolean Operations 215

5.4 **Further Exercises 215**

5.5 **Bibliographic Notes 216**

Chapter 6 **The Constraint Database Approach 217**

6.1 **An Abstract Model: Infinite Relations 218**

6.1.1 Flat Relations 218
6.1.2 Nested Relations 223
6.1.3 Conclusion 225

6.2 **A Discrete Model: Constraint Relations 225**

6.2.1 Spatial Modeling with Constraints 225
6.2.2 The Linear Constraint Data Model 229
6.2.3 Relational Algebra for Constraint Relations 230

6.3 **Implementation of the Constraint Model 239**

6.3.1 Representation of Relations 239
6.3.2 Representation of Symbolic Relations (Constraint Formulas) 239
6.3.3 Data Loading and Conversion 240
6.3.4 Normalization of Symbolic Tuples 250
6.3.5 Implementation of Algebra Operations 254

6.4 **Further Exercises 257**

6.5 **Bibliographic Notes 259**

Chapter 7 **Spatio-Temporal Indexing 261**

7.1 **Geometric Preliminaries 262**

7.1.1 Indexing Multidimensional Space with the R-tree Family 262
7.1.2 Duality 266
7.1.3 External Partition Tree 267
7.1.4 Catalog Structure 270
7.1.5 External Priority Search Tree 271
7.1.6 External Range Tree 272

7.2 **Requirements for Indexing Moving Objects 274**

7.2.1 Specifics of Spatio-Temporal Index Structures 274
7.2.2 Specification Criteria for Spatio-Temporal Index Structures 277
7.2.3 A Survey of STAMs in the Past 279

7.3 **Indexing Current and Near-Future Movement 281**

7.3.1 General Strategies 282
7.3.2 The TPR-tree 283
7.3.3 The Dual Data Transformation Approach 292
7.3.4 Time-Oblivious Indexing with Multilevel Partition Trees 299
7.3.5 Kinetic B-trees 301
7.3.6 Kinetic External Range Trees 301
7.3.7 Time-Responsive Indexing with Multiversion Kinetic B-trees 303
7.3.8 Time-Responsive Indexing with Multiversion External Kinetic Range Trees 304

7.4 **Indexing Trajectories (History of Movement) 306**

7.4.1 The STR-tree 307
7.4.2 The TB-tree 310
7.4.3 Query Processing 312

7.5 **Further Exercises 316**

7.6 **Bibliographic Notes 319**

Chapter 8 **Outlook 321**

8.1 **Data Capture 321**

8.2 **Generating Test Data 322**

8.3 **Movement in Networks 323**

8.4 **Query Processing for Continuous/Location-Based Queries 325**

8.5 **Aggregation and Selectivity Estimation 326**

Solutions to Exercises in the Text 329

Bibliography 357

Citation Index 371

Index 375

About the Authors 389

Foreword

How can you represent a hurricane in a database? How can you represent an ocean's waves and currents? How can you represent a fleet of ships operating in that environment? If you have a representation, can it answer the interesting and difficult questions, such as what is the average current and windspeed experienced by these ships? These are challenging spatial database problems—but they are *static*. Now consider the more realistic problem when the hurricane, currents, and ships are moving. How would you structure and index the database and what kind of query language would you provide to answer questions such as: How long will it take each rescue ship and helicopter to arrive at the scene of the emergency?

With the advent of wireless and mobile computing, RFIDs, and sensor networks, it seems that every problem we encounter forces us to deal with objects moving in the 4D universe of space and time. Manufacturing, environmental monitoring, transportation and distribution, emergency services, and telecommunications all have challenging problems in representing and querying databases describing moving objects.

These data representation and data query problems were intractable 15 years ago—each had to be handled manually or approximated. But there has been huge progress in spatial databases, temporal databases, database indexing, and data querying over the last decade. We have learned how to represent 3D objects in compact ways, and have learned how to represent and reason about time and dynamics. The last five years have seen a synthesis of these spatial and temporal ideas into spatio-temporal data types and methods.

This book represents a milestone in that synthesis of temporal and spatial database concepts and techniques. It unifies and organizes the existing research into a coherent whole; and it also presents substantial new results and approaches in many areas. In each case it begins with what is known, then it introduces the new concepts in an abstract and general model, and then it translates the ideas into a pragmatic representation of data structures or SQL-like query language extensions. As such, the book makes both an excellent text and an excellent reference. It also takes you to the frontiers of our understanding, so it is a great point of departure for a new researcher who wants to advance this field.

Ralf Güting and Markus Schneider have been leaders in the unification of spatio-temporal databases. I have been working in an area peripheral to spatio-temporal databases and so was aware of some of the advances. But, in reading the preprint, I found myself saying "Aha!" more than once as each chapter progressed. As Alan Kay observed, "Perspective is worth 100 points of IQ"—meaning that if you look at a problem in the right way, it is easy to understand the problem and the solution. This book has lots of "perspective." I am now eager to apply this perspective to my problems.

Jim Gray
Microsoft Research

Preface

This book is about *moving objects databases*, a relatively new research area that has received a lot of interest in recent years. The general goal of this research is to allow one to represent moving entities in databases and to ask queries about such movements. Moving entities could be cars, trucks, aircraft, ships, mobile phone users, terrorists, or polar bears. For these examples, usually only the time-dependent position in space is relevant, not the extent; hence, we can characterize them as *moving points*. However, there are also moving entities with an extent—for example, hurricanes, forest fires, oil spills, armies, epidemic diseases, and so forth. These we would characterize as *moving regions*.

Moving objects are essentially time-dependent geometries, and database support for them is a specific flavor of *spatio-temporal databases*. The term *moving objects* emphasizes the fact that geometries can now change continuously, in contrast to most of the earlier work on spatio-temporal databases that supported only discrete changes. Note that discrete changes are a special case of continuous developments, and moving objects databases support both.

Some of the interest in this field is spurred by current trends in consumer electronics. Wireless network–enabled and position-aware (i.e., GPS equipped) devices, such as personal digital assistants, on-board units in vehicles, or even mobile phones, have become relatively cheap and are predicted to be in widespread use in the near future. This will lead to many kinds of new applications, such as location-based services. Similarly, big retail companies are moving toward tracking their products by indoor location devices (e.g. using RFID tags). Both trends mean that a huge volume of movement information (sometimes called trajectories) will become available and will need to be managed and analyzed in database systems.

The focus of the book is on the underlying database technology to support such applications. Extending database technology to deal with moving objects means—as for many other nonstandard database applications—to provide facilities in a DBMS data model for describing such entities and to extend the query language by constructs for analyzing them (e.g., for formulating predicates about them). Second, it means that the implementation of a DBMS must be extended. The two major strategies for this are: to build a layer on top of an existing DBMS and so to map moving object representations and predicates to existing facilities of the DBMS or to actually extend the DBMS by providing data structures for moving objects, methods for evaluating operations, specialized indexes and join algorithms, and so forth.

There are two major ways of looking at moving objects in databases: to be interested in maintaining continuously information about the current position and predict near future positions; and to consider whole histories of movements to be stored in the database and to ask queries for any time in the past or possibly the future (if we allow "histories" to include the future). This book treats both perspectives in depth.

Purpose and Audience

This book has three major purposes:

- It is intended as a textbook for teaching graduate students or advanced undergraduates.
- By providing a clear and concise presentation of the major concepts and results in the new field of moving objects databases, it should be interesting to researchers who want to get access to the area.
- Domain experts from industry, such as spatial data analysts, GIS experts, and software developers can obtain an introduction into state-of-the-art research on moving objects databases.

Structure and Organization

Chapter 1 gives an introduction to the theme of the book and briefly describes the essential features of database management systems, spatial database systems, and temporal database systems. It then shows that traditional database technology is unable to model and implement moving objects and that new concepts and techniques are needed. A number of applications are listed that demonstrate the necessity of concepts for moving objects.

Chapter 2 gives an overview of two precursors of today's spatio-temporal models. The first approach is based on a temporal extension of simplicial complexes. The second approach is event-based.

Chapter 3 deals with location management, which is related to current and near-future movements. The most prominent model is the MOST model, whose components and main concepts are described in detail. Additional topics are the query language FTL, based on temporal logic; the problem of balancing update cost and imprecision; and the uncertainty of the trajectory of a moving object.

Chapter 4 describes the authors' approach for modeling and querying histories of movement or evolutions of spatial objects over time. This concept is based on abstract data types that can be embedded as attribute types in database schemas. At two different abstraction levels, we present an abstract model with spatio-temporal data types and operations as well as a discrete model providing finite representations for the types of the abstract model. Additionally, the abstract model is enhanced by a concept of spatio-temporal predicates that can be employed for the formulation of spatio-temporal selections and joins.

Chapter 5 presents data structures and algorithms for the data types and operations of the abstract model. Data structures are designed in the context of, and according to, the needs of database systems. Algorithms are designed for operations on temporal data types and for lifted operations. Lifted operations on moving objects are operations that are derived from static operations on corresponding spatial objects in a certain systematic way.

Chapter 6 deals with the constraint approach for moving objects. As an abstract model for geometric entities in a k-dimensional space, the constraint approach uses infinite relations. A corresponding discrete model is based on constraint relations. Finally, an implementation of the discrete model is described.

Chapter 7 focuses on spatio-temporal indexing. Starting with some needed geometric preliminaries, which make this book independent from other textbooks, requirements for indexing moving objects are introduced. Then, index structures are presented for current and near-future movements as well as for histories of movement.

Chapter 8 provides a brief overview of further research areas in moving objects databases that are beyond the scope of this book.

The text of this book has been used as course material at Fernuniversität Hagen and is designed for self-study. Each chapter provides exercises within the text. The reader is encouraged to work on these exercises when they occur. Solutions can be found at the end of the book. Further exercises are provided at the end of each chapter; these can be used for homework assignments. Each chapter also provides bibliographic notes explaining the sources for the presented material and related work.

Prerequisites and Possible Courses

This book should be accessible to anyone with a general background on the concepts of database systems. A deeper knowledge on the implementation of database systems is helpful but not required. A background on spatial and temporal database systems is useful but not needed; brief introductions to these fields are provided in Chapter 1.

At Fernuniversität Hagen, the material of the book is used in two ways:

- The complete text is used for a one-semester graduate course, covering modeling and implementation issues.

- A short course, focusing only on the modeling aspects, consists of Chapters 1 through 4.

At the University of Florida, the text of the book is currently used for a one-semester, graduate research class in seminar form. After a broad introduction into the field by the instructor, graduate students are assigned chapters for extensive individual study. The bibliographic notes at the end of the chapters lead them to further material. Students have to give a detailed presentation about their assigned topic and write a report. In addition, the class performs a prototypical implementation project together.

Other selections of subsets for short courses are possible:

- A short course on modeling might consist of Chapters 1 through 4, but replace Section 4.4 with Sections 6.1 and 6.2, to include the constraint model.
- The approaches of Chapters 3, 4, and 6 are alternative—hence, can be read in any order or be omitted. To get a balanced view we recommend including at least Chapters 1 and 3 and Sections 4.1 through 4.3.
- Chapter 5 describes the implementation for the model of Chapter 4 (Sections 4.1 through 4.3).
- Section 7.3 describes indexing for current and near-future movement—hence, is related to the model in Chapter 3. Section 7.4 covers indexing of trajectories or histories of movement and is related to the model in Chapter 4. Nevertheless, one can study the indexing problems without detailed knowledge of these chapters.

Acknowledgments

Writing this book is in some way a result of our research work on moving objects databases, and we are most grateful to several of our colleagues with whom we had the pleasure to work. The CHOROCHRONOS project, funded by the European Union in the late 1990s, has been very influential. This was led by Timos Sellis and Manolis Koubarakis; we thank them for their great leadership and organization of the project and for inviting us to participate initially. We greatly enjoyed meetings and discussions with them and the other members of the project—namely, Andrew Frank, Stéphane Grumbach, Christian Jensen, Nikos Lorentzos, Yannis Manolopoulos, Enrico Nardelli, Barbara Pernici, Hans-Jörg Schek, Michel Scholl, Babis Theodoulidis, and Nectaria Tryfona.

The presentation of our own approach in Chapters 4 and 5 is based on joint work and papers with our coauthors, and we owe a great thanks to Martin Erwig, Luca Forlizzi, Enrico Nardelli, Christian Jensen, Jose Antonio Cotelo Lema, Mike Böhlen, Nikos Lorentzos, and Michalis Vazirgiannis. It was a pleasure to collaborate with them and we are proud of the outcome of our joint work.

Special thanks go to Christian Jensen for continued support and advice and to Ouri Wolfson for many interesting discussions and his great hospitality on the occasion of Ralf's visit to Chicago.

Both of us thank the research agencies partially supporting our work: for Ralf this is the DFG (Deutsche Forschungsgemeinschaft), grant Gu293/8-1; and for Markus this is the NSF (National Science Foundation), grant NSF-CAREER-IIS-0347574.

Our book proposal received a warm welcome and later enthusiastic support by Jim Gray and the editors at Morgan Kaufmann Publishers, Rick Adams and Diane Cerra. We are grateful for that and were impressed by the speed and professionalism by which they set up a board of expert reviewers. We thank the reviewers, Ouri Wolfson, Shashi Shekhar, Vassilis Tsotras, Max Egenhofer, Cyrus Shahabi, and Agnès Voisard, for providing careful and critical reviews of the book proposal in an amazingly short period of time. Thanks to all of them for supporting the project and providing many useful suggestions. Some of these suggestions we will only be able to realize in an expanded second edition . . . Thanks also to Ouri Wolfson, Vassilis Tsotras, and Agnès Voisard for providing detailed second-round reviews on selected chapters.

We thank the research assistants, Dirk Ansorge, Helge Bals, Thomas Behr, and Markus Spiekermann at Fernuniversität Hagen, for reading the course material and providing corrections and especially for developing the homework exercises; they did a great job.

We also thank the students at Fernuniversität Hagen who worked through the course and provided feedback and corrections. Here we mention especially Matthias Ruth, Stefan Schmidt, and Marten Jung.

Ralf Hartmut Güting
Hagen, Germany

Markus Schneider
Gainesville, Florida, USA

February, 2005

1 Introduction

The topic of this book is the extension of database technology to support the representation of moving objects in databases, termed *moving objects databases*. This is an exciting new research area, which developed during the second half of the 1990s. Moving objects are basically geometries changing over time; hence, this is a specific flavor of spatio-temporal databases, which, in turn, have their roots in spatial databases, dealing with descriptions of geometry in databases, and temporal databases, addressing the development of data over time. The term *moving objects databases* emphasizes the fact that geometries may now change continuously, in contrast to earlier work on spatio-temporal databases that supported only discrete changes.

In this first chapter, we provide some overview and background. We first review briefly the role of database management systems. This is followed by short introductions to the fields of spatial and temporal databases. We then describe the topic of this book in more depth, explaining different views of moving objects databases and describing classes of moving objects and applications.

1.1 Database Management Systems

Although we assume that you are familiar with the general concepts of database systems, let us briefly review their major aspects.

A *database management system* (DBMS) is a piece of software that manages a *database*, a repository of interrelated data items that are often central to the business of an enterprise or institution. A database is generally used by many diverse applications and multiple users, each of which may need only a fraction of the data. One role of the database is to provide a single representation to all these applica-

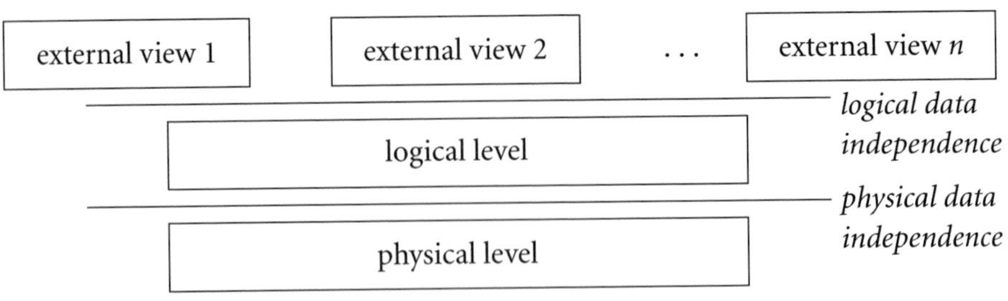

Figure 1.1 The three level architecture.

tions, avoiding redundancies and possible inconsistencies that would occur if each application managed its data separately.

A DBMS provides to applications a high-level *data model* and a related *query and data manipulation language*. The data model is a logical view of how data are organized, which is generally very different from the way data are actually laid out on physical storage media. One of the most popular data models is the relational model, which provides users with the view that data are organized in simple tables. The query language is based on the concepts offered in the data model. For example, in the relational model it is possible to derive new tables from given tables by selecting rows with certain properties or a subset of the columns.

The separation between the logical view of data given in the data model and the actual physical representation is called the principle of *data independence*, one of the most fundamental contributions of DBMS technology. In the three-level architecture for database systems, a widely accepted architectural model, data independence actually occurs at two different levels (Figure 1.1). Here the physical level describes how data are organized on storage media; the logical level defines data in terms of the data model mentioned previously, and the top level offers each application its own view of a part of the data from the logical level, possibly transformed in some way. Physical data independence means that we can reorganize the physical organization of data without affecting the representation at the logical level, and logical data independence allows us to change the logical level to some extent without affecting the view of data of specific applications. It is the task of the DBMS to map efficiently between the levels. In particular, the *query optimizer* component needs to transform queries posed at the logical level into efficient access plans at the physical level.

Data in a database are a valuable resource, and one major functionality of the DBMS is to protect data from being corrupted. To this end, changes to a database performed by an application are encapsulated within *transactions*; either all of the changes within a transaction are applied to the database or none of them is applied, so that a transaction transforms a database from a consistent state to another consistent state. The DBMS manages concurrent access to the database by multiple applications and isolates them from each other; changes performed within a transaction T become visible to all other applications only after transaction T is completed. The DBMS also keeps track of all physical changes performed during a transaction and is able to recover the consistent state before the transaction in most cases of failure (e.g., if the application software or even the DBMS itself crashes, and even in many cases of hardware failure).

Other aspects of data protection include facilities in the data model to formulate *integrity constraints*, rules about certain relationships between data items that need to hold, and the management of *access rights* for various user groups.

The classical database management systems were conceived for relatively simple business applications. For example, the data types available for attribute types in the relational model are simple: basically integers, floating-point numbers, or short text strings. One goal of database research in the last two decades has been to widen the scope, so that as much as possible any kind of data used by any application can be managed within a DBMS, described by a high-level data model, and accessed by a powerful query language. For example, we would like to store images, geographic maps, music, videos, CAD documents, data from scientific experiments, meteorological measurements, and so on. For all these kinds of data, we are interested in appropriate extensions of data model and query language, so that any kind of question about these data can be formulated in a manner as simple as possible and be answered efficiently (i.e., *fast*) by the DBMS. For example, we would like to retrieve images containing shapes similar to a given one ("find the images containing an airplane") or produce a map of the distribution of rainfall over some terrain.

With respect to the topic of this book, moving objects databases, we observe the following limitations of classical databases and the standard relational model.

1. We would like to represent geometric shapes, such as the region belonging to a country. There is no reasonable way to do this, except for very simple objects such as points, for which the coordinates can be represented in numeric attributes.
2. We would like to represent the development of entities over time. But because the data represented in a database generally reflect the current state of the world, there is no easy way to talk about the past.
3. We would like to represent objects moving around right now or in the past. For currently moving objects, this would mean that positions are continuously updated, which is not really feasible.

These limitations are addressed in the following three sections.

1.2 Spatial Databases

The goal of spatial database research has been to extend DBMS data models and query languages to be able to represent and query geometries in a natural way. The implementation of a DBMS needs to be extended by corresponding data structures for geometric shapes, algorithms for performing geometric computations, indexing techniques for multidimensional space, and extensions of the optimizer (translation rules, cost functions) to map from the query language to the new geometry-related components.

The major motivation for studying spatial databases is the support of geographic information systems (GIS). Early GIS made only limited use of DBMS technology—for example, by storing nonspatial data in a DBMS but managing geometries separately in files. However, spatial database technology has matured, so now all the major DBMS vendors (e.g., Oracle, IBM DB2, Informix) offer spatial extensions. Hence, it is easier now to build GIS entirely as a layer on top of a DBMS (i.e., store all the data in the DBMS).

While GIS have been the major driving force, spatial databases have a wider scope. Besides geographic space, there are other spaces of interest that may be represented in a database, such as:

- The layout of a VLSI design (often a large set of rectangles)
- A 3D model of the human body
- A protein structure studied in molecular biology

An important distinction concerns *image databases* and *spatial databases.* Although geographic space can be represented by images obtained by aerial photographs or satellites, the focus of spatial DBMS is to represent entities in space with a clearly defined location and extent. Image databases manage images as such. Of course, there are connections. For example, feature extraction techniques can be used to identify spatial entities within an image that can be stored in a spatial database.

1.2.1 Modeling Spatial Concepts

What are the entities to be stored in a spatial database? Considering geographic space, obviously anything qualifies that might appear on a paper map—for example, cities, rivers, highway networks, landmarks, boundaries of countries, hospitals, subway stations, forests, corn fields, and so forth.

To model these diverse entities, we can offer concepts to model *single objects* and *spatially related collections of objects.*

For modeling single objects, three fundamental abstractions are *point*, *line*, and *region*. A *point* represents (the geometric aspect of) an object, for which only its location in space, but not its extent, is relevant. Examples of point objects are cities on a large-scale map, landmarks, hospitals, or subway stations. A *line* (in this context always meaning a curve in space) is the basic abstraction for moving through space, or connections in space. Examples of line objects are rivers, highways, or

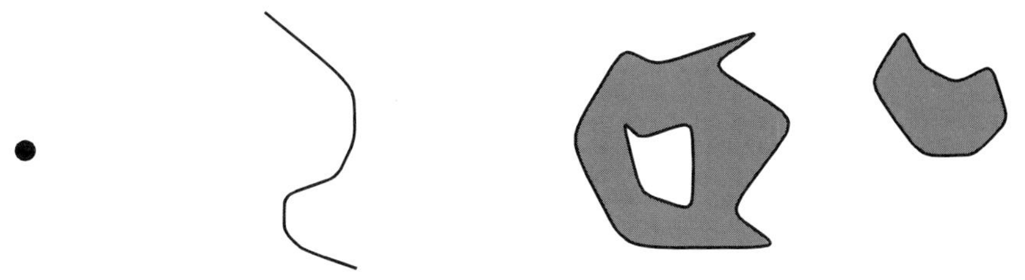

Figure 1.2 The three basic abstractions: point, line, and region.

telephone cables. Finally, a *region* is the abstraction for an entity having an extent in the 2D space. A region may in general have holes and consist of several disjoint pieces. Examples of region objects are countries, forests, or lakes. The three basic abstractions are illustrated in Figure 1.2.

The two most important instances of spatially related collections of objects are *partitions* (of the plane) and *networks*. A *partition* (Figure 1.3) can be viewed as a set of region objects that are required to be disjoint. The adjacency relationship is of particular interest—that is, there are often pairs of region objects with a common boundary. Partitions can be used to represent so-called thematic maps.

A *network* (Figure 1.4) can be viewed as a graph embedded into the plane, consisting of a set of point objects forming its nodes and a set of line objects describing the geometry of the edges. Networks are ubiquitous in geography—for example, highways, rivers, public transport, or power supply lines.

We have mentioned only the most fundamental abstractions that are supported in a spatial DBMS. For example, other interesting spatially related collections of objects are nested partitions (e.g., a country partitioned into provinces partitioned into districts, etc.) or a digital terrain (elevation) model.

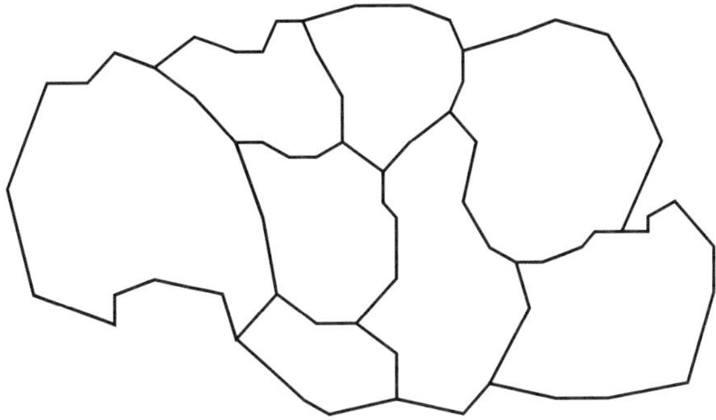

Figure 1.3 A partition.

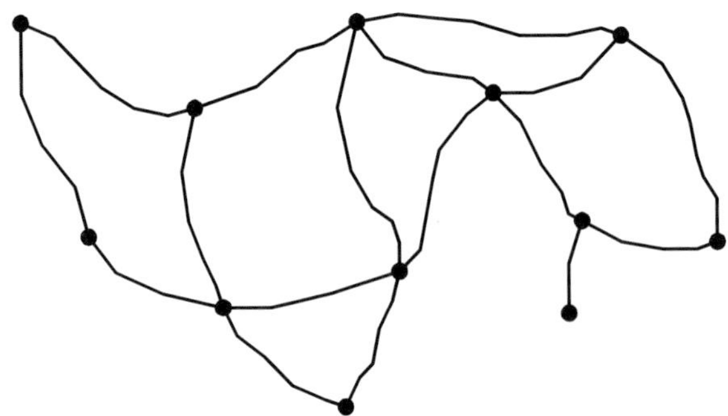

Figure 1.4 A network.

1.2.2 Extending Data Model and Query Language

We now consider how the basic abstractions can be embedded into a DBMS data model. For the single object abstractions, point, line, and region, it is natural to introduce corresponding abstract data types, or *spatial data types* (SDTs). An SDT encapsulates the structure—for example, of a region—with operations. These may be predicates (e.g., testing whether two regions are adjacent or one is enclosed by the other); operations constructing new SDT values (e.g., forming the difference of two regions or the intersection of a line with a region); numeric operations, such as computing the area of a region or the distance between a point and a line; or operations on sets of SDT values (e.g., aggregating a collection of regions into a single region or finding in a collection of points the one closest to a query point).

A collection of spatial data types with related operations forms a *spatial algebra*. Important issues in the design of such algebras are closure under operations and completeness. The data types should be chosen carefully so that closure can be achieved. For example, the intersection of two line values yields in general a set of

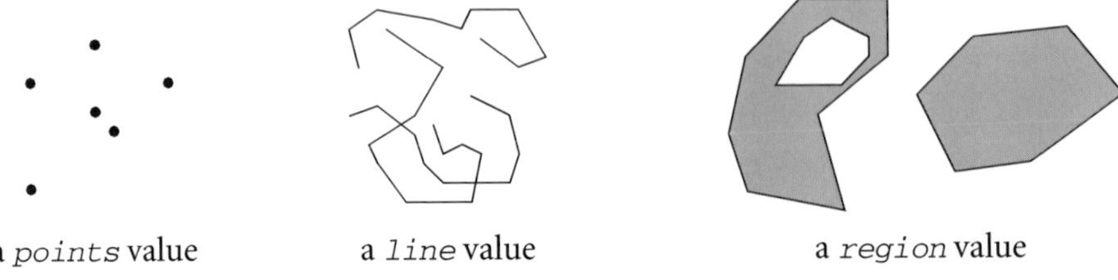

Figure 1.5 The spatial data types `points`, `line`, and `region`.

points,[1] and the difference of two regions, even if each argument is a simple region without holes, may yield a region consisting of several disjoint components containing holes. An algebra with nice closure properties, the ROSE algebra, offers data types called `points`, `line`, and `region`,[2] whose structure is illustrated in Figure 1.5. Here type `points` offers a set of points, type `line` a set of polylines, and type `region` a set of polygons with holes. So we can offer operations such as

intersection:	*line* × *line*	→ *points*
minus:	*region* × *region*	→ *region*
contour:	*region*	→ *line*
sum:	*set*(*line*)	→ *line*
length:	*line*	→ *real*

Once spatial data types are defined, they can be embedded into a DBMS data model in the role of *attribute types*. Hence, in addition to the standard types, such as *int*, *real*, and *string*, we may have spatial types: *points*, *line*, and *region*. These types can be used in any kind of DBMS data model; it does not matter whether it is relational, object oriented, or something else. In a relational setting we may have relations to represent cities, rivers, and countries—for example:

```
cities (name: string, population: int, location: points)
rivers (name: string, route: line)
highways (name: string, route: line)
states (name: string, area: region)
```

Queries can then be formulated by using SDT operations on spatial attributes within a standard query language such as SQL. Let us assume that predicates are available:

inside:	*points* × *region*	→ *bool*
adjacent:	*region* × *region*	→ *bool*

We can then formulate queries:

What is the total population of cities in France?

[1] There may also be line values in the intersection, if there are overlapping parts of the argument lines. These will normally be returned by another operation.
[2] Actually the names used for the second and third data type in the ROSE algebra are *lines* and *regions*. We rename them here to be consistent with later parts of the book.

```
SELECT SUM(c.pop)
FROM cities AS c, states AS s
WHERE c.location inside s.area AND s.name = 'France'
```

Return the part of the river Rhine that is within Germany.

```
SELECT intersection(r.route, s.area)
FROM rivers AS r, states AS s
WHERE r.name = 'Rhine' AND s.name = 'Germany'
```

Make a list, showing for each country the number of its neighbor countries.

```
SELECT s.name, COUNT(*)
FROM states AS s, states AS t
WHERE s.area adjacent t.area
GROUP BY s.name
```

Exercise 1.1 Formulate the following queries, using SQL and data type operations. In each case, first define new SDT operations, if necessary, and then write the query.

1. How many people live within 10 kilometers from the river Rhine? (Cities are modeled as points; hence, if the point is within that distance we count the whole population.)
2. With which of its neighbor countries does Germany have the longest common border?
3. Find the locations of all bridges of highways crossing rivers. Return them as a relation with the name of the highway, the name of the river, and the location.

You may use the following notations in formulating queries.

Assignments. The construct `LET <name> = <query>` assigns the result of a query to a new object called *name*, which can then be used in further steps of a query.

Multistep Queries. A query can be written as a list of assignments, separated by semicolons, followed by one or more query expressions. The latter are the result of the query.

Defining Derived Values. We assume that arbitrary ADT operations over new and old data types can occur anywhere in a WHERE clause and can be used in a SELECT clause to produce new attributes, with the notation `<expression> AS <new attrname>`. ■

1.2.3 Implementation Strategy

To implement such a model, obviously we need data structures for the types and algorithms implementing the operations. Moreover, we need to support selection and join by spatial criteria. For selection, specialized index structures are needed. One popular candidate is the R-tree, which hierarchically organizes a set of rectangles. The actual SDT values (e.g., `region`) are represented in such an index by their minimum bounding rectangle (*MBR*, also called *bounding box*). To support spatial join, there are also specialized algorithms available, some of which make use of spatial indexes.

To integrate these components into a DBMS, an extensible DBMS architecture is needed. The DBMS should offer interfaces to register components such as the following:

- Data structures for the types
- Algorithms for the data type operations
- Spatial index structures with appropriate access methods
- Spatial join methods
- Cost functions for all methods, for use by the query optimizer
- Statistics about the distribution of objects in space, needed for selectivity estimation
- Extensions of the optimizer (e.g., in the form of translation rules)
- Registration of types and operations in the query language
- User interface extensions to handle presentation of spatial data, possibly input of spatial values for querying

Such extensible architectures have been investigated in research since about the mid-1980s. In the past few years, some of these capabilities have become available in commercial systems. In particular, extensibility by attribute data types and operations is well understood; we can add such an algebra as a *data blade*, *cartridge*, or *extender* in the various systems. Extensibility by index structures and extensions of the query optimizer are a much more thorny issue, but limited capabilities of this kind have also been realized.

1.3 Temporal Databases

1.3.1 Managing Time in Standard Databases

The databases managed by standard DBMS normally describe the current state of the world as far as it is known in the database. A change in the current state of the world will be reflected a bit later in some update to the database, after which the previous state is lost.

Of course, for many (perhaps most) applications, it is not sufficient to maintain just the current state; they need to keep track of some kind of history. In a standard DBMS this is possible, if the application manages time itself, by adding explicit time attributes and performing the right kind of computations in queries. For example, suppose a company has an employee table of the form:

```
employee (name: string, department: string, salary: int)
```

If the company wishes to keep track of previous departments and salaries for its employees, the table may be extended:

```
employee (name: string, department: string, salary: int,
start: date, end: date)
```

Standard DBMS offer a very limited support for this in the form of data types such as `date` or `time` (discussed later in this section).

However, dealing with time in this form by the application is difficult, error prone, and leads to complex query formulations and often inefficient query execution. For example, in a join of two tables extended by time attributes as shown previously, it is necessary to make sure that only tuples with overlapping time intervals are joined, by adding explicit conditions in the query. These conditions are several inequalities on the time attributes. A standard DBMS is often not very good at handling inequalities in query optimization (focusing more on equi-joins)—hence, an inefficient execution may result. In contrast, if true temporal support is built into the DBMS, this can be done automatically; no conditions are needed in the query, and execution will be tuned to perform this kind of join very efficiently.

The goal of temporal database research has been to integrate temporal concepts deeply into the DBMS data model and query language and to extend the system accordingly to achieve efficient execution.

1.3.2 The Time Domain

First of all, let us consider how time itself can be modeled. Time is generally perceived as a one-dimensional space extending from the past to the future. There are some options: The time space can be viewed as *bounded* or *infinite*. A bounded model assumes some origin and also an end of time.

Time can be viewed as *discrete*, *dense*, or *continuous*. Discrete models are isomorphic to the natural numbers or integers. Dense models are isomorphic to either the rationals or the reals: between any two instants of time another instant exists. Continuous models are isomorphic to the real numbers. While most people perceive time as being continuous, for practical reasons temporal database models often use discrete representations of time. In contrast, later in this book continuous models will be used, since this is more appropriate for dealing with moving objects.

In the continuous model, each real number corresponds to a "point in time"; in the discrete model, each natural number corresponds to an "atomic" time interval called a *chronon*. Consecutive chronons can be grouped into larger units called *granules* (e.g., hours, weeks, years).

We can also distinguish between *absolute* and *relative* time (also called *anchored* and *unanchored* time, respectively). For example, "January 22, 2002, 12:00 P.M." is an absolute time, and "three weeks" is a relative time.

These concepts of time can be captured in a number of data types:

- `instant`, a particular chronon on the timeline in the discrete model or a point on the timeline in a continuous model.
- `period`, an anchored interval on the timeline.
- `periods`, a set of disjoint anchored intervals on the timeline, usually called a *temporal element* in the literature. We call the type `periods` to be consistent with later parts of the book.
- `interval`, a directed, unanchored duration of time—that is, a time interval of known length with unspecified start and end instants.

Some additional more "practical" data types, present in the SQL-92 standard, are:

- `date`, a particular day from a year in the range 1 through 9999 A.D.
- `time`, a particular second within a range of 24 hours
- `timestamp`, a particular fraction of a second (usually a microsecond) of a particular day

1.3.3 Time Dimensions

We now turn to the semantics of the time domain. While many different semantics can be thought of, the two most important "kinds" of time are the so-called *valid time* and *transaction time*. The *valid time* refers to the time in the real world when an event occurs or a fact is valid. The *transaction time* refers to the time when a change is recorded in the database or the time interval during which a particular state of the database exists.

In this context, standard databases are called *snapshot databases*; those dealing with valid time only are called *valid-time* or *historical databases*; those handling only transaction time are called *transaction-time* or *rollback databases*; and those treating both kinds of time are called *bitemporal databases*. The term *temporal database* refers to a model or system offering any kind of time support.

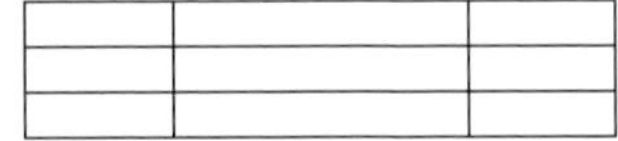

Figure 1.6 A snapshot relation.

The four kinds of databases are illustrated in Figures 1.6 through 1.9. Figure 1.6 shows a simple standard relation with three tuples and three attributes, now called a snapshot relation. As usual, rows of the table represent tuples; columns correspond to attributes.

Figure 1.7 introduces the valid-time dimension. We can see that for each of the three tuples there are different versions for certain valid-time intervals in the past. Indeed, there is a fourth tuple that is not valid at the current time.

Figure 1.8 shows the transaction-time dimension. Here, a first transaction has inserted three tuples into the relation. A second transaction has added a fourth tuple. Then, the third transaction has deleted the second and inserted yet another tuple.

Finally, Figure 1.9 shows a bitemporal relation. Here, an initial transaction creates two tuples valid from now on. The second transaction modifies the value of the second tuple and inserts a third one, also valid from now on. The third transaction deletes the second and the third tuple from the database (indicated by the gray shading, so these tuples are no longer valid). In addition, it changes the start time of the second tuple (presumably the previous start time was wrong). The first tuple is still valid.

Note that what is represented in the figures is the content of the respective database at the current time. For example, in the transaction-time figures we can access all the previous states of the database.

1.3.4 Extending the Data Model

The question now is how time can be incorporated into the DBMS data model. The general approach in temporal databases has been to consider elements of the DBMS

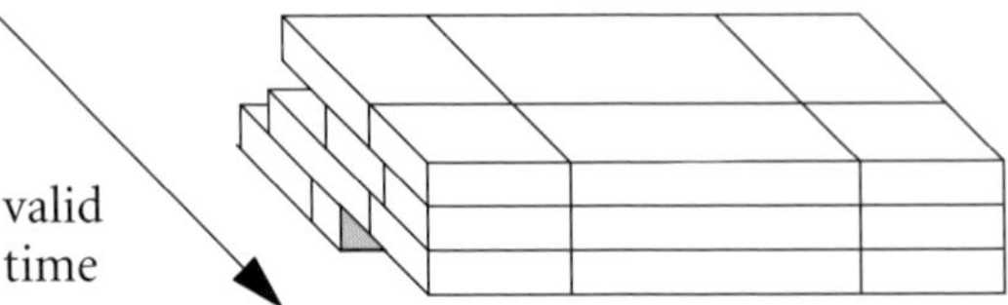

Figure 1.7 A valid-time relation.

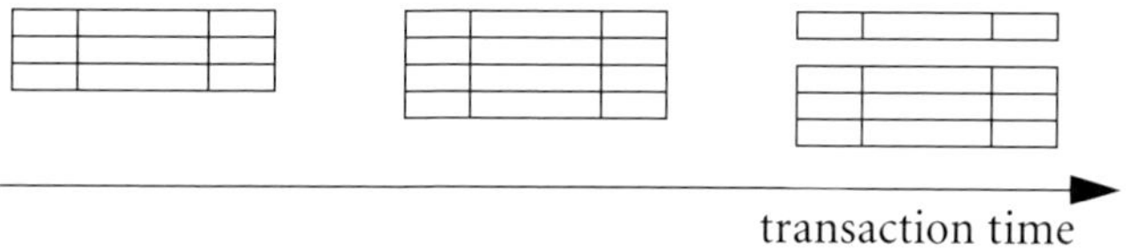

Figure 1.8 A transaction-time relation.

data model (e.g., tuples) as *facts* and to associate elements of the time domain with them to describe when facts are valid (*timestamps*). There are some choices:

- The data model extended: the most important choices are *relational* and *object-oriented* models.
- The granularity of facts: the most relevant are *tuples/objects* and *attributes.*
- The kind of timestamp used: a single chronon (`instant`), single time interval (`period`), set of time intervals = temporal element (`periods`).
- The time dimension: support of *valid time*, *transaction time*, or *bitemporal.*

A vast number of data models have been proposed in the literature (around 40 according to Zaniolo et al., 1997, Part II: Temporal Databases [see Bibliography]) that can be classified along these criteria. We show only a few of them in Table 1.1. Most of these models are relational. Some of them are mentioned only in one field of the table, even though they do address both time dimensions. The name mentioned in the table is either the name of the model or of the author proposing it; details can be found in the bibliographic notes at the end of the chapter.

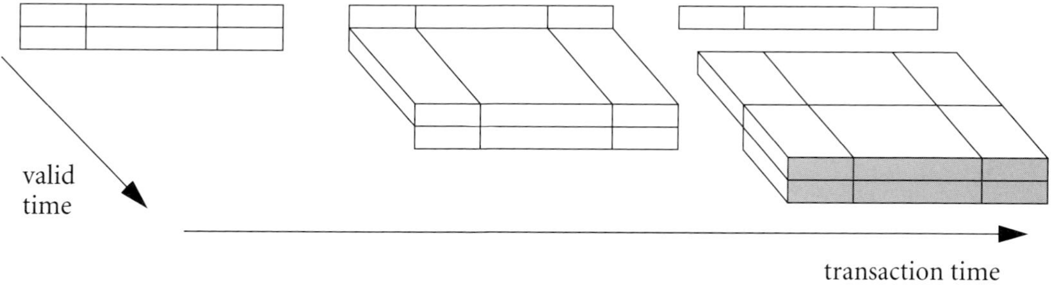

Figure 1.9 A bitemporal relation.

Table 1.1 Classification of temporal data models.

		Instant	*Period*	*Temporal Element*
Valid time	Timestamped attribute values	Lorentzos	Tansel	HRDM
	Timestamped tuples	Segev	Sarda	BCDM
Transaction time	Timestamped attribute values	Caruso	—	Bhargava
	Timestamped tuples	Ariav	Postgres	BCDM

We now discuss a few representative models using a very simple example. The first model, by Segev, timestamps tuples with the instant when they became valid. The example in Table 1.2 describes the history of two employees, Lisa and John, working in different departments during a particular month, say, January 2002. On January 1, Lisa started to work in the toys department. On January 8, she moved to the books department. She returned to the toys department on January 14 and quit the company on January 16. John started to work on the January 11 in the books department and still works there. In this model, a separate tuple with null values in all non-key attributes is required to record termination of a valid-time interval.

The next model, by Sarda, uses period timestamps. In this model, the same information appears as shown in Table 1.3. Here, null values are not needed any-more. The symbol "∞" denotes "forever" in valid time (i.e., an end of the valid-time period is not yet known).

Instead of tuples, it is also possible to timestamp attribute values. In the historical relational data model, HRDM, attribute values are functions from time into

Table 1.2 Model by Segev.

Name	*Department*	*Time*
Lisa	Toys	1
Lisa	Books	8
Lisa	Toys	14
Lisa	Null	17
John	Books	11

Table 1.3 Model by Sarda.

Name	*Department*	*Time*
Lisa	Toys	[1–7]
Lisa	Books	[8–13]
Lisa	Toys	[14–16]
John	Books	[11–∞]

some domain (Table 1.4). Here, the whole employment history can be represented in two tuples, one for each value of the key attribute.

Exercise 1.2 Mr. Jones takes a trip from London to Edinburgh on December 5, where he stays at the Grand Hotel for three nights. On December 8, he decides that the Grand Hotel is too expensive and moves to a cheaper place called Traveler's Inn, where he spends another week. On December 15, after the business part of his trip is finished, he starts a short skiing vacation in the ski resort of Aviemore, where he spends a weekend staying at the Golf Hotel. On Sunday, December 17, he goes back home.

In the meantime, his wife Anne finds it boring to stay at home alone, so on December 7 she visits her friend Linda in Brighton and stays with her for five days. On December 12, she goes back home. On December 16, she visits her parents and stays with them for a while. Today, on December 20, she is still there.

Represent this information in the data models by Segev, Sarda, and the HRDM, starting on December 5. ■

Table 1.4 HRDM.

Name	*Department*
1 → Lisa ... 16 → Lisa	1 → Toys ... 7 → Toys 8 → Books ... 13 → Books 14 → Toys ... 16 → Toys
11 → John 12 → John ...	11 → Books 12 → Books ...

These three models have dealt with valid time only. We extend our previous example to a bitemporal one by considering how information about Lisa and John was recorded in the database. This happened in the following transactions:

1. On January 6, the administration was informed that Lisa had started to work in the toys department on January 1 and was going to work there until January 15.
2. On January 10, it became known and entered into the database that Lisa had moved to the books department on January 8. She was still expected to work until January 15.
3. On January 12, it was decided that Lisa would move back to toys on January 14 and would stay there a while longer, until January 20. Also, it became known that a new employee, John, had started the day before in the books department.
4. On January 20, it was entered that Lisa had actually quit the company on January 16.

An illustration of the bitemporal space is shown in Figure 1.10. Here, transaction time is on the horizontal axis and valid time on the vertical axis. The left part of the figure shows the state of the database after the second transaction; the right side shows the final state. An arrow to the right indicates that this information is valid with reference to transaction time "until changed." An upward arrow indicates an unknown end of interval with reference to the valid time. Note that by drawing a vertical line in such a diagram, we can see what was known in the database at that

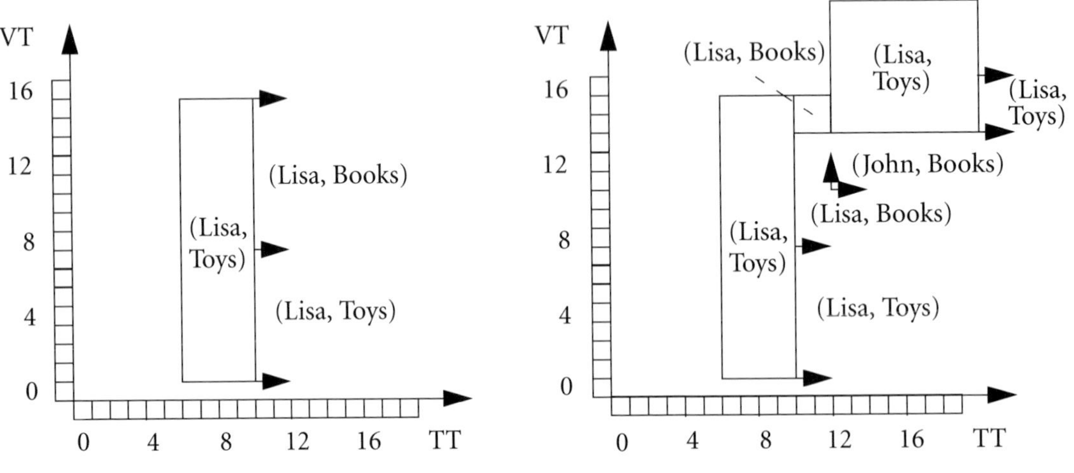

Figure 1.10 Bitemporal space.

Table 1.5 Bhargava's model.

Name	*Department*
$[6, 9] \times [1, 15]$ Lisa	$[6, 9] \times [1, 15]$ Toys
$[10, uc] \times [1, 13]$ Lisa	$[10, uc] \times [1, 7]$ Toys
$[10, 11] \times [14, 15]$ Lisa	$[10, uc] \times [8, 13]$ Books
$[12, 19] \times [14, 20]$ Lisa	$[10, 11] \times [14, 15]$ Books
$[20, uc] \times [14, 16]$ Lisa	$[12, 19] \times [14, 20]$ Toys
	$[20, uc] \times [14, 16]$ Toys
$[12, uc] \times [11, \infty]$ John	$[12, uc] \times [11, \infty]$ Books

particular time. For example, at the current time (say, January 20) we have the same information about employment history as in the valid-time tables.

The model by Bhargava is a bitemporal model using attribute-value timestamping. A timestamp is a rectangle in the bitemporal space. Here, our example (Figure 1.10, right) looks as shown in Table 1.5. The value *uc* ("until changed") denotes an open-ended interval in transaction time.

Exercise 1.3 We extend the example from Exercise 1.2 by considering what Anne's mother Jennifer knew about the locations of her daughter and her son-in-law (of course, she calls him by his first name, Keith). We start on December 1. On this day, Jennifer assumed both of them to be at home as they had been before. Her knowledge was then changed by the following events:

1. On December 6, Anne called her on the phone and told her that Keith had yesterday gone on a business trip to Edinburgh. He would stay there for two weeks. She herself was planning to visit Linda for a week, starting tomorrow.
2. On December 13, Anne called again and told her that she was already back home since yesterday.
3. On December 16, Anne arrived. What a pleasant surprise!
4. On December 19 she received a postcard from Keith in Aviemore, describing his skiing vacation. He wrote that he had arrived on Friday (yesterday), and would go home tomorrow.

Draw figures of the bitemporal space corresponding to Jennifer's knowledge, as of December 13 and 19. Draw separate figures for Keith and Anne, since otherwise figures get too crowded. ■

Table 1.6 BCDM (at time 20).

Name	*Department*	*Time*
Lisa	Toys	{(6, 1), ..., (6, 15), ..., (9, 1), ..., (9, 15), (10, 1), ..., (10, 7), ..., (19, 1), ..., (19, 7), (*uc*, 1), ..., (*uc*, 7), (12, 14), ..., (12, 20), ..., (19, 14), ..., (19, 20), (*uc*, 14), ..., (*uc*, 16)}
Lisa	Books	{(10, 8), ..., (10, 13), ..., (19, 8), ..., (19, 13), (*uc*, 8), ..., (*uc*, 13), (10, 14), (10, 15), (11, 14), (11, 15)}
John	Books	{(12, 11), (12, 12), ..., (12, ∞), (13, 11), ..., (13, ∞), ..., (19, 11), ..., (19, ∞), (*uc*, 11), ..., (*uc*, ∞)}

The final model we mention here is the bitemporal conceptual data model BCDM. This model uses tuple timestamping. Timestamps are bitemporal elements that are finite sets of bitemporal chronons. No two value-equivalent tuples are allowed in a relation instance; hence, the complete history of any given fact is represented in a single tuple. In this model, our example bitemporal database looks as that shown in Table 1.6.

So, the BCDM simply enumerates all the bitemporal chronons forming the bitemporal element of a tuple. This seems like an unnecessarily large representation. However, the purpose of the BCDM is not to determine an efficient representation but rather to have simple semantics. The idea is that this model is then mapped in an implementation to some more space-efficient representation. For example, we can compute a minimal decomposition of the temporal element into rectangles, similar to Bhargava's model.

If you look at the translation from Figure 1.10 to Table 1.6 in detail, some questions come up. How is the translation of open-ended time intervals involving the symbols "∞" (in valid time) and "*uc*" (in transaction time) done? We have stated previously that temporal elements are *finite* sets of chronons, so how can this be achieved?

The answer is as follows. The BCDM uses a *bounded* model of time. For valid time this is a set of chronons $\{t_1, ..., t_k\}$, where t_1 is the origin of time and t_k the end of time, assumed to lie in the past and the future, respectively. For transaction time it is the set of chronons $\{t'_1, ..., t'_l\} \cup \{uc\}$. A valid-time interval $[t_j, \infty]$ is therefore interpreted as a set of chronons $\{t_j, ..., t_k\}$. For transaction time, things are slightly more subtle. The value *uc* is assumed to move with the current time. At time t'_m = *now* a transaction-time interval $[t'_j, uc]$ is interpreted as the interval $[t'_j, ..., t'_{m-1}, uc]$. At every tick of the clock, the bitemporal elements in a relation instance are updated by adding new chronons for the current time. Therefore, it is important to state in Table 1.6 that we consider the relation instance at time 20. For the tuple

(John, Books), at this time, the transaction-time chronons are {12, 13, ..., 19, *uc*}. At time 21 they will be {12, 13, ..., 19, 20, *uc*}.

1.3.5 Extending the Query Language: TSQL2

As an example of a temporal query language we consider TSQL2, which is based on the BCDM data model. It was designed jointly by a committee of 18 researchers who had proposed temporal models and query languages earlier. TSQL2 is a superset of SQL-92 and has also been incorporated into the SQL3 standard.

In TSQL2 a bitemporal relation can be defined as follows. As a richer example, let us assume we wish to represent prescriptions in a doctor's database, recording for each patient which drugs were prescribed for which period of time. This can be done by a data definition command:

```
CREATE TABLE prescription (
  name char(30),
  drug char(30),
  dosage char(30),
  frequency interval minute)
AS VALID STATE DAY AND TRANSACTION
```

Here, `name` is the name of the patient, `frequency` the number of minutes between drug administrations. The clause `as valid state day and transaction` says this is a *bitemporal state relation*, where the granularity with reference to the valid time is one day. For the transaction time, the granularity is system dependent, something like milliseconds.

There are six different kinds of relations in TSQL2:

- Snapshot relations
- Valid-time state relations (specified: `as valid state`)
- Valid-time event relations (`as valid event`)
- Transaction-time relations (`as transaction`)
- Bitemporal state relations (`as valid state and transaction`)
- Bitemporal event relations (`as valid event and transaction`)

The difference between *state* and *event* relations is that a state relation records facts that are true over certain periods of time, whereas an event relation records events that occurred at certain instants of time. Each tuple records a kind of event and is timestamped with the instants when this event occurred. An event relation might record the days when a patient visited the doctor:

```
CREATE TABLE visit (
  name char(30))
AS VALID EVENT DAY AND TRANSACTION
```

Let us now formulate a few queries. First of all, it is possible to get an ordinary relation from a (bi)temporal relation by using the keyword `snapshot`.

Who has ever been prescribed any drugs?

```
SELECT SNAPSHOT name
FROM prescription
```

This returns an ordinary (snapshot) relation containing the names of all patients who ever were prescribed drugs.

In contrast, the normal behavior of queries is to return the complete history with respect to valid time, assuming a version of the database (transaction time) as of *now*. In other words, the evaluation is based on our current knowledge of the past.

Which drugs were prescribed to Lisa?

```
SELECT drug
FROM prescription
WHERE name = 'Lisa'
```

will return a valid-time relation containing one tuple for each drug that Lisa was prescribed, associated with one or more maximal periods when Lisa was taking that drug. Note that in the prescription relation, after selecting for the name Lisa and the current time, there may be several tuple instances for a given drug, with different dosage and frequency values. These are all merged into a single tuple, joining their respective periods of valid time. This is an important operation in temporal databases called *coalescing*.

Which drugs have been prescribed together with aspirin?

```
SELECT p1.name, p2.drug
FROM prescription AS p1, prescription AS p2
WHERE p1.drug = 'aspirin' AND p2.drug <> 'aspirin'
  AND p1.name = p2.name
```

Here, the correlation variables `p1` and `p2` can be bound to pairs of tuples from `prescription`; it is automatically ensured that the valid-time intervals of these tuples overlap. The result is a set of tuples containing the name of a patient and a drug, together with the maximal periods of time when both that drug and aspirin were prescribed to the patient.

So far, the timestamp of result tuples was determined by the intersection of the timestamps of the argument tuples. This default can be overridden by a *valid-clause.*

Which drugs was Lisa prescribed during 1999?

```
SELECT p.drug
VALID INTERSECT(VALID(p), PERIOD '[1999]' DAY)
FROM prescription AS p
WHERE p.name = 'Lisa'
```

The intersect operation is applied to two intervals—namely, the valid-time interval of the tuple and the year 1999, specified as an interval of days. Result tuples will have valid-time intervals restricted to the time interval of that intersection.

We can also go back to some earlier state of the database: What did the physician believe on September 10, 1998, was Lisa's prescription history?

```
SELECT drug
FROM prescription AS p
WHERE name = 'Lisa'
  AND TRANSACTION(p) OVERLAPS DATE '1998-09-10'
```

In fact, there is a default predicate on transaction time that was implicitly appended to all the earlier queries:

```
TRANSACTION(p) OVERLAPS CURRENT_TIMESTAMP
```

This should suffice to illustrate a few of the capabilities of a temporal query language such as TSQL2. The language is powerful, and quite complex queries are possible.

1.4 Moving Objects

The goal of research on moving objects databases is to extend database technology so that any kind of moving entity can be represented in a database, and powerful query languages are available to formulate any kind of questions about such movements. In this section, we look at the motivation for this research in more detail, and consider examples of moving objects and questions one might ask about them.

There are actually two different approaches leading to the idea of moving objects databases, which can be described as the *location management* perspective and the *spatio-temporal data* perspective.

1.4.1 The Location Management Perspective

This approach considers the problem of managing the positions of a set of entities in a database—for example, the positions of all taxicabs in a city. At a given instant of time, this is no problem. We might have a relation with a taxi ID as a key and attributes for x- and y-coordinates to record the position. However, taxis are moving around. To keep the location information up-to-date, the position has to be updated frequently for each taxicab. Here we encounter an unpleasant trade-off. If updates are sent and applied to the database very often, the error in location information in the database is kept small, yet the update load becomes very high. Indeed, to keep track of a large set of entities, this is not feasible any more. Conversely, if updates are sent less frequently, the errors in the recorded positions relative to the actual positions become large.

This led to the idea of storing in the database for each moving object not the current position but rather a *motion vector*, which amounts to describing the position as a function of time. That is, if we record for an object its position at time t_0 together with its speed and direction at that time, we can derive expected positions for all times after t_0. Of course, motion vectors also need to be updated from time to time, but much less frequently than positions.

Hence, from the location management perspective, we are interested in maintaining dynamically the locations of a set of currently moving objects and in being able to ask queries about the current positions, the positions in the near future, or any relationships that may develop between the moving entities and static geometries over time.

Note that from the point of view of temporal databases, what is stored in such a location management database is not a temporal database at all; it is a snapshot database maintaining the current state of the world. No history of movement is kept. We will consider moving objects databases based on the location management perspective in Chapter 3.

1.4.2 The Spatio-Temporal Data Perspective

Here, the approach is to consider the various kinds of data that might be stored in a (static) spatial database and to observe that clearly such data may change over time. We wish to describe in the database not only the current state of the spatial data but also the whole history of this development. We would like to be able to go back in time to any particular instant and to retrieve the state at that time. Moreover, we would like to understand how things changed, analyze when certain relationships were fulfilled, and so forth.

Two basic questions come up:

1. Which kinds of data are stored in spatial databases?
2. Which kinds of change may occur?

For the first question, we have seen in Section 1.2.1 that spatial databases support abstractions for single objects such as *point*, *line*, or *region*, as well as spatially related collections of objects among which *networks* and *partitions* are the most relevant.

Regarding kinds of change, a major distinction concerns *discrete changes* and *continuous changes.*

Classical research on spatio-temporal databases has focused on discrete changes for all the spatial entities mentioned previously. In contrast, continuous changes are the topic of this book, and this is what is usually meant by the term *moving object.*

While discrete changes occur on any kind of spatial entity, continuous changes seem most relevant for *point* and *region.*[3] Hence, a *moving point* is the basic abstraction of a physical object moving around in the plane or a higher-dimensional space, for which only the position, but not the extent, is relevant. The *moving region* abstraction describes an entity in the plane that changes its position as well as its extent and shape (i.e., a moving region may not only move but also grow and shrink).

1.4.3 Moving Objects and Questions about Them

Let us look at some examples of moving entities and possible questions about them. We consider moving points (Table 1.7) and moving regions (Table 1.8). With the exception of countries, all of them change continuously. Whether they have been or can be observed continuously is a different issue, discussed later.

Clearly, there are many kinds of interesting moving entities, and one can ask questions about them ranging from simple to very complex. The goal of moving objects database research is to design models and languages that allow us to formulate these questions in a simple yet precise way.

1.4.4 A Classification of Spatio-Temporal Data

In Tables 1.7 and 1.8, we have emphasized entities capable of continuous movement. Nevertheless, there are also many applications involving spatial data that change only in discrete steps. To understand the scope of the more traditional spatio-temporal database research, let us introduce a classification of time-dependent point and region data.

Spatio-temporal data can be viewed in a natural way as being embedded in a space that is the cross-product of the original spatial domain and of time. Here we consider 2D space and restrict attention to a single time dimension—namely, valid time. Hence data "live" in a 3D space, as illustrated in Figure 1.11.

[3] It seems much harder to think of examples of continuously moving lines, networks, or partitions, although such examples can certainly be found.

We now characterize application data with respect to their "shape" in this 3D space, obtaining the following categories:

1. *Events in space and time—(point, instant)*. Examples are: archaeological discoveries, plane crashes, volcano eruptions, earthquakes (at a large scale where the duration is not relevant).
2. *Locations valid for a certain period of time—(point, period)*. Examples are: cities built at some time, still existing or destroyed; construction sites (e.g., of buildings, highways); branches, offices, plants, or stores of a company; coal mines, oil wells, being used for some time; or "immovables," anything that is built at some place and later destroyed.

Table 1.7 Moving points and questions.

Moving Point Entities	*Questions*
People: politicians, terrorists, criminals	■ When did Bush meet Arafat? ■ Show the trajectory of Lee Harvey Oswald on November 22, 1963.
Animals	■ Determine trajectories of birds, whales, . . . ■ Which distance do they traverse, at which speed? How often do they stop? ■ Where are the whales now? ■ Did their habitats move in the last 20 years?
Satellites, spacecraft, planets	■ Which satellites will get close to the route of this spacecraft within the next four hours?
Cars: taxi cabs, trucks	■ Which taxi is closest to a passenger request position? ■ Which routes are used regularly by trucks? ■ Did the trucks with dangerous goods come close to a high-risk facility?
Airplanes	■ Were any two planes close to a collision? ■ Are two planes heading toward each other (going to crash)? ■ Did planes cross the air territory of state X? ■ At what speed does this plane move? What is its top speed? ■ Did Iraqi planes pass the 39th degree?
Ships	■ Are any ships heading toward shallow areas? ■ Find "strange" movements of ships, indicating illegal dumping of waste.
Military vehicles: rockets, missiles, tanks, submarines	■ All kinds of military analyses.

3. *Set of location events—sequence of (point, instant)*. Entities of class (1) when viewed collectively. For example, the volcano eruptions of the last year.
4. *Stepwise constant locations—sequence of (point, period)*. Examples are: the capital of a country; the headquarters of a company; the accommodations of a traveler during a trip; the trip of an email message (assuming transfer times between nodes are zero).
5. *Moving entities—moving point*. Examples are: people, planes, cars, and so on; see Table 1.7.

Table 1.8 Moving regions and questions.

Moving Region Entities	*Questions*
Countries	▪ What was the largest extent ever of the Roman Empire? ▪ On which occasions did any two states merge (e.g., reunification)? ▪ Which states split into two or more parts? ▪ How did the Serb-occupied areas in former Yugoslavia develop over time? When was the maximal extent reached?
Forests, lakes	▪ How fast is the Amazon rain forest shrinking? ▪ Is the Dead Sea shrinking? ▪ What is the minimal and maximal extent of river X during the year?
Glaciers	▪ Does the polar ice cap grow? Does it move? ▪ Where must glacier X have been at time Y (backward projection)?
Storms	▪ Where is the hurricane heading? When will it reach Florida?
High/low pressure areas	▪ Where do they go? Where will they be tomorrow?
Scalar functions over space (e.g., temperature)	▪ Where has the 0-degree boundary been last midnight?
People	▪ Movements of the Celts in the second century B.C.
Troops, armies	▪ Hannibal traversing the Alps. Show his trajectory. When did he pass village X?
Cancer	▪ Can we find in a series of X-ray images a growing cancer? How fast does it grow? How big was it on June 1, 1995?
Continents	▪ History of continental shift
Diseases	▪ Show the area affected by mad cow disease for every month in 1998.
Oil spills	▪ Which parts of the coast will be touched tomorrow?

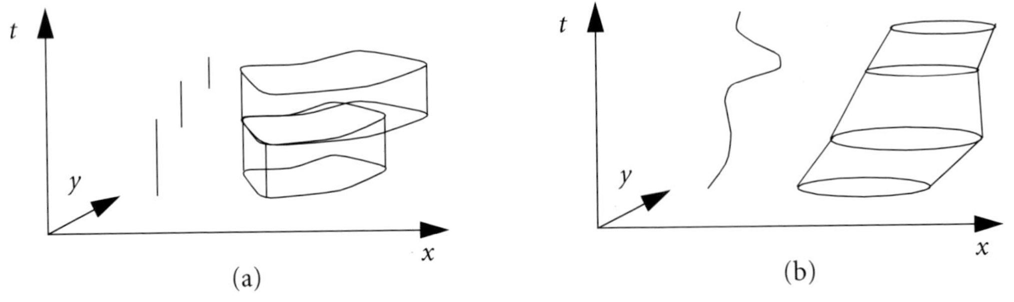

Figure 1.11 Discretely changing point and region (a); continuously changing point and region (b).

6. *Region events in space and time—(region, instant)*. For example, a forest fire at large scale.
7. *Regions valid for some period of time—(region, period)*. Example: an area closed for a certain time after a traffic accident.
8. *Set of region events—sequence of (region, instant)*. Example: the Olympic games viewed collectively, at a large scale.
9. *Stepwise constant regions—sequence of (region, period)*. Examples are: countries, real estate (changes of shape only through legal acts), agricultural land use, and so on.
10. *Moving entities with extent—moving region*. Examples are: forests (growth); forest fires at small scale (i.e., we describe the development); people in history; see Table 1.8.

These classes of data will be useful to characterize the scope of two approaches to spatio-temporal modeling that are described next.

1.4.5 Temporal Databases with Spatial Data Types

A straightforward idea to deal with spatio-temporal applications is the following: Use any temporal DBMS with its system-maintained tuple timestamps and enhance it by spatial data types. For example, assuming the TSQL syntax from Section 1.3.5 and the spatial data types from Section 1.2.2, we might create a table for real estate:

```
CREATE TABLE real_estate (
  owner char(30),
  area region)
AS VALID STATE DAY
```

Such a table would manage discretely changing regions, as shown in Figure 1.11(a). We can ask queries combining the features of the temporal query language with operations on spatial data types: show the properties adjacent to the property of Charles Smith as of March 17, 1977:

```
SELECT r2.area
FROM real_estate AS r1, real_estate AS r2
WHERE r1.owner = 'Charles Smith' AND
  VALID(r1) OVERLAPS DATE '[1977-03-17]' AND
  r1.area ADJACENT r2.area
```

This is something like the cross-product of spatial and temporal databases. Capabilities of spatial and temporal systems are combined without any specific integration effort. This approach is natural, and it appears that its technology is already well understood, since techniques from both fields can be used. Considering the classification of Section 1.4.4, this approach can support classes 1 through 4 and 6 through 9 of spatio-temporal data. However, it cannot deal with moving objects, classes 5 and 10.

In Chapter 2, we consider this approach in more detail, studying two representative data models.

1.4.6 Spatio-Temporal Data Types

An alternative idea is to extend the strategy used in spatial databases to offer abstract data types with suitable operations: In this case we offer *spatio-temporal data types*, such as moving point (type `mpoint` for short) or moving region (`mregion`). A value of such a data type captures the temporal development of a point or a region over time. Hence, a value of type `mpoint` is a continuous function *f*: `instant` → `point`, and a value of type `mregion` is a continuous function *g*: `instant` → `region`. Geometrically, such values correspond to the 3D shapes shown in Figure 1.11(b). As in spatial databases, such types can be embedded into relational or other DBMS data models. Here, we can describe the real estate data of the previous subsection as:

```
real_estate (owner: char(30), area: mregion)
```

This is possible since a data type capable of describing continuous movement can also describe discrete changes. However, with this approach it is also possible to describe truly continuous changes and have relations describing the movements of airplanes or storms:

```
flight (id: string, from: string, to: string, route: mpoint)
weather (id: string, kind: string, area: mregion)
```

The data types include suitable operations such as:

intersection:	*mpoint* × *mregion*	→ *mpoint*
distance:	*mpoint* × *mpoint*	→ *mreal*
trajectory:	*mpoint*	→ *line*
deftime:	*mpoint*	→ *periods*
length:	*line*	→ *real*
min:	*mreal*	→ *real*

We discover quickly that in addition to the main types of interest, *mpoint* and *mregion*, related spatial and temporal as well as other time-dependent types are needed. For example, the distance between two moving points is a real valued function of time, captured here in a data type *mreal* ("moving real"). These operations have the following meaning: **Intersection** returns the part of a moving point whenever it lies inside a moving region, which is a moving point (*mpoint*) again. **Distance** was mentioned previously. **Trajectory** projects a moving point into the plane, yielding a *line* value. **Deftime** returns the set of time intervals when a moving point is defined, a *periods* value, as introduced in Section 1.3.2. **Length** returns the length of a *line* value, and **min** yields the minimal value assumed over time by a moving real.

Given such operations, we may formulate queries:

Find all flights from Düsseldorf that are longer than 5,000 kms.

```
SELECT id
FROM flight
WHERE from = 'DUS' AND length(trajectory(route)) > 5000
```

Retrieve any pairs of airplanes, which, during their flight, came closer to each other than 500 meters!

```
SELECT f.id, g.id
FROM flight AS f, flight AS g
WHERE f.id <> g.id AND min(distance(f.route, g.route)) < 0.5
```

At what times was flight BA488 within the snowstorm with ID S16?

```
SELECT deftime(intersection(f.route, w.area))
FROM flight AS f, weather AS w
WHERE f.id = 'BA488' AND w.id = 'S16'
```

Clearly, the approach using spatio-temporal data types can manage continuous as well as discrete changes and support all 10 classes of spatio-temporal data discussed in Section 1.4.4. On the other hand, time is not managed "automatically" by the system, as in the temporal databases in Section 1.3. We will consider this approach in more detail in Chapter 4.

1.5 Further Exercises

Exercise 1.4 Arctic Expedition

Mr. Jones is going to do an expedition in an arctic region. The exact schedule, which he made together with the crew from Alpha Station on June 12, looks as follows:

- June 12: preparation for the expedition at Alpha Station
- June 13–15: crossing White Plains
- June 16: arrival at Beta Station
- June 17–20: crossing Snowy Mountains
- June 21: arrival at Gamma Station, documenting the trip

According to schedule, Mr. Jones's team departs from Alpha Station on June 13. Due to heavy snowfall, the team doesn't manage to get through to Beta Station in time. On June 15, Mr. Jones contacts Alpha Station using his radio transmitter and informs it that he will arrive one day later and that the schedule must be corrected by one day (all stations are connected and therefore this information is also available to the other stations now). On June 17, the team finally arrives, rests for a day, and leaves on June 18.

On the way over the mountains, the team encounters a heavy snowstorm again. Unfortunately, Mr. Jones loses the radio transmitter during that storm on June 19. Gamma Station realizes that the contact is lost but can't send a rescue team because of the heavy storm.

The rescue team, which unfortunately is not equipped with a mobile transmitter, departs from Gamma Station on June 21. Its plan is to follow the direct route to Beta Station within four days and to arrive there on June 24. At that time the team assumes that Mr. Jones is still somewhere in the mountains and must be found.

Surprisingly, Mr. Jones's team returns to Beta Station safely on June 23. On his arrival, Mr. Jones tells the station's crew that after he lost the radio transmitter on June 19, the team tried to head forward to Gamma Station but was forced to stop because of the storm. The team camped in the mountains for one day (June 20) and then decided to go back to Beta Station. He also tells the crew that his new plan is to go to Gamma Station together with the rescue team from June 26 to June 29.

Finally, both teams arrive there in time. Gamma Station submits this joyful message to everybody. After documenting the expedition, Mr. Jones sends last greetings to all stations and leaves.

Draw separate figures of the bitemporal space corresponding to the knowledge of Alpha Station about Mr. Jones's team and to the knowledge of the rescue team about Mr. Jones's team.

1.6 Bibliographic Notes

In Section 1.1, we briefly discussed database systems in general. Of course, there are many good books, of which we can mention only a few. Some good books are Garcia-Molina et al., 2002; Elmasri and Navathe, 2003; Kifer et al., 2005.

A very good book on spatial databases has appeared recently (Rigaux et al., 2002); other good books include Shekhar and Chawla, 2003; Worboys and Duckham, 2004; Laurini and Thompson, 1992. Spatial database technology as available in the Oracle System is described in Kothuri et al., 2004.

Section 1.2 is based on the survey article by Güting, 1994a. The ROSE algebra and its implementation is described in Güting and Schneider, 1995; Güting et al., 1995.

A good book that summarizes many of the research results in temporal databases up to 1993 is Tansel et al., 1993. A nice, shorter introduction to temporal databases, on which Section 1.3 is based, can be found in Zaniolo et al., 1997, Part II: Temporal Databases. The language TSQL2 is described in detail in Snodgrass, 1995. There is also a survey article on temporal databases (Özsoyoglu and Snodgrass, 1995).

A classical article that established the distinction between valid time and transaction time is Snodgrass and Ahn, 1986. The data models by Segev and Sarda are described in Segev and Shoshani, 1987, and Sarda, 1990, respectively. The HRDM model is presented in Clifford and Croker, 1987. Bhargava's model can be found in Bhargava and Gadia, 1993. The bitemporal conceptual data model BCDM is the model underlying TSQL2; it is described in detail in Snodgrass, 1995, Chapter 10. Details on the other models mentioned in Table 1.1 can be found also in Snodgrass, 1995, Chapter 10, or in Özsoyoglu and Snodgrass, 1995.

Section 1.4, introducing the basic ideas of moving objects databases, is based on articles by Wolfson and colleagues (e.g., Wolfson et al., 1998b) for the location management perspective, and by Güting and colleagues (e.g., Erwig et al., 1999) for the spatio-temporal data type perspective. Later chapters will examine these approaches in more depth and provide further references.

There is also an edited book covering many aspects of moving objects databases (Koubarakis et al., 2003). It summarizes the results of the CHOROCHRONOS project, in which the authors also participated.

Another book related to moving objects is Schiller and Voisard, 2004, which focuses on location-based services—that is, services depending on the current location of a user. Some chapters of the book also address database issues; others provide case studies of applications or the technology of capturing position data, for example, by GPS (see also Section 8.1).

2 Spatio-Temporal Databases in the Past

Classical research on spatio-temporal databases has focused on *discrete* changes of spatial objects over time. Applications here predominantly have a "man-made" nature. For example, cadastral applications deal with the management of land parcels, whose boundaries can change from time to time due to specific legal actions such as splitting, merging, or land consolidation. Political boundaries can suddenly disappear, as the reunification of West and East Germany shows. Road networks are extended by new streets.

In the following, we give two representative examples of early spatio-temporal models dealing with this kind of application. In the sense of Section 1.3.5, the first model leads to bitemporal state relations, while the second model supports bitemporal event relations.

2.1 Spatio-Bitemporal Objects

The basic idea of the first model is to provide a unified approach for spatial and temporal information. This is achieved by combining concepts of purely spatial modeling based on so-called two-dimensional simplicial complexes with concepts of purely temporal modeling incorporating the two orthogonal time dimensions of transaction and valid time (Section 1.3.3).

2.1.1 An Application Scenario

As a motivating example, let us consider a highly simplified and fictitious scenario of land ownership. Information related to land ownership usually comprises spa-

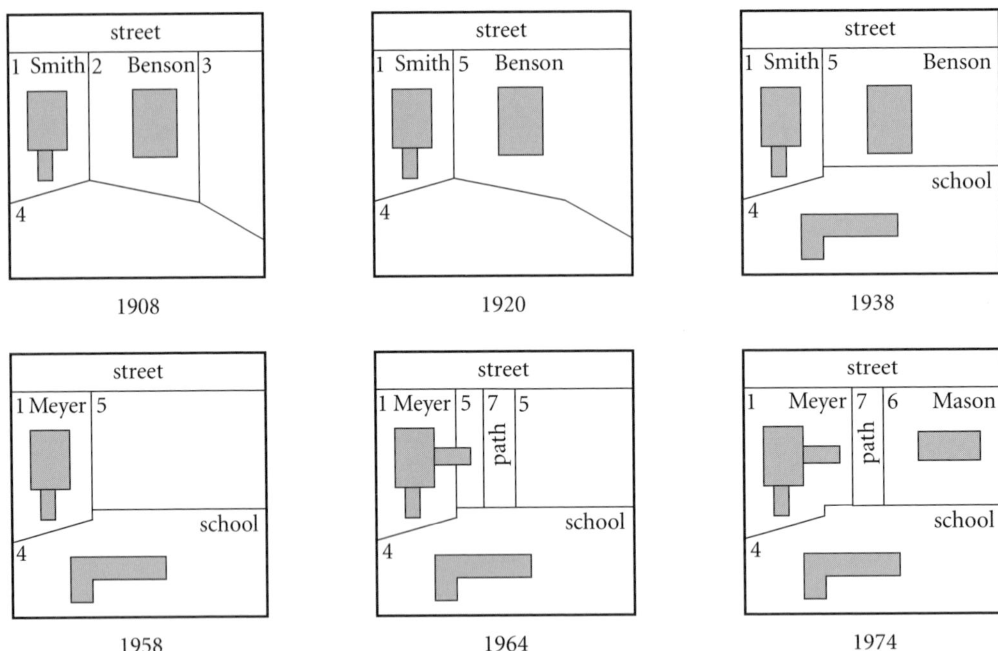

Figure 2.1 Spatio-temporal change of land ownership.

tial, temporal, legal, and other aspects. Spatial aspects refer to the geometry of land parcels. Temporal aspects relate to the duration of ownership. Legal and other aspects of ownership are affected by contracts, death and inheritance, legal proceedings, fire, and so on. Figure 2.1 shows the spatial and ownership variation of a land area through some decades of the century. The chronology of these changes is as follows:

- 1908: The land area under consideration consists of a street, a land parcel owned by Bill Smith (parcel 1), a land parcel owned by Jane Benson (parcel 2), and other parcels.
- 1920: Jane Benson has bought parcel 3, which together with her old parcel 2 is now named parcel 5.
- 1938: Jane Benson has sold a part of her parcel in favor of the construction of a new school on parcel 4.
- 1958: Jane Benson's house has been destroyed by fire, and she has died. Jack Meyer now owns the land and the buildings of parcel 1.

- 1960: The council announces to build a path through parcel 5 in 1962 in order to give better access to the school.
- 1962: The construction of the path on the new parcel 7 is postponed until 1964.
- 1964: Jack Meyer has built an extension, which partly trespasses on parcel 5. The council has built the path through parcel 5.
- 1974: Jack Meyer has included a part of parcel 5 by illegal possession into his ownership. Jill Mason has bought the remaining part of parcel 5, which is now named parcel 6, and built a house on it.

This scenario incorporates both transaction time and valid time. For example, in 1962 (transaction time) the information is available that the path, originally forecast in 1960 (transaction time) to be built in 1962 (valid time), is postponed until 1964 (valid time).

2.1.2 Bitemporal Elements

Formally, the model is based on bitemporal elements (Section 1.3.4) and simplicial complexes. With bitemporal elements, transaction times and valid times are measured along two orthogonal time axes. We assume that the domain T_V of valid time contains the special elements $-\infty$ and ∞, indicating the indefinite past (or initial state) and indefinite future (or final state), respectively. T_T shall denote transaction time.

Definition 2.1 A *bitemporal element* (BTE) is defined as the union of a finite set of disjoint Cartesian products of periods of the form $I_T \times I_V$, where I_T is a period of T_T and I_V is a period of T_V. ■

The concept of *period* is used here in the sense of Section 1.3.2. Using a geometric interpretation, this definition specifies a BTE as a point set in the plane rather than a finite set of rectangles, where each rectangle corresponds to the point set formed by the cross-product of a transaction-time period and a valid-time period. The semantics expressed by a BTE T is that $(t_T, t_V) \in T$ if, and only if, at transaction time t_T the database contains the information that the object bitemporally referenced by T exists at valid time t_V.

As an example, Figure 2.2 shows the graphical representation of a BTE T for a fictitious boundary part b of a parcel. The horizontal axis denotes transaction time and the vertical axis denotes valid time. In transaction time 1990, there is no valid time in which b exists. In transaction time 1991, b exists from valid time 1991 into the indefinite future, since a transaction has taken place providing information about the determination of b. The validity up to the indefinite future (∞) is not

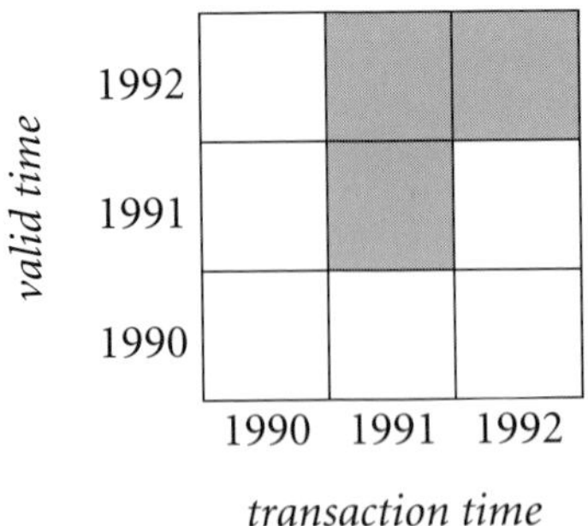

Figure 2.2 Example of a bitemporal element (BTE).

specially marked in the graphical representation of a BTE. In transaction time 1992, it turns out that the knowledge at transaction time 1991 about b was erroneous and that b exists from valid time 1992 into the definite future. That is, the determination of the boundary part b was postponed to 1992. Altogether, $T = (1991 \times 1991) \cup (1991 \times 1992) \cup (1992 \times 1992)$, where a year is regarded, for example, as a period of days, weeks, or months.

2.1.3 Spatial Objects Modeled as Simplicial Complexes

The geometric part of the model is based on algebraic topology. *Algebraic topology,* also called *combinatorial topology,* plays an important role in the mathematical field of algebra. It investigates topological structures for classifying and formally describing point sets by using algebraic means. Its techniques rest on problem translation and algebraic manipulation of symbols that represent spatial configurations and their relationships. The basic method consists of three steps: conversion of the problem from a spatial environment to an algebraic environment; solving the algebraic form of the problem; and conversion of the algebraic solution back to the spatial environment. The intersection of two lines, for example, becomes the search for common nodes. The coincidence of two line objects, the neighborhood of two region objects, and the neighborhood of a line and a region object result in a search for common edges or common nodes (depending on the definition of neighborhood) of the lines and the boundaries of regions.

Spatial objects, which are assumed to be embedded in the two-dimensional Euclidean space, are represented as *simplicial complexes,* which themselves are composed of *simplexes.*

Definition 2.2 Given $k + 1$ points $v_0, \ldots, v_k \in \mathbb{R}^n$, where the k vectors $\{v_1 - v_0, v_2 - v_0, \ldots, v_k - v_0\}$ are linearly independent, the set $\{v_0, \ldots, v_k\}$ is called *geometrically independent,* and the point set

$$\sigma = \sigma_k = \{p \in \mathbb{R}^n \mid p = \sum_{i=0}^{k} \lambda_i v_i \text{ with } \sum_{i=0}^{k} \lambda_i = 1, \lambda_i \in \mathbb{R}, \lambda_0, \ldots, \lambda_k \geq 0\} \subset \mathbb{R}^n$$

is called the (closed) *simplex* of dimension k (or the *k-simplex*) with the vertices v_0, ..., v_k, or the *k-simplex spanned* by $\{v_0, \ldots, v_k\}$. ■

This formula collects all points that together form σ. The condition that the sum of all λ_i's has to be equal to 1 ensures that only those points are captured for σ that are located on the boundary of σ or within the interior of σ.

For a given dimension k, a k-simplex is the minimal and elementary spatial object (i.e., a building block from which all more complex spatial objects of this dimension can be constructed). In the three-dimensional space, a 0-simplex is a single point or a node, a 1-simplex is a straight line or an edge between two distinct points including the end points, a 2-simplex is a filled triangle connecting three noncollinear points, and a 3-simplex is a solid tetrahedron connecting four noncoplanar points (Figure 2.3).

Any k-simplex is composed of $k + 1$ geometrically independent simplexes of dimension $k - 1$. For example, a triangle, a 2-simplex, is composed of three 1-simplexes, which are geometrically independent if no two edges are parallel and no edge has length 0. A *face* of a simplex is any simplex that contributes to the composition of the simplex. For example, a node of a bounding edge of a triangle and a bounding edge itself are faces.

Definition 2.3 A (*simplicial*) *k-complex* C is a finite set of simplexes so that each face of a simplex in C is also in C, and the intersection of two simplexes in C is either empty or a face of both simplexes. The *dimension* k of C is the largest dimension of the simplexes in C. ■

This definition is the first of two so-called *completeness principles*. The principle it describes is called *completeness of incidence*. It implies that no two distinct simplexes in C exist that (partially) occupy the same space and that the intersection of

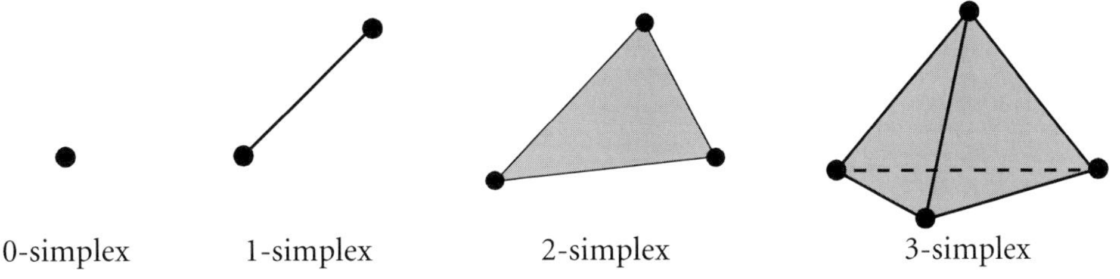

Figure 2.3 Simplex structures of different dimensions.

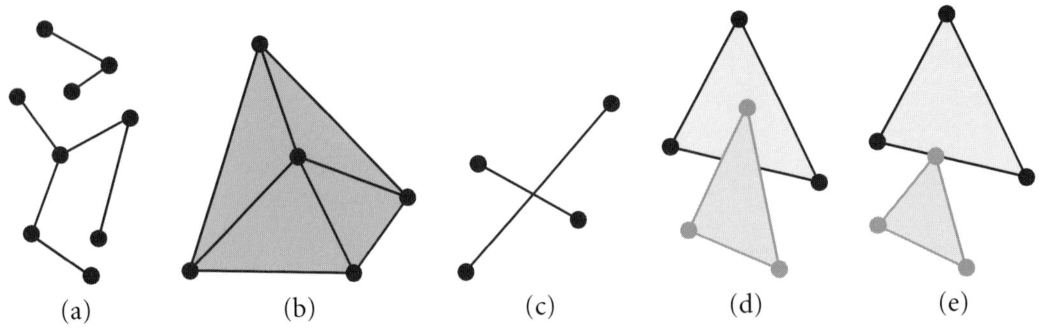

Figure 2.4 Examples of a 1-complex (a); a 2-complex (b); and three configurations that are not simplicial complexes, because the intersection of some of their simplexes is either not a face (c), (d) or not a simplex (e).

lines at points that are neither start nor end points of lines is excluded. Figure 2.4 shows some examples of allowed and forbidden spatial configurations of simplicial complexes.

The second principle, which we will not assume here, is called *completeness of inclusion*. It requires that every l-simplex in C with $l < k$ is a face (boundary simplex) of an $(l + 1)$-simplex in C. This avoids geometric anomalies. For example, for $k = 2$, every point is then a start or end point of a line (no isolated points exist), and every line is part of the boundary of a triangle (no dangling lines exist).

Definition 2.4 An *oriented k-simplex* is obtained from a k-simplex σ with vertices $v_0, \ldots, v_k$ by choosing an order for the vertices. We write an oriented k-simplex as an ordered sequence $\sigma = \langle v_0 v_1 v_2 \ldots v_k \rangle$. An *oriented simplicial complex* is obtained from a simplicial complex by assigning an orientation to each of its simplexes. ■

We now distinguish different parts of a simplex and complex, respectively, and specify what their *boundary* and *interior* are.

Definition 2.5 The *boundary* of a k-simplex σ_k, denoted by $\partial\sigma_k$, is the union of all its $k + 1$ $(k - 1)$-simplexes. The *boundary* of a k-complex C, denoted by ∂C, is the smallest complex that contains the symmetric difference of the boundaries of its constituent k-simplexes. The *interior* of a k-complex C, denoted by C°, is the union of all $(k - 1)$-simplexes which are not part of the boundary of C. ■

For instance, the boundary of a 2-simplex (triangle) $\sigma = \langle v_0 v_1 v_2 \rangle$ is $\partial\sigma = \{\langle v_0 v_1 \rangle, \langle v_1 v_2 \rangle, \langle v_2 v_0 \rangle\}$, which is a set of three 1-simplexes (edges). The boundary of a 2-complex $C = \{\langle x_1 y_1 z_1 \rangle, \ldots, \langle x_n y_n z_n \rangle\}$ is $\partial C = \Delta(\partial\langle x_1 y_1 z_1 \rangle, \ldots, \partial\langle x_n y_n z_n \rangle)$, where Δ denotes the symmetric difference operation with $\Delta(A, B) = (A \backslash B) \cup (B \backslash A)$ for two

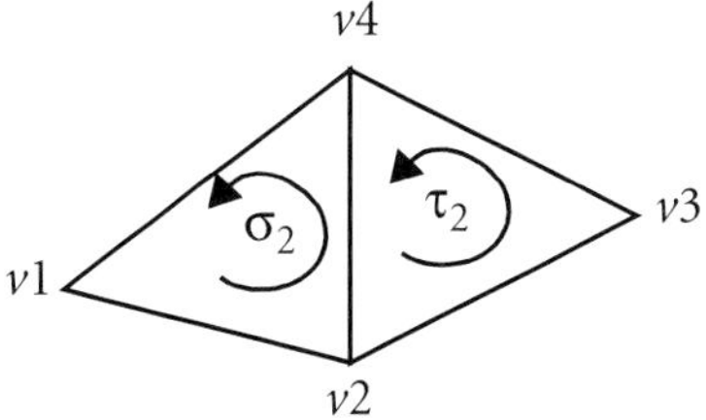

Figure 2.5 Example of a complex consisting of two simplexes.

sets A and B. The common edges of the 2-dimensional simplexes of C form the interior of C.

As an example, which also demonstrates how algebraic computation works in algebraic topology, the computation of the boundary of a 2-complex C_2, consisting of two adjacent-oriented 2-simplexes $\sigma_2 = \langle v_1 v_2 v_4 \rangle$ and $\tau_2 = \langle v_2 v_3 v_4 \rangle$ is illustrated in Figure 2.5. We obtain $\partial\sigma_2 = \langle v_2 v_4 \rangle - \langle v_1 v_4 \rangle + \langle v_1 v_2 \rangle$ and $\partial\tau_2 = \langle v_3 v_4 \rangle - \langle v_2 v_4 \rangle + \langle v_2 v_3 \rangle$. Then, $\partial C_2 = \partial\sigma_2 + \partial\tau_2 = \langle v_2 v_4 \rangle - \langle v_1 v_4 \rangle + \langle v_1 v_2 \rangle + \langle v_3 v_4 \rangle - \langle v_2 v_4 \rangle + \langle v_2 v_3 \rangle = \langle v_1 v_2 \rangle + \langle v_2 v_3 \rangle + \langle v_3 v_4 \rangle - \langle v_1 v_4 \rangle = \langle v_1 v_2 \rangle + \langle v_2 v_3 \rangle + \langle v_3 v_4 \rangle + \langle v_4 v_1 \rangle$.

For later operation definitions, we will need the concept of *common refinement* of two simplicial complexes, which corresponds to a special kind of geometric union and identifies common parts (i.e., two simplicial complexes become acquainted with each other). Its definition makes use of the concept of *planar embedding*, which we define first.

Definition 2.6 For a given simplicial complex $C = \{s_1, \ldots, s_n\}$, its *planar embedding* is given as:

$$emb(C) = \bigcup_{i=1}^{n} s_i.$$

Definition 2.7 A *common refinement* of two simplicial complexes C_1 and C_2, denoted by *refine*(C_1, C_2), is a simplicial complex that has the same planar embedding as the union of the embeddings of C_1 and C_2: $emb(refine(C_1, C_2)) = emb(C_1) \cup emb(C_2)$.

This construction is in general not unique, due to possible different decompositions into simplex structures (see Figure 2.6).

2.1.4 Spatio-Bitemporal Objects

The combination of bitemporal elements and simplicial complexes leads us to *spatio-bitemporal objects*. The main idea is to attach BTEs (Definition 2.1) as labels to components of simplicial complexes (Definition 2.3).

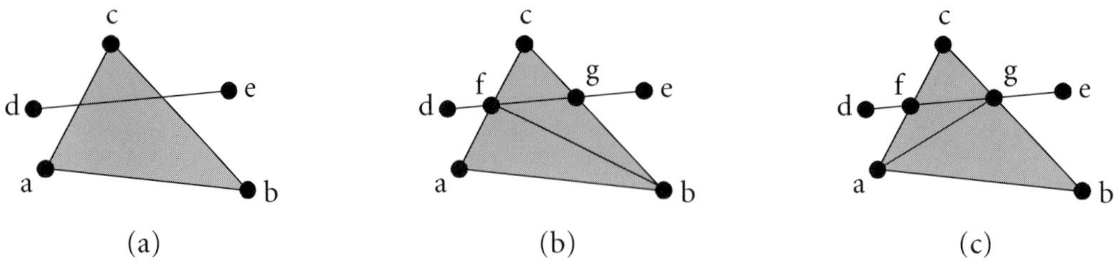

Figure 2.6 Complexes *abc* and *de* (a) and two possible common refinements (b), (c).

Definition 2.8 An *ST-simplex* is an ordered pair (S, T), where S is a simplex and T is a BTE. For an ST-simplex $R = (S, T)$, let $\pi_s(R) = S$ and $\pi_t(R) = T$. ■

An ST-simplex R indicates that a spatial configuration S exists over a given range T of transaction and valid times. π_s and π_t are spatial and bitemporal projection functions.

The concept of *ST-complex* is introduced now for describing the structure of a general, bitemporally referenced spatial configuration.

Definition 2.9 An *ST-complex* C is a finite set of ST-simplexes fulfilling the following properties:

1. The spatial projections of ST-simplexes in C are pairwise disjoint.
2. Taken together, these spatial projections form a simplicial complex.
3. $\forall\, R, R' \in C : \pi_s(R)$ is a face of $\pi_s(R') \Rightarrow \pi_t(R) \supseteq \pi_t(R')$. ■

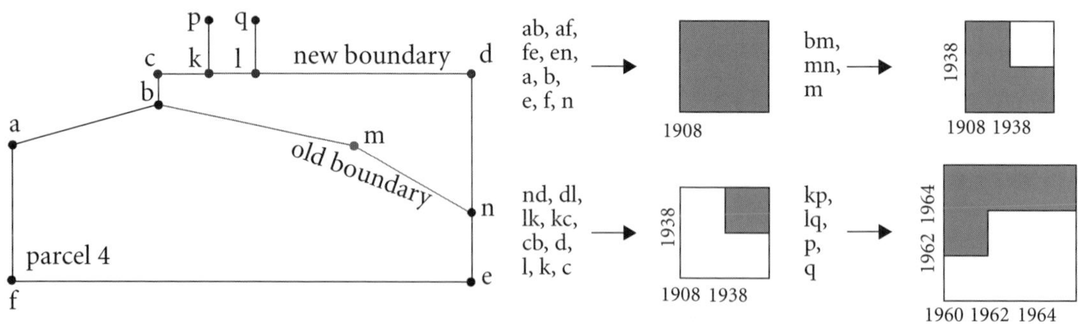

Figure 2.7 ST-complex example: boundary and face annotation with BTEs of parcel 4.

Condition 1 implies that the same simplex may not occur with different BTEs in the same ST-complex. Condition 2 requires that the underlying geometric structure is a simplicial complex. The reason for condition 3 is that a simplex cannot exist without its faces.

As an example, in the left part of Figure 2.7 we consider the temporal development of the boundary of parcel 4 in Figure 2.1 as an ST-complex. Areal properties are not represented here; they would require a representation of the parcel by triangular simplexes. The right part of Figure 2.7 shows which BTEs are associated with which boundary segments and vertices. Remember that in the graphical representation of each BTE, the horizontal axis denotes transaction time and the vertical axis valid time.

2.1.5 Spatio-Bitemporal Operations

Besides purely spatial and purely temporal operations, which we will not mention here, spatio-bitemporal operations can be defined on ST-complexes. Some of them will be introduced and explained in the following text. We first list their signatures (Table 2.1).

For the predicate definitions of the subset relationship and the equality of two ST-complexes C and C', we consider C and C' as embedded in four-dimensional space comprising two spatial and two temporal dimensions.

Table 2.1 A collection of spatio-bitemporal operations.

$=$:	ST-complex × ST-complex	$\rightarrow$ Boolean	(ST-equal)
$\subset_{ST}$:	ST-complex × ST-complex	$\rightarrow$ Boolean	(ST-subset)
∂:	ST-complex	$\rightarrow$ ST-complex	(ST-boundary)
π_s:	ST-complex	$\rightarrow$ S-complex	(S-project)
π_t:	ST-complex	$\rightarrow$ BTE	(T-project)
$\times_\beta$:	ST-complex × ST-complex	$\rightarrow$ ST-complex	(ST-β-product)
$\cup_{ST}$:	ST-complex × ST-complex	$\rightarrow$ ST-complex	(ST-union)
$\cap_{ST}$:	ST-complex × ST-complex	$\rightarrow$ ST-complex	(ST-intersection)
$\setminus_{ST}$:	ST-complex × ST-complex	$\rightarrow$ ST-complex	(ST-difference)
${\sigma^s}_X$:	ST-complex	$\rightarrow$ ST-complex	(S-select)
${\sigma^t}_\phi$:	ST-complex	$\rightarrow$ ST-complex	(T-select)

Definition 2.10 Let C and C' be two ST-complexes. Then

1. $C \subset_{ST} C' \Leftrightarrow \forall (x, y, w, z) \in (S, T) \in C \exists (S', T') \in C' : (x, y, w, z) \in (S', T')$
2. $C =_{ST} C' \Leftrightarrow C \subset_{ST} C' \wedge C' \subset_{ST} C$ ■

For defining the boundary of an ST-complex, we make use of the purely spatial boundary operation ∂ (Definition 2.5).

Definition 2.11 For an ST-complex C, let $\partial C = \{(S, T) \mid S \in \partial(\pi_s(C))\}$. ■

Projection operators are needed to map either to the spatial or to the temporal domain and then to continue computation purely in that domain. Intuitively, the spatial projection of an ST-complex is a complex representing the entire knowledge one has ever had about the spatial extent of the ST-complex over all transaction and valid times. The bitemporal projection of an ST-complex is a BTE gathering all transaction and valid times at which parts of the ST-complex have existed. The projection operators extend the ones on simplexes.

Definition 2.12 Let ST-complex $C = \{(S_1, T_1), \ldots, (S_n, T_n)\}$. Then:

1. $\pi_s(C) = \{S_1, \ldots, S_n\}$
2. $\pi_t(C) = \bigcup_{1 \leq i \leq n} T_i$ ■

The next operation we discuss is the so-called *spatio-bitemporal* β*-product.* It allows the composition of two ST-complexes that are parameterized by a so-called β-operation. A β*-operation* is a binary operation with the signature β: $BTE \times BTE \rightarrow BTE$.

Definition 2.13 Let us assume two ST-complexes C_1 and C_2 and a β-operation on BTEs. Let simplicial complex R be a common refinement of $\pi_s(C_1)$ and $\pi_s(C_2)$. We define $C_1 \times_\beta C_2$ to be the smallest ST-complex (with respect to the ST-subset relationship introduced in Definition 2.10) that contains the set of ST-simplexes $\{(S, \beta(T_1^S, T_2^S)) \mid S \in R\}$, where T_1^S and T_2^S are the BTEs associated with the smallest faces of $\pi_s(C_1)$ and $\pi_s(C_2)$, respectively, that contain S. ■

This "dense" definition can be explained by giving an algorithm computing $C_1 \times_\beta C_2$. In a first step, we compute the spatial part of the result, which is given as a common refinement R of the spatial projections of C_1 and C_2. In a second step, for each constituent face (simplex) S of R, we determine the pertaining BTE as follows: We know that S must explicitly exist either in the spatial projection of C_1, in the spatial projection of C_2, or in both. Otherwise, it would not be part of R. If this is the case, then we can directly take the pertaining BTE T_1^S, T_2^S, or both. If S does not explicitly exist in one of the spatial projections of C_1 or C_2, the BTE of the smallest face containing S is taken as $T_1{}^S$ or $T_2{}^S$, respectively. We then apply β to $T_1{}^S$ and $T_2{}^S$. In a third step, we remove all those faces S from the result with an empty BTE. The definition will also become clearer later, when we look at some examples for β.

The result of $C_1 \times_\beta C_2$ depends on the choice of the common refinement R, which in general is not unique. But because all possible common refinements have the same planar embedding (i.e., comprise the same point set), the different results will all be ST-equal.[1] The reason is that different common refinements of $\pi_s(C_1)$ and $\pi_s(C_2)$ only produce different subdivisions (e.g., triangulations, splitting of edges) of $\pi_s(C_1)$ and $\pi_s(C_2)$ with the same planar embedding. This fact does not affect the BTE attached to the same point of each possible common refinement. In other words, a point can belong to different faces due to different common refinements, but the pertaining BTE does not change.

We now consider a few important applications of the ST-β-product. With $\beta \in \{\cup_{ST}, \cap_{ST}, \setminus_{ST}\}$, the ST-$\beta$-product can be used to define set-theoretic *union*, *intersection*, and *difference* operations on two ST-complexes.

Definition 2.14 Let C_1 and C_2 be two ST-complexes. Then:

1. $C_1 \cup_{ST} C_2 = C_1 \times_\cup C_2$
2. $C_1 \cap_{ST} C_2 = C_1 \times_\cap C_2$
3. $C_1 \setminus_{ST} C_2 = C_1 \times_\setminus C_2$ ■

Figure 2.8 illustrates these definitions for union (d) and intersection (e) on the basis of two ST-complexes C_1 (a) and C_2 (b) with the common refinement of their spatial projections (c) and the BTEs attached to their single spatial simplexes. The union contains all the elements of the refined spatial projections of C_1 and C_2, where each spatial simplex has associated with it the union of the BTEs associated with that element in C_1 and C_2. The intersection yields an ST-complex whose spatial simplexes are shared by the refined spatial projections of C_1 and C_2, with a non-empty intersection of corresponding BTEs in C_1 and C_2. If an empty BTE is calculated for a common spatial simplex, the spatial simplex is omitted from the resulting complex.

The set of ST-simplexes $\{(S, \beta(T_1{}^S, T_2{}^S)) \mid S \in R\}$ does not necessarily form an ST-complex. However, there is always a unique minimum ST-complex that contains this set. An example is the difference of the two ST-complexes C_1 and C_2 in Figure 2.8(a) and (b). The faces of interest are the 1-simplex *de* and the two

[1] More precisely, these operations act on equivalence classes of ST-equal ST-complexes and not on single ST-complexes. For notational simplicity, we allow operations to act on single ST-complexes.

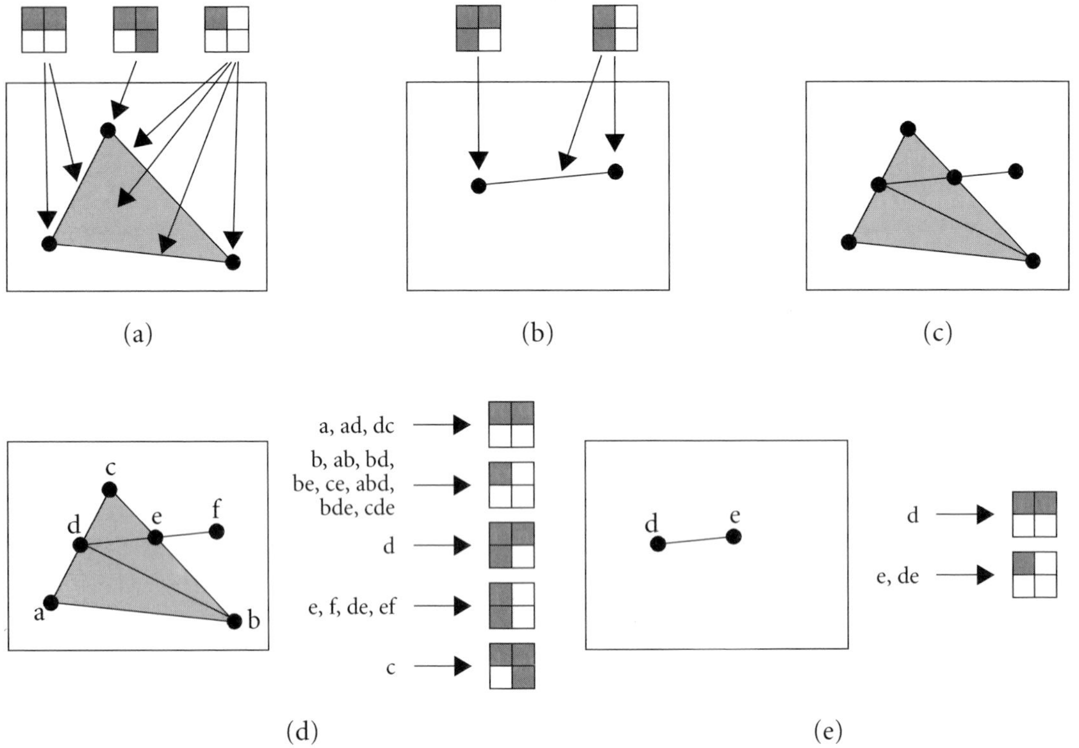

Figure 2.8 ST-complex C_1 (a); ST-complex C_2 (b); a common refinement of $\pi_s(C_1)$ and $\pi_s(C_2)$ (c); the ST-union of C_1 and C_2 (d); and the ST-intersection of C_1 and C_2 (e).

0-simplexes *d* and *e*, which (you should check this) all are associated with the empty BTE. This means that all three simplexes should be omitted from the resulting complex. While this is correct for *de* and *e*, this is incorrect for *d*, since *d* is also the bounding node of the simplex *de*, which becomes incomplete. Consequently, *d* has to be maintained and obtains the BTE as the maximum BTE of all its incident edges.

The *spatial selection* $\sigma^s{}_X(C)$ is another operation that can be expressed using the ST-β-product. It allows us to choose from an ST-complex *C* all those ST-simplexes whose spatial projection is contained in a given simplicial complex *X*.

Definition 2.15 Let $X = \{S_1, \ldots, S_n\}$ be a simplicial complex, and let $D_X = \{(S_1, T_T \times T_V), \ldots, (S_n, T_T \times T_V)\}$ be the ST-complex, where each simplex of *X* is associated with the universal BTE $T_T \times T_V$. The *spatial selection* on an ST-complex *C* with respect to *X* is then defined as $\sigma^s{}_X(C) = C \cap_{ST} D_X$. ■

For example, the spatial selection on C_1 in Figure 2.8(a) with respect to the spatial projection of C_2 in Figure 2.8(b) is again shown in Figure 2.8(e).

For the definition of the next and last operation considered here we need the two auxiliary concepts of *ST-comparable* and *ST-minimum*.

Definition 2.16 The elements of a set $\{C_1, \ldots, C_n\}$ of ST-complexes are *comparable* if, and only if, $\forall\ 1 \leq i < j \leq n : C_i \subset_{ST} C_j \lor C_j \subset_{ST} C_i$. ■

Definition 2.17 The *minimum* of a set $\{C_1, \ldots, C_n\}$ of comparable ST-complexes is defined as $min_{ST}(\{C_1, \ldots, C_n\}) = C$, such that:

1. $C \in \{C_1, \ldots, C_n\}$
2. $\forall\ 1 \leq i \leq n : C =_{ST} C_i \lor C \subset_{ST} C_i$ ■

We are now able to define the *temporal selection* $\sigma^t_\phi(C)$, which selects from an ST-complex C the smallest ST-complex, each of whose simplicial components fulfills a temporal condition specified by a formula ϕ.

Definition 2.18 Let $\phi(t)$ be a first-order formula, which may contain BTEs as constants, β-operations for functions, and a single free variable t. The *temporal selection* on an ST-complex C with respect to ϕ is then defined as $\sigma^t_\phi(C) = min_{ST}(\{C' \mid C' = \{(S, T) \in C \mid \phi(T)\}\})$. ■

For example, if we take the ST-complex C_1 in Figure 2.8(a) and the BTE B in Figure 2.9(a), the result of the temporal selection $\sigma^t_{t \supseteq B}(C_1)$ is shown in Figure 2.9(b).

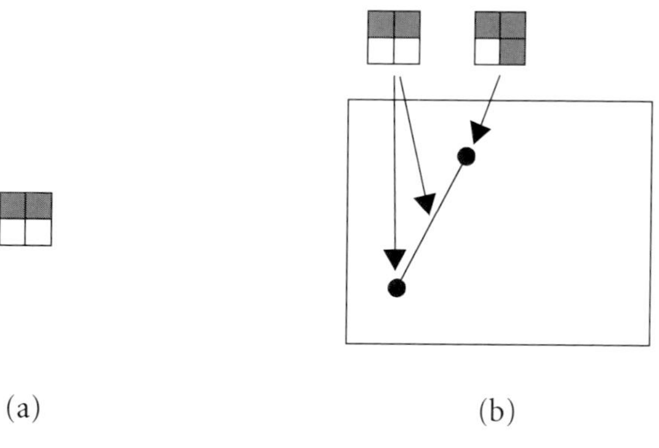

Figure 2.9 BTE B (a) and the temporal selection $\sigma^t_{t \supseteq B}(C_1)$ (b).

2.1.6 Querying

An essential feature of a (spatio-temporal) database system is that it provides a language for posing queries. The spatio-temporal data model described so far can be taken as the basis of a *query algebra*. We will illustrate this by integrating the spatio-bitemporal data type *ST-complex* into the relational setting and incorporating the spatio-bitemporal operations (Table 2.1) into the well-known standard database query language SQL. For reasons of user friendliness, readability, and compatibility with SQL, we will not employ the mathematical notations for the operations but replace them with the purely textual terms given in parentheses in Table 2.1.

Again, we take the land owner scenario and assume that the land parcel data are stored in a relation with the scheme:

```
parcels (parcel-id: integer, owner: string,
          area: ST-complex, building: ST-complex)
```

This schema stores information about the parcel identifier, the owner of a parcel, and the development of the parcel area, as well as the building on the parcel over space and time. Parcel identifier and owner together form the key of the schema. It is striking that the nonstandard spatio-bitemporal data type *ST-complex* is used in the same way as an attribute type as the standard data types *integer* and *string*. This is possible, because the type *ST-complex* is modeled and used as an *abstract data type*—that is, only its name is visible outward but its internal, complex structure is hidden from the user in the data type representation.

We are now able to formulate some queries:

"What did the building on parcel 1 look like in 1958?"

```
SELECT S-project(T-select((_, 1958), building))
FROM parcels
WHERE parcel-id = 1 AND (_, 1958) IN T-project(building)
```

In the `WHERE` clause, the first part selects all those tuples belonging to parcel 1. The second part identifies that tuple with a building attribute value whose BTE contains 1958 as a valid time. The underscore "_" serves as a wildcard for transaction time here. In the `SELECT` clause, we first determine the spatio-bitemporal complex for the year 1958 by temporal selection and then compute the spatial projection. Note that we have slightly changed the signature of `T-select` and positioned the temporal selection condition as the first operand.

"How has the building on parcel 1 been extended during 1958 and 1974?"

```
SELECT S-project(ST-difference(T-select((_, 1974), building),
                               T-select((_, 1958), building)))
FROM parcels
WHERE parcel-id = 1
```

The WHERE clause selects parcel 1. By temporal selection, the SELECT clause first determines the snapshots of the building on parcel 1 in the years 1974 and 1958 as ST-complexes and then computes their difference, yielding an ST-complex again; it finally calculates the spatial projection of the result that just describes the geometric difference of the building.

"Does the path currently pass through land that was ever part of Jane Benson's house?"

```
SELECT NOT isempty(S-intersection(
                    S-project(T-select((nowDB, _), p.area)),
                    S-project(q.building))) AS is_part
FROM parcels AS p, parcels AS q
WHERE p.parcel-id = 7 AND p.owner = 'public' AND
      q.owner = 'Jane Benson'
```

The WHERE clause joins parcel 7, which belongs to the path, with all properties Jane Benson ever had. The SELECT clause computes a Boolean value for the new attribute is_part as follows: First, the ST-complex belonging to the area of the path is temporally restricted to nowDB, which indicates a BTE representing all bitemporal times with database time now, and afterward its spatial projection is determined. Then, the spatial projection of the ST-complex describing the buildings owned by Jane Benson is computed. The resulting two spatial complexes are intersected by the operation S-intersection. Finally, the assumed predicate isempty checks whether the intersection result is empty. If the result is not empty, the path and the building under consideration have shared a part in the past.

"Has Jack Meyer's house ever shared a common boundary with the path?"

```
SELECT NOT isempty(ST-intersection(
                    ST-boundary(p.area),
                    ST-boundary(q.building))) AS is_part
FROM parcels AS p, parcels AS q
WHERE p.parcel-id = 7 AND p.owner = 'public' AND
      q.owner = 'Jack Meyer'
```

The `SELECT` clause determines the boundaries of the two ST-complexes that describe the path area and Jack Meyer's building and computes their intersection.

Exercise 2.1 Where exactly does the "discrete" nature of this approach become visible? ■

Exercise 2.2 Formulate the following queries in the SQL-like style presented previously and design extensions to the language if necessary:

1. When was a parcel owned by a specific person not a developed real estate?
2. When was the school (as the first building) constructed on parcel 4? ■

2.2 An Event-Based Approach

The second model to be presented propagates the event-based approach. In this time-based approach, location in time becomes the primary organizational basis for recording change. An event represents a change in state at some instant, such as the change of a value associated with a location in space at some time t. In this model, only valid time is of importance. The treatment of transaction time is not included.

2.2.1 The Model

The time associated with each change (i.e., each event) is stored in increasing order from an initial time t_0 (e.g., March 1, 1963) to the latest recorded change at time t_n. This means that the representation of change is organized as a function of a *discrete* time domain to some codomain of interest. Mostly, the length of any temporal period (i.e., the temporal distance between t_{i-1} and t_i) and any other such period will vary. The idea now is to associate with each timestamp t_i only the changes (the "deltas") that occurred between t_{i-1} and t_i but not the complete changed snapshot. All changes between t_{i-1} and t_i are collected in a set c_i. The only exception is at time t_0, when the initial scenario or base map *BM* has to be recorded once. This is illustrated in the event list in Figure 2.10(a). Figure 2.10(b) gives more insight as to how changes are recorded at time t_i. In this approach, the geometry is stored as a bitmap, or image, so that changes at time t_i relate to a set of individual locations (x_{ik}, y_{ik}) with altered values v_{ik}.

From a representation point of view, a main drawback of this method is that the number of triplets (x, y, v) to be stored in c_i depends directly on the total number of discrete locations whose values changed between t_{i-1} and t_i. An improvement is to group together all individual locations that share the same common value v. Such a value-specific group is called a *component*, and the shared value v is called its *descriptor*. Instead of once for every location per event, each new value is stored

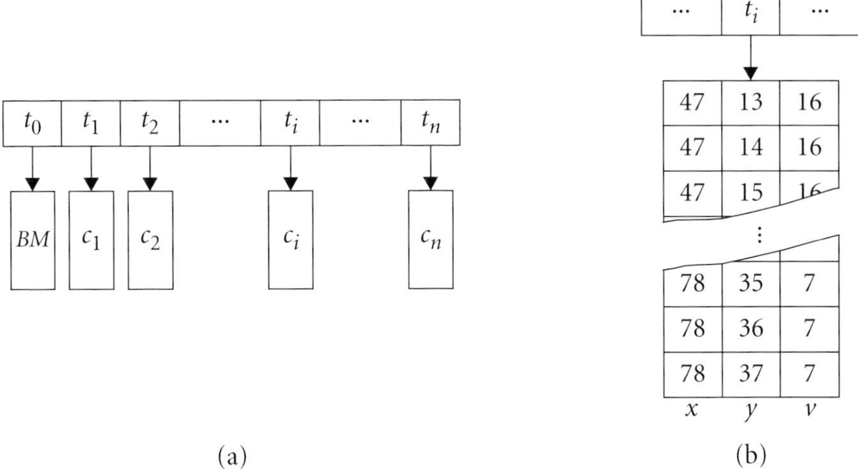

Figure 2.10 Example of an event list, where t_i contains a time value (e.g., day, month, and year), *BM* is the base map, and c_i contains all changes that occurred between the times t_{i-1} and t_i (a); structure of the changes in c_i that comprises a collection of triplets (x_{ik}, y_{ik}, v_{ik}), each of which describes the new value v_{ik} at t_i for location (x_{ik}, y_{ik}) (b).

only once per event with all locations that map to this value. This leads to a separate component for each new value.

A further improvement is to apply raster run-length encoding within each component in order to reduce the amount of storage space required for recording locations. This means that, if in a row of the image with the same *x*-coordinate, several consecutive *y*-coordinates share the same value *v*, these *y*-coordinates can be summarized by an interval which usually leads to a much shorter representation. Figure 2.11 gives an example. In Figure 2.11(a) a simplified map consists of light-shaded and dark-shaded locations. Each location is labeled with a numerical value. The light-shaded locations visualize the development of the base map *BM* after the changes at the times $t_1, \ldots, t_{i-1}$. The dark-shaded locations represent the changes at time t_i. Figure 2.11(b) shows the event components for the changes at time t_i, including their descriptors.

The temporal ordering of events in the event list enables search and retrieval of particular time periods and also of change to specific values in these time periods. Such an ordering also facilitates the comparison of different temporal sequences for different thematic domains or of the same thematic domain in different geographical areas. A comparison of only the times at which events occur (i.e., looking for temporal patterns) can be performed by retrieving the times alone directly from the event list; it is not necessary to retrieve associated values and locations. Due to grouping according to values, the spatial locations carrying this new value can be easily determined. In particular, we can pose the following queries dealing with a single temporal sequence:

1. Retrieve all locations that changed at a given time t_i.
2. Retrieve all locations that changed at a given time t_i to a given value.
3. Retrieve all locations that changed at a given time t_i with their new values.
4. Retrieve all locations that changed between t_i and t_j.
5. Retrieve all locations that changed between t_i and t_j to a given value.
6. Retrieve all locations which changed between t_i and t_j with their new values.
7. Calculate the total change in an area to a given value between t_i and t_j.
8. Did location (x, y) change to a new value at a given time t_i?
9. Did location (x, y) change to a new value between t_i and t_j?
10. When did location (x, y) change to a new value?

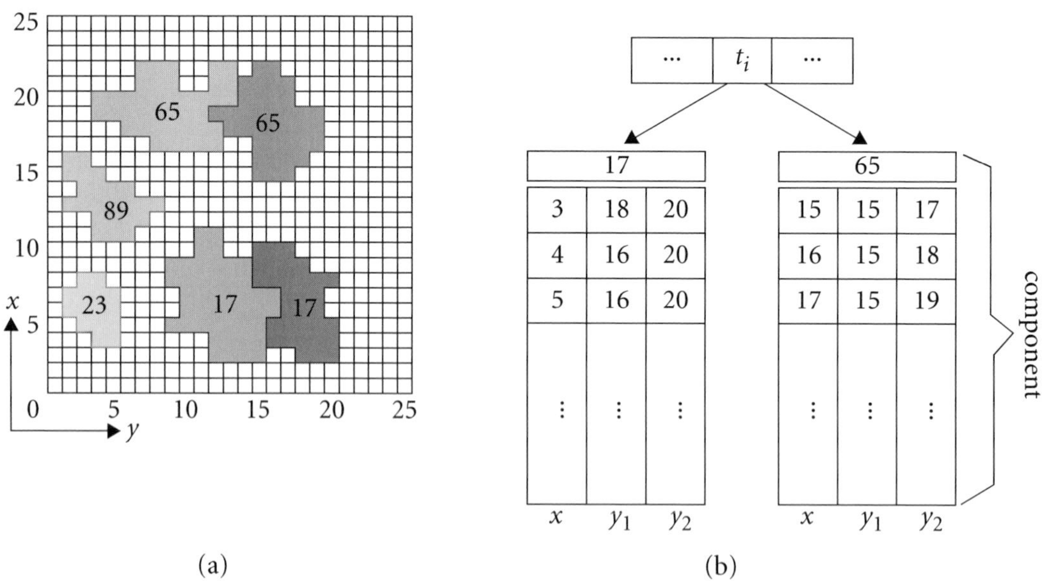

Figure 2.11 Status of a simplified map (light shaded) after applying the "deltas" at times $t_1, \ldots, t_{i-1}$ to a base map, *BM*, and the changed (dark shaded) locations at time t_i (a); the corresponding event components (b).

2.2.2 Query Processing Algorithms

This time, we will not show how these queries can be formulated in a database query language as we did in Section 2.1.6, but we will demonstrate how algorithms can be designed for executing them during the query processing stage. We will also determine the run time complexity of these algorithms.

We begin with the design of an algorithm for evaluating query 2 from the previous list, which requires a two-stage search. The first stage of the search is to find the event with the desired timestamp t in the event list *el* (see Figure 2.10), which is arranged in increasing temporal order. If the entire event list occurred after the desired time (i.e., $t_0 > t$), the search returns the empty list. Otherwise, the search continues until the time t_e associated with an event e is larger than or equal to the desired time t (i.e., $t_e \geq t$). Here, the assumption is that t need not necessarily match any timestamp stored in the event list. If $t_e \neq t$ for all events e we use the simple rule of closest temporal distance as to whether t_e or t_{e-1} is selected. This decision can, of course, change depending on the application. The second stage is to determine the component c associated with this event, whose descriptor matches the given value *gv*. All *xy*-locations within that component are then returned by a function *xylist*. This leads us to the following algorithm:

Algorithm *GetChangedLocsAtInstantForValue*(*el*, *t*, *gv*)

Input: event list *el*, time *t*, value *gv*;

Output: list *xylist* of locations changing to value *gv* at time *t*;

Method:

```
if t_0 > t then return null endif;
for each event e in el do
   if t_e >= t then
      if t <= (t_e + t_{e-1})/2 then ev := e-1 else ev := e endif;
      for each component c of event ev do
         if descriptor(c) = gv then return xylist(c) endif
      endfor
   endif
endfor
```

end.

Both the search of the event list and the search of the component descriptors within the desired event, once found, are linear searches. Hence, the worst time complexity is $O(n_e + c_e + k_c)$, where n_e is the total number of events in the event list, c_e is the maximum number of components for any given event, and k_c is the maximum number of changes stored in any component c. Note that n_e and c_e are input parameters, while k_c is an output parameter. This result can be improved to $O((\log n_e) + c_e + k_c)$ by using any $O(\log n)$ search, where n denotes the total number of elements to be searched.

Exercise 2.3 A snapshot model would store the complete map, including the changes for each event, at a time t_i. Describe roughly (without algorithmic notation) an algorithm performing the same task and utilizing the snapshot model. What are the differences? What is the run-time behavior of the algorithm? ■

Next, we deal with an algorithm for query 5 in the previous list asking for changes to a given value in a given temporal interval.

Algorithm *GetChangedLocsInIntervalForValue*(el, t_1, t_2, gv)

Input: event list *el*, start time t_1, end time t_2, value *gv*;

Output: list *xylist* of locations changing to value *gv* in $[t_1, t_2]$;

Method:

```
if t0 > t2 then return null endif;
for each event e in el do
   if t1 <= te <= t2 then
      for each component c of event e do
         if descriptor(c) = gv then return xylist(c) endif
      endfor
   endif
endfor
```

end.

This algorithm is a slight variation of the preceding one and uses a range of temporal values at the first stage of search and retrieves all locations stored in components with a descriptor *gv* for all events from a starting time t_1 to a finishing time t_2. For the sake of simplicity, we assume that the temporal interval $[t_1, t_2]$ is wide enough so that at least one event will be found in between.

The run-time complexity of this algorithm is $O((\log n_e) + n_f \cdot (c_e + k_c))$, where $\log n_e$ is the amount of time needed to search the event list for the starting event; n_f is the number of events retrieved sequentially up to the finishing event so that $t_1 \leq t_e \leq t_2$, c_e is the maximum number of components for any event *e* and k_c is the maximum number of changes stored in any component *c*. Note that n_e, n_f, and c_e are input parameters, while k_c is an output parameter. The worst-case scenario in terms of efficiency is the case where the starting time coincides with the first event in the event list and the finishing time coincides with the last event in the event list. In this case, the run-time complexity is $O(n_e \cdot (c_e + k_c))$.

Finally, we discuss an algorithm evaluating query 7, which asks for the total change to a given value *gv* in an area during a given temporal interval. The amount of areal change for a given value at some time t_i is determined by the total number of areal units represented within the corresponding component or within an *xylist*(c) returned (e.g., by either of the previous algorithms). Since run-length coding is employed for both of these, counting the total number of changed areal units is rather simple, as the following algorithm shows. This algorithm assumes an input *xylist* as a run-length-encoded list of (x, y)-locations associated with our desired value *gv* of interest.

Algorithm *Area*(*xylist*)

Input: run-length-encoded list *xylist* of (x, y)-locations;

Output: area as an integer value

Method:

```
area := 0;
for each entry (x, y1, y2) in xylist do
    area := area + (y2 − y1 + 1)
endfor;
return area
```

end.

Obviously, the run-time complexity is a linear function of the number of entries in the list *xylist*.

Exercise 2.4 Discuss algorithms for the evaluation of the remaining queries listed previously. Determine their run-time complexity. ■

2.3 Further Exercises

Exercise 2.5 Railway Networks

In this exercise, we want to study a fictitious scenario regarding how railway companies expand their networks and which connections exist at which time. Let us assume there are two companies named Western-Pacific and Central-Pacific. The chronology of their routes is as follows:

- 1850: Western-Pacific started to connect the cities *U* and *F*; the completion was scheduled for 1852.

- 1851: Central-Pacific announced the opening of its first route between *K* and *M* for 1852.
- 1852: The opening of route *UF* was postponed to 1853. Western-Pacific planned to build the short distance between *F* and *M* next year.
- 1853: The tracks *KM*, *UF*, and *FM* were finished.
- 1855: Central-Pacific planned a direct connection between *U* and *K*, which should be usable in 1857 but was finished in 1858.
- 1860: A new railway between *F* and *N* was opened by Western-Pacific.
- 1863: The route *FN* was closed for one year because a bridge was destroyed.
- 1864: Western-Pacific sold the track between *M* and *F* to Central-Pacific.

Draw the railway connections of 1864. Define all segments and vertices of the two networks as ST-simplexes and prove that the net of Western-Pacific forms an ST-complex. Represent the BTEs as in Figure 2.7. Group all simplexes together that have the same BTE.

Exercise 2.6 A Law in the ST Algebra

Prove that for all spatio-temporal complexes *A*, *B*, and *C*:

$$(A \cup_{ST} B) \cup_{ST} C =_{ST} A \cup_{ST} (B \cup_{ST} C).$$

Such laws are helpful, for example, when designing a query optimizer.

2.4 Bibliographic Notes

The presentation of the spatio-temporal model in Section 2.1 is based on Worboys, 1994. We have added a more detailed discussion of spatial complexes as one of the two main underlying pillars of this model and the description of an embedding of the query algebra into a SQL-like query language context. Literature about algebraic topology can be found in Armstrong, 1983; Croom, 1978. Here, only the basic concepts are of interest.

A number of articles exploit algebraic topology for spatial modeling. Frank and Kuhn (1986) propose a topological model, which is based on simplicial complexes (cell complexes). An algebra for complexes is introduced that provides a variety of operations, such as creating an initial complex, adding a point or line to a complex, connecting two points in a complex with a line, deleting a point, or deleting a line. These operations can, for example, be used for computing a common refinement or the spatial part of a spatio-bitemporal operation. In a continuation of this work, Egenhofer et al. (1989) show the simplicity of an implementation of simplicial structures. They present a simplicial algebra with only a small set of operations that fulfill closure properties (that is, an operation manipulating one or more simplicial complexes can produce only a simplicial complex). Update operations are consistent, and the completeness principles are ensured after each modification. Algorithms proposed relate to the insertion of a node, a line, and a polygon into a simplicial decomposition. Finally, in Egenhofer, 1989; Egenhofer, 1991, simplicial topology is applied for the definition of topological relationships.

The presentation of the spatio-temporal model in Section 2.2 is based on Peuquet and Duan, 1995. The authors denote their approach as an event-based spatio-temporal data model (ESTDM).

Two survey articles summarizing the earlier work on spatio-temporal databases such as the models presented in this chapter are Abraham and Roddick, 1999; Peuquet, 2001. The latter includes some of the work on moving objects.

3 Modeling and Querying Current Movement

In this chapter, we consider moving objects databases from the location management perspective. Suppose we need to manage in a database the locations of a set of mobile units (e.g., cars, trucks, helicopters, people carrying mobile phones) that are moving around *right now.* We wish to be able to retrieve their current positions. In fact, if it is known in the database not only where they are but also how they are moving right now, we should also be able to ask queries about the future.

After discussing some basic assumptions and issues in Section 3.1, we introduce a data model called MOST (moving objects spatio-temporal model) to describe current and expected future movement (Section 3.2). Associated with it is a query language called FTL (future temporal logic), which allows us to express queries about future development (Section 3.3). We also study the problem of how often and when mobile objects should transmit updates of their current position, and speed, to the database in order to keep the inherent imprecision in the DBMS knowledge about their locations bounded (Section 3.4). Finally, in Section 3.5 we consider *uncertain trajectories*—that is, motion plans with an associated bound on the uncertainty of the time-dependent position.

3.1 Location Management

There are various applications that need to keep track of the locations of moving objects. For example, a query to a database representing the locations of taxicabs in a city might be: Retrieve the three free cabs closest to Königsallee 48 (a customer request position). For a trucking company database, queries might be: Which trucks are within 10 kilometers of truck T68 (which needs assistance)? or: Will truck T70 reach its destination within the next half hour? In a military application, a query might be: Retrieve the friendly helicopters that will arrive in the valley within the next 15 minutes.

Managing continuously changing positions in a database obviously is a problem, since normally data in a database are assumed to be constant until these data are explicitly updated. Sending very frequent updates would allow one to approximate the continuous movement by stepwise constant locations, but this incurs a very high update load and is not feasible for a large number of objects.

The basic idea developed in this chapter is to store a moving object not by its position directly but instead by its motion vector (i.e., its position as a function of time). In this way, the position represented in the database will change continuously, even without any explicit update to the database. It is still necessary to update the motion vector occasionally, but much less frequently than would be the case with stored positions.

It is important to note that within the DBMS data model, motion vectors are not visible explicitly (e.g., by a special data type, as sketched in Section 1.4.6). Instead, a concept of a *dynamic attribute* is introduced: an attribute that changes its value with time without explicit updates. The stored motion vector serves as an implementation for this more abstract view of dynamic attribute. Hence, the data type of a dynamic attribute is the same as the corresponding static data type (e.g., `point`), and queries are formulated as if they refer to static positions. However, since the value of a dynamic attribute changes over time, so does the result of a query: The same query posed at different times will in general yield different results, even if the database contents are the same.

Clearly, if dynamic attributes are available, then the database represents knowledge not only about current but also about expected future positions. Hence, we should be able to ask about the state of the database 10 minutes from now, or even about a sequence of relationships between moving objects in the future. The language FTL (future temporal logic) is designed for this purpose.

Answers to queries referring to the future are always tentative, since it is possible that the database is changed by an explicit update to a dynamic attribute (i.e., its underlying motion vector is changed). For example, suppose, according to its motion vector, a truck is expected to arrive in a city within the next 10 minutes. After this result has been given to a user, the truck stops (and sends a corresponding update of its motion vector). So, in fact, it does not arrive within 10 minutes. Nevertheless, the answer given previously has to be regarded as correct, according to what was known in the database at that time.

When answers to queries can change over time even without updates to the database, the issue of *continuous queries* needs to be considered in a new light. For example, suppose a car is traveling along a highway and the driver issues a query: Retrieve cheap motels within 5 kilometers from the current position. It makes sense to ask for this query to be continuously reevaluated, since the answer changes while the car moves. While in classical databases continuous queries (such as triggers) need to be reevaluated on each relevant update, here it is not obvious how they can be executed. In the following text, a strategy is described to evaluate a continuous query only once; reevaluation is only needed on explicit updates.

Another important issue is the problem of inherent imprecision and uncertainty that is related to the frequency of updates. Clearly, the motion of an object as represented by its motion vector will normally not represent the real motion exactly. The distance between the database position and the real position is called the *deviation*. Assuming that with an update the real position and speed are transmitted, the deviation at the update time[1] is 0, and then it generally grows with time. The database should be aware not only of the expected position but also of the range of possible deviations at a given time.

To keep the deviation and hence the uncertainty about an object's position bounded, we will assume a kind of "contract" between a moving object and the database managing its position: Whenever the deviation reaches a certain threshold, the moving object sends an update to inform the database about its current position and speed. Various policies exist for doing this; these are discussed in Section 3.4.

3.2 MOST—A Data Model for Current and Future Movement

3.2.1 Basic Assumptions

We now introduce the MOST (moving objects spatio-temporal) data model used in the remainder of the chapter. First, let us recall some standard assumptions. A database is a set of object classes. Each object class is given by its set of attributes.

It is also assumed that spatial data types, such as point, line, and polygon with suitable operations, are available. Here, the modeling is done a bit differently (compared with Section 1.2). Some object classes are designated as *spatial*, which means they have an attribute representing a spatial value, such as a point or a polygon. The object itself is then called a *point object* or a *polygon object*. Also, the operations on the spatial values (SDT operations in Section 1.2) are here applied to the objects directly. So, for example, if we have two point objects p_1 and p_2 and a polygon object *pol*, we can apply spatial operations such as DIST(p_1, p_2), returning the distance between the point attribute values of p_1 and p_2, or INSIDE(p_1, *pol*), testing whether the point attribute value of p_1 lies inside the polygon attribute value of *pol*. For all of this to work, it is necessary that each object has *exactly one* spatial attribute.

More specifically, we assume that each spatial object class is either a point class, a line class, or a polygon class.

[1] We assume that updates are executed instantaneously (i.e., there is no time difference between sending the update and performing the update in the database). In other words, valid time and transaction time are equal.

Of particular interest in this model are point objects. A first way of modeling point objects lets them have a special attribute called *pos*, which, in turn, has two components, called *subattributes*, denoted *pos.x* and *pos.y* (in case of a 2D coordinate system). The data types of the subattributes may be `int` or `real`.

Besides object classes, a database contains a special object called *Time*, which yields the current time at every instant. Time is discrete (i.e., the time domain is the natural numbers [represented as `int`]), and the value of the *Time* object increases by one at each *clock tick*.

3.2.2 Dynamic Attributes

The fundamental new idea in the MOST model is the so-called *dynamic attributes*. Each attribute of an object class is classified to be either *static* or *dynamic*. A static attribute is as usual. A dynamic attribute changes its value with time automatically. For example, the schema for an object class describing cars moving freely in the x, y-plane might be given as:

```
car (license_plate: string,
  pos: (x: dynamic real, y: dynamic real))
```

Not all attribute types are eligible to be dynamic. It is assumed that such a type has a value 0 and an addition operation. This holds for numeric types such as `int` or `real` but could be extended to types such as `point`.

Formally, a dynamic attribute A of type T (denoted A: T) is represented by three subattributes, *A.value*, *A.updatetime*, and *A.function*, where *A.value* is of type T, *A.updatetime* is a time value, and *A.function* is a function f: `int` $\rightarrow T$ such that at time $t = 0$, $f(t) = 0$. The semantics of this representation are called the *value* of A at time t and defined as:

$$value(A, t) = A.value + A.function(t - A.updatetime) \qquad \text{for } t \geq A.updatetime$$

An update sets *A.updatetime* to the current *time* value and changes *A.value*, *A.function*, or both.

If a query refers to the attribute A, its dynamic *value* is meant and used in the evaluation. Hence, the result depends on the time when the query is issued. It is also possible to refer to the subattributes directly and so access the representation of a dynamic attribute. For example, a user can ask for objects for which *pos.x.function* = 5 (meaning $f(t) = 5\ t$) to find objects whose speed in x-direction is 5.

While dynamic attributes are intended to support description of movement, they may be used to describe other time-dependent values (e.g., temperature).

3.2.3 Representing Object Positions

We have already seen the first method to describe moving point objects by dynamic x and y subattributes of the position attribute *pos*. This is appropriate for objects moving freely in the x, y-plane.

For vehicles, a more realistic assumption is that they move along road networks. The second method of modeling uses an attribute *loc* with six subattributes, called *loc.route*, *loc.startlocation*, *loc.starttime*, *loc.direction*, *loc.speed*, and *loc.uncertainty*. Here, *loc.route* is (a pointer to) a line spatial object, which describes the geometry of a path over the traffic network (i.e., the route along which the object is moving). *Loc.startlocation* is a point on *loc.route*, the location of the moving object at time *loc.starttime*. *Loc.direction* is a Boolean indicating the direction along the route (relative to east-west, north-south, or the end points of the route). *Loc.speed* is a function f giving the distance[2] from the *loc.startlocation* as a function of the time elapsed since the last location update, that is, since *loc.starttime*. It is assumed that every update sets *loc.starttime* and *loc.startlocation* to the position at that time. Again, we require $f(0) = 0$. In the most simple form, *loc.speed* stores a constant v, hence, the distance from *loc.startlocation* at time *loc.starttime* + t is $v \cdot t$. *Loc.uncertainty* is either a constant or a function of the number of time units elapsed since the last location update. It represents a threshold on the deviation of the object; whenever the threshold is reached, the object will send a location update. *Loc.uncertainty* is used and further discussed in Section 3.4.

The semantics of the *loc* attribute are again a time-dependent position (x, y) in the plane, which also happens to lie on the network. At time *loc.starttime*, it is *loc.startlocation*; at time *loc.starttime* + t, it is the position on *loc.route* at distance *loc.speed* $\cdot\, t$ from *loc.startlocation* in the direction *loc.direction*. Query evaluation may take the uncertainty into account—that is, the answer to a query for the location of object m at time t may be: The object is on the route *loc.route* at most *loc.uncertainty* before or behind position (x, y).

The *uncertainty* subattribute is, of course, not specific to the network modeling; it might be added to the *pos* attribute as well. In this case the answer to the query would be: The object is within a circle of radius *uncertainty* around position (x, y).

3.2.4 Database Histories

Queries in traditional database systems refer to the current state of the database. Queries in the MOST model may also refer to future states that are given implicitly by the dynamic attributes. First, we need to be more precise about what is meant by a database state.

[2] By distance, the distance along the route is meant.

A *database state* is a mapping that associates each object class with a set of objects of the appropriate type and associates the *Time* object with a time value. For any object o in a database, we denote its attribute A as $o.A$; if A has a subattribute B it is denoted as $o.A.B$. The value of $o.A$ in the database state s is denoted by $s(o.A)$, and $s(Time)$ gives the time value of database state s. For each dynamic attribute A, its value in state s is $value(A, s(Time))$.

A *database history* is an infinite sequence of database states, one for each clock tick. It starts at some time u and extends infinitely into the future—hence, is s_u, s_{u+1}, s_{u+2}, and so on. We denote the history starting at time u by H_u. The value of an attribute A in two consecutive database states s_i, s_{i+1} can be different, either due to an explicit update of A or because A is a dynamic attribute whose value has changed implicitly. At any time t the database states with a lower timestamp than t are called *past database history*; the infinite remainder of the sequence with higher timestamps is called *future database history*.

Note that an explicit update at a time $t > u$ affects all states from t on of a given history H_u. Suppose until $t - 1$, the history H_u is:

$$s_u, s_{u+1}, s_{u+2}, \ldots, s_{t-1}, s_t, s_{t+1}, s_{t+2}, \ldots$$

Then, from time t on, the history is

$$s_u, s_{u+1}, s_{u+2}, \ldots, s_{t-1}, s'_t, s'_{t+1}, s'_{t+2}, \ldots$$

Hence, with each clock tick, we get a new database state, and with each update, we get a new history. We denote a history starting at time u and as of time $u + k$ (i.e., updates have been performed until and including time $u + k$) by $H_{u,k}$. Hence, $H_{u,0} = H_u$ and with $t = u + k$ the history before the update is $H_{u,k-1}$, and after the update it is $H_{u,k}$.

Note that database histories are just a concept to define the semantics of queries; they are not stored or manipulated explicitly, which obviously would be impossible.

3.2.5 Three Types of Queries

Queries are predicates over database histories rather than just a single state. This leads to a distinction between three different types of queries, called *instantaneous*, *continuous*, and *persistent*. The same query can be posed in each of the three modes, with different results; these are explained next.

As we will see in Section 3.3, a query has an implicit concept of the current time. For example, there will be language constructs to express a condition "within the next 10 time units," which means within 10 time units from the current time. If nothing is said about time, the database state at the current time is meant. The current time is normally the time when the query is issued. We denote by $Q(H, t)$ a query Q evaluated on a database history H assuming a current time t.

A query Q posed at time t as an *instantaneous* query is evaluated as:

$Q(H_t, t)$ (*instantaneous query*)

That is, it is evaluated on the history starting at t, assuming t as the current time. For example, a query issued at time t by a car driver, "Find all motels within five kilometers from my position," will return all the motels within five kilometers from the car's position at time t.

It is important to observe that the concept of an instantaneous query does not imply that only the current database state is used. For example, the driver might also pose the query "find all motels that I will reach within 10 minutes," and this query refers to all database states having a timestamp between the current time and 10 minutes later.

The second type of query is the continuous query. Query Q posed at time t as a *continuous query* is evaluated as a sequence of queries:

$Q(H_t, t), Q(H_{t+1}, t+1), Q(H_{t+2}, t+2), \ldots$ (*continuous query*)

In other words, it is reevaluated on each clock tick as a new instantaneous query. The answer to the query also changes over time; at instant u the result of the instantaneous query $Q(H_u, u)$ is valid. If the result of the continuous query is displayed to the user, the contents of the display may change without user interaction. For example, the car driver may decide to run the query, "Find all motels within five kilometers from my position," as a continuous query in order to be informed when suitable motels become available.

Of course, reevaluating the query on each clock tick is not feasible. Instead, an evaluation algorithm is given that computes the answer to a continuous query just once, in the form of a set of tuples annotated with time stamps. For each tuple, its timestamp indicates the period of time during which it belongs to the result. When time progresses, tuples whose time period is entered are added to the answer set, and tuples whose time period expires are removed from the answer set.

As already discussed in the introduction to this chapter, the answer to a future query is tentative. For a continuous query, this means that the result set (tuples with timestamps) may become invalid due to an explicit update. Hence, a continuous query needs to be reevaluated on an update that may change its result set.

The third type of query, *persistent query*, is motivated by the fact that so far with continuous queries it is impossible to recognize certain kinds of developments over time. As an example, consider the query, Q = Find all cars whose speed has doubled within five minutes. Suppose this is posed as a continuous query at time $t = 20$ (and let time units be minutes). Let o be a car with *o.loc.speed* = 40. Further, let the speed of o be explicitly updated to 60 at time 22 and to 80 at time 24.

When the continuous query is evaluated as $Q(H_{20}, 20)$, in all future states the speed of o is 40; hence, it is not in the result. When it is evaluated as $Q(H_{22}, 22)$, in all future states the speed is 60. Similarly, when evaluated as an instantaneous query at time 24, in all future states the speed is 80. So o is never in the result.

Query Q posed at time t as a *persistent query* is evaluated as a sequence of queries:

$$Q(H_{t,0}, t), Q(H_{t,1}, t), Q(H_{t,2}, t), \ldots \qquad \textit{(persistent query)}$$

Hence, a persistent query is continuously evaluated on the history starting at time t and its answer changes when that history changes due to explicit updates.

Considering our example, when the fifth query in the previous sequence, $Q(H_{24}, 20)$, is evaluated, the fact that the speed of o has doubled from time 20 to time 24 is recognized, and o is returned as a result.

Again, reevaluation does not really occur on each clock tick; instead, it is done on each update that might affect its result, as is done for continuous queries.

We have included persistent queries in the discussion in order to show the different kinds of "continuous" queries that are possible from a semantic point of view. However, to evaluate persistent queries, it is necessary to keep information about past contents of the database (in other words, to use a kind of temporal version of the MOST data model, such as the models in Section 1.3). So far, the MOST model is nontemporal in the sense that values of subattributes are rewritten on updates and the previous values are lost. Extending the MOST model in this way is beyond the scope of this chapter, and we will not consider the evaluation of persistent queries further.

3.3 FTL—A Query Language Based on Future Temporal Logic

In this section, we describe FTL, a query language that allows us to express conditions about the future. We first introduce the language by some examples (Section 3.3.1), then define the syntax (Section 3.3.2) and semantics (Section 3.3.3) of the language precisely. Finally, in Section 3.3.4, an algorithm for evaluating FTL queries is presented.

3.3.1 Some Example Queries

Several example queries for moving objects applications have already been mentioned; let us see how some of them would be expressed in FTL.

Example 3.1 Which trucks are within 10 kilometers of truck T68?

```
RETRIEVE t
FROM trucks t, trucks s
WHERE s.id = 'T68' ∧ dist(s, t) ≤ 10
```
■

The general form of a query is:[3]

```
RETRIEVE <target-list> FROM <object-classes>
WHERE <FTL-formula>
```

The FTL formula is the interesting part. In the first example, nothing special happens yet. The syntax used is a "theoretical" one; in practice, we would replace the logical connective ∧ by a keyword "and" and type "<=" instead of ≤. Observe that the distance operator **dist** is applied to the objects directly rather than to point attributes, as discussed in Section 3.2.1.

The FTL language as such only deals with instantaneous queries. How we can get from instantaneous to continuous queries has been explained in the previous section. But to require a query to be evaluated as a continuous query is not within the scope of the language; it has to be specified externally (e.g., at the user interface).

Hence, the previous query is evaluated instantaneously at the time when it is issued. We assume trucks have a dynamic location (*loc*) attribute, and the distance is evaluated on the current positions of trucks *s* (T68) and *t*. The distance function **dist** is also assumed to operate over the network; hence, it involves a shortest-path computation.

Observe that the query is beautifully (and perhaps deceivingly) simple; nothing needs to be said about time, yet the query refers to the current situation and its result will change when posed at different times.

Example 3.2 Will truck T70 reach its destination within the next half hour?

As formulated, the query would require a boolean (yes or no) result, which is not directly possible. Instead, we will retrieve truck T70 if it reaches its destination in time; otherwise, the result will be empty.

We assume destinations to be modeled as a point object class *destinations*, where points lie on the traffic network. The *trucks* object class has an attribute *dest* giving its destination in form of a reference to such a destination object.

```
RETRIEVE t
FROM trucks t
WHERE t.id = 'T70' ∧ eventually_within_30 (dist(t, t.dest) = 0)
```

[3] In the original literature describing FTL the FROM clause is omitted; a single implicit class of moving objects is assumed.

Here, we assume again that time units are minutes. New is the temporal operator **eventually_within_c**, where c is a numeric constant referring to time units. It can be applied to a predicate p. The meaning of **eventually_within_c**(p) is: Within the next c time units, p will become true. ■

Example 3.3 To make the next example more interesting, we modify our helicopter query a bit: Retrieve the friendly helicopters that will arrive in the valley within the next 15 minutes and then stay in the valley for at least 5 minutes.

```
RETRIEVE h
FROM helicopters h
WHERE eventually_within_15 (inside(h, Valley) ∧
  always_for_5 (inside(h, Valley)))
```

Here, *Valley* is a polygon object and **inside** an operation comparing a point object with a polygon object. We assume that helicopters represented in this object class are all friendly; hence, there is no explicit condition for that.

Note that the condition says that within 15 minutes a database state will be reached such that helicopter h is inside the valley, and for the next five time units, this will always be true. ■

We can see that it is possible in the language to specify sequences of conditions that must become true in a certain order and to specify bounds on the periods of time involved. In the next section, we define the structure of the language precisely.

3.3.2 Syntax

The interesting part of the FTL language is the FTL formulas. FTL is similar to first-order logic; hence, the language consists of constants, variables, function symbols, predicate symbols, and so forth.

Definition 3.1 The FTL language consists of the following *symbols*:

1. *Constants*. These may be of the atomic data types (e.g., 54, "T68") or named objects in the database (e.g., *Valley*). The special database object *Time* is also a constant.
2. For each $n > 0$, a set of n-ary *function symbols*. Each function symbol denotes a function taking n arguments of particular types and returning a value of some type. Examples are +, * on type `int`, or the " ." operator, which takes an object of some object class and an attribute name and returns a value of the attribute type.

3. For each $n \geq 0$, a set of n-ary *predicate symbols*. Each predicate symbol denotes a relation with n arguments of specified types. For example, $\leq$, $\geq$ denote the usual arithmetic comparison operators.
4. *Variables*. These are typed and can range over object classes or atomic types. For example, h_{truck} is a variable ranging over the *truck* class, and j_{int} an integer variable. Usually the index denoting the domain of the variable is omitted.
5. Logical connectives $\wedge$, $\neg$.
6. The *assignment quantifier* $\leftarrow$.
7. Temporal modal operators **until**, **nexttime**.
8. Brackets and punctuation symbols "(", ")", "[", "]", and ",". ■

The MOST model and FTL language are designed to be implemented on top of a DBMS providing its own nontemporal query language (e.g., OQL). FTL allows us to embed so-called *atomic queries* from that underlying language. These are queries returning single values from atomic types (e.g., an integer). For example, the query:

```
RETRIEVE d.name FROM destinations d WHERE d.id = 'd12'
```

is such an atomic query returning a `string` value. Within FTL, this atomic query is viewed as a *constant* symbol. It is also possible that such a query contains a variable. For example, the query:

```
RETRIEVE d.name FROM destinations d WHERE d.id = y
```

has a free variable y. This is viewed as a function symbol denoting a unary function that returns for a given argument a `string` value.

Definition 3.2 A *term* is one of the following:

1. A constant c
2. A variable v
3. An attribute access $v.A$
4. An application of a function to terms of appropriate types $f(t_1, \ldots, t_n)$ ■

For example, 10, $x + 3$, **dist**(x, y), *d.name* are terms, and "retrieve d.name from destinations d where d.id = y" is also a term.

Definition 3.3 A *well-formed formula* is defined as follows:

1. If R is an n-ary predicate symbol and $t_1, \ldots, t_n$ are terms of appropriate types, then $R(t_1, \ldots, t_n)$ is a well-formed formula.
2. If f and g are well-formed formulas, then $f \wedge g$ and $\neg f$ are well-formed formulas.
3. If f and g are well-formed formulas, then f **until** g and **nexttime** f are well-formed formulas.
4. If f is a well-formed formula, x is a variable, and t is a term of the same type as x, then $([x \leftarrow t]\ f)$ is a well-formed formula. A variable in a formula is *free* if it is not in the scope of an assignment quantifier of the form $[x \leftarrow t]$. ■

The semantics of all this are defined in the next section. Observe that FTL does not have the existential and universal quantifiers of first-order logic;[4] instead, the assignment quantifier is offered that allows us to bind a variable to the result of a query in one of the states of a database history. In particular, it is possible to capture an atomic value at some point in time and relate it to other values at later points in time.

We have not yet discussed some constructs, such as **eventually_within_c**, occurring in the previous examples. These will be shown to be derivable from the primitives of the language and will be discussed in the following text.

3.3.3 Semantics

Let s_u be the state of the database when the query "retrieve <target-list> from <object-classes> where f" is entered. The semantics of formula f are defined with respect to the history starting with s_u, that is, history H_u.

First, we need to define the meaning of the symbols of the language.

1. *Constants* represent corresponding values from their domain. For example, 54 represents an integer, "T68" a character string, and *Valley* and *Time* represent database objects.
2. *Function symbols* have their standard interpretation or denote functions defined in the text. For example, the symbols + and * represent the standard addition and multiplication functions. The **dist** symbol represents the distance function described in Section 3.3.1.

[4] It is argued that this is to avoid problems of safety, which are more severe in the context of database histories. See standard database textbooks for a discussion of safety of the relational calculus, for example.

3. *Predicate symbols* also have their standard interpretation. For example, $\leq$ denotes the standard less than or equal relation.

In the sequel, we do not distinguish in notation between such symbols and their interpretation. For example, for a constant symbol *c*, the value represented is also denoted as *c*.

Definition 3.4 A *variable assignment* for formula *f* is a mapping μ that assigns to each free variable in *f* a value from its domain. We denote by $\mu[x/u]$ the mapping obtained from μ by assigning the value *u* to variable *x* and leaving all other variables unchanged. ■

Example 3.4 Let us assume that in the *truck* object class in Example 3.1, there are truck objects with object identifiers T_1 through T_{100}. Consider the formula:

```
s.id = 'T68' ∧ dist(s, t) ≤ 10
```

A possible variable assignment is $\mu = \{(s, T_{10}), (t, T_{20})\}$. ■

Definition 3.5 For a term *t*, its *evaluation* in a state *s* with respect to a variable assignment μ, denoted $\varphi_{s,\mu}[t]$, is defined as follows:

1. If *t* is a constant *c*, then $\varphi_{s,\mu}[c] = s(c)$.
2. If *t* is a variable *v*, then $\varphi_{s,\mu}[v] = \mu(v)$.
3. If *t* is an attribute access *v.A*, then $\varphi_{s,\mu}[v.A] = s(\mu[v].A)$.
4. If *t* is an application of function *f* to arguments $t_1, \ldots, t_n$, then $\varphi_{s,\mu}[f(t_1, \ldots, t_n)] = f(\varphi_{s,\mu}[t_1], \ldots, \varphi_{s,\mu}[t_n])$. ■

Observe that constants are evaluated in a database state; this is needed in particular for the constant *Time*. Also dynamic attributes are evaluated with respect to the current state.

We now define the satisfaction of a formula at a state *s* on a history *H* with respect to a variable assignment μ. Satisfaction is defined inductively on the structure of formulas.

Definition 3.6 Formula *f* is *satisfied* at state *s* on history *H* with respect to variable assignment μ [satisfied at (s, μ), for short]:

1. $R(t_1, \ldots, t_n)$ is satisfied $:\Leftrightarrow R(\varphi_{s,\mu}[t_1], \ldots, \varphi_{s,\mu}[t_n])$ holds.
2. $f \wedge g$ is satisfied $:\Leftrightarrow$ both *f* and *g* are satisfied at (s, μ).
3. $\neg f$ is satisfied $:\Leftrightarrow f$ is not satisfied at (s, μ).

4. f **until** g is satisfied :⇔ either g is satisfied at (s, μ), or there exists a future state s' on history H such that (g is satisfied at $(s', \mu) \wedge$ for all states s_i on history H before state s', f is satisfied at (s_i, μ)).
5. **nexttime** f is satisfied :⇔ f is satisfied at (s', μ), where s' is the state immediately following s in H.
6. $([x \leftarrow t]\, f)$ is satisfied :⇔ f is satisfied at $(s, \mu[x/\varphi_{s,\mu}[t]])$. ■

The assignment quantifier can be used in combination with the **nexttime** operator to detect change.

Example 3.5 The formula ($[x \leftarrow$ **dist**$(a, b)]$ (**nexttime** **dist**$(a, b) > x$)) is evaluated as follows. Let us assume it is evaluated in a state s, for which s' is the next state.

($[x \leftarrow$ **dist**$(a, b)]$ (**nexttime dist**$(a, b) > x$)) is satisfied at state s
⇔ (**nexttime dist**$(a, b) > \alpha$) is satisfied at state s, where α is the distance between objects a and b, evaluated in state s
⇔ (**dist**$(a, b) > \alpha$) is satisfied at state s'
⇔ $(\beta > \alpha)$ where β is the distance between objects a and b, evaluated in state s'

So the formula is satisfied if the distance between objects a and b increases from the current state to the next state. ■

Based on the given syntactical primitives for constructing formulas whose meanings are now well defined, some derived notations can be defined as follows.

First, in addition to the logical connectors $\wedge$ and $\neg$, we can also use $\vee$ and $\Rightarrow$, which can be defined in terms of the first two.

Second, temporal operators **eventually** and **always** can be defined as follows.

- **Eventually** g means that g will be fulfilled at some future state. It can be defined as *true* **until** g.
- **Always** g means that g is satisfied at all future states, including the present state. It is defined as $\neg$ (**eventually** $(\neg g)$).

In addition, it is useful to have related operators that have bounded, rather than infinite, periods of time. First, we define bounded versions of the **until** operator:

- g **until_within_c** h asserts that there exists a future time within at most c time units from now such that h holds, and until then g will be continuously satisfied.
- g **until_after_c** h asserts that there exists a future time after at least c time units from now such that h holds, and until then g will be continuously satisfied.

Exercise 3.1 Define the semantics of the **until_within_c** and the **until_after_c** operators in terms of existing constructs of the FTL language.

Based on these, we can define other bounded temporal operators:

- **Eventually_within_c** g asserts that the formula g will be fulfilled within c time units from the current state, defined as *true* **until_within_c** g.
- **Eventually_after_c** g means that g holds after at least c units of time, defined as *true* **until_after_c** g.
- **Always_for_c** g asserts that the formula g holds continuously for the next c units of time, defined as g **until_after_c** *true*.

So, finally, we have arrived at a definition of the temporal operators used in Exercises 3.2 and 3.3.

3.3.4 Evaluating FTL Queries

An interesting issue now is how FTL queries are processed and evaluated by an algorithm. From the set of FTL queries that can be formed according to Section 3.3.2, we here only consider the subset of so-called *conjunctive* formulas. Such a formula is constructed:

- Without negations
- Without the **nexttime** operator
- Without any reference to the *Time* object (Section 3.2.1)

The reason for excluding negations is safety (i.e., finiteness of the result), since negations may introduce infinite answers. The condition of excluding the time variable in queries implies that for every query q that is on the right side of an assignment in f (i.e., as in $[x \leftarrow \theta]$), the value returned by q at any time is independent of the time when it is evaluated; it is only the result of a *function* application assigning values to the free variables in q; and it depends only on the current positions of the objects. This condition also ensures that satisfaction of a nontemporal predicate when an object is at a particular position depends only on the position of the object but not on the time when the object reached the position.

The bounded temporal operators such as **eventually_within_c** are admitted, however. Since the *Time* object must not be used, the evaluation algorithm will handle the two basic operators **until_within_c** and **until_after_c** explicitly.

As an additional constraint, only instantaneous and continuous but not persistent queries are allowed.

The basic idea for evaluating an FTL formula is to compute for each formula f with free variables $x_1, \ldots, x_k$ a relation $R_f(x_1, \ldots, x_k, t_{start}, t_{end})$. That relation has one attribute for each of the free variables in f and two additional attributes t_{start}, t_{end} describing a time interval. Each tuple $(o_1, \ldots, o_k, t_1, t_2)$ of R_f represents one instantiation $\rho = <o_1, \ldots, o_k>$ of the variables $x_1, \ldots, x_k$ such that the formula is true for this instantiation during the time interval $[t_1, t_2]$.

Furthermore, for two tuples with the same *instantiation* $\rho = <o_1, \ldots, o_k>$ of the variables $x_1, \ldots, x_k$, the time intervals are disjoint and nonadjacent.

A set of tuples T with the same instantiation ρ and set of time intervals I represents a combination of objects $<o_1, \ldots, o_k>$ that fulfills f during times I.

An FTL formula is structured into subformulas according to Definition 3.3. The idea for evaluation is to compute relations for the atomic formulas first and then to evaluate formulas bottom-up, translating connectives into relation operations.

At the beginning of this section, we said that we consider a restricted class of formulas where negation and **nexttime** are missing and **until_within_c** and **until_after_c** are treated explicitly. Here is an update of Definition 3.3 for that case.

Definition 3.7 A *well-formed formula* (in the restricted case) is defined as follows:

1. If R is an n-ary predicate symbol and $t_1, \ldots, t_n$ are terms of appropriate types, then $R(t_1, \ldots, t_n)$ is a well-formed formula.
2. If f and g are well-formed formulas, then $f \wedge g$ is a well-formed formula.
3. If f and g are well-formed formulas, then f **until** g is a well-formed formula.
4. If f and g are well-formed formulas, then f **until_within_c** g is a well-formed formula.
5. If f and g are well-formed formulas, then f **until_after_c** g is a well-formed formula.
6. If f is a well-formed formula, x is a variable, and t is a term of the same type as x, then $([x \leftarrow t]\ f)$ is a well formed formula. A variable in a formula is *free* if it is not in the scope of an assignment quantifier of the form $[x \leftarrow t]$. ■

We now consider each of these cases in turn. Let h be a subformula with free variables $x_1, \ldots, x_l$.

Case 1: $h \equiv R(x_1, \ldots, x_l)$

Example: $h \equiv dist(x_1, x_2) < 8$

We assume that for each such atomic predicate an algorithm exists returning for each possible instantiation $<o_i, o_j>$ the time intervals when the predicate holds.

Compute a relation R_h with all such tuples $<o_1, \ldots, o_l>$ and associated time intervals.

Case 2: $h \equiv f \wedge g$

Let R_f and R_g be the relations computed for the subformulas—for example:

- $R_f(x_1, x_2, x_5, t_s, t_e)$
- $R_g(x_1, x_4, x_5, x_7, t_s, t_e)$

Then the result relation will have the schema:

- $R_h(x_1, x_2, x_4, x_5, x_7, t_s, t_e)$

Suppose for an instantiation $<o_1, o_2, o_4, o_5, o_7>$, f is satisfied during I_1 and g is satisfied during I_2. Then $f \wedge g$ is satisfied during $I_1 \cap I_2$. Therefore, compute the result relation R_h as follows. Compute a join of R_f and R_g; common variables must be equal, and time intervals must intersect. For each result tuple its time interval is the intersection of the time intervals of the two joining tuples.

Case 3: $h \equiv f$ until g

Let R_f and R_g be the relations computed for the subformulas, with $p + 2$ and $q + 2$ attributes, respectively.

Consider tuple t_1 in R_f. Let T_1 be the set of all tuples with the same values in the first p attributes (same instantiation). Let I_1 be the set of time intervals in T_1. Similarly, consider t_2 in R_g, T_2, and I_2.

Figure 3.1 shows tuples t_1 and t_2 with overlapping time intervals. Clearly, if f holds for the instantion of t_1 during its time interval, and if g holds for the instantiation of t_2 during its time interval, then f **`until`** g holds for the union of their time intervals.

Now consider the complete sets of time intervals I_1 and I_2 for these two instantiations (Figure 3.2). When does f **`until`** g hold?

Figure 3.1 Overlapping time intervals for two instantiations of formulas f and g.

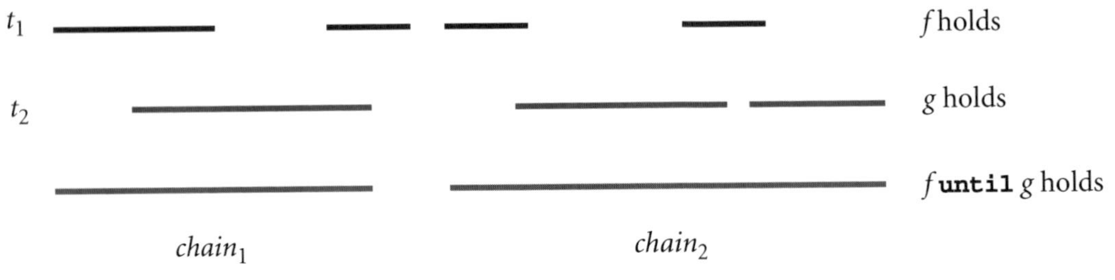

Figure 3.2 Time intervals for *f* **until** *g*.

Remember the semantics of *f* **until** *g*:

> *f* **until** *g* is satisfied :⇔ either *g* is satisfied at (s, μ), or there exists a future state s' on history H such that (g is satisfied at $(s', \mu) \wedge$ for all states s_i on history H before state s', f is satisfied at (s_i, μ)).

Therefore, *f* **until** *g* holds for periods of time when there are chains of intervals alternating between t_1 and t_2 up to the end of a t_2 interval, as illustrated in Figure 3.2.

Hence, compute R_h as follows: Compute a join of R_f and R_g matching pairs of (sets of) tuples with relation to their variable instantiations. For the two resulting sets of intervals I_1 and I_2, compute their *maximal chains*. For each maximal chain, construct one result tuple, with time interval corresponding to the extent of the chain.

An alternative formulation is: Compute solution intervals for any suitable pair of intervals of t_1 and t_2. Merge all sequences of overlapping solution intervals into one, and return this in a result tuple.

Exercise 3.2 Let us assume a set of tuples with the same instantiation ρ for the free variables but arbitrary and different time intervals. Sketch an algorithm that merges overlapping or consecutive intervals appropriately and achieves a transformation into a set of tuples with disjoint time intervals. ■

Case 4: *h* ≡ *f* until_within_c g

Recall the semantics of this case:

> *f* **until_within_c** *g* asserts that there is a future time within at most *c* time units from now such that *g* holds, and until then *f* will be continuously satisfied.

This case is illustrated in Figure 3.3.

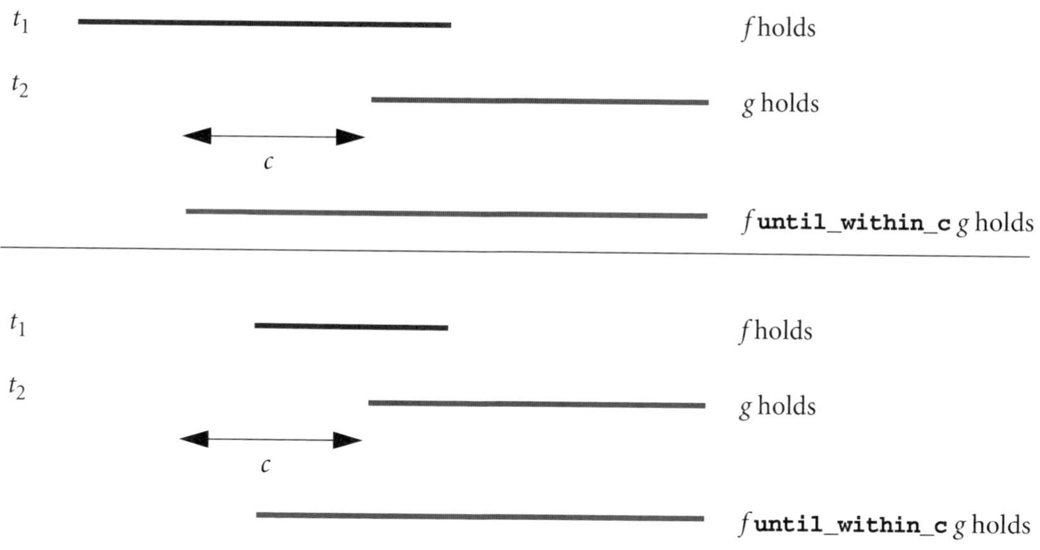

Figure 3.3 Time intervals for *f* **until_within_c** *g*.

Let t_1, t_2 be matching pairs of tuples from R_f and R_g with overlapping time intervals. Let $d = \max\{t_1.l, t_2.l - c\}$.[5] Then, *f* **until_within_c** *g* holds in the interval $[d, t_2.u]$. Extend to chains as before—that is, merge any overlapping solution intervals so discovered into one. The result relation is computed in a join, similar to Case 3.

Case 5: *h* ≡ *f* until_after_*c* g

This case is left to the exercises.

Exercise 3.3 Make a drawing and analyze Case 5 as was done for Case 4. ■

Case 6: *h* ≡ [*y* ← *q*] *f*

Here, *q* is a query yielding an atomic result—for example:

$$y \leftarrow \text{height}(o)$$

Let R_f be the result relation for *f*. The term *q* is in general a query and has to yield an atomic result so that it can be assigned to *y*. It usually contains some free variables. The result relation R_q for $[y \leftarrow q]$ is assumed to have $p + 3$ attributes, where the first *p* attributes relate to the free variables in *q*; the number $(p + 1)$ attribute

[5] We denote by *t.l* the left end of the time interval for tuple *t* and by *t.u* the right end.

stores the value of q; and the remaining two attributes represent a time interval. Each instantiation of the free variables in q leads to a result value stored as the number $(p + 1)$ attribute value, and if this value holds during n disjoint time intervals, n corresponding tuples are stored in R_q.

In our example, R_q has four attributes. The first attribute keeps the object id, the third and fourth attributes describe a time interval, and the second attribute gives the height of the object during this interval.

The result relation R_h for h is computed by joining R_q and R_f with the join condition that for any two tuples t_1 from R_q and t_2 from R_f the attribute values corresponding to common variables are equal; the attribute value corresponding to the y-value in R_f is equal to the query result value in t_1; and the time intervals of both tuples intersect. The output tuple consists of all variable attribute values stemming from t_1 and t_2, except for the attributes corresponding to variable y and the intersection of the intervals in t_1 and t_2.

This is what is described in the literature for Case 6. We believe there is a problem with this description—namely, the predicate f contains y as a free variable. The relation R_f has to be computed for all possible bindings of y but without any knowledge of the possible values for y. Note that in the other cases variables were ranging over object classes—hence, they could be bound to all existing object identifiers. It does not seem feasible to let y range over all integers if *height* would return an integer result, not to mention reals, if *height* returned a real number.

It seems that some additional trick is needed. For example, we might compute the relation R_q first. We could then project on the attribute corresponding to y and use the resulting set of values as a domain for the possible bindings of y in formula f.

This concludes the description of the algorithm for evaluating FTL formulas.

The result relation *Answer*(Q) can be used in the following way to answer continuous and instantaneous queries. For a continuous query Q at each clock tick t, the instantiations of the tuples having an interval that contains t are shown to the user. Let us assume, for example, that *Answer*(Q) includes the tuples (2, 10, 15) and (5, 12, 14). Then, the object with $id = 2$ is shown between the clock ticks 10 and 15 and between the clock ticks 12 and 14 the object with $id = 5$ is displayed. In the case of an instantaneous query Q the instantiations of all tuples having an interval that contains the current clock tick are presented.

Exercise 3.4 We consider a simplified highway network with some trucks with the identifiers T12, T42, and T70. (See Figure 3.4.)

The three trucks all move in the direction of the arrow and toward (and beyond) *T-City*. The raster units indicated on the network correspond to 10 kilometers. For each truck, its current position is the start point of the arrow. Truck T12 moves at a speed of 60 kilometers per hour, T42 at 100 kilometers per hour, and T70 at 120 kilometers per hour.

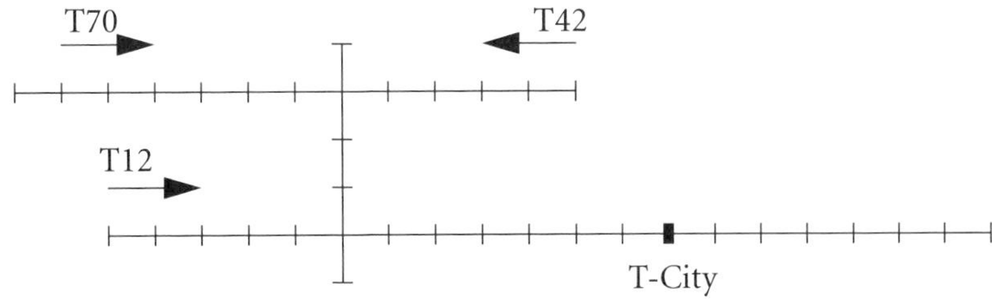

Figure 3.4 A highway network with three trucks.

Apply the algorithm described previously to evaluate the query:

```
RETRIEVE t
FROM trucks t
WHERE eventually_within_30 (dist(t, T_City) <= 20)
```

3.4 Location Updates—Balancing Update Cost and Imprecision

3.4.1 Background

The motion of spatial objects over time necessitates the transmission of updates of their current position and speed to the database in order to provide the database with up-to-date information for retrieval and query tasks and to keep the inherent imprecision in the database bounded. The main issue here is when and how often these position updates should be made. Frequent updating may be expensive in terms of cost and performance overhead; infrequent updates result in outdated answers to position queries. Consequently, the location of a moving object is inherently imprecise, since the object location stored in the database, which we will call *database location*, cannot always be identical to the actual location of the object. This holds regardless of the policy employed to update the database location of an object. Several *location update policies* may be applicable (e.g., the database location is updated every *n* clock tick). In this section, we introduce so-called *dead-reckoning* policies. These update the database whenever the distance between the actual location of a moving object and its database location exceeds a given *threshold th*, say 100 meters. Thus, this threshold determines and bounds the location imprecision. For a moving object *m*, a query "What is the current location of *m*?" will then be answered by the DBMS with "The current location of *m* is (x, y) with a deviation of at most 100 meters." Here, the issue is how to determine the update threshold *th* in dead-reckoning policies.

The feature of imprecision leads us to two related but different concepts: deviation and uncertainty. The *deviation* of a moving object m at a specific instant t is the distance between m's actual location at time t and its database location at time t. In our example, the deviation is the distance between the actual location of m and (x, y). The *uncertainty* of m at an instant t is the size of the area comprising all possible, current positions of m. In our example, the uncertainty is the size of the area of a circle with a radius of 100 meters. Both deviation and uncertainty are afflicted with a cost in terms of incorrect decision making. The deviation (uncertainty) cost is proportional to the size of the deviation (uncertainty). We will see that the ratio between the costs of an uncertainty unit and a deviation unit depends on the interpretation of an answer.

To be able to update the database location of a moving object, we need an appropriate localization mechanism. In moving objects applications, each moving object is usually equipped with a *Global Positioning System (GPS)* and can thus generate and transmit the updates by using a wireless network. This introduces a third cost factor: communication or transmission cost. Furthermore, we can recognize an obvious trade-off between communication and imprecision in the sense that the higher the communication cost, the lower the imprecision, and vice versa. This leads to the issue of an information cost model in moving objects databases that balances imprecision and update cost. The model should also be able to cope with the situation where a moving object becomes disconnected and cannot send location updates.

3.4.2 The Information Cost of a Trip

The first issue we deal with relates to an information cost model for a trip taken by a moving object. We have seen that during a trip a moving object causes a deviation cost and an uncertainty cost, which both can be regarded as a penalty due to incorrect decision making. Moreover, a moving object causes update cost, since location update messages have to be sent to the database.

For a moving object the *deviation cost* depends both on the size of the deviation as well as on the duration for which it lasts. The size of the deviation affects the decision-making process. The higher the deviation is, the more difficult and imprecise it is to make a reliable decision based on the moving object's current position. To see that the duration for which the deviation persists plays a role for calculating the cost, we assume that there is one query per time unit that retrieves the location of a moving object. If the deviation lasts for n time units, its cost will be n times the cost of the deviation lasting for a single time unit, because all queries instead of only one have to pay the deviation penalty. Formally, for a given moving object, the cost of the deviation between a starting time t_1 and an ending time t_2 can be described by the *deviation cost function* $COST_d(t_1, t_2)$ yielding a nonnegative number. Assuming that the penalty for each unit of deviation during a time unit is weighted by the constant 1, the deviation cost function can be defined as:

$$COST_d(t_1, t_2) = \int_{t_1}^{t_2} d(t)dt$$

where $d(t)$ describes the deviation as a function of time. We also denote this function as *uniform* deviation cost function. It is the basis for all later descriptions of update policies. Of course, other deviation cost functions are conceivable. An example is the step deviation cost function. This function yields a penalty of 0 for each time unit in which the deviation falls below a given threshold *th*, and it yields a penalty of 1 otherwise.

The *update cost* C_1 covers the effort for transmitting a single location update message from a moving object to the database. It is difficult to determine it precisely, because it can be different from one moving object to another, or even vary for a single moving object during a trip (e.g., due to changing availability of resources such as bandwidth or computation). Of course, we have to measure the update cost by using the same kind of unit as for the deviation cost. With respect to the ratio between the update cost and the cost of a deviation unit per time unit, we can state that it is equal to C_1, since the latter cost factor is assumed to be 1. We can also conclude that in order to reduce the deviation by 1 during a time unit, the moving object will need $1/C_1$ messages.

The *uncertainty cost* depends on the size of uncertainty and on the duration for which it lasts. A higher degree of uncertainty conveys less reliable information for answering a query. Formally, for a given moving object, the cost of the uncertainty between a starting time t_1 and an ending time t_2 can be described by the *uncertainty cost function* $COST_u(t_1, t_2)$ yielding a nonnegative number. Let the *uncertainty unit cost* C_2 be the penalty for each uncertainty unit during a time unit. This implies that C_2 is defined as the ratio between the cost of an uncertainty unit and the cost of a deviation unit, since the latter cost is assumed to be equal to 1. Then, the *uncertainty cost function* $COST_u(t_1, t_2)$ can be defined as:

$$COST_u(t_1, t_2) = \int_{t_1}^{t_2} C_2 u(t)dt$$

where $u(t)$ is the value of the *loc.uncertainty* attribute (see Section 3.2.3) of the moving object as a function of time. We can now exert influence on the weighting and thus the importance of the uncertainty factor and the deviation factor. If for answering the query "The current location of the moving object *m* is (x, y) with a deviation of at most *u* units" the uncertainty aspect is to be stressed, C_2 should be set higher than 1, and lower than 1 otherwise. In a dead-reckoning update policy, each update message to the database determines a new uncertainy, which is not necessarily lower than the previous one. Hence, an increase of communication reduces the deviation but not necessarily the uncertainty.

We are now in the position to define the information cost of a trip taken by a moving object. Let t_1 and t_2 be the times of two consecutive location update messages. Then, the *information cost* in the half open interval $[t_1, t_2[$ is:

$$COST_I([t_1, t_2[) = C_1 + COST_d([t_1, t_2[) + COST_u([t_1, t_2[)$$

The result contains the message cost at time t_1 but not at time t_2. Since each location update message writes the actual current position of the moving object in the database, the deviation is reduced to 0. The total information cost is calculated by summing up all $COST_I([t_1, t_2[)$ values for every pair of consecutive update instants t_1 and t_2. Formally, let $t_1, t_2, \ldots, t_n$ be the instants of all update messages sent from a moving object. Let 0 be the time point when the trip started and t_{n+1} be the time point when the trip ended. Then, the *total information cost* of a trip is:

$$COST_I([0, t_{n+1}[) = COST_d([0, t_1[) + COST_u([0, t_1[) + \sum_{i=1}^{n} COST_I([t_i, t_{i+1}[)$$

3.4.3 Cost-Based Optimization for Dead-Reckoning Policies

Next, we consider the issue of information cost optimality. We know that the essential feature of all dead-reckoning update policies consists of the existence of a threshold *th* at any instant. This threshold is checked against the distance between the location of a moving object *m* and its database location. Hence, both the DBMS and the moving object must have knowledge of *th*. When the deviation of *m* exceeds *th*, *m* sends a location update message to the database. This message contains the current location, the predicted speed, and the new deviation threshold *K*. The goal of dead-reckoning policies is to set *K*, which is stored by the DBMS in the *loc.uncertainty* subattribute, such that the total information cost is minimized.

The general strategy is the following: First, *m* predicts the future behavior and direction of the deviation. This prediction is used as a basis for computing the average cost per time unit between now and the next update as a function *f* of the new threshold *K*. Then, *K* is set to minimize *f*. The proposed method of optimizing *K* is not unique. The optimization is related to the average cost *per time unit* and not to the total cost between the two instants t_1 and t_2, because the total cost increases as the time interval until the next update increases. For the case that the deviation between two consecutive updates is described by a linear function of time, we can determine the optimal value *K* for *loc.uncertainty*.

Let C_1 denote the update cost and C_2 denote the uncertainty cost. We assume that t_1 and t_2 are the instants of two consecutive location updates, that the deviation $d(t)$ between t_1 and t_2 is given by the linear function $a(t - t_1)$ with $t_1 \leq t \leq t_2$ and a positive constant a, and that *loc.uncertainty* is fixed at K between t_1 and t_2. The statement is then that the total information cost per time unit between t_1 and t_2 is minimal if $K = \sqrt{(2aC_1)/(2C_2+1)}$. This can be shown as follows: We take the formula for computing the information cost in an interval $[t_1, t_2[$ and insert our assumptions. We obtain:

$$\begin{aligned} COST_I([t_1, t_2[) &= C_1 + \int_{t_1}^{t_2} a(t-t_1)dt + \int_{t_1}^{t_2} C_2 K dt \\ &= C_1 + 0.5a(t_2 - t_1)^2 + C_2K(t_2 - t_1) \end{aligned}$$

Let $f(t_2) = COST_I([t_1, t_2[)/(t_2 - t_1)$ denote the average information cost per time unit between t_1 and t_2 for the update time t_2. We know that t_1 and t_2 are two consecutive update times. Hence, at t_2 the deviation exceeds the threshold *loc.uncertainty* so that $K = a(t_2 - t_1)$. We can now replace t_2 in $f(t_2)$ by $K/a + t_1$ and obtain $f(K) = aC_1/K + (0.5 + C_2)K$. Using the derivative the minimum of $f(K)$ is at $K = \sqrt{(2aC_1)/(2C_2+1)}$.

What is the interpretation of this result? Let us assume that m is currently at instant t_1. This means that its deviation has exceeded the uncertainty threshold *loc.uncertainty*. Hence, m needs to compute a new value for *loc.uncertainty* and transmit it to the database. Let us further assume that m predicts a linear behavior of the deviation. Then, *loc.uncertainty* has to be assigned a value that will remain fixed until the next update. In order to minimize the information cost, the recommendation then is that m should set the threshold to $K = \sqrt{(2aC_1)/(2C_2+1)}$.

Finally, we try to detect disconnection of a moving object from the database. Then, the moving object cannot send location updates. In this case, we are interested in a dead-reckoning policy in which the uncertainty threshold *loc.uncertainty* continuously decreases between updates. As an example of decrease, we consider a threshold *loc.uncertainty decreasing fractionally* and starting with a constant K. This means that during the first time unit after the location update u, the value of the threshold is K; during the second time unit after u the value is $K/2$; and during the ith time unit after u the value is K/i, until the next update, which determines a new K. Assuming a linear behavior of the deviation, the total information cost per time unit between t_1 and t_2 is given by the function $f(K) = (C_1 + 0.5K + C_2K(1 + 1/2 + 1/3 + \ldots + 1/\sqrt{K/a})) / \sqrt{K/a}$.

Exercise 3.5 Prove the correctness of $f(K)$.

The interpretation of this result is similar to the previous one. In order to optimize the information cost, the moving object should set K to the value that minimizes $f(K)$.

3.4.4 Dead-Reckoning Location Update Policies

A *location update policy* is a position update prescription or strategy for a moving object that determines when the moving object propagates its actual position to the database and what the update values are. We discuss here a few *dead-reckoning* location update policies that set the deviation bound (i.e., the threshold *th*) stored in the subattribute *loc.uncertainty* in a way so that the total information cost is minimized.

The first strategy is called the *speed dead-reckoning* (*sdr*) *policy.* At the beginning of a trip, the moving object *m* fixes an uncertainty threshold in an ad hoc manner and transmits it to the database into the *loc.uncertainty* subattribute. The threshold remains unchanged for the duration of the whole trip, and *m* updates the database whenever the deviation exceeds *loc.uncertainty.* The update information includes the current location and the current speed. A slight, more flexible variation or extension of this concept is to take another kind of speed (e.g., the average speed since the last update, the average speed since the beginning of the trip, or a speed that is predicted based on terrain knowledge).

The *adaptive dead-reckoning* (*adr*) *policy* starts like the *sdr* policy, with an initial deviation threshold th_1 selected arbitrarily and sent to the database by *m* at the beginning of the trip. Then, *m* tracks the deviation and sends an update message to the database when the deviation exceeds th_1. The update consists of the current speed, the current location, and a new threshold th_2 stored in the *loc.uncertainty* attribute. The threshold th_2 is computed as follows: Let us assume that t_1 denotes the number of time units from the beginning of the trip until the deviation exceeds th_1 for the first time and that I_1 is the deviation cost (according to the formula in Section 3.4.2) during that interval. Let us assume further $a_1 = 2I_1 / t_1 2$. Then, $th_2 = \sqrt{(2a_1C_1)/(2C_2 + 1)}$, where C_1 is the update cost and C_2 is the uncertainty unit cost. When the deviation reaches th_2, a similar update is sent. This time the threshold is $th_3 = \sqrt{(2a_2C_1)/(2C_2 + 1)}$, where $a_2 = 2I_2 / t_2 2$, I_2 is the deviation cost from the first update to the second update, and t_2 is the number of time units elapsed since the first location update. That is, a difference between a_1 and a_2 results in a difference between th_2 and th_3. Further thresholds th_i are computed in a similar way.

The main difference between the *sdr* policy and the *adr* policy is that the first policy pursues an ad hoc strategy for determining a threshold, while the latter policy is cost based. At each update instant p_i, the *adr* policy optimizes the information cost per time unit and assumes that the deviation following instant p_i will behave according to the linear function $d(t) = 2tI_i / t_i 2$, where t is the number of time units after p_i, t_i is the number of time units between the preceding update and the current one at time p_i, and I_i is the deviation cost during the same time interval. This prediction of the future deviation can be explained as follows. *Adr* approximates the current deviation from the time of the preceding update to time p_i by a linear function with slope $2I_i / t_i 2$. At time p_i this linear function has the same deviation cost (i.e., I_i) as the actual current deviation. Due to the locality principle, the prediction of *adr* after the update at time p_i leads to a behavior of the deviation according to the same approximation function.

Exercise 3.6 Let us assume that at the beginning of a trip the moving object m sends a location update message giving its route, its location on the route, *loc.speed* = 0.2 miles/minute, and *loc.uncertainty* = 0.5 miles. Suppose that after four minutes the deviation exceeds the threshold 0.2 and that then m transmits its current location on the route, its current speed, and a new value for *loc.uncertainty.* The integral of the deviation from the beginning of the trip at time 0 to time 4 in minutes shall be 1, and $C_1 = 8$, and $C_2 = 1$. Compute the new value for *loc.uncertainty* according to the *adr* policy. Suppose that 10 minutes later the deviation reaches this new threshold and that the integral of the deviation from time 4 to time 14 is 1.5. Compute again the new value for *loc.uncertainty.* ■

The last strategy we discuss is the *disconnection detection dead-reckoning* (*dtdr*) *policy.* This policy is an answer to the problem that updates are not generated because the deviation does not exceed the uncertainty threshold, but because the moving object m is disconnected. At the beginning of the trip, m sends an initial, arbitrary deviation threshold th_1 to the database. The uncertainty threshold *loc.uncertainty* is set to a fractionally decreasing value starting with th_1 for the first time unit. During the second time unit, the uncertainty threshold is $th_1/2$ and so on. Then, m starts tracking the deviation. At time t_1, when the deviation reaches the current uncertainty threshold (i.e., th_1/t_1), m sends a location update message to the database. The update comprises the current speed, the current location, and a new threshold th_2 to be stored in the *loc.uncertainty* subattribute.

For computing th_2, we use the function $f(K) = (C_1 + 0.5K + C_2K(1 + 1/2 + 1/3 + \ldots + 1/\sqrt{K/a_1}))/\sqrt{K/a_1}$ (see Section 3.4.3). Since $f(K)$ uses the slope factor a of the future deviation, we first estimate this deviation. Let I_1 be the cost of the deviation since the beginning of the trip, and let $a_1 = 2I_1/t_{12}$. The formula for $f(K)$ does not have a closed form. Hence, we approximate the sum $1 + 1/2 + 1/3 + \ldots + 1/\sqrt{K/a_1}$ by $\ln(\sqrt{K/a_1})$, since $\ln(n)$ is an approximation of the nth harmonic number. Thus the approximation function of $f(K)$ is $g(K) = (C_1 + 0.5K + C_2K(1 + \ln(\sqrt{K/a_1})))/\sqrt{K/a_1}$. The derivation of $g(K)$ is 0 when K is the solution of the equation $\ln(K) = d_1/K - d_2$ with $d_1 = 2C_1/C_2$ and $d_2 = 1/C_2 + 4 - \ln(a_1)$. By using the well known Newton-Raphson method, we can find a numerical solution to this equation. The solution leads to the new threshold th_2, and m sets the uncertainty threshold *loc.uncertainty* to a fractionally decreasing value starting with th_2.

After t_2 time units, the deviation exceeds the current uncertainty threshold, which is equal to th_2/t_2, and a location update containing th_3 is transmitted. The value th_3 is computed as previously but with a new slope a_2. I_2 is the deviation cost during the previous t_2 time units. This process, which continues until the end of the trip at each update instant, determines the next optimal threshold by incorporating the constants C_1 and C_2 and the slope a_i of the current deviation approximation function.

Exercise 3.7 Let us assume that at the beginning of a trip the moving object m sends a location update message giving its route, its location on the route, *loc.speed* = 0.2 miles/minute, and *loc.uncertainty* = 0.5 miles. A time unit is one minute. Determine the threshold for the first minute and for the second minute according to the *dtdr* policy. Suppose that during the second minute of the trip the deviation exceeds the current threshold and that then m transmits its current location on the route, its current speed, and a new value for *loc.uncertainty*. The integral of the deviation from the beginning of the trip at time 0 to time 2 shall be 0.5, and $C_1 = 8$, and $C_2 = 1$. Compute the slope a_1 of the deviation estimator and the new value for *loc.uncertainty*. Suppose that five minutes later the deviation reaches its new current threshold and that then the integral of the deviation from time 2 to time 7 is 1.2. Compute the current threshold, the new slope a_2 of the deviation estimator, and the new value for *loc.uncertainty*. ■

An interesting question now is which of the three discussed dead-reckoning location update policies causes the lowest information costs. This has been empirically investigated in a simulation testbed used to compare the information cost of the three policies on the assumption that the uncertainty threshold is arbitrary and fixed. The result of this comparison is that the *adr* policy is superior to the other policies and hence has the lowest information cost. It may even have an information cost that is six times lower than that of the *sdr* policy.

3.5 The Uncertainty of the Trajectory of a Moving Object

We have seen that uncertainty is an inherent feature in databases storing information about the current and near-future locations of moving objects. Unless uncertainty is captured in the model and query language, the burden of coping with it and reflecting it in the answers to queries will inevitably, and at the same time hopelessly, be left to the user. In this section, we consider the issue of *uncertainty* of the *trajectory* of a moving object.

The concept of trajectory goes beyond the simple model of motion vectors treated so far in this chapter. A trajectory can be viewed as a motion plan for the future, but it can also be used to represent a history of movement, the topic of the next chapter. Nevertheless, we treat it in this chapter, since also bounded uncertainty is involved, which is related to the update policies discussed in the previous section.

3.5.1 A Model of a Trajectory

Usually, the trajectory of a moving object is modeled as a polyline in three-dimensional space (see Chapter 4). Two dimensions relate to space and the third dimension to time. If we in addition aim at capturing the uncertainty aspect, we can model the trajectory as a cylindrical volume in three-dimensional space. We can then ask for objects that are inside a particular region during a particular time interval. Due to the uncertainty aspect, we can go a step further and take into account the *temporal uncertainty* and the *regional uncertainty* of objects. We can then query the objects that are inside the region *sometime* or *always* during the time interval (temporal uncertainty). Similarly, we may ask for the objects that are *possibly* or *definitely* inside the region. This allows us to pose queries such as:

- Retrieve the current location of the trucks that will *possibly* be inside a region *R* *sometime* between 1:00 P.M. and 1:10 P.M.
- Retrieve the number of planes that will *definitely* be inside the region *R* *sometime* between 4:30 P.M. and 4:45 P.M.
- Retrieve the police cars that will *possibly* be inside the region *R* *always* between 9:20 A.M. and 9:50 A.M.

We now characterize the spatio-temporal nature of a moving object by the following definition of a trajectory:

Definition 3.8 A *trajectory* of a moving object is a polyline in the three-dimensional space, where two dimensions refer to space and the third dimension to time. It is represented as a sequence of points $\langle(x_1, y_1, t_1), \ldots, (x_n, y_n, t_n)\rangle$ with $t_1 < \ldots < t_n$. For a given trajectory *tr*, its spatial projection on the *xy*-plane is called the *route* of *tr*. ■

The location of a moving object is here given as an implicit function of time. The object is at position (x_i, y_i) at time t_i, and during each period $[t_i, t_{i+1}]$, the object is assumed to move along a straight line from (x_i, y_i) to (x_{i+1}, y_{i+1}) at a constant speed.

Definition 3.9 For a given trajectory *tr*, the *expected location* of the moving object at a point in time *t* between t_i and t_{i+1} with $1 \le i < n$ is obtained by linear interpolation between the positions (x_i, y_i) and (x_{i+1}, y_{i+1}). ■

The trajectory can be thought of as a set of points describing the future *motion plan* of the object. This set of points is visited and traversed by the object. Between two consecutive points we assume the object is moving along the shortest path (i.e., on a straight line, with constant speed).

3.5.2 Uncertainty Concepts for Trajectories

To express the uncertainty of a trajectory or motion plan, we associate an uncertainty threshold *th* with each line segment of the trajectory. In total, we thus obtain a three-dimensional, cylindrical “buffer zone” around the trajectory. For a given motion plan, the corresponding buffer zone has the following meaning for the moving object and the server: The moving object will update the server if its actual location deviates from its expected location by the distance *th* or more.

In practice, we can imagine that the on-board computer of the moving object is equipped with a GPS device, which receives an update every two seconds so that it knows its actual position. In addition, the moving object is aware of its motion plan and thus its trajectory so that, on the assumption of constant speed, it can interpolate its expected location at any instant. The deviation can then be simply computed as the distance between the actual and the expected location.

More formally, we can describe these uncertainty concepts for trajectories by the following definitions.

Definition 3.10 Let *th* be a positive real number and *tr* be a trajectory. The corresponding *uncertainty trajectory* is the pair (*tr*, *th*). The value *th* is called the *uncertainty threshold*. ■

Next, we give a definition for the buffer zone.

Definition 3.11 Let $tr = \langle (x_1, y_1, t_1), \ldots, (x_n, y_n, t_n) \rangle$ be a trajectory and *th* be the uncertainty threshold. For each point (x, y, t) along the time axis, its *th-uncertainty area*, or *uncertainty area* for short, is given by a horizontal circle with radius *th* centered at (x, y, t), where (x, y) is the expected location at time $t \in [t_1, t_n]$. ■

An interesting issue now is which motion curves are allowed in the uncertainty area so that a location update does *not* have to be propagated to the database.

Definition 3.12 Let $tr = \langle (x_1, y_1, t_1), \ldots, (x_n, y_n, t_n) \rangle$ be a trajectory and *th* be the uncertainty threshold. A *possible motion curve* is the image of any function of the set $PMC_{tr,th} = \{f: [t_1, t_n] \rightarrow \mathbb{R}^2 \mid f \text{ is continuous} \wedge \text{for all } t \in [t_1, t_n], f(t) \text{ is located inside the } th\text{-uncertainty area of the expected location of } tr \text{ at time } t\}$. Its two-dimensional, spatial projection is called *possible route*. ■

Consequently, a moving object does not have to update the database as long as it is on some possible motion curve of its uncertain trajectory. We are now able to define the buffer zone around a line segment of the trajectory.

Definition 3.13 For an uncertain trajectory (*tr*, *th*) and two end points (x_i, y_i, t_i) and $(x_{i+1}, y_{i+1}, t_{i+1})$ of *tr*, the *segment trajectory volume* of (*tr*, *th*) between t_i and t_{i+1} is the set of all points (x, y, t) such that (x, y, t) belongs to a possible motion curve of *tr* and $t_i \leq t \leq t_{i+1}$. The two-dimensional, spatial projection of the segment trajectory volume is called the *segment uncertainty zone.* ■

This definition can now be easily generalized to the whole trajectory.

Definition 3.14 For a trajectory $tr = \langle(x_1, y_1, t_1), \ldots, (x_n, y_n, t_n)\rangle$ and an uncertainty threshold th, the *trajectory volume* of (tr, th) is the set of all segment trajectory volumes between t_i and t_{i+1} for all $1 \leq i < n$. The two-dimensional, spatial projection of the trajectory volume is called the *uncertainty zone.* ■

Definitions 3.12, 3.13, and 3.14 are illustrated in Figure 3.5. Each segment trajectory volume between t_i and t_{i+1} has a cylindrical body. Its axis is the vector from (x_i, y_i) to (x_{i+1}, y_{i+1}), which specifies the three-dimensional trajectory line segment, and its bases are the circles with radius th in the planes at $t = t_i$ and $t = t_{i+1}$. This cylindrical body is different from a tilted cylinder. The intersection of a tilted cylinder with a horizontal xy-plane yields an ellipse, whereas the intersection of the cylindrical body, which we have obtained here, with such a plane yields a circle.

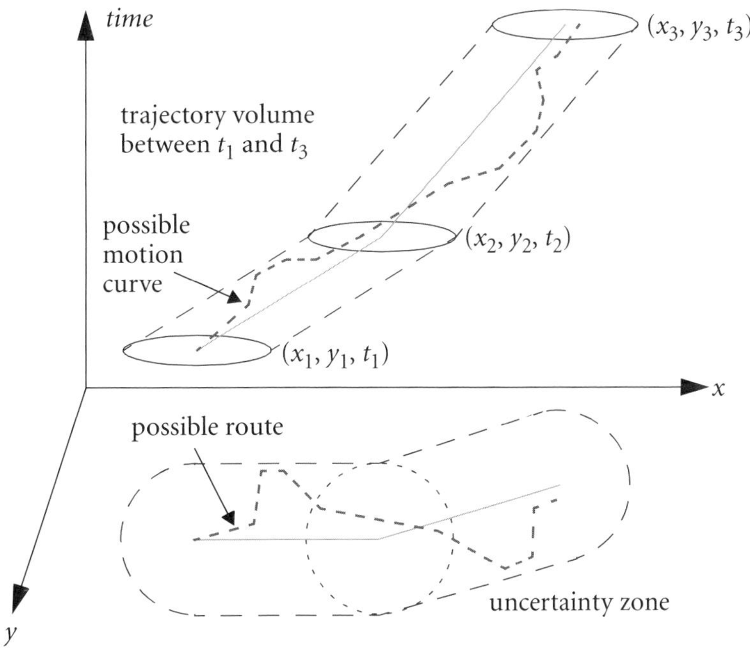

Figure 3.5 A possible motion curve, its possible route, and its trajectory volume.

Exercise 3.8 Let v_{x_i} and v_{y_i} denote the x- and y-components of the velocity of a moving object along the ith segment of the route—that is, between (x_i, y_i) and (x_{i+1}, y_{i+1}). Show that the segment trajectory volume between t_i and t_{i+1} is the set of all points (x, y, t) that satisfy $t_i \leq t \leq t_{i+1}$ and $(x - (x_i + v_{x_i} \cdot t))^2 + (y - (y_i + v_{y_i} \cdot t))^2 \leq r^2$. ■

3.5.3 Querying Moving Objects with Uncertainty

The interesting issue now is: How can we query moving objects with uncertainty given by their trajectories, and what are the most essential operators for doing this? First, we can identify two operators that relate to a single trajectory. This leads us to *point* queries. Second, we present a collection of six operators specifying Boolean conditions that assess a qualitative description of the relative position of a moving object with respect to a given region within a given time interval. This leads us to a concept for *spatio-temporal predicates.* The application of each of these eight operators corresponds to a spatio-temporal *range* query.

The two operators for point queries are named **whereAt** and **whenAt** with the following signatures:

whereAt:	*trajectory* × *time* → *point*
whenAt:	*trajectory* × *point* → *instants*

The operator **whereAt**(tr, t) returns the expected location (i.e., a two-dimensional point), on the route of tr at time t. The operator **whenAt**(tr, l) returns the times at which an object moving along trajectory tr is at an expected location l. Here, the answer may be a set of times captured by a value of a type *instants*, in case the moving point passes through a certain location more than once. If the route of tr does not traverse l, we determine the set C of all those points on this route that are closest to l. The operator then returns the set of times at which the moving object is expected to be at each point in C.

Next, we consider six Boolean predicates, which all share the property that they are satisfied if a moving object is inside a given region R during a given time interval $[t_1, t_2]$. This means we can use them for spatio-temporal range queries. Their differences result from existential and all quantifications with respect to three aspects. First, we can temporally quantify the validity of a predicate and ask whether the moving object satisfies the condition *sometime* or *always* within $[t_1, t_2]$. Second, we can spatially quantify the validity of a predicate and ask whether the object satisfies the condition *somewhere* or *everywhere* within the region R. Third, we can quantify the validity of a predicate with respect to uncertainty and ask whether the object satisfies the condition *possibly* or *definitely.*

Since we have three kinds of quantification, there are 3! different orders (permutations) to arrange them. For each fixed order, we have 2^3 possibilities to combine the three quantification aspects. This results in $2^3 \cdot 3! = 48$ possible operators. Since it is not reasonable to require that a point object is *everywhere* in R, we do not consider this quantification in the following. This means that the spatial quantifier *somewhere* is the default. Hence, we only obtain $2^2 \cdot 2! = 8$ possible operators. These eight predicates π_i all have the signature:

π_i: *uncertainTrajectory* × *region* × *time* × *time* → *bool*

and are now defined.

Definition 3.15 Let r be a *simple* query region (i.e., a region whose interior is connected and that does not have holes). Let $ut = (tr, th)$ be an uncertain trajectory. We can then define the following *spatio-temporal predicates*:

1. The predicate **PossiblySometimeInside**(ut, r, t_1, t_2) is *true* if there is a possible motion curve c of ut and there is a time $t \in [t_1, t_2]$ such that c is inside r at t.
2. The predicate **SometimePossiblyInside**(ut, r, t_1, t_2) is *true* if predicate **PossiblySometimeInside**(ut, r, t_1, t_2) is *true*.
3. The predicate **PossiblyAlwaysInside**(ut, r, t_1, t_2) is *true* if there is a possible motion curve of ut that is inside r for every $t \in [t_1, t_2]$.
4. The predicate **AlwaysPossiblyInside**(ut, r, t_1, t_2) is *true* if for every instant $t \in [t_1, t_2]$ a possible motion curve of ut exists that will intersect r at time t.
5. The predicate **AlwaysDefinitelyInside**(ut, r, t_1, t_2) is *true* if at every time $t \in [t_1, t_2]$ every possible motion curve of ut is in r.
6. The predicate **DefinitelyAlwaysInside**(ut, r, t_1, t_2) is *true* if predicate **AlwaysDefinitelyInside**(ut, r, t_1, t_2) is *true*.
7. The predicate **DefinitelySometimeInside**(ut, r, t_1, t_2) is *true* if for every possible motion curve of ut a time $t \in [t_1, t_2]$ exists in which this motion curve is inside r.
8. The predicate **SometimeDefinitelyInside**(ut, r, t_1, t_2) is *true* if an instant $t \in [t_1, t_2]$ exists at which every possible motion route of ut is inside r. ■

Intuitively, the validity of the predicate in item 1 implies that the moving object may take a possible route within its uncertainty zone, such that this route will intersect r between t_1 and t_2. In item 3, the predicate is satisfied if the motion of the object follows at least one particular two-dimensional possible route, which is completely contained within r during the whole query time interval. Item 4 requires for the validity of the defined predicate that for each instant of the query time interval a possible motion curve can be found which intersects r at that instant. In item 5, the validity of the predicate is given if, for whatever possible motion curve the object chooses, it is guaranteed to be located within the query region r throughout the entire query time interval. Item 7 expresses that no matter which possible motion curve within the uncertainty zone the moving object takes, it will intersect the query region at some instant of the query time interval and thus fulfill the predicate. However, the time of intersection may be different for different possible motion curves. Satisfaction of the predicate in item 8 means that, for whatever possible motion curve the moving object takes, at the particular instant *t* the object will be inside the query region.

Due to the semantic equivalence of the predicates **PossiblySometimeInside** and **SometimePossiblyInside** (items 1 and 2), as well as the semantic equivalence of the predicates **AlwaysDefinitelyInside** and **DefinitelyAlwaysInside** (items 5 and 6), we can reduce the number of spatio-temporal predicates from eight to six. These two semantic equivalences could also have been formulated in two lemmas, whose proofs are then based on the two logical rules $\exists x \exists y\, P(x, y) \Leftrightarrow \exists y \exists x\, P(x, y)$ and $\forall x \forall y\, P(x, y) \Leftrightarrow \forall y \forall x\, P(x, y)$, respectively. Figure 3.6 illustrates two-dimensional, spatial projections of the six predicates. Dashed lines show the possible motion curve(s) to which the predicates are satisfied. Solid lines indicate the routes and the boundaries of the uncertainty zone.

The predicates **PossiblyAlwaysInside** and **AlwaysPossiblyInside** (items 3 and 4), as well as the predicates **SometimeDefinitelyInside** and **Definitely-SometimeInside** (items 7 and 8), are not equivalent. Instead, only **Possibly-**

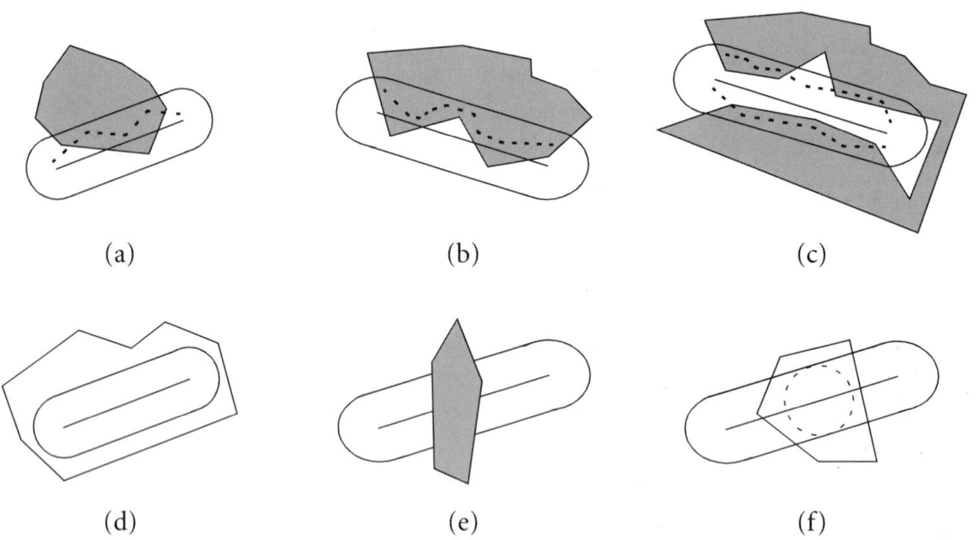

Figure 3.6 Examples (of the spatial projections) of the spatio-temporal predicates **PossiblySometimeInside** (a), **PossiblyAlwaysInside** (b), **AlwaysPossiblyInside** (c), **DefinitelyAlwaysInside** (d), **DefinitelySometimeInside** (e), **SometimeDefinitelyInside** (f).

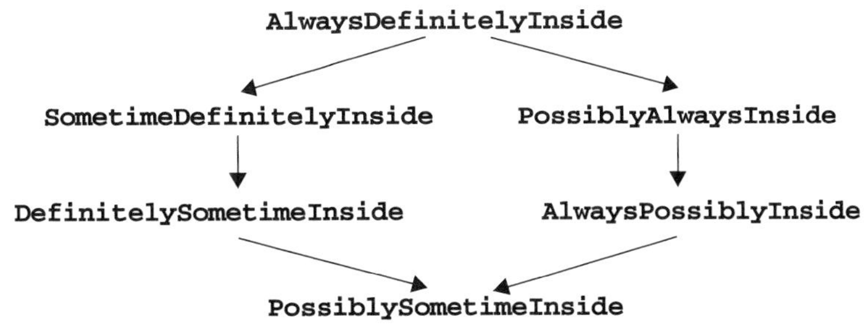

Figure 3.7 Relationships among the spatio-temporal predicates.

AlwaysInside(ut, r, t_1, t_2) $\Rightarrow$ **AlwaysPossiblyInside**(ut, r, t_1, t_2), and **SometimeDefinitelyInside**(ut, r, t_1, t_2) $\Rightarrow$ **DefinitelySometimeInside**(ut, r, t_1, t_2) hold. The proofs rest on the logical rule that $\exists x \forall y\, P(x, y) \Rightarrow \forall y \exists x\, P(x, y)$. Thus, the condition on the left side of the implication symbol is stronger than the condition on the right side. If r denotes a *convex* simple region, the special case can be proved that **PossiblyAlwaysInside**(ut, r, t_1, t_2) $\Leftrightarrow$ **AlwaysPossiblyInside**(ut, r, t_1, t_2). Figure 3.6(b) and (c) illustrate that the predicate **AlwaysPossiblyInside** may be satisfied by two or more possible motion curves together, none of which satisfies **PossiblyAlwaysInside** by itself. Similarly, in Figure 3.6(b) the query region fulfills **DefinitelySometimeInside**, but since it does not contain the uncertainty zone for any time point, it does not satisfy the predicate **SometimeDefinitelyInside**.

The relationship between the six predicates is depicted in Figure 3.7, where an arrow denotes an implication. More complex query conditions can be formulated by composition of the operators. For instance, the query "Retrieve all the objects that are possibly within a region r, always between the times the object A arrives at the locations l_1 and l_2" can then be formulated as:

PossiblyAlwaysInside(ut, r, **whenAt**(ut_A, l_1), **whenAt**(ut_A, l_2))

3.5.4 Algorithms for Spatio-Temporal Operations and Predicates

The algorithms for implementing the two operators for point queries are straightforward. The **whereAt** operator applied to a trajectory with n line segments can be implemented in time O(log n). This time includes a binary search to determine the line segment between (x_i, y_i) and (x_{i+1}, y_{i+1}) for some $1 \leq i < n$ such that $t_i \leq t \leq t_{i+1}$ and a linear interpolation in constant time to compute the location at time t. The **whenAt** operator is implemented in O(n). Each line segment is examined in constant time for a time t when tr is at location l.

Next, we present algorithms for the six spatio-temporal predicates. These algorithms follow straightforward applications of computational geometry techniques with well-known run-time complexities. The essential idea is to reduce three-dimensional geometric problems to the two-dimensional case, where they can be solved in a much easier way. For reasons of simplicity, we here restrict query polygons to *convex* polygons. Optimizations of part of the described algorithms and a generalization to concave query regions can be found in the literature (see Section 3.7).

Let t_1 and t_2 be two instants. Two-dimensional spatial objects moving over time can be considered as three-dimensional objects with time as the third dimension. A query polygon r with the query time interval $[t_1, t_2]$ can then be represented as a prism $p(r) = \{(x, y, t) \mid (x, y) \in r \wedge t_1 \leq t \leq t_2\}$, which is called *query prism*. Further, each segment trajectory volume between times t_i and t_{i+1} is approximated by a *minimum bounding volume* (MBV), whose faces are all parallel to the three possible planes. These MBVs serve as filters and as a three-dimensional indexing scheme for accelerating query processing. During the *filtering* step, those line segments of trajectories are retrieved whose MBV intersects with $p(r)$. These form the *candidate set* we have to deal with. In the *refinement* step, the line segments of the candidate set are investigated by an exact algorithm. The algorithms in the following will assume the existence of a candidate set and restrict themselves to a description of the refinement step. Let $v(ut)$ denote the trajectory volume of a given uncertain trajectory $ut = (tr, th)$ between t_1 and t_2, and let $v(ut, r) = v(ut) \cap p(r)$ be the intersection of the trajectory volume and the query prism. Finally, let $\pi(tr)$ denote the spatial projection of tr on the xy-plane (i.e., its route).

For the algorithms we also need the concept of the *Minkowski sum*, denoted by the symbol $\oplus$. This operation takes a polygon q and a disk $d(c)$ with radius c as operands and computes $q \oplus d(c)$ comprising all points in the plane that are either elements of the boundary of q, elements of the interior of q, or elements of the "sweep" of $d(c)$ when its center moves along the edges of q. Hence, for a convex polygon the boundary of $q \oplus d(c)$ consists of straight line segments between vertices of q and of arcs at the vertices of q (Figure 3.8). If q has n edges, we know from computational geometry that the run-time complexity to compute $q \oplus d(c)$ is $O(n)$.

The predicate `PossiblySometimeInside` is obviously true if, and only if, the intersection of the trajectory volume and the query prism is nonempty (i.e., if $v(ut, r) \neq \emptyset$). This leads us to the following algorithm:

algorithm *PossiblySometimeInside* (ut, r, t_1, t_2)
    construct $r \oplus d(th)$;
    if $\pi(tr) \cap (r \oplus d(th)) = \emptyset$ **then return** *false* **else return** *true* **endif**
end.

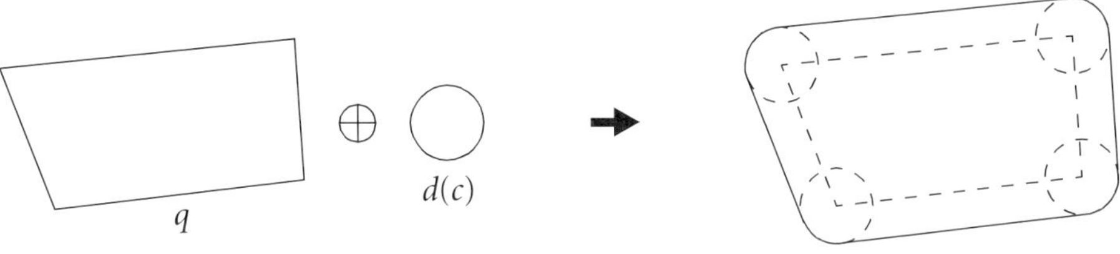

Figure 3.8 Minkowski sum of a convex polygon with a disk.

In other words, $v(ut, r)$ is nonempty if, and only if, $\pi(tr)$ intersects the expanded polygon $r \oplus d(th)$. The complexity of the algorithm is $O(kn)$, where k is the number of line segments of tr between t_1 and t_2, and n is the number of edges of r.

For the predicate **`PossiblyAlwaysInside`**, we can prove that it yields true if, and only if, $v(ut, r)$ contains a possible motion curve between t_1 and t_2. The algorithm is then as follows:

algorithm *PossiblyAlwaysInside* (ut, r, t_1, t_2)
  construct $r \oplus d(th)$;
  if $\pi(tr)$ lies completely inside $r \oplus d(th)$ **then return** *true* **else return** *false* **endif**
end.

Again, the complexity is $O(kn)$. Since we have confined ourselves to convex polygons, we can apply this algorithm also for the predicate **`AlwaysPossiblyInside`**.

For the predicate **`DefinitelyAlwaysInside`**, we can prove that it yields true if, and only if, $v(ut, r) = v(ut)$. As an algorithm we obtain:

algorithm *DefinitelyAlwaysInside* (ut, r, t_1, t_2)
  for each straight line segment of *tr* **do**
    if the uncertainty zone of the segment is not inside r **then return** *false* **endif**
  endfor;
  return *true*
end.

The algorithmic step to find out if the uncertainty zone of a segment of *tr* is not contained in r can be processed by checking if the route segment has a distance from some edge of r that is less than *th*. This requires $O(kn)$ time.

For the predicate **`SometimeDefinitelyInside`**, we can prove that it yields true if, and only if, $v(ut, r)$ contains an entire horizontal disk. This holds for concave polygons as well. The algorithm can be formulated as follows:

algorithm *SometimeDefinitelyInside* (ut, r, t_1, t_2)
  for each straight line segment s of tr with $\pi(s) \cap r \neq \emptyset$ **do**
    if r contains a circle with radius th centered at some point on s **then**
      return *true*
    endif
  endfor;
  return *false*
end.

The run-time complexity of this algorithm is again $O(kn)$.

For the last predicate, we need to define the property of connectivity. This property usually requires the existence of some *path* between any two points in a given set, which in our case is a subset of $\mathbb{R}^3$. Given any two points a and b in $\mathbb{R}^3$, a path from a to b is any continuous function f: $[0, 1] \rightarrow \mathbb{R}^3$ such that $f(0) = a$ and $f(1) = b$. For two instants t_1 and t_2, a set $S \subseteq \mathbb{R}^3$ is called *connected between* t_1 and t_2, if two points $(x_1, y_1, t_1), (x_2, y_2, t_2) \in S$ exist that are connected by a path in S. We can now prove that the predicate **`DefinitelySometimeInside`** yields true if, and only if, $v(ut) \setminus p(r)$ is not connected between t_1 and t_2. Otherwise, a possible motion curve exists between t_1 and t_2 that is completely in $v(ut) \setminus p(r)$ so that the predicate is not fulfilled.

Let $uz(ut)$ be the uncertainty zone of the trajectory volume of ut, and let $uz'(ut)$ be equal to $uz(ut)$ without the uncertainty areas at t_1 and t_2, which are two circles c_1 and c_2. Let B be the boundary of $uz'(ut)$. B consists of (at most) $2k$ straight line segments and $k + 1$ arcs (at most one around the vertices of each segment). Let $B' = B \setminus (c_1 \cup c_2)$. Thus, B' consists of two disjoint lines l_1 and l_2 on the left and right sides of the route of tr. Figure 3.9 demonstrates some of the introduced concepts. The line l_2 has an arc at the end of the first route segment. The dashed semicircles

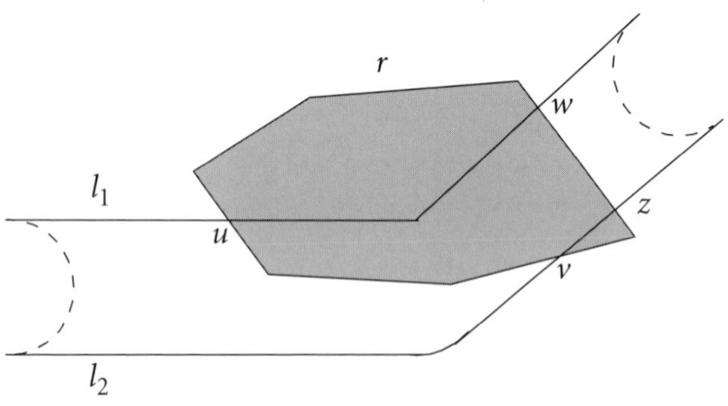

Figure 3.9 Processing of the **`DefinitelySometimeInside`** predicate.

belong to the boundaries of the uncertainty areas at t_1 and t_2. They are removed when evaluating the predicate. For the query region r, two paths can be found that make the predicate true—namely, the path from u to v and the path from w to z.

algorithm *DefinitelySometimeInside* (ut, r, t_1, t_2)
  if there exists a path P between a point on l_1 and a point on l_2 that consists
    completely of (parts of) edges of r **and** P is completely in $uz'(ut)$ **then**
    return *true*
  else
    return *false*
  endif
end.

This algorithm requires $O(kn^2)$ time.

3.6 Further Exercises

Exercise 3.9 FTL Query Language

In this task we consider some aspects of the FTL syntax and query evaluation.

1. Translate the statement in Exercise 3.3 into an FTL formula and explain terms, predicates, subformulas, and free variables.
2. Evaluate the query:

```
RETRIEVE f.id, g.id FROM flights f, g
WHERE (dist(f, g) > 16 AND dist(f, g) < 30)
  until_after_1 (dist(f, g) < 10)
```

The relation *flights* has three tuples with the following values:

motion (units/minute)	*id*
$(0, 0) + (2, 1)\cdot a\cdot t$	LT
$(5, 0) + (-1, 2)\cdot b\cdot t$	IB
$(10, 2) + (-2, 1)\cdot c\cdot t$	AA

In order to make the calculation as easy as possible, three assumptions are made: the planes are nearly at the same altitude and the same velocity, so the third dimension was left out and $a = b = c = 1$; the current time corresponds to $t = 0$; the **dist** function is defined as follows:

$$\textbf{dist}(f, g) = < f.motion(t) - g.motion(t),\ f.motion(t) - g.motion(t) >$$

with $<\cdot,\cdot>$ denoting the Euclidean scalar product.

Note: The motion function is given in units per minute; since we can scale the units with an arbitrary length, every speed can be modeled. For example, if a unit stands for 7 kilometers the planes will have a velocity of approximately 900 kilometers/hour.

Exercise 3.10 Choosing an Optimal Threshold

Section 3.4.3 shows how to choose the uncertainty threshold K in order to minimize the average information cost per time unit. In that section, it is assumed that the future deviation is given by a linear function $a(t - t_1)$, where a is a positive constant and t_1 is the time at which the new threshold must be chosen. Now, we examine a slightly different scenario. We assume that the estimated future deviation is given by a quadratic function $a(t - t_1)^2$ between t_1 and t_2. This new deviation function yields a new formula for information cost. Find the new optimal value for K that minimizes the average information cost per time unit (i.e., perform an analysis analogous to the analysis in Section 3.4.3 but with the different deviation function).

Exercise 3.11 Adaptive Dead Reckoning Policy

This exercise asks you to apply the adaptive dead-reckoning policy to a simple example. We assume that the update cost is $C_1 = 50$, and the uncertainty unit cost is $C_2 = 1$. The threshold K is initially set to 12. At each location update, the moving object transmits its current speed and its current direction to the database. The moving object moves linearly from (0, 0) to (10, 0) within the time interval [0, 20] (i.e., the location as a function of time is defined as $(t/2, 0)$). Subsequently, the moving object moves linearly from (10, 0) to (0, 0) within the time interval [20, 30]. In this scenario, answer the following questions:

1. When are location updates sent?
2. What is the value of the threshold K at time 30?
3. What is the information cost of this trip?

Remember that the moving object sends a location update at time 0. The deviation at time t is the Euclidean distance between the moving object's actual location and its location according to the database. The deviation cost (needed for computing the new threshold, Section 3.4.3) of a time interval is the integral of the deviation function over that time interval. You should not confuse this [observed] deviation with the deviation estimation by a linear function in Section 3.4.3. The deviation estimation by a linear function is a mathematical assumption used for deriving a formula for the optimal value of K. If that formula is applied to a real situation, we insert the observed deviation into that formula, not the estimated deviation.

Exercise 3.12 Spatio-Temporal Predicates

Let r be a simple query region and $ut = (tr, th)$ be an uncertain trajectory. Show that the following implications don't hold:

1. **PossiblySometimeInside**(ut, r, t_1, t_2)
   $\Rightarrow$ **DefinitelySometimeInside**(ut, r, t_1, t_2)
2. **PossiblySometimeInside**(ut, r, t_1, t_2)
   $\Rightarrow$ **AlwaysPossiblyInside**(ut, r, t_1, t_2)
3. **SometimeDefinitelyInside**(ut, r, t_1, t_2)
   $\Rightarrow$ **AlwaysDefinitelyInside**(ut, r, t_1, t_2)
4. **PossiblyAlwaysInside**(ut, r, t_1, t_2)
   $\Rightarrow$ **AlwaysDefinitelyInside**(ut, r, t_1, t_2)

3.7 Bibliographic Notes

The presentation in this chapter is based on Sistla et al., 1997; Sistla et al., 1998; Wolfson et al., 1998a; Wolfson et al., 1999a; Wolfson et al., 1998b. These publications introduce a concept that focuses on capturing the *current* motion of moving points and their anticipated locations in the *near future*. The concept of dynamic attributes (Section 3.1), the MOST data model (Section 3.2), and the query language FTL, as well as the evaluation of FTL queries (Section 3.3), are described in Sistla et al., 1997; Sistla et al., 1998. The basic framework of the FTL language had been introduced in an earlier article by Sistla and Wolfson, 1995; this article provides some additional details (e.g., about bounded temporal operators). Sistla et al., 1998, also treat a more general case than what has been presented here, where object positions may have an associated uncertainty (e.g., by providing a lower and upper bound on the speed).

The problem of balancing location update costs and imprecision (Section 3.4) is discussed in Wolfson et al., 1998a; Wolfson et al., 1999a; Wolfson et al., 1998b. A related recent article discussing update policies is by Civilis et al., 2004.

The problem of inherent uncertainty associated with the location of moving points (Section 3.5) is addressed in Trajcevski et al., 2002. An extension and more detailed discussion of the uncertainty aspect can be found in Trajcevski et al., 2004. Related works on uncertain trajectories include Pfoser and Jensen, 1999; Mokhtar and Su, 2004. Pfoser and Jensen, 1999, discuss the relationship between the sampling rate of GPS observations and the known precision of the trajectory. Mokhtar and Su, 2004, offer a probabilistic model of uncertain trajectories. A trajectory is viewed as a vector of uniform stochastic processes. They describe the evaluation of a class of queries called "universal range queries": The result is a set of pairs, <*o*, *p*>, where *o* is an object and *p* the probability that *o* has been in the range all the time. Probabilistic query evaluation for uncertain object locations is also discussed in Cheng et al. 2004; they consider range queries and nearest neighbor queries.

The model described in this chapter has been realized in a prototype called DOMINO, which has been presented in several stages of implementation at various conferences (Wolfson et al., 1999b; Wolfson et al., 2000; Wolfson et al., 2002).

Some related work on query processing for continuous queries such as those introduced with the MOST model is mentioned in Section 8.4.

4 Modeling and Querying History of Movement

In this chapter, we develop a data model and query language dealing with histories of movement, rather than the current and near-future movement. To this end, we take up the idea of *spatio-temporal data types*, discussed briefly in Section 1.4.6. The first section (Section 4.1) describes the approach and discusses some basic issues related to it. In particular, the distinction between an *abstract model* and a *discrete model* is introduced. Section 4.2 then develops a precise design of spatio-temporal types and operations at the level of such an abstract model. Abstract models need to be translated into discrete models to be implementable, and this is the topic of Section 4.3.

Finally, in Section 4.4, we discuss perhaps the most important operations on spatio-temporal objects—namely, predicates—in more detail and develop techniques for composing them temporally to obtain predicates describing so-called *developments* of configurations of moving objects.

4.1 An Approach Based on Abstract Data Types

4.1.1 Types and Operations

Let us recall some ideas that were already sketched in Section 1.4.6. We assume that the time-dependent spatial entities of interest, in particular *moving point* and *moving region*, are represented by abstract data types with suitable operations (called `mpoint` and `mregion`). Such types may be embedded as attribute types into any DBMS data model (relational, object oriented, etc.). Beyond the main types of interest, we need a collection of related types, including base types (e.g., `int`, `bool`), spatial types (e.g., `line`, `region`), and time types (e.g., `instant`, `periods` = set of time intervals). We call types whose values are functions from time into some domain *temporal types*. For them, we can distinguish between types allowing for continuous changes and those that are capable only of discrete changes.

Continuous changes:

- *mpoint*: *instant* → *point*
- *mregion*: *instant* → *region*
- *mreal*: *instant* → *real*

Discrete changes:

- *mint*: *instant* → *int*
- *mstring*: *instant* → *string*
- *mbool*: *instant* → *bool*

To have a uniform terminology, we call all these types "moving" and speak of *moving reals*, *moving integers*, or *moving booleans* as well. The time dimension is assumed to represent *valid time*. Moving point and moving region are embedded in a 3D (2D + time) space, whereas moving real, as well as the discretely changing types, "live" in a 2D (1D + time) space, as shown in Figure 4.1.

Note that temporal types are generally partial functions (i.e., the value may be undefined, or empty, for certain periods of time). This occurs naturally through some operations—for example, if we reduce a moving point to the times when it was within some region.

The study of operations on these types leads to the definition of related types. For example, it is desirable for all temporal types to have their projections available into their domain (which is time, or `instant`) and range (which varies according to the type). The projection into the domain is a set of time intervals—hence, we

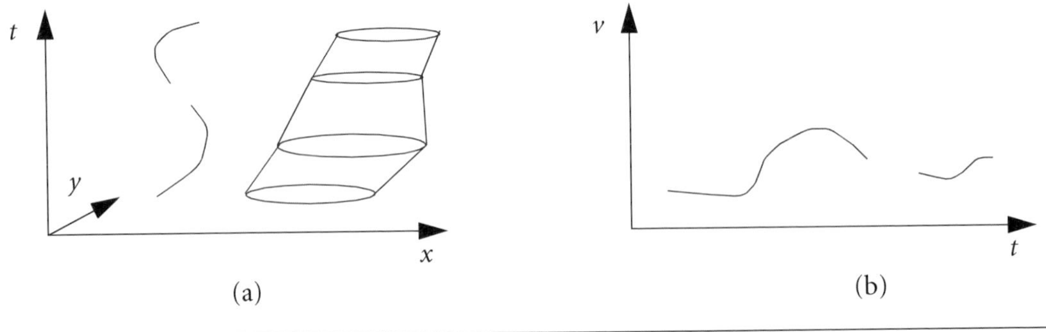

Figure 4.1 Moving point and moving region (a); moving real (b).

need a data type for them; let's call it *periods*. This operation, by the way, does not depend on the particular temporal data type; hence, it is generic, and can be described as:

deftime:	*moving*(α)	$\rightarrow$ *periods*

for $\alpha \in$ {*int*, *real*, *string*, *bool*, *point*, *region*}. Here, *moving* is, in fact, a type constructor, which yields for a given argument type α the type whose values are partial functions from *instant* into α.

For a moving point or a moving region, we consider its projection into the range (the 2D space). For a moving point, this projection is usually a curve in the 2D plane and for a moving region it is a region; therefore, we need spatial types *line* and *region* and can then define operations:

trajectory:	*moving*(*point*)	$\rightarrow$ *line*
traversed:	*moving*(*region*)	$\rightarrow$ *region*

The projection of a moving real into its range (the real numbers), on the other hand, yields a set of real intervals. Since we need sets of intervals more often, it makes sense to introduce a type constructor for them; let's call it *range*, which yields for an argument type α (which must represent a one-dimensional domain in this case) the corresponding type whose values are sets of intervals over α. This leads to a projection operation:

rangevalues:	*moving*(α)	$\rightarrow$ *range*(α)

for $\alpha \in$ {*int*, *string*, *bool*, *real*, *instant*}, which may be instantiated, for example, to:

rangevalues:	*moving*(*real*)	$\rightarrow$ *range*(*real*)

Since the *periods* type introduced previously represents sets of intervals over the time domain *instant*, we discover that *periods* = *range*(*instant*).

We would like to observe time-dependent numeric properties of moving points or moving regions, such as distance, speed, the size of a region, or the number of components (disjoint faces) of a region. To represent the results of such operations, we need data types such as *moving*(*real*) or *moving*(*int*). We can then define operations such as:

distance:	*moving*(*point*) × *moving*(*point*)	$\rightarrow$ *moving*(*real*)
speed:	*moving*(*point*)	$\rightarrow$ *moving*(*real*)
area:	*moving*(*region*)	$\rightarrow$ *moving*(*real*)
no_components:	*moving*(*region*)	$\rightarrow$ *moving*(*int*)

These examples may suffice to show how the study of desirable operations leads to requirements for new data types. These in turn need to be equipped with adequate operations so that results of such types can be evaluated further in a query.

Once this basic idea is given, the next task is to design carefully such a system of related types and operations so that all interesting questions can be posed and some kind of closure is achieved. More formally, this means that we need to design a *many-sorted algebra*. This involves two steps:

1. Define operations together with their argument and result types (i.e., define a *signature*). Formally, a signature consists of *sorts* (names for the types) and *operators* (names for the operations).
2. Define the semantics for this signature (i.e., associate an algebra) by defining *carrier sets* for the sorts and *functions* for the operators. So the carrier set for a type *t* contains the possible values for *t* and the function associated with an operation ω is a mapping between the corresponding carrier sets.

4.1.2 Abstract versus Discrete Models

Now, a fundamental question that needs to be clarified before proceeding is at which *level of abstraction* the semantics should be defined. There are two possible levels, which we will call *abstract* and *discrete* models, respectively. Table 4.1 shows examples of possible definitions at the two levels. Note that these definitions are

Table 4.1 Definitions at the abstract and the discrete level.

Abstract Continuous Infinite	Concrete **Discrete** Finite
A `region` is a closed subset of $\mathbb{R}^2$ with non-empty interior.	A `region` is a set of polygons that may have polygonal holes.
A `line` is a curve in $\mathbb{R}^2$ (i.e., a continuous function f: $[0, 1] \rightarrow \mathbb{R}^2$).	A `line` is a polyline (e.g., a list of line segments).
A *moving*(`point`) is a function from time into `point` values.	A *moving*(`point`) is a polyline in the 3D space.
	. . . is a cubic spline in 3D.
A *moving*(`real`) is a function from time into `real` values.	A *moving*(`real`) is a piecewise quadratic polynomial.
A *moving*(`region`) is a function from time into `region` values.	A *moving*(`region`) is a polyhedron in 3D. . . . is a sequence of affine mappings.

only sketched, since the purpose is not to give precise definitions but to explain the difference between the two levels of abstraction.

There are three pairs of terms that characterize the difference between these levels: *abstract* versus *concrete*, *continuous* versus *discrete*, and *infinite* versus *finite*. It is essential that at the abstract level we are allowed to make definitions in terms of infinite sets, whereas at the discrete level, only finite representations can be used.

The difference between these levels can be described as follows:

- The abstract level is conceptually more simple. Formal definitions for the semantics of types (i.e., carrier sets) are much simpler than at the discrete level. In fact, the abstract level appears to be the conceptual model that we are interested in: We do not think of an airplane as moving along a polyline but rather as moving continuously (i.e., having a position that is a continuous function of time).
- The abstract level is more uniform. For example, observe that all the *moving* types have the same kind of definition; they are all functions from time into the respective domain. At the discrete level, we need to distinguish between various structures.
- The abstract level is generic, whereas the discrete level represents a particular choice, which may not be suitable for all applications. For example, if at the discrete level we represent a moving region by a polyhedral shape, then rotations can only be very badly represented. On the other hand, there exists a representation as a sequence of time intervals; within each time interval the development of the shape is described by an affine mapping, which allows for rotation, translation, and scaling. This model can represent rotations easily and exactly. However, it cannot represent arbitrary changes of shape, which are better supported in the polyhedral model.
- The abstract level is not directly implementable, since we cannot represent infinite sets (as such) in computers. It is mandatory to find a finite representation. Only discrete models are implementable.

If we attempt to design a spatio-temporal algebra directly at the discrete level, we will run into a lot of difficulties. One is that the formal definitions of the semantics of types and operations quickly become very complicated. Another is that we need to make choices directly, like the one between polyhedral and affine mappings discussed previously. Some choices at the discrete level prevent the definition of operations that are otherwise quite natural. For example, on a *moving*(`real`) it is natural to have a *derivative* operation. However, on the discrete level, it is quite hard to find a representation that is closed under *derivative*. So if we have fixed such a discrete representation, then it is impossible to include the *derivative* operation into the design. For all these reasons, it is a good strategy to proceed in two steps:

1. Design the spatio-temporal algebra at the abstract level.
2. Design one or more discrete models as instantiations of the abstract model (and then implement these).

We will follow this strategy. In Section 4.2, a design at the abstract level is presented. Section 4.3 then develops a corresponding discrete model. The implementation of that discrete model is the topic of Chapter 5.

4.1.3 Language Embedding of Abstract Data Types

We have already seen in Chapter 1 how abstract data types can be embedded into a DBMS data model and its query language. In this section, we describe more precisely some facilities that we assume to be available in the DBMS query language—possibly in a different notation—that are needed to achieve a smooth interplay with ADT operations. We will later use these facilities in example queries.

Assignments. The construct `LET <name> = <query>` assigns the result of a query to a new object called *name*, which can then be used in further steps of a query.

Multistep queries. A query can be written as a list of assignments, separated by semicolons, followed by one or more query expressions. The latter are the result of the query.

Conversions between sets of elements and atomic values. In a relational setting, this means that a relation with a single tuple and attribute can be converted to a typed atomic value and vice versa. We use the notations `ELEMENT(<query>)` and `SET(<attrname>, <value>)` for this.

Example 4.1 We assume an (object-) relational environment and an example relation:

```
employee(name: string, salary: int, permanent: bool)
```

The expression:

```
ELEMENT(SELECT salary FROM employee
  WHERE name = 'John Smith') * 2
```

is a product of two integers. The expression:

```
SET(name, 'John Smith')
```

returns a relation with a single attribute *name* and a single tuple with value "John Smith." ■

Defining derived values. We assume that arbitrary ADT operations over new and old data types may occur anywhere in a WHERE clause and can be used in a SELECT clause to produce new attributes, with the notation `<expression> AS <new attrname>`.

Defining operations. We allow for the definition of new operations derived from existing ones in the form `LET <name> = <functional expression>`. A functional expression has the form `FUN <parameter list> expression`; it corresponds to lambda abstraction in functional languages.

Example 4.2 A new operation *square* could be defined and used as:

```
LET square = FUN (m:int) m * m; square(100)
```

■

Defining aggregate functions. Any binary, associative, and commutative operation on a data type can be used as an aggregate function over a column of that data type, using the notation `AGGR(<attrname>, <operator>, <neutral element>)`. In case the relation is empty, the neutral element is returned. In case it has a single tuple, then that single attribute value is returned. Otherwise, the existing attribute values are combined using the given operator. Furthermore, a name for the aggregate function can be defined by `LET <name> = AGGREGATE(<operator>, <neutral element>)`.

Example 4.3 We can determine whether all employees have permanent positions by:

```
LET all = AGGREGATE(and, TRUE);
SELECT all(permanent) FROM employee
```

■

Later, we will see examples of aggregate functions involving spatial operations.

4.2 An Abstract Model

In this section, we precisely design a system of spatio-temporal data types and operations suitable to represent and query moving objects. The design pursues the following goals:

- *Closure.* The type system should have a clear structure; in particular, type constructors should be applied systematically and consistently. For example, this means that:
  - For all base types of interest, we have corresponding time-dependent (temporal, or "moving") types.

— For all temporal types, we have types to represent their projections into domain and range.

- *Genericity.* There will be a relatively large number of data types (about 20). If we design operations for each of them independently, we can easily end up with a manual-like description with hundreds of operations. It is essential to develop a more abstract view of the available types and to design relatively few generic operations applicable to as many types as possible.
- *Consistency between nontemporal and temporal types.* For example, the definitions of static and moving regions should agree in the sense that a moving region evaluated at any instant of time yields a static region, and the full structure of a static region is able to evolve continuously in a moving region. This would be violated if, for example, a static region were allowed to have several disjoint parts and a moving region would have only a single component at any time.
- *Consistency between nontemporal and temporal operations.* For example, the definition of *distance* between two static points should agree with the definition of a distance function that returns the distance between two moving points as a moving real.

All of this will help to obtain a relatively simple, yet powerful, model and query language.

4.2.1 Data Types

We start with describing the available data types, or the *type system*. We first give an informal overview and then become more precise in the definition of the type system and the semantics of types.

Clearly, there must be the standard data types available in any data model, such as `int`, `real`, `bool`, and `string`. We will call them *base types* from now on. Second, there are four *spatial types*, called `point`, `points`, `line`, and `region`, illustrated in Figure 4.2.

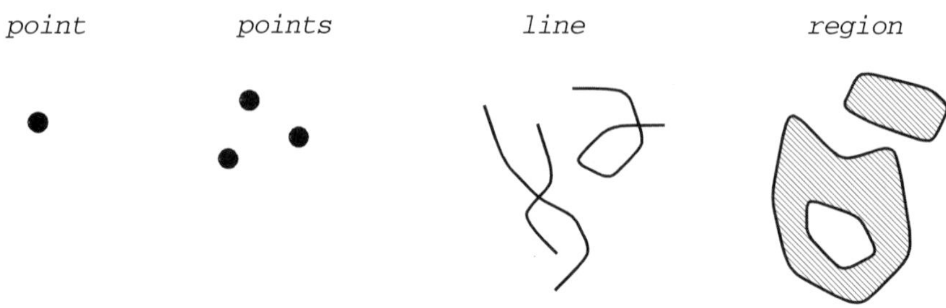

Figure 4.2 The spatial data types.

Then there are data types to represent time—namely, `instant` and `periods`—the latter representing a set of disjoint time intervals.

For each of the base types and spatial types, we have a corresponding time-dependent, or *temporal*, type, obtained by a type constructor, *moving*. Hence, we have types *moving*(`int`), . . ., *moving*(`region`).

A further type constructor `range` yields for each of the base types a corresponding type offering sets of intervals.

Finally, there is a type constructor called `intime`, which, for each of the base types or the spatial types, yields a corresponding type whose values are pairs, consisting of an instant of time and a value of the respective argument type. For example, a value of type `intime`(`int`) is a pair consisting of an `instant` and an `int` value.

An overview of the available types, which also explains some of their motivation, is shown in Figure 4.3. Only the `intime` types are omitted there. In particular, we want to have types able to represent the projections of temporal types into domain and range, as mentioned previously. For the spatial types, the projections into the range (i.e., the 2D plane) are a bit involved. A *moving*(`point`) may move around continuously, which yields a projection as a curve, or a `line` value, but it may also

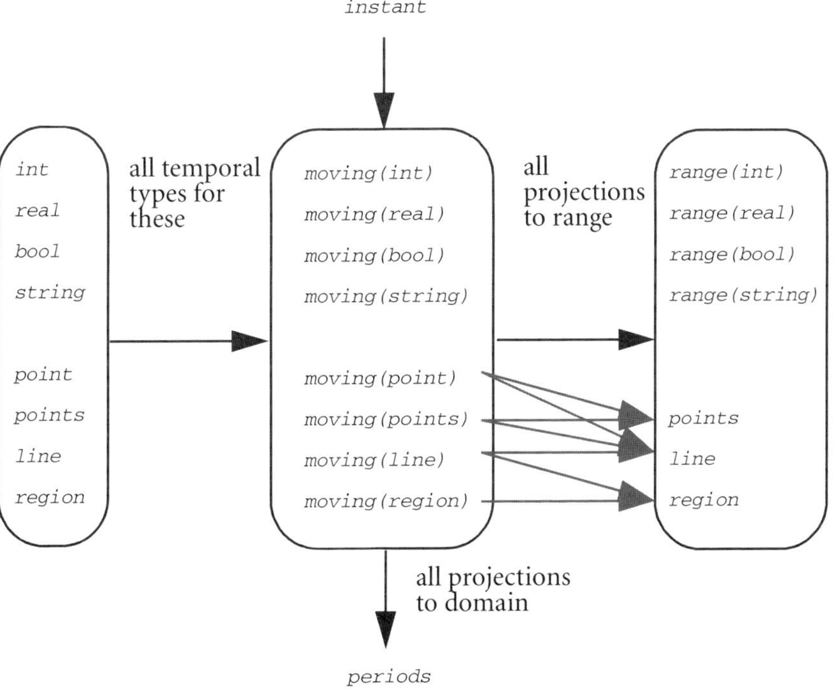

Figure 4.3 Structure of the type system.

Table 4.2 Type system as a signature.

Type constructor	*Signature*	
int, *real*, *string*, *bool*		→ BASE
point, *points*, *line*, *region*		→ SPATIAL
instant		→ TIME
range	BASE ∪ TIME	→ RANGE
moving, *intime*	BASE ∪ SPATIAL	→ TEMPORAL

"jump around" in discrete steps (e.g., consider the classes [1] through [4] of the classification given in Section 1.4.4), in which case the projection is a *points* value. Similarly, in a *moving*(*line*), the curve may jump around and yield a projection as a *line*, rather than the more natural projection of a continuously moving curve as a *region*. We will later introduce specialized projection operations to obtain typed projection results (e.g., one projection operation to get the *points* part of the projection of a moving point and another one to get the *line* part of the projection).

The type system can be described more precisely in the form of a signature, as shown in Table 4.2. Remember that a signature has sorts and operators. In this case, the sorts are called *kinds*[1] and denote collections of types; the operators are *type constructors*. The signature generates a set of *terms*, which are exactly the *types* offered by this type system. Note that type constructors without arguments (*int*, *point*) are called *constant* and are types directly.

4.2.2 Formal Definition of Data Types

For each data type α we need to define the set of possible values and its *carrier set*, which is denoted as A_α.

Base types

The four base types *int*, *real*, *string*, and *bool* have the usual interpretation except that their domain is extended by the value $\perp$ (undefined).

Definition 4.1 The carrier sets for the base types are:

$$A_{int} := \mathbb{Z} \cup \{\perp\}$$

$$A_{real} := \mathbb{R} \cup \{\perp\}$$

[1] We write kinds in capitals.

$A_{string} := V^* \cup \{\bot\}$, where V is a finite alphabet

$A_{bool} := \{FALSE, TRUE\} \cup \{\bot\}$ ■

The undefined value is included because it is natural for operations on temporal types—whose values are partial functions of time—to return undefined values. For example, if the size of a moving region is evaluated at an instant when the region is undefined (or empty), the result is undefined. We introduce a shorthand notation $\bar{A}$ to refer to a carrier set without the undefined value (i.e., $\bar{A}_\alpha = A_\alpha \setminus \{\bot\}$).

Spatial types

The four spatial types have already been illustrated in Figure 4.2. Informally, they have the following meaning. A value of type `point` represents a point in the Euclidean plane or is undefined. A `points` value is a finite set of points. A `line` value is a finite set of continuous curves in the plane. A `region` is a finite set of disjoint parts called *faces*, each of which may have holes. It is allowed that a face lies within a hole of another face. Each of the three set types may be empty.

Definition 4.2 The carrier sets for the types `point` and `points` are:

$A_{point} : = \mathbb{R}^2 \cup \{\bot\}$

$A_{points} : = \{P \subset \mathbb{R}^2 \mid P \text{ is finite}\}$ ■

While the definitions for `point` and `points` are quite simple, those for `line` and `region` are a bit involved. We will not give the full formal definition from the original literature (see the bibliographic notes at the end of this chapter), but will discuss the structure of these definitions briefly.

The definition of `line` is based on the concept of a curve.

Definition 4.3 A *curve* is a continuous mapping f: $[0, 1] \to \mathbb{R}^2$, such that:

$$\forall a, b \in [0,1] : f(a) = f(b) \Rightarrow (a = b \vee \{a, b\} = \{0,1\})$$ ■

This means curves are not self-intersecting; only the start and end points $f(0)$ and $f(1)$ may be equal. For a curve, only the set of points from $\mathbb{R}^2$ forming its range is of interest, defined as $rng(f) = \{p \in \mathbb{R}^2 \mid \exists a \in [0,1]: f(a) = p\}$. Two curves are *equivalent* if their ranges are equal.

A `line` value is a subset of $\mathbb{R}^2$ (hence, an infinite set of points) that can be represented as a union of (the ranges of) a finite set of such curves.

There is an important requirement: The curves used must be selected from some class of curves that are *simple* in the sense that the intersection of any two curves from this class yields only a finite number of proper intersection points (disregarding common parts that are curves themselves). As we have discussed, the abstract model described here will later be implemented by a discrete model. Then, a particular class of curves (e.g., polygonal lines or cubic splines) will be selected. We only require that the class of curves selected fulfills this simplicity requirement. This is needed, for example, to ensure that the result of the **`intersection`** of two *`line`* values can be represented as a *`points`* value.

Furthermore, observe that many different sets of curves may result in the same *`line`* value. We are interested in finding a canonical representation (i.e., a unique set of curves defining this *`line`* value). Now, a finite set of curves defines a graph structure whose nodes are intersections of curves and whose edges are intersection-free pieces of curves. This is the intended canonical representation. This is illustrated in Figure 4.4.

The formal definitions, therefore, introduce the concept of a *C-complex*, which is basically a finite set of curves that may only meet in end points and therefore correspond precisely to the edges of the graph structure. For such a C-complex C, $points(C)$ denotes the points in $\mathbb{R}^2$ covered by it (i.e., the union of the ranges of all its curves). Let $CC(S)$ denote the set of all C-complexes using curves from a class of simple curves, S.

Definition 4.4 Let S be a class of simple curves. The carrier set of *`line`* is:

$$A_{line} := \{Q \subset \mathbb{R}^2 \mid \exists C \in CC(S) : Q = points(C)\}$$

Since for a given *`line`* value Q, there is a unique defining C-complex, we can denote it by $sc(Q)$ (the simple curves of Q).

A *`region`* value is defined as a point set in the plane with a certain structure. Similar to *`line`*, we first define the structure, called an *R-complex* now, and its associated point set, and then define a region as a point set that could belong to such an R-complex.

In region values, we do not want to have certain anomalies such as isolated points, dangling lines, or missing points or lines within a "covered area." To avoid this, we need the concept of a regular closed set. A set of points in the plane, $Q \subset \mathbb{R}^2$, is called *regular closed*, if it is equal to the closure of its interior: $Q = closure(interior(Q))$.[2] For example, an isolated point will disappear because it is not in the interior of a point set and also not in the closure of the interior.

Two regular closed sets Q, R are called *quasi-disjoint* if $Q \cap R$ is finite.

[2] These are concepts from topology. The interior of a point set is the point set without its boundary; closure adds the points of the boundary.

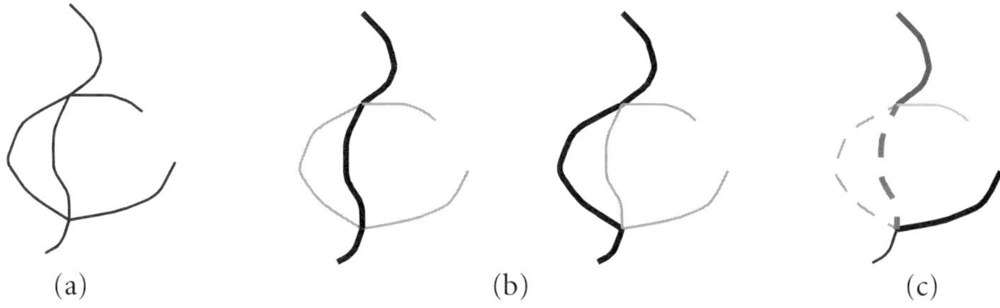

Figure 4.4 A line value (a); two possible interpretations of this line value as two curves (b); the canonical set of curves making up the C-complex (c).

An R-complex then is essentially a finite set R of nonempty, regular closed sets such that any two distinct elements of R are quasi-disjoint. Furthermore, its boundary must be representable as a C-complex (hence, as a `line` value). We require that the same class of curves be used in the definition of `line` and (boundaries of) `region` values. The set of all R-complexes with boundaries from the class of curves S is denoted as $RC(S)$.

Hence, a region can be viewed as a finite set of components called *faces*, each of which is a regular closed set. Any two distinct faces are disjoint except possibly for finitely many "touch points" at the boundary. Boundaries of faces are simple in the same sense as line values—for example, the intersection of the boundaries of faces may produce only finitely many intersection points. The boundary of a face may have outer as well as inner parts (i.e., the face may have holes).

Definition 4.5 Let S be a class of simple curves. The carrier set of `region` is:

$$A_{\mathtt{region}} := \{Q \subset \mathbb{R}^2 \mid \exists R \in RC(S) : Q = points(R)\}$$ ■

Since, for a given region value Q, its R-complex is uniquely defined, we can denote it by $faces(Q)$.

For the spatial types `points`, `line`, and `region` the possible values are sets, which may be empty. These empty sets play a role similar to the undefined value for the other types. Hence, we extend the shorthand $\bar{A}$ to the spatial types and to all other types for which the elements of the carrier set are sets of values, and define $\bar{A}_\alpha = A_\alpha \setminus \{\varnothing\}$.

Time type

Type `instant` represents a point in time, or is undefined. Time is considered to be linear and continuous (i.e., isomorphic to the real numbers).

Definition 4.6 The carrier set of type `instant` is:

$$A_{instant} := \mathbb{R} \cup \{\perp\}$$ ■

Range types (sets of intervals)

Definition 4.7 Let α be a data type to which the *range* type constructor is applicable (and hence on which a total order $<$ exists). An α-*interval* is a set $X \subseteq \bar{A}_\alpha$ such that:

$$\forall x, y \in X, \forall z \in \bar{A}_\alpha : x < z < y \Rightarrow z \in X$$

Two α-intervals are *adjacent* if they are disjoint and their union is an α-interval. An α-*range* is a finite set of disjoint, nonadjacent intervals. For an α-range R, *points*(R) denotes the union of all its intervals. ■

Definition 4.8 Let α be a data type to which the *range* type constructor is applicable. The carrier set for *range*(α) is:

$$A_{range(\alpha)} := \{X \subseteq \bar{A}_\alpha \mid \exists \text{ an } \alpha\text{-range } R : X = points(R)\}$$ ■

We introduce an additional name `periods` for the data type *range*(`instant`).

Temporal types

From the base types and spatial types we derive corresponding temporal types using the type constructor *moving*.

Definition 4.9 Let α, with carrier set A_α, be a type to which type constructor *moving* is applicable. Then the carrier set for *moving*(α) is:

$$A_{moving(\alpha)} := \{f \mid f : \bar{A}_{instant} \rightarrow \bar{A}_\alpha \text{ is a partial function} \wedge \Gamma(f) \text{ is finite}\}$$ ■

Hence, each value f is a function describing the development over time of a value from the carrier set A_α. The condition "$\Gamma(f)$ is finite" ensures that f consists only of a finite number of continuous components.[3] This is needed for certain operations—for example, to guarantee that the result of the projection of a moving

[3] $\Gamma(f)$ is the set of maximal continuous components of f defined in Güting et al., 2000. This is based on a generalized concept of continuity defined there and also discussed in Section 4.2.6.

object into the plane consists of only a finite number of components, and also to make the abstract design implementable.

The temporal types obtained through the *moving* constructor are infinite sets of pairs (instant, value). It is useful to have types to represent single elements of such sets. This is achieved through the *intime* type constructor.

Definition 4.10 Let α, with carrier set A_α, be a data type to which the *intime* constructor is applicable. The carrier set for *intime*(α) is:

$$A_{intime(\alpha)} := A_{instant} \times A_\alpha$$ ■

4.2.3 Overview of Operations

The design of operations follows three principles: Design operations to be as generic as possible; achieve consistency between operations on nontemporal and temporal types; and capture the interesting phenomena.

The first principle is crucial, since the type system is quite large. To avoid a proliferation of operations, a unifying view of collections of types is needed. The basic idea to achieve this is to relate each data type to either a one-dimensional or a two-dimensional space and to distinguish within each space between types whose values are single elements of the respective space (called *point types*) and types whose values are subsets of the space (called *point set types*). For example, we consider a space called *Integer* (representing the one-dimensional space of integers) for which type *int* describes single values and is the point type, whereas *range*(*int*) describes sets of values and is the point set type. Another space is called *2D* and represents the 2D plane. Here, *point* is the point type and there are three different point set types: *points*, *line*, and *region*. We will then define generic operations just in terms of spaces and their available point and point set types.

Second, to achieve consistency of operations on nontemporal and temporal types, we proceed in two steps. In the first step, we carefully design operations on nontemporal types. In the second step, we systematically and uniformly extend these operations to the temporal variants of the respective types by a technique called *lifting*.

Third, to obtain a powerful query language, it is necessary to include operations from various domains (or branches of mathematics). While simple set theory and first-order logic are the most fundamental and best understood parts of query languages, operations based on order relationships, topology, metric spaces, and so on are also needed. While there is no clear recipe to achieve closure of "interesting phenomena," this motivates the inclusion of operations such as distance, size of a region, relationships of boundaries, and so forth.

In the design to be presented, there are three classes of operations: operations on nontemporal types, operations on temporal types, and operations involving sets of database objects. These are described in the following three sections.

Table 4.3 Operations on nontemporal types.

Class	*Operations*
Predicates	**isempty** =, ≠, **intersects**, **inside** <, ≤, ≥, >, **before** **touches**, **attached**, **overlaps**, **on_border**, **in_interior**
Set Operations	**intersection**, **union**, **minus** **crossings**, **touch_points**, **common_border**
Aggregation	**min**, **max**, **avg**, **center**, **single**
Numeric	**no_components**, **size**, **perimeter**, **duration**, **length**, **area**
Distance and Direction	**distance**, **direction**
Base Type Specific	**and**, **or**, **not**

4.2.4 Operations on Nontemporal Types

Although the focus is on moving objects (hence, on temporal types), the definitions of operations on nontemporal types are essential, since these operations will later be lifted to obtain operations on temporal types. Table 4.3 shows the six classes of operations on nontemporal types and lists the names of these operations. The signatures and meanings of these operations will be discussed shortly.

As mentioned previously, the nontemporal types are classified into point types and point set types. This is shown in Table 4.4. Note that the term *temporal type* refers to types whose values are functions of time; hence, *instant* and *periods* are not temporal types in this sense. The table also shows a distinction between continuous and discrete spaces (and types), which is needed for certain numeric operations.

Table 4.4 Classification of nontemporal types.

			Point Type	*Point Set Types*
1D Spaces	*discrete*	*Integer*	*int*	*range(int)*
		Boolean	*bool*	*range(bool)*
		String	*string*	*range(string)*
	continuous	*Real*	*real*	*range(real)*
		Time	*instant*	*periods*
2D Space		*2D*	*point*	*points, line, region*

Notations for signatures

Based on the spaces defined in Table 4.4, we introduce notations for writing "generic" signatures. Let π and σ be *type variables* ranging over all point types and point set types of Table 4.4, respectively.

Example 4.4 We will define the signature of an operation **inside** as:

inside:	$\pi \times \sigma$	$\to$ *bool*

This means that for any given space, **inside** takes a first argument of one of its point types and a second argument of one of its point set types and returns a *bool* value. This is an abbreviation for the signatures:

inside:	*int* × *range*(*int*)	$\to$ *bool*
	bool × *range*(*bool*)	$\to$ *bool*
	string × *range*(*string*)	$\to$ *bool*
	real × *range*(*real*)	$\to$ *bool*
	instant × *periods*	$\to$ *bool*
	point × *points*	$\to$ *bool*
	point × *line*	$\to$ *bool*
	point × *region*	$\to$ *bool*

A signature $\sigma_1 \times \sigma_2 \to \alpha$ means that the type variables σ_1 and σ_2 can be instantiated independently; nevertheless, they have to range over the same space. In contrast, the signature $\sigma \times \sigma \to \alpha$ says that both arguments have to be of the same type. The notation $\alpha \otimes \beta \to \gamma$ is used if any order of the two argument types is valid; it is an abbreviation for the signatures $\alpha \times \beta \to \gamma$ and $\beta \times \alpha \to \gamma$.

Some operations are restricted to certain classes of spaces; these classes are denoted as 1D = {Integer, Boolean, String, Real, Time}, 2D = {2D}, 1Dcont = {Real, Time}, 1Dnum = {Integer, Real, Time}, and cont = {Real, Time, 2D}. A signature is restricted to a class of spaces by putting the name of the space behind it in square brackets. For example, a signature $\beta \to \gamma$ [1D] is valid for all one-dimensional spaces.

Generic operations may have more appropriate names when applied to specific types. For example, there is a generic **size** operation for point set types. When it is applied to a *periods* argument, the name **duration** is more appropriate. In such a case, we introduce the more specific name as an *alias* with the notation **size**[**duration**].

In defining semantics u, v, ... denote single values of a π type and U, V, ... sets of values corresponding to a σ type. For binary operations, u or U refers to the first and v or V to the second argument. For example, the semantics of the **inside** operation are defined as:

$$u \in V$$

Furthermore, we use μ to denote moving object arguments and t (T) to refer to *instant* (*periods*) argument values.

Example 4.5 We introduce the following example relations, representing cities, countries, rivers, and highways in Europe.

```
city (name:string, pop: int, center: point)
country (name: string, area: region)
river (name: string, route: line)
highway (name: string, route: line)
```

■

Predicates

We consider unary and binary predicates. At this abstract level, we can ask whether a point is undefined or whether a point set is empty. The generic predicate **isempty**[**undefined**] is used for this purpose (Table 4.5).

To achieve some completeness, the design of binary predicates is based on the following strategy. First, we consider possible relationships between two points (single values), two point sets, and a point versus a point set. Second, predicates are based on set theory, order relationships, and topology. Order relationships exist only in the 1D spaces. Topology means we consider interiors and boundaries of sets. This design is shown in Table 4.6. Here, the notations ∂Q and Q° refer to the boundary and the interior of point set Q, respectively.

Table 4.6 was constructed by studying systematically the possible relationships between sets and single values and then, if necessary, inventing a name for such a relationship (e.g., **touches**). The expressions in the table are directly the semantics definitions for the operations.

Exercise 4.1 Write down the generic signatures for the binary predicates, as in Table 4.5. The *semantics* column is not needed. When appropriate, try to apply the notations described in "Notations for signatures."

■

Table 4.5 Unary predicate.

Operation	*Signature*	*Semantics*
isempty[**undefined**]	$\pi \rightarrow$ *bool*	$u = \perp$
	$\sigma \rightarrow$ *bool*	$U = \varnothing$

Table 4.6 Design of binary predicates.

	Sets	*Order (1D Spaces)*	*Topology*
point versus point	$u = v$, $u \neq v$	$u < v$, $u \leq v$, $u \geq v$, $u > v$	
point set versus point set	$U = V$, $U \neq V$ $U \cap V \neq \emptyset$ (**intersects**) $U \subseteq V$ (**inside**)	$\forall u \in U, \forall v \in V: u \leq v$ (**before**)	$\partial U \cap \partial V \neq \emptyset$ (**touches**) $\partial U \cap V^{\circ} \neq \emptyset$ (**attached**) $U^{\circ} \cap V^{\circ} \neq \emptyset$ (**overlaps**)
point versus point set	$u \in V$ (**inside**)	$\forall u \in U: u \leq v$ (**before**) $\forall v \in V: u \leq v$	$u \in \partial V$ (**on_border**) $u \in V^{\circ}$ (**in_interior**)

There are no predicates related to distance or direction (e.g., "north"). However, such predicates can be built via numeric operations defined in the following text.

Set operations

Set operations are fundamental and are available for all point set types. Where feasible, we also allow set operations on point types, allowing expressions such as u **minus** v and U **minus** v. Singleton sets or empty sets resulting from such operations are interpreted as point values. For example, the result of $\{u\} \setminus \{v\}$ can be {u} or $\emptyset$, which is translated to u or $\perp$, respectively. Permitting set operations on point types is especially useful when these are lifted to operations on temporal types, as we will see later. The signatures of set operations are shown in Table 4.7.

In Table 4.7, the signatures are divided into five groups. The first two concern point versus point and point versus point set. The next two deal with point set versus point set interactions in one-dimensional spaces and in 2D. The last group introduces specialized operations to get lower-dimensional results.

The definition of result types and in particular of the semantics of operations has to take into account that in 1D we deal with arbitrary open or closed sets (see Definition 4.7, the *range* type constructor), whereas in 2D we have regular closed sets only.[4] Therefore, in 1D spaces the set operations have the usual semantics, whereas in 2D so-called regularized set operations are used. Note that in general the result of a set operation may be a mixture of of zero-, one-, and two-dimensional parts. For example, an intersection between two *region* values may result in a point set that can be divided into *point*, *line*, and *region* values. Regularized set operations keep only the part of the result with the highest dimension, and apply closure to it.

Based on these principles, here are some comments on Table 4.7. Group 1: There is no **union** for two point arguments, since this is not representable as a point type.

[4] Why the 1D and the 2D cases are treated differently is discussed in Güting et al., 2000.

Table 4.7 Set operations.

	Operation	*Signature*		
1.	**intersection**, **minus**	$\pi \times \pi$	$\to \pi$	
2.	**intersection**	$\pi \otimes \sigma$	$\to \pi$	
	minus	$\pi \times \sigma$	$\to \pi$	
		$\sigma \times \pi$	$\to \sigma$	
	union	$\pi \otimes \sigma$	$\to \sigma$	
3.	**intersection**, **minus**, **union**	$\sigma \times \sigma$	$\to \sigma$	[1D]
4.	**intersection**	$\sigma_1 \times \sigma_2$	$\to min(\sigma_1, \sigma_2)$	[2D]
	minus	$\sigma_1 \times \sigma_2$	$\to \sigma_1$	[2D]
	union	$\sigma \times \sigma$	$\to \sigma$	[2D]
5.	**crossings**	*line* × *line*	→ *points*	
	touch_points	*region* ⊗ *line*	→ *points*	
		region × *region*	→ *points*	
	common_border	*region* ⊗ *line*	→ *line*	
		region × *region*	→ *line*	

Group 4: Operations in this group use the regularized set operation semantics just discussed. For **intersection**, the result type is the minimum of the two argument types in an assumed dimensional order, *points* < *line* < *region*. For **minus**, the result type is that of the first argument, since subtracting a lower-dimensional value returns the first argument unchanged, and subtracting a higher-dimensional value does not increase the dimension of the first argument. For **union**, only arguments of the same dimension make sense, since for arguments of different dimension the result is always the higher-dimensional argument.

In group 5, **crossings** returns the isolated points in the result of a *line*/*line* intersection, whereas **intersection** returns common *line* parts. Operations **touch_points** and **common_border** form intersections of the boundaries of *region* and of *line* values. Formal definitions of the semantics for all operations can be found in the original literature.

Exercise 4.2 Provide formal definitions of semantics for the following cases:

1. **intersection**: $\pi \times \pi \to \pi$
2. **intersection**: $\pi \times \sigma \to \pi$

3. **minus**: $\sigma \times \pi \rightarrow \sigma$
4. **minus**: $\sigma \times \sigma \rightarrow \sigma$ [1D]
5. **minus**: $\sigma \times \sigma \rightarrow \sigma$ [2D]
6. **union**: $\sigma \times \sigma \rightarrow \sigma$ [2D]

The following notations may be helpful: Predicates *is1D* and *is2D* allow us to check whether the argument is of a one-dimensional or a two-dimensional type. Notations $\rho(Q)$, ∂Q, and Q° refer to the closure of point set Q, its boundary, and its interior, respectively. ■

The following example illustrates that with union and intersection we also have the corresponding aggregate functions available, using the general mechanisms described in Section 4.1.3.

Example 4.6 Compute the region of Europe from the regions of its countries.

```
LET sum = AGGREGATE(union, TheEmptyRegion);
LET Europe = ELEMENT(SELECT sum(area) FROM country)
```

Here, *TheEmptyRegion* is a constant defined in the database containing an empty `region` value. *Europe* is a `region` value after evaluation. ■

Aggregation

Aggregation reduces point sets to points. Operations are shown in Table 4.8. For the **min** and **max** operation on open intervals in a 1D space, the infimum or supremum is returned instead of an undefined value. The **single** operation returns the element of a singleton set. For **min** and **max** on `periods` values, we introduce the alias names **start** and **end**. We show the semantics only for some of the operations.

Table 4.8 Aggregate operations.

Operation	*Signature*			*Semantics*
min, **max**	σ	$\rightarrow \pi$	[1D]	$min(\rho(U))$, $max(\rho(U))$
avg	σ	$\rightarrow \pi$	[1Dnum]	
avg[**center**]	σ	$\rightarrow \pi$	[2D]	
single	σ	$\rightarrow \pi$		if $\exists\, u$: $U = \{u\}$ then u else $\bot$
min[**start**], **max**[**end**]	`periods` $\rightarrow$ `instant`			

Example 4.7 Find the point where the highway A1 crosses the river Rhine.

```
LET RhineA1 = ELEMENT(
  SELECT single(crossings(R.route, H.route))
  FROM river AS R, highway AS H
  WHERE R.name = 'Rhine' AND H.name = 'A1' )
```

Through the use of **single**, the result *RhineA1* is a *point* value instead of a *points* value as returned by **crossings**. If anything unexpected happens within this computation (e.g., there is no river Rhine in the database), the result point will have the value $\perp$. ■

Numeric properties of sets

For sets of points, a number of well-known numeric properties may be computed (Table 4.9). The number of components is the number of disjoint maximal connected subsets (i.e., the number of faces for a *region*, connected components for a *line* graph, and intervals for a *range* value in 1D). The **size** is defined for all continuous set types (i.e., for *range*(*real*), *periods*, *line*, and *region*). It is the sum of the lengths of intervals in 1D, the total length of curves for *line*, and the area for *region* values. The **perimeter** is the length of the boundary of a *region*. The second part of the table just defines some alias names. Formal semantics are omitted.

Example 4.8 How long is the common border of France and Germany?

```
LET France =
  ELEMENT(SELECT area FROM country WHERE name = 'France');
LET Germany =
  ELEMENT(SELECT area FROM country WHERE name = 'Germany');
length(common_border(France, Germany))
```
■

Table 4.9 Numeric operations.

Operation	*Signature*		
no_components	σ	$\rightarrow$ *int*	
size	σ	$\rightarrow$ *real*	[cont]
perimeter	*region*	$\rightarrow$ *real*	
size[**duration**]	*periods*	$\rightarrow$ *real*	
size[**length**]	*line*	$\rightarrow$ *real*	
size[**area**]	*region*	$\rightarrow$ *real*	

Table 4.10 Numeric operations.

Operation	*Signature*	
distance	$\pi \times \pi$	$\rightarrow$ *real* [cont]
	$\pi \otimes \sigma$	$\rightarrow$ *real* [cont]
	$\sigma \times \sigma$	$\rightarrow$ *real* [cont]
direction	*point* $\times$ *point*	$\rightarrow$ *real*

Distance and direction

A distance measure exists for all continuous types. The **distance** function determines the minimum distance among all pairs of points from the first and second argument. The distance is the absolute value of the difference in 1D and the Euclidean distance in 2D. (See Table 4.10.)

The direction function returns the angle of the line from the first to the second point, measured in degrees, relative to a horizontal line. Hence, if q is exactly north of p, then **direction**$(p, q) = 90$. If $p = q$, then the result is $\perp$.

Example 4.9 Find the cities north of and within 200 kms of Munich.

```
LET Munich =
  ELEMENT(SELECT center FROM city WHERE name = 'Munich');
SELECT name FROM city
WHERE distance(center, Munich) < 200
  AND direction(Munich, center) >= 45
  AND direction(Munich, center) <= 135
```

■

Specific operations for base types

The standard operations **and**, **or**, and **not** are needed although they are not related to the point versus point set view. We mention them because they have to be included in the set of operations subject to temporal *lifting*, called the *kernel algebra*.

The kernel algebra

The kernel algebra is defined to consist of the types in BASE $\cup$ SPATIAL, together with all operations defined in this section, restricted to those types.

4.2.5 Operations on Temporal Types

Recall that values of temporal types (i.e., types *moving*(α)) are partial functions of the form $f: \bar{A}_{instant} \rightarrow \bar{A}_{\alpha}$. An overview of operations on such types is given in

Table 4.11 Operations on temporal types.

Class	*Operations*
Projection to Domain and Range	**deftime**, **rangevalues**, **locations**, **trajectory**, **routes**, **traversed**, **inst**, **val**
Interaction with Domain and Range	**atinstant**, **atperiods**, **initial**, **final**, **present**, **at**, **atmin**, **atmax**, **passes**
Rate of Change	**derivative**, **speed**, **mdirection**, **turn**, **velocity**
Lifting	(all new operations inferred)
When	**when**

Table 4.11. We first discuss three classes of specialized operations on such types and then the general technique of lifting, which is also the basis for implementing the **when** operator.

Projection to domain and range

The first class of operations deals with projections of temporal values—which are functions—into domain and range (Table 4.12). The operation **deftime** returns the set of time intervals when a temporal function is defined. The operation **rangevalues** performs the projection into the range for the one-dimensional types. These two operations are illustrated for the case of a *moving*(*real*) in Figure 4.5.

Table 4.12 Projection operations.

Operation	*Signature*		
deftime	*moving*(α)	→ *periods*	
rangevalues	*moving*(α)	→ *range*(α)	[1D]
locations	*moving*(*point*)	→ *points*	
	moving(*points*)	→ *points*	
trajectory	*moving*(*point*)	→ *line*	
	moving(*points*)	→ *line*	
routes	*moving*(*line*)	→ *line*	
traversed	*moving*(*line*)	→ *region*	
	moving(*region*)	→ *region*	
inst	*intime*(α)	→ *instant*	
val	*intime*(α)	→ α	

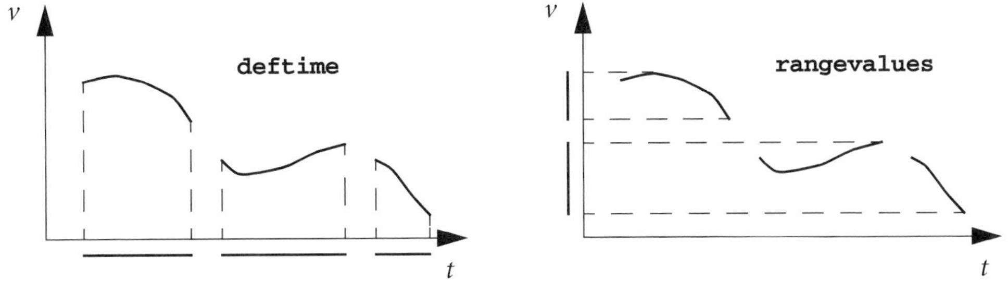

Figure 4.5 Projection operations **deftime** and **rangevalues**.

For the 2D data types, operations are offered to return the parts of the projections corresponding to our data types. For example, the projection of a *moving*(`point`) into the plane may consist of points and lines; these are returned by the operations **locations** and **trajectory**, respectively. For the values of `intime` types, which are just pairs, the two trivial projection operations **inst** and **val** are offered to access the components.

All the infinite point sets that result from domain and range projections are represented in collapsed form by the corresponding point set types. For example, a set of instants is represented as a `periods` value, and an infinite set of regions is represented by the union of the points of all the regions, as a `region` value. That these projections can be represented as finite sets of intervals, faces, and so on is due to the continuity condition for types *moving*(α) in Definition 4.9. The resulting design is complete in that all projection values in domain and range can be obtained.

Example 4.10 We use the example relations from Chapter 1 also in this section. Data types *moving*(`point`), *moving*(`real`), and so on are denoted *mpoint*, *mreal*, and so forth as attribute types.

```
flight (id: string, from: string, to: string, route: mpoint)
weather (id: string, kind: string, area: mregion)
```

Example 4.11 How large was the area in France affected by hurricane Lizzy?

```
LET Lizzy = ELEMENT(SELECT area FROM weather
  WHERE id = 'Lizzy');
area(intersection(traversed(Lizzy), France))
```

At what time did hurricane Lizzy start?

```
start(deftime(Lizzy))
```

Table 4.13 Interaction with values in domain and range.

Operation	*Signature*		
atinstant	$moving(\alpha) \times instant$	$\rightarrow intime(\alpha)$	
atperiods	$moving(\alpha) \times periods$	$\rightarrow moving(\alpha)$	
initial, **final**	$moving(\alpha)$	$\rightarrow intime(\alpha)$	
present	$moving(\alpha) \times instant$	$\rightarrow bool$	
	$moving(\alpha) \times periods$	$\rightarrow bool$	
at	$moving(\alpha) \times \beta$	$\rightarrow moving(\alpha)$	[1D]
	$moving(\alpha) \times \beta$	$\rightarrow moving(min(\alpha, \beta))$	[2D]
atmin, **atmax**	$moving(\alpha)$	$\rightarrow moving(\alpha)$	[1D]
passes	$moving(\alpha) \times \beta$	$\rightarrow bool$	

Interaction with points and point sets in domain and range

In this section, we define operations that relate the functional values of *moving* types with values in either their (time) domain or their range. With such operations we can answer questions such as: Does a moving point pass a given point or region in the plane? or Does a moving real ever assume the value 42? We can also restrict the moving entity to the given domain or range values.

In Table 4.13, the first group of operations concerns interaction with time domain values, the second interaction with range values. Operations **atinstant** and **atperiods** restrict the function to a given instant of time or set of time intervals, respectively (illustrated for a *moving(real)* in Figure 4.6). **Initial** and **final** return the (instant, value) pairs for the first and last instant of the definition time. The **present** predicate allows one to check whether the temporal function is defined at an instant of time, or is ever defined during a given set of time intervals.

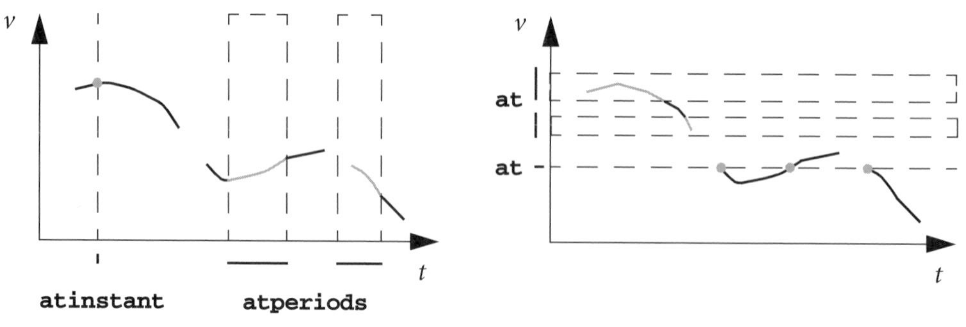

Figure 4.6 Operations **atinstant**, **atperiods**, and **at** on a **moving**(**real**).

Operation **at** restricts to a point or point set in the range of the function (Figure 4.6). In a one-dimensional space, the result is of the same type as the function argument. In two dimensions, for arguments of types *moving*(α) and β, the result type is the minimum of α and β, with respect to the order *point* < *points* < *line* < *region*. For example, if a *moving*(*point*) is restricted by a *region*, the result is a *moving*(*point*) again. If a *moving*(*region*) is restricted by a *point* value, the result is a *moving*(*point*), too (which is the second argument point at all times when it is inside the moving region).

Somewhat similar to **initial** and **final**, **atmin** and **atmax** reduce the function to the times when it was minimal or maximal, respectively. Since this depends on an order, obviously these operations can only be defined for a one-dimensional space. **Passes** is a predicate analogous to **present** checking whether the function ever assumed (one of) the value(s) from the range given as the second argument.

Example 4.12 How long was hurricane Lizzy over France?

```
duration(deftime(at(Lizzy, France)))
```

Where was flight KLM066 while Lizzy was over France?

```
trajectory(
  atperiods(ELEMENT(SELECT route FROM flight
    WHERE id = 'KLM066'),
  deftime(at(Lizzy, France))))
```

■

For further examples, we need a notation for time constants (i.e., to denote certain instants or periods of time). We introduce a few operations that allow us to derive such constants from integers (Table 4.14).

Table 4.14 Some operations to construct time constants.

Operation	*Signature*	
year	*int*	→ *periods*
month	*int* × *int*	→ *periods*
day	*int* × *int* × *int*	→ *periods*
hour	*int* × *int* × *int* × *int*	→ *periods*
minute	*int* × *int* × *int* × *int* × *int*	→ *periods*
second	*int* × *int* × *int* × *int* × *int* × *int*	→ *periods*
period	*periods* × *periods*	→ *periods*

Each of the operations in the first group constructs a `periods` value as a single closed time interval. For example, **year**(1990) denotes the time interval from the first to the last instant of the year 1990, and **second**(1990, 5, 15, 6, 30, 27) denotes the closed time interval for the second at 6:30:27 on May 15, 1990. Furthermore, the operation **period** allows us to construct from two given `periods` values the closed time interval extending from the minimal to the maximal instant of time present in any of the arguments. Hence, the expression **period**(**day**(2000, 5, 9), **minute**(2001, 3, 8, 12, 5)) constructs the time interval ranging from the first instant of May 9, 2000, 0:00:00 A.M. to the last instant of March 8, 2001, 12:05:59 P.M. You should be aware of the fact that we assume a continuous time domain; hence, even a second is a time interval, not an instant.

To denote instants of time, we can use the **start** and **end** operations on `periods` values. For example, the expression **start**(**minute**(2001, 3, 8, 12, 5)) denotes the first instant of March 8, 2001, 12:05:00 P.M.

Exercise 4.3 Suppose we have a table describing volcano eruptions in Europe.

```
volcano (name: string, eruptions: mpoint)
```

Formulate the following queries:

1. Show the locations of all volcanoes. (Return the result as a `points` value. Hint: It will be necessary to construct an intermediate table.)
2. Were there any eruptions in Italy in the seventeenth century? (Return the names of the volcanoes involved, if any.)
3. How many times did Etna erupt? ■

The operations in Table 4.13 are all of interest from a language design point of view. Some of them may also be expressed in terms of other operations. For example, for an `instant` t, we have:

present(f, t) = **not**(**isempty**(**val**(**atinstant**(f, t))))

Exercise 4.4 Which further operations in Table 4.13 can be derived from others? Show the equivalent expressions. ■

Rate of change

An important property of any time-dependent value is its rate of change (i.e., the derivative). To understand to which of our data types this concept is applicable, consider the definition of the derivative:

$$f'(t) = \lim_{\Delta t \to 0} \frac{f(t+\Delta t) - f(t)}{\Delta t}$$

This definition is applicable to any data type *moving*(α), whose range type α supports a difference operation and supports division by a real number.

Type *real* obviously qualifies as a range type, leading to operation **derivative** with the usual meaning. For type *point*, there are three kinds of differences that are of interest: the Euclidean distance, the direction between the two points, and the vector difference (considering a *point* value as a vector in 2D). This leads to three different derivative operations called **speed**, **mdirection**, and **velocity**, respectively (Table 4.15).

Here, **speed** yields the usual concept of speed of a *moving*(*point*) at all times as a *moving*(*real*), and **mdirection** is the direction of movement (i.e., the angle between the x-axis and a tangent to the trajectory of the *moving*(*point*)). **Turn** is an additional operation that yields the *change of direction* at all times.[5] Finally, **velocity** returns the derivative of the movement as a vector-valued function.

For further examples, we need a notation to denote interval constants to be used in queries. Similarly as for time constants, we introduce a few operations supporting this. (See Table 4.16.)

In Table 4.16, **range** forms the closed interval of the given argument values. To be able to construct open or half-open intervals, the operations **open**, **closed**,

Table 4.15 Derivative operations.

Operation	*Signature*		*Semantics*
derivative	*mreal*	→ *mreal*	μ' where $\mu'(t) = \lim_{\delta \to 0}(\mu(t+\delta) - \mu(t))/\delta$
speed	*mpoint*	→ *mreal*	μ' where $\mu'(t) = \lim_{\delta \to 0} f_{\mathbf{distance}}(\mu(t+\delta), \mu(t))/\delta$
mdirection	*mpoint*	→ *mreal*	μ' where $\mu'(t) = \lim_{\delta \to 0} f_{\mathbf{direction}}(\mu(t+\delta), \mu(t))/\delta$
turn	*mpoint*	→ *mreal*	μ' where $\mu'(t)$ $= \lim_{\delta \to 0}(f_{\mathbf{mdirection}}(\mu(t+\delta)) - f_{\mathbf{mdirection}}(\mu(t)))/\delta$
velocity	*mpoint*	→ *mpoint*	μ' where $\mu'(t) = \lim_{\delta \to 0}(\mu(t+\delta) - \mu(t))/\delta$

[5] The description of derivative operations here is slightly different from that in the original article by Güting et al., 2000; we follow a small revision suggested in Cotelo Lema et al., 2003.

Table 4.16 Some operations to construct intervals.

Operation	*Signature*	
range	$\alpha \times \alpha$	$\rightarrow$ *range*(α)
open, **closed**, **leftclosed**, **rightclosed**	*range*(α)	$\rightarrow$ *range*(α)
minint, **maxint**		$\rightarrow$ *int*
minreal, **maxreal**		$\rightarrow$ *real*
mininstant, **maxinstant**		$\rightarrow$ *instant*

leftclosed, and **rightclosed** are provided. Applied to a *range* value, these operations manipulate the bottom and top boundary. To be able to construct ranges describing the positive or negative numbers, the constants **minint** and so on are provided, where **minint** corresponds to $-\infty$.

Example 4.13 Let *LizzyArea* be a *moving*(*real*) describing the time-dependent size of hurricane Lizzy. We will see shortly how *LizzyArea* can be computed from *Lizzy*. Based on that, we can ask: At what times did the area of hurricane Lizzy shrink?

```
LET negative = open(range(minreal, 0));
deftime(at(derivative(LizzyArea), negative))
```

■

Example 4.14 Show the parts of the route of flight KLM066, when the airplane's speed was at least 800 kilometers/hour.

```
LET KLM066 = ELEMENT(SELECT route FROM flight
  WHERE id = 'KLM066');
trajectory(atperiods(KLM066,
  deftime(at(speed(KLM066), range(800, maxreal)))))
```

■

Lifting operations to time-dependent operations

We now complete the plan described in Section 4.2.3 of first defining operations on nontemporal types and then making them all uniformly time dependent. The technique described next is applied to all operations of the *kernel algebra*, defined in Section 4.2.4.

Consider an operation **op** of the kernel algebra with signature:

$$\alpha_1 \times \alpha_2 \times \ldots \times \alpha_n \rightarrow \beta$$

The idea of *lifting* is to allow any of the argument types to be replaced by the respective temporal type and also to return a corresponding temporal type. Hence, the lifted version of **op** has signatures:

$$\alpha_1' \times \alpha_2' \times \ldots \times \alpha_n' \rightarrow \mathit{moving}(\beta)$$

where $\alpha_i' \in \{\alpha_i, \mathit{moving}(\alpha_i)\}$.

Example 4.15 The equality operation on real numbers with signature:

=	*real* × *real*	→ *bool*

has lifted versions

=	*moving*(*real*) × *real*	→ *moving*(*bool*)
=	*real* × *moving*(*real*)	→ *moving*(*bool*)
=	*moving*(*real*) × *moving*(*real*)	→ *moving*(*bool*)

The **intersection** operation with signature:

intersection	*point* × *region*	→ *point*

has lifted versions

intersection	*moving*(*point*) × *region*	→ *moving*(*point*)
intersection	*point* × *moving*(*region*)	→ *moving*(*point*)
intersection	*moving*(*point*) × *moving*(*region*)	→ *moving*(*point*)

■

This lifting of operations generalizes existing operations that did not appear to be of great utility to operations that are quite useful. For example, an operator that computes the intersection between a *point* and a *region* does not seem to be very useful. However, computing the intersection between a *moving*(*point*) and a *region*—which means: Compute the part of the *moving*(*point*) when it was inside the *region*—is quite important. This is the reason why in Section 4.2.4 set operations were defined carefully for all argument types including single points.

The semantics of lifted operations can be defined as follows. Given **op** with signature:

$$\alpha_1 \times \alpha_2 \times \ldots \times \alpha_n \rightarrow \beta$$

any lifted version of the signature can be described by the set $L \subseteq \{1, \ldots, n\}$ of lifted indexes. For example, the signature $\mathit{moving}(\alpha_1) \times \alpha_2 \times \mathit{moving}(\alpha_3) \rightarrow \mathit{moving}(\beta)$ is given by $L = \{1, 3\}$.

Let f_{op} be the semantics of **op**—hence, the result of applying **op** to arguments x_1, ..., x_n is $f_{\text{op}}(x_1, \ldots, x_n)$. We define the semantics for each lifted version of **op** as f^L_{op}. Observe that in a lifted version an argument x_i is replaced by a corresponding temporal function $x_i(t)$. We define what it means to apply a *possibly lifted argument* (function) to an `instant` t by:

$$x_i^L(t) = \begin{cases} x_i(t) & \text{if } i \in L \\ x_i & \text{otherwise} \end{cases}$$

We can then define the function f^L_{op} pointwise for each instant of time by:

$$f^L_{\text{op}}(x_1, \ldots, x_n) = \{(t, f_{\text{op}}(x_1^L(t), \ldots, x_n^L(t))) \mid t \in A_{\mathit{instant}}\}$$

We now have available in our query language all the operations of the kernel algebra (Table 4.3) in their lifted versions—that is, we have time-dependent:

- Predicates
- Set operations
- Aggregation operations
- Numeric operations
- Distance and direction operations
- Boolean operations

The result is a very powerful query language! Let us see some examples.

Example 4.16 We can now easily define the time-dependent size of hurricane Lizzy used in Exercise 4.13:

```
LET LizzyArea = area(Lizzy)
```

Example 4.17 At what time did hurricane Lizzy split into two separate parts?

```
inst(initial(at(no_components(Lizzy), range(2,2))))
```

Here, **no_components** returns a *moving*(*int*), which, by the **at** operation, is reduced to the times when it has value 2. There are other possible ways to formulate this—for example:

```
start(deftime(at(no_components(Lizzy) = 2, true)))
```

Here, the *moving*(*int*) resulting from the expression **no_components**(*Lizzy*) is compared using the lifted equality operation to the value 2, resulting in a *moving*(*bool*). This in turn is reduced to the times when it has value *true*. Then, the initial instant is determined in a slightly different way than before. ■

Exercise 4.5 Define derived operations **always**, **sometimes**, and **never** (using the LET ... = FUN ... mechanism), all with signature *moving*(*bool*) → *bool*. Here, **always** means that the *moving*(*bool*) has value *true* whenever it is defined (similar for the other operations). Note that *false* < *true*. ■

Exercise 4.6 Define a **closest** operator with signature *moving*(*point*) × *point* → *intime*(*point*) returning the time and position when a moving point is (for the first time) closest to a given static point. Furthermore, assuming we have a relation about interesting sites to visit of the form:

```
site (name: string, pos: point)
```

containing, for example, an entry about the Eiffel tower, formulate the query: At what time was flight LH078 closest to the Eiffel tower? ■

Example 4.18 Assume we have a table listing the locations of airports:

```
airport (id: string, pos: point)
```

Compute for each airport the minimal distance it was from the center of hurricane Lizzy.

```
SELECT id, val(initial(atmin(distance(center(Lizzy), pos))))
FROM airport
```
■

Example 4.19 At what times was hurricane Lizzy heading north (let's say, within 10 degrees of the exact north direction)?

```
deftime(at(mdirection(center(Lizzy)), range(80, 100)))
```
■

Table 4.17 The **when** operation.

Operation	Signature	Semantics	Syntax
when	$moving(\alpha) \times (\alpha \rightarrow bool) \rightarrow moving(\alpha)$	$\{(t, y) \in \mu \mid p(y)\}$	$arg_1\ op[arg_2]$

The when operation

It would be nice if we had an operation that allows us to restrict a temporal value (or moving object) to the times when an arbitrary condition is fulfilled. That is, we would like to have an operation **when** with the signature shown in Table 4.17.

So the second argument is a predicate on the underlying nontemporal type. For this operator we specify a special syntax, as shown in the rightmost column, which means that we begin by writing the first argument and then the operator followed by the second argument in square brackets. Such an operator might be used in a query: Return the hurricane Lizzy whenever its size was more than 500 km^2.

```
Lizzy when[FUN (r: region) area(r) > 500]
```

In the definition of semantics, μ is the first argument, a function—hence, an infinite set of (instant, value) pairs. By *p* we denote the predicate given as a second argument.

So the operator would be very useful, and it has a quite simple and clear definition of semantics. The only question is whether it makes any sense to define such an operator, since it seems impossible to implement. Namely, μ is an infinite set, and to evaluate **when**, we need to call for evaluation of the user-defined predicate an infinite number of times.

Surprisingly, it *is* possible to implement the operator, and the key to it is the technique of *lifting* introduced previously. More precisely, it is possible to implement the operator if all operators in the parameter predicate belong to the kernel algebra. This means their lifted versions are available as well. This query can be implemented by the expression:

```
atperiods(Lizzy, deftime(at(area(Lizzy) > 500, true)))
```

The reason why the effect of the apparently unimplementable **when** can be achieved is that we do not call for evaluation of the original **area** operation on infinitely many instances of parameter *r*, but instead we call the lifted version of **area** on the original argument *Lizzy*, a *moving*(*region*) value. In terms of implementation, there will be two different algorithms: one working on *region* values and the other one working on *moving*(*region*) values directly.

The general translation of the **when** operator is the following:

$$x\ \mathbf{when}[\mathrm{FUN}\ (y{:}\ \alpha)\ p(y)] = \mathbf{atperiods}(x, \mathbf{deftime}(\mathbf{at}(\ p(y)\{y/x\}, true))$$

where $p(y)\{y/x\}$ denotes the predicate p where each occurrence of y has been replaced by x. So, based on lifting and rewriting, the **when** operator can indeed be effectively implemented.

4.2.6 Operations on Sets of Objects

All operations defined so far (Sections 4.2.4 and 4.2.5) apply to "atomic" data types only (i.e., attribute data types with respect to a DBMS data model). However, sometimes in the design of an algebra for new applications it is necessary to define operations that manipulate sets of "database objects" (i.e., tuples in the relational model or objects in an OO model) with attributes of the new data types. In the design presented here, only a single such operation is needed, called **decompose**. Its purpose is to make the components of our point set types accessible in a query. "Components" are the same as those that are counted in the **no_components** operation: In *range* types, a component is an interval, in *points* a single point, in *line* a connected component, and in *region* a face. Furthermore, in temporal types, a component is a maximal continuous part of the function value. For example, the *moving*(*real*) in Figure 4.5 has three such components.

The concept of continuity is well known for real-valued functions. For other temporal types—for example, *moving*(*points*) or *moving*(*region*)—it is not so obvious what continuity means. We will discuss this issue in the following text.

Basically, we would like to define the **decompose** operation as mapping a value of type α into a value of type *set*(α)—for example, *region* $\rightarrow$ *set*(*region*)—where in the result set, each value contains only a single face. However, not all DBMS data models allow us to manipulate sets of atomic values as such. For example, the relational model does not have sets of atomic values. Since the design should be as widely usable as possible, **decompose** is defined as an operation on a set of database objects instead, transforming, for example, a relation into another relation. The signature is shown in Table 4.18.

The first argument of **decompose** is a set of database objects (e.g., of tuples in the relational model); the second is a function mapping such an object into a value of one of our point set types (e.g., an attribute name). The third argument is a name for a new attribute that will be added to each result object.

The result set of objects is computed as follows: For each object u with an attribute value that has k components, **decompose** returns k copies of u, each of which is extended by one of the k component values.

Table 4.18 The **decompose** operation.

Operation	*Signature*		*Syntax*
decompose	$set(\omega_1) \times (\omega_1 \rightarrow \sigma) \times ident$	$\rightarrow set(\omega_2)$	$arg_1\ op[arg_2, arg_3]$
	$set(\omega_1) \times (\omega_1 \rightarrow moving(\alpha)) \times ident$	$\rightarrow set(\omega_2)$	

Example 4.20 Consider the *country* relation introduced earlier with schema:

```
country (name: string, area: region)
```

The expression:

```
country decompose[area, part]
```

returns a relation with schema:

```
(name: string, area: region, part: region)
```

Each tuple in the result will contain in its *part* attribute one component of the *area* attribute. ■

Example 4.21 Find the volcano eruptions that lasted for more than two days!

```
LET oneday = duration(day(2000, 1, 1));
LET volcano2 = volcano decompose[eruptions, eruption];
SELECT eruption FROM volcano2
WHERE duration(deftime(eruption)) > 2 * oneday
```

We use an arbitrary day to determine the duration of a day as a real number. ■

Let us now consider what the concept of "continuity" could mean for types other than *moving*(`real`) (e.g., *moving*(`region`)). A definition of continuity should allow us to capture discrete changes. A discrete change occurs when, for example, a new point appears in a `points` value, a `line` suddenly turns by 90 degrees, or a `region` value suddenly has a new position or shape. Intuitively, discontinuity means that "from one instant to the next" a value changes without traversing all the intermediate stages.

The idea for defining this formally is to introduce a function that measures dissimilarity between two values of a given data type. Let α be a type and ψ: $\bar{A}_\alpha \times \bar{A}_\alpha \rightarrow \mathbb{R}$. The value of ψ applied to two equal arguments should be 0, and it should approach 0 when the argument values get more and more similar. Given ψ, we can define continuity as follows.

Definition 4.11 Let f: $\bar{A}_{\mathit{instant}} \rightarrow \bar{A}_\alpha$, and $t \in \bar{A}_{\mathit{instant}}$. f is ψ-continuous in t

$$:\Leftrightarrow \forall \gamma > 0\ \exists \varepsilon > 0 \text{ such that } \forall \delta < \varepsilon : \psi(f(t \pm \delta), f(t)) < \gamma$$

where $\gamma, \delta, \varepsilon \in \mathbb{R}$ and ψ: $\bar{A}_\alpha \times \bar{A}_\alpha \rightarrow \mathbb{R}$. ■

This is a slightly modified version of the usual definition of continuity for real-valued functions.

Definition 4.12 Here are definitions of ψ for some of the data types α, to which the *moving* constructor is applicable:

$$\alpha \in \{int, string, bool\} \qquad \psi(x, y) = \begin{cases} 0 & \text{if } x = y \\ 1 & \text{otherwise} \end{cases}$$

$$\alpha = real: \qquad \psi(x, y) = |x - y|$$

$$\alpha = point: \qquad \psi(p_1, p_2) = d(p_1, p_2)$$

Here, $d(p_1, p_2)$ denotes the Euclidean distance between points p_1 and p_2. For the remaining types `points`, `line`, and `region`,the definitions are left to the exercises. ■

Exercise 4.7 Define an appropriate function ψ to define dissimilarity between `region` values. ■

Exercise 4.8 Assume we have two relations describing states and cities in history:

```
historic_states (name: string, area: mregion)
historic_cities (name: mstring, pos: point)
```

For the states we assume that their area changed over time,[6] but the name was always the same. At any time in history a state name was unique—that is, no two states with the same name existed. A state may have disappeared for some time, then reappeared; it is still the same state. On the other hand, we assume a state cannot change its name; rather, in such a case, a new state begins to exist. For the cities, we assume that their location is fixed, yet the name may have changed over time. So the identity of a city is determined by its position. Hence, *name* is a key for *historic_states*, and *pos* is a key for *historic_cities*.

Formulate the following queries (some of them from Table 1.8):

1. What was the largest extent ever of the Roman Empire? Return the extent as a number, the time period, and the region of the maximal extent.

[6] Clearly, for states, the area changes only in discrete steps, but that case is also covered by this model.

2. On which occasions did any two states merge? Return the time when it happened, the names and regions before the merge, and the name and region after the merge.
3. List all names of the city now called Istanbul.
4. Which states contained Istanbul? For each state, list the names the city had during the respective period. ■

This completes the description of the abstract model. It provides a rich set of types and operations for modeling and querying moving objects. The data types have been defined at a conceptual level as infinite sets. The next task is to come up with finite representations for all the data types so that the design becomes implementable.

4.3 A Discrete Model

In this section, we develop a *discrete model* to implement the abstract model of the previous section. Remember the discussion in Section 4.1.2: Many choices exist to represent the infinite point sets of the abstract level. Hence, this is not going to be the one and only discrete model, but just one instance of such a model. Other discrete models—for example, supporting curved surfaces—may be designed as well and be more suitable for certain applications.

4.3.1 Overview

The task now is to design and define formally finite representations for all the data types (or type constructors) of the abstract model. Let us reconsider the type system of that model (Tables 4.2 and 4.19).

Table 4.19 Type system of the abstract model.

Type constructor	*Signature*	
int, real, string, bool		→ BASE
point, points, line, region		→ SPATIAL
instant		→ TIME
range	BASE ∪ TIME	→ RANGE
intime	BASE ∪ SPATIAL	→ TEMPORAL
moving	BASE ∪ SPATIAL	→ TEMPORAL

The base types *int*, *real*, *string*, and *bool* can be directly implemented in terms of corresponding types of a programming language. The spatial types *point* and *points* also have direct discrete representations, whereas for *line* and *region* we will define linear approximations (in terms of polylines and polygons). Type *instant* can be represented as a programming language real number. The *range* types represent finite sets of intervals, and the *intime* types represent pairs (instant, value). Finite representations for them are also straightforward.

Note that a constant type constructor at the discrete level will be mapped to a data structure in the implementation, and a type constructor with arguments will be mapped to a parameterized data structure. In programming languages, arrays or template classes are examples of such parameterized data structures. So far, all the type constructors of the abstract model will have direct counterparts in the discrete model. However, for the *moving* constructor there is no way to have a data structure that automatically assembles given data structures for the (static) argument types into data structures for corresponding temporal types (representing functions of time). As a result, the discrete type system does not have a *moving* constructor but replaces it by the type constructors shown in Table 4.20.

For the representation of the temporal types we will use the so-called *sliced representation*. The basic idea is to decompose the temporal development of a value along the time dimension into fragment intervals called *slices*, such that within each slice this development can be represented by some kind of "simple" function. This idea is illustrated in Figure 4.7.

In terms of data types, the sliced representation is built by a type constructor *mapping* representing a set of slices and data types for the various kinds of slices (simple functions), which we call *unit types*. For example, to represent pieces of a *moving*(*real*), we have a type *ureal* ("real unit") and a *moving*(*real*) as a whole

Table 4.20 Type system of the discrete model.

Type constructor	*Signature*	
int, *real*, *string*, *bool*		→ BASE
point, *points*, *line*, *region*		→ SPATIAL
instant		→ TIME
range	BASE ∪ TIME	→ RANGE
intime	BASE ∪ SPATIAL	→ TEMPORAL
const	BASE ∪ SPATIAL	→ UNIT
ureal, *upoint*, *upoints*, *uline*, *uregion*		→ UNIT
mapping	UNIT	→ TEMPORAL

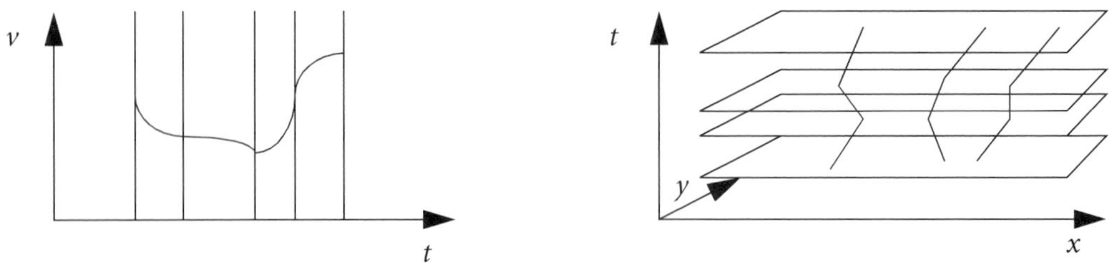

Figure 4.7 Sliced representation of a *moving*(*real*) and a *moving*(*points*) value.

is represented by the type *mapping*(*ureal*). A value of a unit type, called a *unit*, is a pair consisting of a time interval and a description of a simple function valid during that time interval.

For the data types *int*, *string*, and *bool*, which admit only discrete changes, the description of the "simple function" is simply the value itself. The type constructor *const* builds unit types for them by just pairing this value with a time interval. Hence, we can represent all the moving types of the abstract model by discrete types, as shown in Table 4.21.

The *const* type constructor is uniformly applicable to all base types and spatial types. Hence, there are also temporal types representing stepwise constant developments, such as *mapping*(*const*(*region*)), for example, but these are not so interesting here.

In the following two sections, we formally define the semantics of the data types of the discrete model. That means that for each type α, we define its domain, or carrier set D_α. In contrast to the definitions in the abstract model, the elements of such carrier sets here must always be described in terms of finite representations.

Table 4.21 Correspondence between abstract and discrete temporal types.

Abstract Type	*Discrete Type*
moving(*int*)	*mapping*(*const*(*int*))
moving(*string*)	*mapping*(*const*(*string*))
moving(*bool*)	*mapping*(*const*(*bool*))
moving(*real*)	*mapping*(*ureal*)
moving(*point*)	*mapping*(*upoint*)
moving(*points*)	*mapping*(*upoints*)
moving(*line*)	*mapping*(*uline*)
moving(*region*)	*mapping*(*uregion*)

Note that beyond saying precisely what we mean by the data types, the purpose of such definitions is to give a high-level specification of data structures. The description is generally given in terms of sets and tuples and constraints on them; this is a bit more abstract than talking about representations in terms of arrays, records, pointers, and so on and still leaves some freedom in mapping to an implementation. It is also a programming language-independent specification.

4.3.2 Nontemporal Types

The standard data types available in programming languages are the basis of our definitions. Such types are denoted as `int`, `real`, and so forth. You can compare these to the corresponding definitions of the abstract model in Section 4.2.2.

Definition 4.13 The carrier sets for the types *int*, *real*, *string*, *bool*, *point*, *points*, and *instant* are defined as follows. Let *Instant* = `real` and *Point* = `real` × `real`.

$$D_{int} = \texttt{int} \cup \{\bot\} \qquad D_{point} = Point \cup \{\bot\}$$
$$D_{real} = \texttt{real} \cup \{\bot\} \qquad D_{points} = 2^{Point}$$
$$D_{string} = \texttt{string} \cup \{\bot\} \qquad D_{instant} = Instant \cup \{\bot\}$$
$$D_{bool} = \texttt{bool} \cup \{\bot\}$$

As mentioned before, the discrete versions of *line* and *region* are based on linear approximations. In the abstract model, a *line* value is a set of curves in the plane viewed as a planar graph, whose nodes are intersections of curves and whose edges are intersection-free pieces of curves. In the discrete model, such an edge curve is represented by a polyline (Figure 4.8). This is equivalent to saying that a *line* value is a set of line segments that may only intersect in their end points.

To define the carrier set for *line*, we first define line segments as ordered pairs of points.

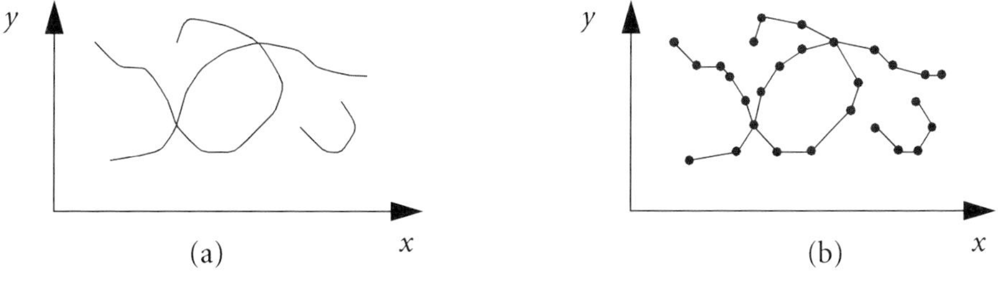

Figure 4.8 A *line* value in the abstract model (a); a *line* value in the discrete model (b).

Definition 4.14 Let

$$Seg = \{(u, v) \mid u, v \in Point, u < v\}$$

be the set of all line segments. The order assumed on points is the lexicographical one—that is, for two points u and v, we have $u < v \Leftrightarrow u.x < v.x \vee (u.x = v.x \wedge u.y < v.y)$.[7] ■

Definition 4.15 The carrier set for `line` is:

$$D_{\mathtt{line}} = \{S \subset Seg \mid S \text{ is finite} \wedge \forall\, s, t \in S: s \neq t \Rightarrow (\neg\, p\text{-}intersect(s, t) \wedge \neg\, touch(s, t))\}$$ ■

Two segments *p-intersect* ("properly intersect") if they intersect in their *interior* (in a point other than an end point); they *touch* if one end point lies in the interior of the other segment.

Exercise 4.9 Formalize these concepts. First, define *points*(s), the infinite point set in the plane forming the line segment s. Then, define *interior*, *p-intersect*, and *touch*. ■

Observe that the values of type `line` (the elements of $D_{\mathtt{line}}$) are certain finite represention; whether these representations have any implied meaning and what that meaning is has not yet been defined anywhere. Of course, by using terms such as *line segment*, we know that a pair $s = (u, v)$ stands for something else. A `line` value of the discrete model is to represent a `line` value of the abstract model. We can formally associate that meaning using a "semantics function" σ to map a value v of the discrete model to a value of the abstract model. Let $l = S \in D_{\mathtt{line}}$ be a `line` value. Its meaning is

$$\sigma(S) = \bigcup_{s \in S} points(s)$$

The set *points*(s) is defined in Exercise 4.9.

For `region` values, the structure is a bit more complex. Basically, a region is a finite set of simple polygons, each of which may have polygonal holes.

[7] By convention, for $p \in Point$, we denote by $p.x$ its first component and by $p.y$ its second component.

Definition 4.16 A *cycle* is (the boundary of) a simple polygon, defined as follows. Let

$Cycle = \{S \subset Seg \mid |S| = n, n \geq 3$, such that:

1. $\forall\, s, t \in S: s \neq t \Rightarrow (\neg\, p\text{-}intersect(s, t) \wedge \neg\, touch(s, t))$
2. $\forall\, p \in endpoints(S): card(p, S) = 2$
3. $\exists \langle s_0, \ldots, s_{n-1}\rangle: \{s_0, \ldots, s_{n-1}\} = S \wedge \forall\, i \in \{0, \ldots, n\text{-}1\}: meet(s_i, s_{(i+1) \bmod n})\ \}$

be the set of all cycles.

In this definition, *endpoints*(*S*) denotes the set of all end points of segments in *S*. The function *card*(*p*, *S*) describes how often *p* occurs as an end point in *S* and hence is defined as $card(p, S) = |\{s \in S \mid s = (p, q) \vee s = (q, p)\}|$. Two line segments *meet*, if they have a common end point. Hence a set of line segments is a cycle if (1) no segments intersect properly or touch, (2) each end point occurs in exactly two segments, and (3) segments can be arranged into a single cycle rather than several disjoint ones (there is an ordered sequence such that any two consecutive segments meet).

A *face* is a pair consisting of an outer cycle and possibly some hole cycles.

Definition 4.17 A *face* is an element of the set

$Face = \{\ (c, H) \mid c \in Cycle, H \subset Cycle$, such that:

1. $\forall\, h \in H: edge\text{-}inside(h, c)$
2. $\forall\, h_1, h_2 \in H: edge\text{-}disjoint(h_1, h_2)$
3. any cycle that can be formed from the segments of *c* or *H* is either *c* or one of the cycles in *H*}

A cycle *c* is *edge-inside* another cycle *d* if its interior is a subset of the interior of *d*, and no edges of *c* and *d* overlap. Two cycles are *edge-disjoint*, if their interiors are disjoint and none of their edges overlap (but their segments may touch or meet). The last condition makes sure that for a given set of line segments there can be only a single interpretation as a set of faces. A `region` value, then, is essentially a set of disjoint faces.

Definition 4.18 The carrier set for `region` is:

$$D_{\mathtt{region}} = \{F \subset Face \mid \forall\, f, g \in F : f \neq g \Rightarrow edge\text{-}disjoint(f, g)\ \}$$

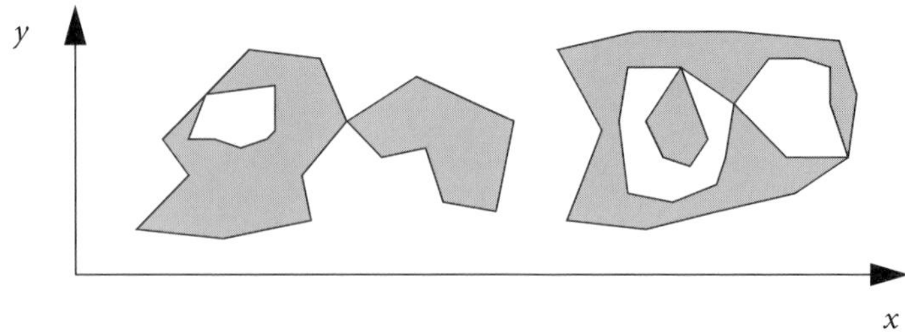

Figure 4.9 A `region` value in the discrete model.

Two faces (c_1, H_1) and (c_2, H_2) are *edge-disjoint if* either their outer cycles c_1 and c_2 are edge-disjoint, or one of the outer cycles is edge-inside a hole of the other face (e.g., c_1 lies in a hole $h \in H_2$). Figure 4.9 shows a `region` value in the discrete model, including some of the slightly pathological situations.

To define the semantics of a region value, we need to start from the semantics of cycle, which is the set of all points *inside* the cycle, including the points on the boundary. A formal definition is omitted here.

We have carefully defined the static spatial data types not only in their own interest, but also because their structure needs to be consistent with the corresponding spatio-temporal types (e.g.. *mapping*(`uregion`)). In fact, the definitions for the temporal unit types will be based on the previous definitions.

Finally, we need to handle the *range* and *intime* constructors.

Definition 4.19 Let $(S, <)$ be a set with a total order. The representation of an interval over S is defined by:

$$Interval(S) = \{ (s, e, lc, rc) \mid s, e \in S, lc, rc \in \texttt{bool}, s \leq e, (s = e) \Rightarrow (lc \wedge rc) \}$$

The meaning of such a representation is:

$$\sigma((s, e, lc, rc)) = \{ u \in S \mid s < u < e\} \cup LC \cup RC$$

where $LC = \{s\}$ if lc and $LC = \emptyset$ otherwise (similar for RC). ■

Definition 4.20 A finite set of disjoint intervals over S is defined by:

$$IntervalSet(S) = \{ V \subseteq Interval(S) \mid \forall\, u, v \in V: u \neq v \Rightarrow (disjoint(u, v) \wedge \neg\, adjacent(u, v)) \}$$ ■

What it means for two intervals to be *disjoint* and *adjacent* should be clear. Intervals must not be adjacent to ensure a minimal representation.

Definition 4.21 The carrier set of the `range` type constructor is for all types α to which it is applicable:

$$D_{\mathtt{range}(\alpha)} = IntervalSet(\overline{D}_\alpha)$$

Here, the notation $\overline{D}_\alpha$ refers to the carrier set without undefined values or empty sets, analogous to the notation $\overline{A}_\alpha$ defined for the abstract model. ■

The `intime` constructor is defined just as in the abstract model.

Definition 4.22 The carrier set for `intime`(α) is:

$$D_{\mathtt{intime}(\alpha)} := D_{\mathtt{instant}} \times D_\alpha$$ ■

4.3.3 Temporal Types

We now define the sliced representation for moving objects described in Section 4.3.1 (see Figure 4.7). This is built from the various unit types and the mapping type constructor.

Unit types

Any unit is a pair consisting of a time interval and a value (which is supposed to describe the "simple function").

Definition 4.23 Let S be a set. Then:

$$Unit(S) = Interval(Instant) \times S$$

A pair (i, v) from $Unit(S)$ is called a *unit*; i is its *unit interval*, and v is called its *unit function*. ■

All the unit types defined in the sequel can be viewed as subtypes of this generic unit type.

The semantics of a unit are a function of time, defined during the unit interval. For a particular unit type $Unit(S_\alpha) = Interval(Instant) \times S_\alpha$, where α is the corresponding non-temporal type, we can assign semantics by defining a function:

$$\iota_\alpha : S_\alpha \times Instant \rightarrow D_\alpha$$

Usually we omit the index α and just denote the function as ι.

Temporal units for base types

The *const* constructor yields unit types with a constant value during the unit interval.

Definition 4.24 Temporal units for all types $\alpha \in$ BASE $\cup$ SPATIAL are given by:

$$D_{const(\alpha)} = Interval(Instant) \times \bar{D}_\alpha$$

The semantics are given by the trivial function, for a unit (i, v) and $t \in Instant$:

$$\iota(v, t) = v$$

■

Among these, we are only interested in the types *const(int)*, *const(string)*, and *const(bool)*, as shown in Table 4.21.

More interesting is the unit type *ureal*, introduced to represent *moving(real)* values.

Definition 4.25 The carrier set for type *ureal* is:

$$D_{ureal} = Interval(Instant) \times \{ (a, b, c, r) \mid a, b, c \in \texttt{real}, r \in \texttt{bool}\}$$

The meaning is:

$$\iota((a, b, c, r), t) = \begin{cases} at^2 + bt + c & \text{if } \neg r \\ \sqrt{at^2 + bt + c} & \text{if } r \end{cases}$$

■

So a real unit can represent a quadratic polynomial in t or a square root of such a polynomial. Why this particular choice? We will represent moving points as well as the other temporal spatial types as moving linearly with time in this discrete model. In that case, the functions obtained by the lifted versions of **distance**, **length**, **perimeter**, or **area** operations are all representable by such real units. For example, **perimeter** and **area** of a moving region are linear and quadratic functions of time, respectively, whereas the **distance** between two moving points is a square root of a quadratic polynomial in t. Note, however, that the operation **derivative** of the abstract model is not closed on this representation. Hence, **derivative** is not implementable in this discrete model.

Temporal units for spatial types

We start by defining a set *MPoint* whose elements describe 2D points moving as linear functions of time.

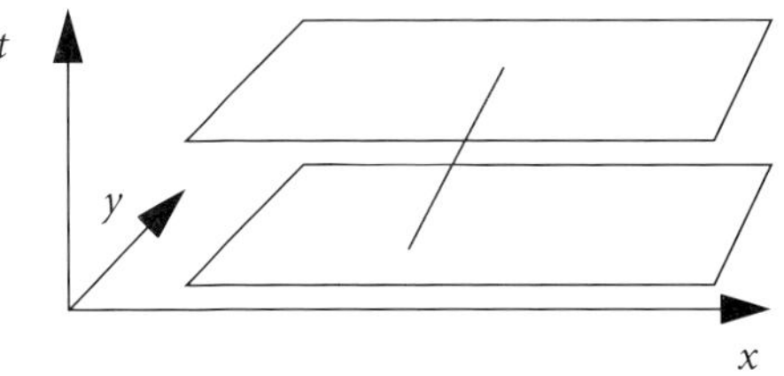

Figure 4.10 A point unit.

Definition 4.26 Let

$$MPoint = \{ (x_0, x_1, y_0, y_0) \mid x_0, x_1, y_0, y_0 \in \texttt{real}\}$$

The meaning is:

$$\iota((x_0, x_1, y_0, y_0), t) = (x_0 + x_1 t, y_0 + y_1 t)$$

This can be used directly to define point units (illustrated in Figure 4.10).

Definition 4.27 The carrier set for type *upoint* is:

$$D_{\texttt{upoint}} = Interval(Instant) \times MPoint$$

The unit type for *points* units, called *upoints*, is slightly more complex. We require that the various points moving around within a *points* unit do not meet (intersect) at any time within the unit interval. The reason is that the evaluation of functions on units should be simple. For example, the lifted **no_components** operation applied to a *points* unit should return a constant value valid through the entire unit interval. If points could meet within a unit, it would be necessary to run an expensive algorithm to discover whether such intersections are present.

Definition 4.28 The carrier set for type *upoints* is:[8]

$$D_{\texttt{upoints}} = \{ (i, M) \mid i \in Interval(Instant), M \subset MPoint, |M| > 0, \text{ such that}$$

$$\forall t \in \sigma(i), \forall k, l \in M : k \neq l \Rightarrow \iota(k,t) \neq \iota(l,t) \quad \}$$

[8] The definition is a bit simpler here than in the original article by Forlizzi et al., 2000. The reason is that we do not allow degeneracies in the start and end times of unit intervals anymore. The same simplification was assumed in the follow-up article on algorithms by Cotelo Lema et al., 2003.

The semantics are given by:

$$\iota(M,t) = \bigcup_{m \in M} \{\iota(m,t)\}$$

■

Remember that $\sigma(i)$ is the set of all instants within time interval i. The result of evaluating M at instant t is a set of points in the plane—hence, a value of type `points`—as it should be. We will generally assume that the ι function distributes through sets and tuples; hence, $\iota(M, t)$ is defined as previously for any set M and for a tuple $r = (r_1, \ldots, r_n)$ we have $\iota(r, t) = (\iota(r_1), \ldots, \iota(r_n))$. This is used, for example, in the definition of the `uregion` type (Definition 4.32).

The constraint $|M| > 0$ ensures that we do not have empty units. An empty unit (i.e., one whose value is undefined or empty during the unit interval) contains no useful information; we will always express the fact that the value is undefined at that time by having no unit at all.

Of course, it is possible that distinct points within a *moving*(`points`) value meet at certain times. This has to be represented by separate units. For example, in Figure 4.11, two points within a *moving*(`points`) value meet in a point p, say, at an instant t_0. This has to be represented within three units: one with an open time interval up to t_0, the second with a closed time interval $[t_0, t_0]$ representing the state only at instant t_0, and the third with an open time interval starting at t_0.

For the representation of moving lines and moving regions, the strategy is to use polyhedral shapes, or linear representations, and to avoid curved surfaces. This is in order to keep algorithms more simple; they are complex enough in the 3D space! Algorithms on linear shapes have been well studied in computational geometry.

As the basis of these temporal representations, we use a *moving segment*, a line segment whose end points move linearly with time and stay within the same 3D plane. This means the segment does not turn while moving; therefore, the resulting 3D shapes will only have plane surfaces.

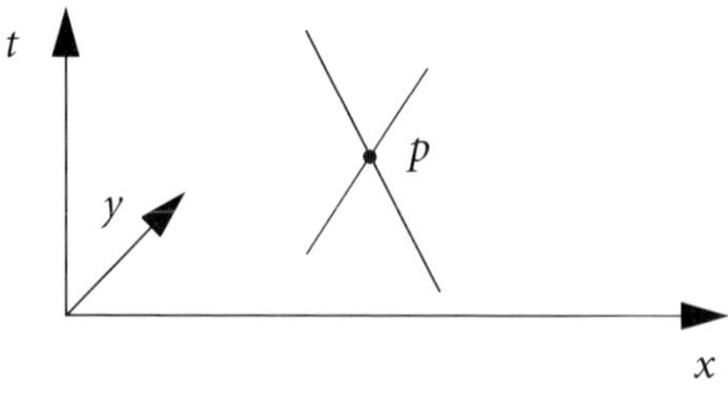

Figure 4.11 Two elements of a *moving*(`points`) value meet.

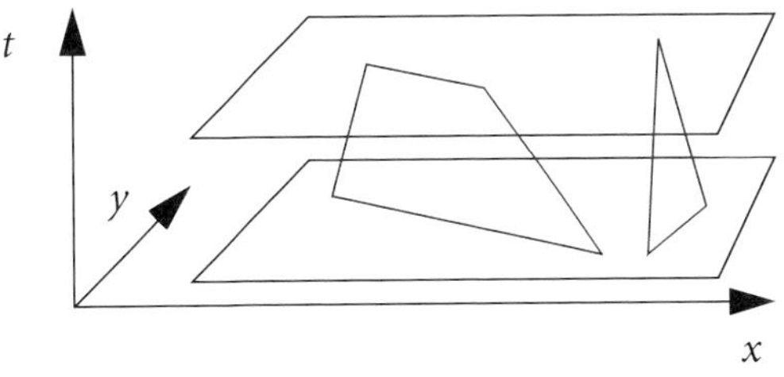

Figure 4.12 Two moving segments.

Definition 4.29 Let the set *MSeg* of *moving segments* be defined as:

$$MSeg = \{ (s, e) \mid s, e \in MPoint, s \neq e, coplanar(s, e)\}$$

A moving segment corresponds to a trapezium in the 3D space and may degenerate into a triangle. In representations of moving lines or regions most often triangles occur. Two examples of moving segments are shown in Figure 4.12.

A moving line is then represented by a set of moving segments. Of course, this is only an approximation of a moving continuous curve, as illustrated in Figure 4.13.

Definition 4.30 The carrier set for type `uline` is:

$$D_{\texttt{uline}} = \{ (i, M) \mid i \in Interval(Instant), M \subset MSeg, \text{ such that } \forall t \in \sigma(i) : \iota(M,t) \in \overline{D}_{\texttt{line}} \}$$

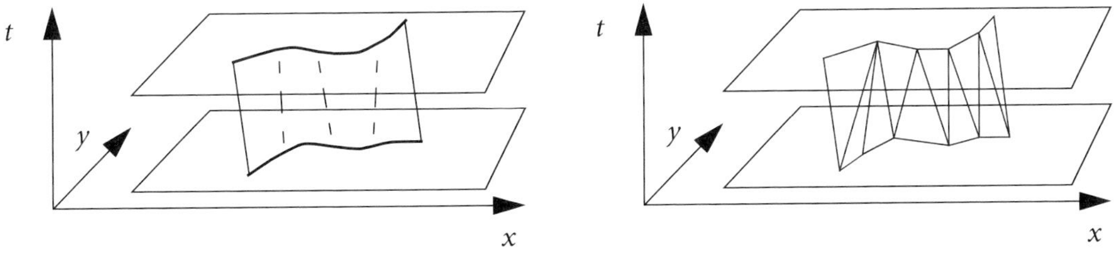

Figure 4.13 A moving curve and its approximation as a line unit.

where:

$$\iota(M,t) = \bigcup_{(s,e)\in M} \iota((s,e),t)$$

$$\iota((s,e),t) = \begin{cases} \{(\iota(s),\iota(e))\} & \text{if } \iota(s) \neq \iota(e) \\ \varnothing & \text{otherwise} \end{cases}$$ ■

So the requirement is that evaluation of a line unit results in a proper, nonempty `line` value at all times during its unit interval. For a moving segment that is degenerated into a triangle, evaluation at the start or end time may result in a point rather than a line segment; such results are removed by the definition of $\iota((s, e), t)$.

For the definition of region units, we mirror the structure of the definitions for static `region` values, replacing segments by moving segments. An example of a region unit is shown in Figure 4.14.

Definition 4.31 Let *MCycle* be the set of *moving cycles* and *MFace* the set of *moving faces*, respectively, defined as:

$$MCycle = \{ \{s_0, \ldots, s_{n-1}\} \mid n \geq 3, \forall\, i \in \{0, \ldots, n\text{-}1\}: s_i \in MSeg\}$$

$$MFace = \{ (c, H) \mid c \in MCycle, H \subset MCycle\}$$ ■

The constraints needed on moving cycles and faces (as in Definitions 4.16 and 4.17) are imposed directly via the `uregion` definition.

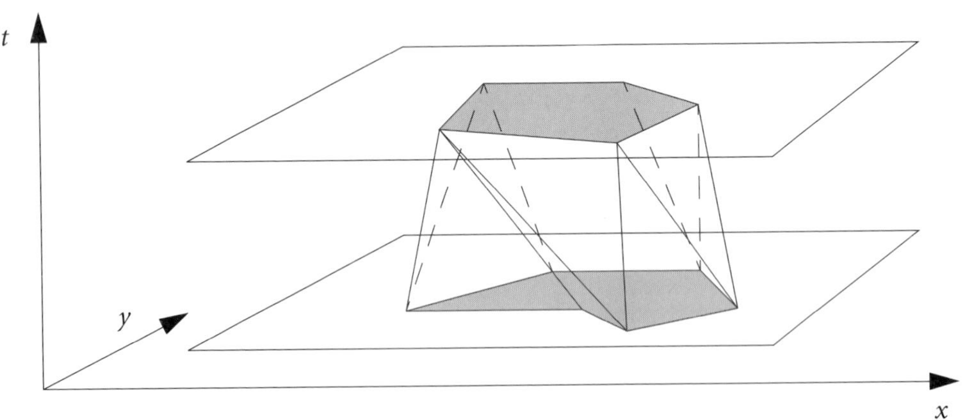

Figure 4.14 A region unit.

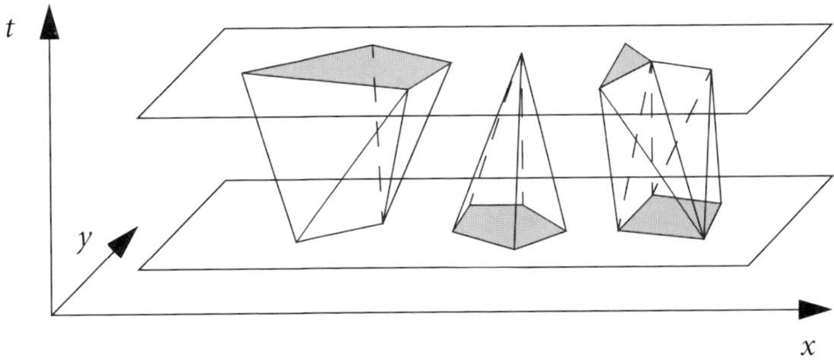

Figure 4.15 A region unit degenerated in the start and end times.

Definition 4.32 The carrier set for type `uregion` is:

$$D_{\texttt{uregion}} = \{\ (i, F) \mid i \in \mathit{Interval(Instant)},\ F \subset \mathit{MFace}, \text{ such that:}$$

$$\forall t \in \sigma(i) : \iota(F, t) \in \overline{D}_{\texttt{region}}\ \}$$

where $\iota(F, t)$ is defined by the fact that i distributes through sets and tuples, and evaluation of a moving segment $\iota((s, e), t)$ is as in Definition 4.30. ■

So a region unit is a set of moving faces, which, in turn, are composed of moving cycles such that evaluation at any instant within the unit interval yields a proper `region` value. Note that we can have region units that degenerate in their start or end times by using an open unit time interval. Such degenerations are shown in Figure 4.15. In this case, we should introduce separate units to represent the state of the moving region at the start or end instant, as discussed for `upoints` previously.

The sliced representation

We complete the discrete model by defining the *mapping* type constructor, which manages a set of units—hence, the sliced representation as a whole.

Definition 4.33 Let S be a set and $\mathit{Unit}(S)$ a unit type.

$$\mathit{Mapping}(S) = \{\ U \subset \mathit{Unit}(S) \mid \forall\ (i_1, v_1) \in U, \forall\ (i_2, v_2) \in U:$$

1. $i_1 = i_2 \Rightarrow v_1 = v_2$
2. $i_1 \neq i_2 \Rightarrow (\mathit{disjoint}(i_1, i_2) \wedge \mathit{adjacent}(i_1, i_2) \Rightarrow v_1 \neq v_2)\ \}$ ■

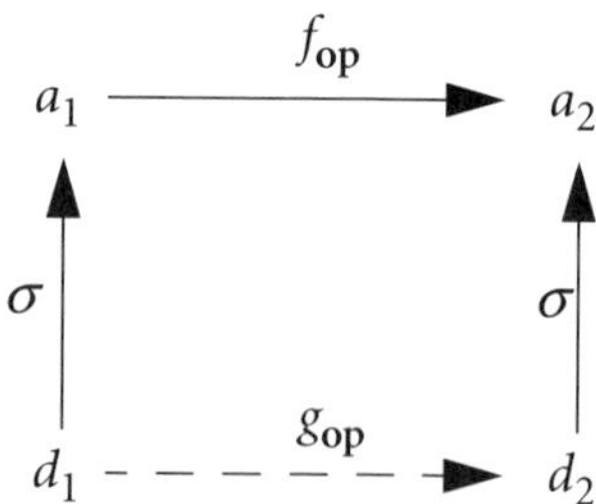

Figure 4.16 Discrete semantics g_{op} are inherited from abstract semantics f_{op}.

So a mapping is a set of units whose time intervals are pairwise disjoint; if they are adjacent, the values must be different, because otherwise one could merge the two units into one. This again ensures a minimal representation.

Definition 4.34 The carrier set of the *mapping* type constructor is for all unit types α:

$$D_{mapping(\alpha)} = Mapping(D_\alpha)$$ ■

Note that it is correct for a value of type *mapping*(α) to be the empty set. This represents a moving object that is undefined at all times.

This completes the description of the discrete model. We do not need to define the semantics of operations again at this level; the semantics of the abstract operations are inherited, as illustrated in Figure 4.16.

Suppose an operation **op** is applied at the discrete level to a value d_1 resulting in a discrete value d_2. The semantics of the discrete operation are given by the fact that the diagram in Figure 4.16 must commute. Here, f_{op} denotes the function, which is the semantics of **op** at the abstract level, and g_{op} the corresponding function at the discrete level; σ is the semantics function that maps a value at the discrete level to the corresponding value at the abstract level. Function g_{op} is determined by the fact that $f_{op}(\sigma(d_1)) = \sigma(g_{op}(d_1))$ must hold.

4.4 Spatio-Temporal Predicates and Developments

A look at the abstract model reveals that a concept of *predicates* for moving spatial objects is so far lacking or, at least, insufficient. Predicates have always played an important role in database systems and especially in query languages. They, in particular, serve as filter conditions in selections and joins. In this section, we introduce the concepts of *spatio-temporal predicates* and *developments* in order to close this gap for moving spatial objects. This enables us to pose queries incorporating *spatio-temporal selections* and *spatio-temporal joins*. Our considerations in this section will be restricted to spatio-temporal predicates between two moving points, between two moving regions, and between a moving point and a moving region. That is, moving lines are not involved, but an extension to spatio-temporal predicates for them is straightforward.

Section 4.4.1 gives an intuitive idea of the nature of a spatio-temporal predicate. Besides the temporal aspect, *topological predicates* for two-dimensional spatial objects, which are just those moving over time and considered by us, form the foundation for the definition of spatio-temporal predicates. Topological relationships, such as *overlap*, *disjoint*, *inside*, or *meet*, make statements about the relative positions of spatial objects to each other without considering metric aspects. We briefly explain the main concepts of topological relationships in Section 4.4.2. Note that the relationships discussed here go far beyond those listed in Table 4.6 in the right column. We also show which topological transitions are possible. In Section 4.4.3, we explain why the temporal lifting of spatial predicates does not lead to spatio-temporal predicates. A way to such predicates is given by *temporal aggregation*, introduced in Section 4.4.4. Based on this concept, we define *basic spatio-temporal predicates* in Section 4.4.5. The temporal composition of spatio-temporal predicates results in *developments*, discussed in Section 4.4.6. Section 4.4.7 presents a concise syntax for developments. Our efforts end in an algebra of spatio-temporal predicates, described in Section 4.4.8. Section 4.4.9 gives some examples, and Section 4.4.10 asks for a canonical collection of spatio-temporal predicates. Finally, Section 4.4.11 demonstrates how spatio-temporal predicates can be embedded into a SQL-like query language and how developments can be employed for querying.

4.4.1 Motivation

So far, we have learned about moving objects, which are spatial objects continuously changing over time. Changes refer to motion, shrinking, growing, shape transformation, splitting, merging, disappearing, or reappearing of spatio-temporal objects. An interesting observation now is that these temporal changes of spatial objects induce modifications of their mutual topological relationships over time. For example, at one time two spatio-temporal objects might be disjoint, whereas some time later they might intersect. These modifications usually proceed continuously over time but can, of course, also happen in discrete steps.

This observation leads us to *spatio-temporal predicates*. To obtain a deeper, intuitive understanding of this concept, we consider the example of an environmental database containing information about the flights of airplanes and about weather conditions. The query whether an airplane *crossed* a certain storm has a spatio-temporal nature and means to check the validity of different topological predicates during a series of events and periods in a given temporal order. This means, more precisely, that we have to examine whether there has been a constellation when the plane and the storm were disjoint for a while, when afterward they met at some time, when then the plane was inside the storm for a while, when after that the plane again reached the border of the storm at some time, and when finally the plane and the storm were disjoint again. We can observe that during certain time periods the topological relationships between both objects are constant and at certain points in time these relationships change. Consequently, we obtain an alternating sequence of time intervals and time points at which the topological relationships between both objects are constant. Roughly speaking, a spatio-temporal relationship is a sequence of (well known) spatial relationships that hold over time intervals or at time points; we call it a *development*.

4.4.2 Topological Predicates for Spatial Objects

Since topological relationships between spatial objects form the basis of spatio-temporal predicates, we need some knowledge of their essential properties. Due to the exclusive consideration of moving points and moving regions, we only have to deal with topological relationships of points and regions. According to Section 4.2.2, for a region A, we can distinguish its *boundary* ∂A and its *interior* A°; here, we also consider its *exterior*, denoted A^- (which is the set of all points in the 2D plane except ∂A and A°). We further simplify in the sense that we only consider single points (i.e., values of type `point`), and *simple* regions (i.e., values of type `region`) with the constraints that they only may consist of a single face and may not have holes. Simple regions are then bounded, regular closed point sets with a connected interior, a connected boundary, and a connected exterior.

The topological predicates between two (single) points are trivial; they are either *disjoint* or they *meet* (which corresponds to equality). Between a point and a region we find three relationships. Either the point is inside the region, outside the region, or on the boundary of the region. This leads to the three predicates *inside*, *disjoint*, and *meet*. For two simple regions, the identification of the possible topological relationships is more difficult. We here employ the so-called 9-*intersection model*, from which a canonical collection of topological relationships can be derived. The model is based on the nine possible intersections of the boundary ∂A, interior A°, and exterior A^- of a region A with the corresponding parts ∂B, B°, and B^- of another region B. Each intersection is tested with regard to the topologically invariant criteria of emptiness and nonemptiness. This can be expressed for two regions A and B by evaluating the following matrix:

$$\begin{bmatrix} \partial A \cap \partial B \neq \varnothing & \partial A \cap B^\circ \neq \varnothing & \partial A \cap B^- \neq \varnothing \\ A^\circ \cap \partial B \neq \varnothing & A^\circ \cap B^\circ \neq \varnothing & A^\circ \cap B^- \neq \varnothing \\ A^- \cap \partial B \neq \varnothing & A^- \cap B^\circ \neq \varnothing & A^- \cap B^- \neq \varnothing \end{bmatrix}$$

For this matrix, $2^9 = 512$ different configurations are possible, from which only a certain subset makes sense. For two simple regions, eight meaningful configurations have been identified that lead to the eight predicates called *equal*, *disjoint*, *coveredBy*, *covers*, *overlap*, *meet*, *inside*, and *contains*. This means that each of these

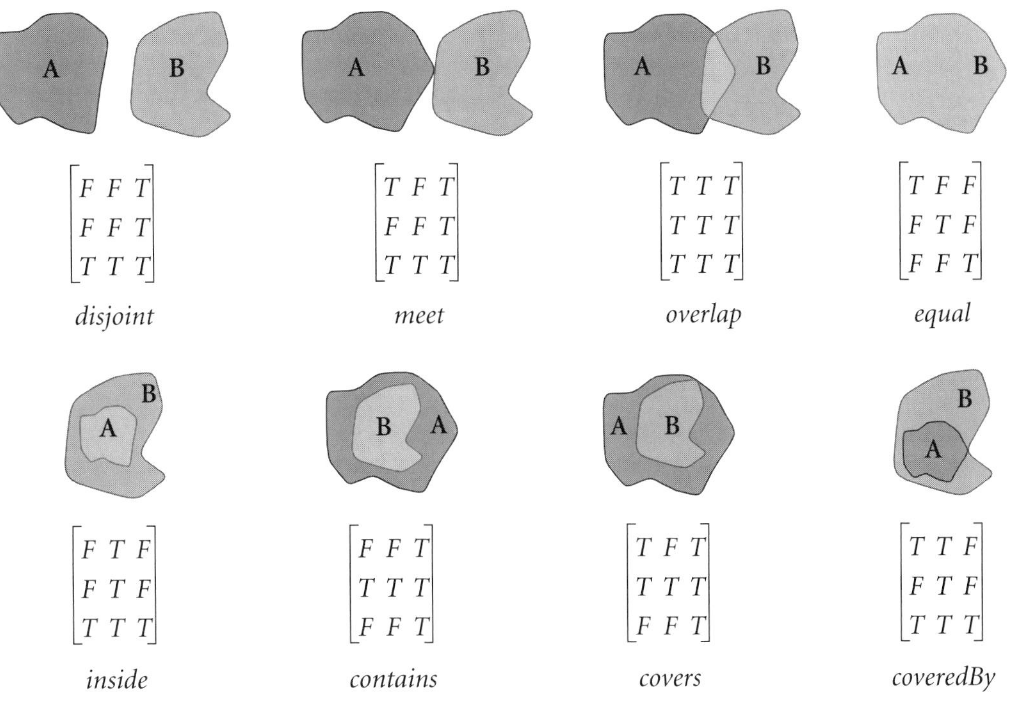

Figure 4.17 The eight topological relationships for two simple regions.

predicates is associated with a unique intersection matrix, so that all predicates are mutually exclusive and complete with regard to the topologically invariant criteria of emptiness and nonemptiness. Figure 4.17 shows examples of the eight predicates together with their intersection matrices.

Topological relationships can also be determined for more complex spatial objects, such as general `points` values and general `region` values. But then the number of possible relationships increases drastically, and their presentation becomes difficult. For instance, five topological relationships can be identified between two `points` values, and thirty-three topological relationships can be found for two `region` values. For our later definition of spatio-temporal predicates, the effect would be that we had to start with the corresponding number of so-called *basic spatio-temporal predicates* (Section 4.4.5). This would lead to a feasible but very lengthy presentation. On the other hand, this means that the design of spatio-temporal predicates is conceptually independent of the underlying system of topological predicates. Only some details of the design would be different.

Exercise 4.10 To understand topological relationships better, determine, characterize, and name the five topological relationships between two complex `points` objects. ■

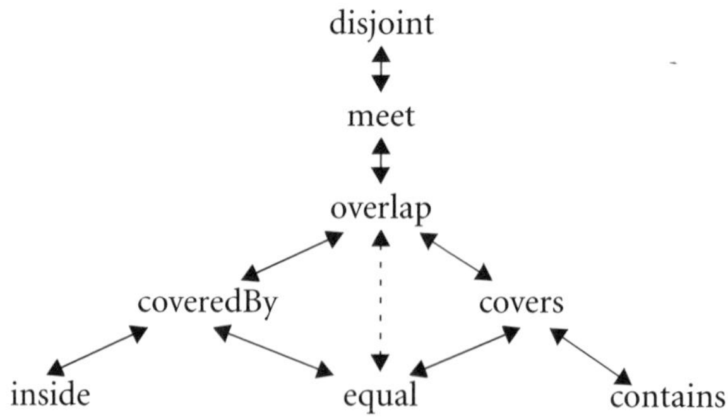

Figure 4.18 Conceptual neighborhood graph for two simple regions.

Possible *topological transitions* (i.e., changes) between topological relationships can be represented in a so-called *conceptual neighborhood graph*, also called *closest-topological relationship graph*. Topological changes occur if the topological relationship between two spatial objects is affected by reshaping or moving one or both objects. Each set of topological relationships concerning any spatial type combination can be organized in such a graph so that similar relationships are close to each other. In such a graph the relationships are the vertices, and the conceptual neighborhood is given by edges between vertices. In the case of the topological relationships between two regions, the conceptual neighborhoods are identified by the so-called *topological distance*, which, for the 9-intersection matrices of any two distinct relationships, is calculated as the number of different *T* and *F* entries. Pairs of relationships with the least, nonzero number of differences are considered to be conceptual neighbors. Figure 4.18 shows the conceptual neighborhood graph for the topological relationships between two simple regions.

An essential feature of this graph is that each of its paths only incorporates a sequence of snapshots of changing topological relationships. Starting from a vertex v all incident edges lead to the *next possible* topological relationships and thus indicate immediately possible qualitative transitions. All other relationships that are not connected to v cannot be directly reached from v. At this point, it should be mentioned that one special case is ignored by the graph due to its construction procedure. In the case that both regions have the same shape and size, a direct transition from **`equal`** to **`overlap`**, and vice versa, is possible. Thus, from this perspective, an edge between the corresponding nodes in the graph could be added.

Time only implicitly plays a role here and is not necessarily important, although it is helpful for an understanding of the graph. This is, of course, not astonishing, since this graph only deals with spatial and not with temporal behavior. The knowledge of possible transitions between topological relationships will later be helpful for an understanding of spatio-temporal predicates.

4.4.3 The Problem of Temporally Lifting Topological Predicates

In Section 4.2.5, we introduced the concept of temporal lifting for time-independent operations. This concept can also be well applied to topological predicates. Since a topological predicate is a function from two spatial data types to *bool*, a temporally lifted topological predicate is a function from two spatio-temporal data types to *moving*(*bool*) (i.e., to temporal Booleans). Hence, the lifted version is not a predicate in the usual sense. Consider the spatial predicate *inside*, for example, which, for points and regions, is defined as:

$$\textbf{inside}: \quad point \times region \quad \rightarrow bool$$

The lifted version of this predicate has the type:

$$\textbf{inside}: \quad moving(point) \times moving(region) \quad \rightarrow moving(bool)$$

with the meaning that it yields true for each time point at which the moving point is inside the evolving region; it yields undefined ($\perp$) whenever the point or the region is undefined, and it yields false in all other cases.

The essence of predicates is, however, that they can be used to express facts that are either true or false. This is especially so in selections and joins of database queries. In the previous example, we can define two spatio-temporal predicates *sometimes-inside* and *always-inside* that yield true if, and only if, the lifted version of **inside** yields true at some time, and at all times, respectively. While the definition for *sometimes-inside* is certainly reasonable, the definition for *always-inside* is questionable, since it yields false whenever the point, the region, or both are undefined. This is a very restrictive view, which also is not intuitive in certain cases. For instance, when the moving point has a shorter lifetime than the moving region and is always located inside the moving region, we would expect *always-inside* to return true.

Our understanding of spatio-temporal predicates is that they are essentially a function that aggregates the Boolean values of a spatial predicate as it evolves over time. In other words, a basic spatio-temporal predicate can be thought of as a temporally lifted spatial predicate yielding a temporal Boolean, which is aggregated by determining whether that temporal boolean was sometimes or always true. Note that while a lifted predicate might well return $\perp$ for some instant of time, this cannot happen for a spatio-temporal predicate. Instead, undefined values will be aggregated into Booleans. Accordingly, we can specify the following definition.

Definition 4.35 A *spatio-temporal predicate* is a function of type $moving(\alpha) \times moving(\beta) \rightarrow bool \backslash \{\perp\}$ for $\alpha, \beta \in \{point, region\}$. ■

4.4.4 Temporal Aggregation

We now have a closer look at how temporal aggregation of the Boolean values works. A lifted spatial predicate yields a defined value only on the intersection of the domains of two spatio-temporal objects. This affects the definition of aggregate operators, such as $\forall$ and $\exists$. A decision has to be made about how "strict" these quantifiers have to be (i.e., whether we map undefined values to true or to false) and whether we aggregate only over a restricted time interval (e.g., the intersection of the two participating moving objects' domains).

We overload the notation of the two quantifiers $\forall$ and $\exists$ from logic and denote universal aggregation by $\forall$ and existential aggregation by $\exists$. Both operators take a spatial predicate and deliver a spatio-temporal predicate—that is, they both have the following (higher order) type:

$$\forall, \exists: (\alpha \times \beta \rightarrow \mathit{bool}) \rightarrow (\mathit{moving}(\alpha) \times \mathit{moving}(\beta) \rightarrow \mathit{bool} \backslash \{\bot\})$$

The semantics of existential quantification causes no difficulties. Let p be a spatial predicate, and let S_1 and S_2 be two spatio-temporal objects. Then, the term $\exists p(S_1, S_2)$ is true if, and only if, p is true for the values of S_1 and S_2 at some time. In the following, we assume that the variable t ranges over type `instant` unless stated otherwise. We define:

$$\exists p := \lambda(S_1, S_2).\exists t : p(S_1(t), S_2(t))$$

This definition uses the lambda notation. A term $\lambda(x_1, \ldots, x_n).e$ denotes a function that takes arguments $x_1, \ldots, x_n$ and returns a value determined by the expression e (here a Boolean predicate quantified over time). When this function is applied to arguments $a_1, \ldots, a_n$ (here, two spatio-temporal objects S_1 and S_2), the body e is evaluated with (all free occurrences of) x_i substituted by a_i.

In contrast to $\exists$, we have several alternatives to define the meaning of $\forall$, depending on the time interval over which the universal quantification is assumed to range. This means that if t_1 and t_2 are the respective domains of the two spatio-temporal objects S_1 and S_2 the result of $\forall p(S_1, S_2)$ depends, in general, on whether quantification ranges over:

1. `instant` **2.** $t_1 \cup t_2$ **3.** t_1 **4.** t_2 **5.** $t_1 \cap t_2$

The first case is the most restrictive one: $\forall p$ can be true only if both objects are totally defined. The second option is also very restrictive, since it actually demands that both arguments have the same domain. This could be intended, for example, if we ask whether two countries have always been neighbors. This means the **`meet`** predicate has to be true for all times any of the two countries exist, which can be true only if the two countries have the same lifetime. Cases (3) and (4) require $t_1 \subseteq t_2$ and

$t_2 \subseteq t_1$, respectively. An example for case (3) is: Did a certain species (always) live in a particular climate region? This requires the **`inside`** predicate to be true during the existence of the species. It does not matter when the lifetime of the climate region properly includes that of the species, but if the species existed before or after the region, the spatio-temporal predicate would be expected to yield false. Case (4) is just the dual case of (3). The last case is least restrictive, since it just demands the predicate to hold on to the two objects' common lifetime. In particular, if $t_1 \cap t_2 = \varnothing$, $\forall p$ yields trivially true. An example is: Was a certain flight able to avoid a storm? This is particularly true at those times when one or the other object does not exist.

If we assess these situations, the first case describes a generally unrealistic assumption, so we do not consider this alternative any further. As we have seen, all the other cases do make sense, and we obtain definitions of four different quantifiers. Hence, the cases (2) to (5) are captured by the quantifiers $\forall_\gamma$, where $\gamma \in \{\cup, \cap, \pi_1, \pi_2\}$ and where $\pi_i(x_1, \ldots, x_i, \ldots, x_n) = x_i$. These quantifiers are defined as follows:

$$\forall_\gamma p := \lambda(S_1, S_2).\forall t \in \gamma(dom(S_1), dom(S_2)) : p(S_1(t), S_2(t))$$

For example, $\forall_{\pi_1}$ *inside* denotes the spatio-temporal predicate:

$$\lambda(S_1, S_2).\forall t \in dom(S_1) : inside(S_1(t), S_2(t))$$

There is a partial ordering among the universal quantifications. This is expressed by the following lemma.

Lemma 4.1 *Quantification ordering.*

1. $\forall_\cup p(S_1, S_2) \Rightarrow \forall_{\pi_1} p(S_1, S_2) \Rightarrow \forall_\cap p(S_1, S_2)$
2. $\forall_\cup p(S_1, S_2) \Rightarrow \forall_{\pi_2} p(S_1, S_2) \Rightarrow \forall_\cap p(S_1, S_2)$ ■

Exercise 4.11 Show the correctness of the first implication of (1) in Lemma 4.1. ■

4.4.5 Basic Spatio-Temporal Predicates

With these notations, we are now able to introduce the concept of *basic spatio-temporal predicates.* These can be defined by temporal lifting and aggregation. The most suitable one of the four meaningful "for all" quantifications is associated with each spatio-temporal version of the eight basic topological predicates (Section 4.4.2) for two regions. In other words, for each lifted spatial predicate there is a "preferred" temporal aggregation. For instance, when we ask by using a *disjoint* predicate whether the route of a plane did not encounter a storm, we usually require disjointedness only on the common lifetime (i.e., the result of this query is not affected by the fact that neither the storm nor the flight started or ended before the respective other object). Thus, the preferred or default interpretation for spatio-temporal *disjoint* is the predicate $\forall_\cap$*disjoint*. In contrast, the query asking for species living in a certain climatic region usually implicitly asks that the species' lifetime be included in that of the climatic region. This means that when we mean spatio-temporal *inside*, we mean $\forall_{\pi_1}$*inside*.

For a few spatio-temporal predicates the default expected aggregation behavior is existential aggregation. For instance, the expected behavior for *meet* and *overlay* is $\exists$*meet* and $\exists$*overlay*, respectively. However, we are mainly interested in working with universal quantifiers in order to be able to construct complex predicates. Therefore, we have chosen a $\forall$ definition for all predicates.

In order to distinguish spatial predicates and lifted spatial predicates, whose names begin with a lowercase letter, from spatio-temporal predicates, we introduce the naming convention that the latter predicates start with a capital letter.

Definition 4.36 *Basic spatio-temporal predicate.* The default aggregation behavior for the spatio-temporal versions of the eight basic topological predicates for two regions is defined as:

Disjoint	:=	$\forall_\cap$ **disjoint**
Meet	:=	$\forall_\cup$ **meet**
Overlap	:=	$\forall_\cup$ **overlap**
Equal	:=	$\forall_\cup$ **equal**
Covers	:=	$\forall_{\pi_2}$ **covers**
Contains	:=	$\forall_{\pi_2}$ **contains**
CoveredBy	:=	$\forall_{\pi_1}$ **coveredBy**
Inside	:=	$\forall_{\pi_1}$ **inside**

■

For a moving point and a moving region we just obtain the three basic predicates **Disjoint**, **Meet**, and **Inside**, which are defined in the preceding list. For two moving points we have the predicates **Disjoint** and **Meet**, which are also defined in the preceding list.

The choice of the default semantics for the basic spatio-temporal predicates is, of course, to some degree debatable. A possibility we always have is to add further predicates with different aggregation behavior.

Exercise 4.12 Assume that for the *meet* and *overlap* situation with respect to two moving regions we are interested in a *directed* definition in addition to their current *symmetric* definition. The term *directed* means that we consider the relationship from the point of view of one of the two operand objects. How can these variations of *meet* and *overlap* be defined and what are appropriate predicate names to express the "directedness"? ■

A further basic spatio-temporal predicate, which will be needed in the following sections, is the predicate that yields true for two arbitrary spatio-temporal objects:

$$\texttt{True} := \lambda(S_1, S_2).true$$

`True` can be thought of as the universal quantification of the spatial predicate **`true`** $= \lambda(s_1, s_2).true$, which yields true for any pair of spatial objects (i.e., **`True`** $=$ $\forall_{\cap}$**`true`** $=$ $\forall_{\cup}$**`true`** $=$ $\forall_{\pi_1}$**`true`** $=$ $\forall_{\pi_2}$**`true`**).

4.4.6 Developments: Sequences of Spatio-Temporal Predicates

Now that we have basic spatio-temporal predicates, the question is how to combine them in order to capture the change of spatial situations over time. That is, the issue is how to specify *developments*. We will demonstrate that particular relationships between two spatio-temporal objects can be appropriately modeled by sequences of spatial and (basic) spatio-temporal predicates.

For that purpose, consider, for example, the following scenario. A moving point P is at time t_2 outside of a moving region R and changes (continuously) its location so that at time t_4 it is inside of R. This could be paraphrased as "*P enters R*." We assume in the following that $i < j \Rightarrow t_i < t_j$. If P at some time t_6 is again outside of R, we could call the whole development of the topological relationships between P and R during a specific time interval "*P crosses R*."

A closer look at the continuous movement of P reveals that P must be located on the boundary of R at some time t_3 and at some time t_5. If at all other times P is located either inside or outside of R (i.e., P does not move along or stay on the boundary of R), we can characterize the whole development more precisely, as shown in Table 4.22.

We can observe two things. First, in order to temporally assemble different spatio-temporal predicates to a development, we need a way to restrict the temporal scope of basic spatio-temporal predicates to intervals. Second, some predicates,

Table 4.22 Development for "*P crosses R*."

Predicate	*Holds*		*Observation*
`Disjoint`(P, R)	during	$I_1 = [t_1, t_3[$	$t_2 \in I_1$
`meet`(P, R)	at	t_3	
`Inside`(P, R)	during	$I_2 =]t_3, t_5[$	$t_4 \in I_2$
`meet`(P, R)	at	t_5	
`Disjoint`(P, R)	during	$I_3 =]t_5, t_7]$	$t_6 \in I_3$

such as **Disjoint** and **Inside**, are used for whole time intervals, whereas other predicates, such as **meet**, are used only at time points.

The first observation leads us to the following definition (where $S|_I$ denotes the partial function that yields $S(t)$ for $t \in I$ and is undefined otherwise).

Definition 4.37 *Predicate constriction.* Let P be a spatio-temporal predicate, and let I be a (half-) open or closed interval. Then:

$$P|_I := \lambda(S_1, S_2).P(S_1|_I, S_2|_I)$$ ■

For an example, consider P and R from previously. It is clear that **Inside**(P, R) is false, but **Inside**$|_{]t_3, t_5[}(P, R)$ is true. In the following, we will abbreviate constrictions of P with open intervals $]t, \infty[$ and $]-\infty, t[$ by simply writing $P_{>t}$ and $P_{<t}$, respectively.

From the definition of constriction and from the definition of function restriction it follows that successive constrictions can be accumulated by intersecting the corresponding constriction intervals.

Lemma 4.2 *Constriction composition.* $(P|_I)|_{I'} = P|_{I \cap I'}$ ■

Exercise 4.13 Show the correctness of Lemma 4.2. ■

The interesting aspect of the second observation is that some predicates actually *cannot* hold at time points. For instance, it is generally not possible in the **disjoint** and **inside** cases to hold only at one time point when describing relationships of spatial objects over some time interval.[9] This is the case for airplanes, which cannot be disjoint from a hurricane only at one point in time; they have the inherent property to be disjoint for a period. On the other hand, any predicate can principally hold for a period of time (e.g., the *meet* relationship holds for a whole interval if the point moves along the border of R or stays stationary on the border for some time). This can be the case for an airplane and a hurricane, which meet at a certain instant or for a whole period.

This means that we can actually identify two classes of predicates: predicates that can be true for an instant in time and predicates that can, in general, only hold for a period of time. Accordingly, we call the former ones *instant predicates* and the latter ones *period predicates.* The classification is given in Table 4.23.

Recall that while period predicates cannot hold at isolated time points, instant predicates can well be used at periods. We will need this distinction of predicates, later when we define the semantics of sequences of predicates.

[9] It is, however, possible that, say, *disjoint* holds only at a time point t if one of the objects exists only at t (i.e., is undefined for $t' \in [t - \varepsilon, t + \varepsilon] - \{t\}, \varepsilon > 0$) or if one of the objects makes a completely discontinuous movement.

Table 4.23 Instant and period predicates.

Instant Predicates	*Period Predicates*
`equal`	`disjoint`
`meet`	`overlap`
`covers`, `coveredBy`	`inside`, `contains`

A further observation with regard to instant/period predicates is that only those developments can be satisfied in which two period predicates are "connected" by an instant predicate. For instance, it is not possible for two spatio-temporal objects to satisfy **`Inside`** immediately after **`Disjoint`** (under the assumption of continuous movement).

Next we define three operations (in infix notation) for combining spatio-temporal and spatial predicates: p ***then*** P defines a spatio-temporal predicate that for some time t_0 checks p and then enforces P for all $t > t_0$; P ***until*** p is defined dually (i.e., P must hold until p is true at some time t_0). Finally, P ***until*** p ***then*** Q is true if there is some time point t_0 when p is true so that P holds before and Q holds after t_0.

Definition 4.38 *Temporal composition.* Let p be a spatial predicate, and let P and Q be spatio-temporal predicates. Then:

$$p \textbf{ then } P := \lambda(S_1, S_2).\exists t : p(S_1(t), S_2(t)) \wedge P_{>t}(S_1, S_2)$$

$$P \textbf{ until } p := \lambda(S_1, S_2).\exists t : p(S_1(t), S_2(t)) \wedge P_{<t}(S_1, S_2)$$

$$P \textbf{ until } p \textbf{ then } Q := \lambda(S_1, S_2).\exists t : p(S_1(t), S_2(t)) \wedge P_{<t}(S_1, S_2) \wedge Q_{>t}(S_1, S_2).$$ ■

These combinators are related in several ways. Our first conclusion is as follows.

Lemma 4.3 *Combinator relationships.* If P ***until*** p ***then*** Q holds for two spatio-temporal objects S_1 and S_2, then so does P ***until*** p and also p ***then*** Q. ■

Exercise 4.14 Show the correctness of Lemma 4.3. ■

It is important to see that the other direction does not hold (i.e., even if both predicates P ***until*** p and p ***then*** Q are true for two objects, this does not necessarily mean that P ***until*** p ***then*** Q is also true). This is because the instants t that make P ***until*** p and p ***then*** Q true can be chosen independently from one another, whereas we need exactly one instant t to make P ***until*** p ***then*** Q true. This means that the latter predicate is really needed and cannot be expressed by a simple conjunction of the other two predicates. We rather have to "synchronize" on the t value. On the other hand, ***until*** and ***then*** are special cases of ***until-then***. This follows from the fact that **True** is a unit for temporal composition.

Lemma 4.4 *Derived compositions.*

1. p ***then*** P = **True** ***until*** p ***then*** P
2. P ***until*** p = P ***until*** p ***then*** **True**

Equation 1 in the preceding list, can be shown as follows: p ***then*** P yields true for two objects S and S' if there is a t such that $p(S(t), S'(t))$ and $P_{>t}(S, S')$ is true. On the other hand, **True** ***until*** p ***then*** P yields true for S and S' if $p(S(t), S'(t))$ and $P_{>t}(S, S')$ and $\mathbf{True}_{<t}(S, S')$ is true, which is identical to the previous condition, since $\mathbf{True}_{<t}(S, S') = \mathbf{True}(S_{<t}, S'_{<t}) = \mathit{true}$. Equation 2 is shown in a similar way. ■

Hence, we can always restrict ourselves to ***until-then*** compositions, knowing that all results extend to ***then*** and ***until*** by the expansion described in Lemma 4.4. In this sense, ***True***, which can in general be employed as an initial, a final, and also intermediate part of a development, serves as a kind of wildcard spatio-temporal predicate, which can be used to express "don't care" or "unknown" parts of developments.

4.4.7 A Concise Syntax for Developments

We will now first show that temporal composition is associative. This fact can then be exploited to define a concise sequencing syntax for predicates.

Lemma 4.5 *Associativity of composition.*

$$P \textbf{ until } p \textbf{ then } (Q \textbf{ until } q \textbf{ then } R) = (P \textbf{ until } p \textbf{ then } Q) \textbf{ until } q \textbf{ then } R$$

This can be proved as follows. We have to show that whenever the left-hand side is true for two objects S and S', then so is the right-hand side and vice versa. If the left-hand side is true, we know that there is a time point t_1, such that $p(S(t_1), S'(t_1))$, $P_{<t_1}(S, S')$, and $(Q \textbf{ until } q \textbf{ then } R)_{>t_1}(S, S')$ is true. The last condition can be reformulated as follows:

$$\begin{aligned} & (Q \textbf{ until } q \textbf{ then } R)_{>t_1}(S, S') \\ = \; & (Q \textbf{ until } q \textbf{ then } R)(S_{>t_1}, S'_{>t_1}) \\ = \; & \exists t_2 : q(S_{>t_1}(t_2), S'_{>t_1}(t_2)) \wedge Q_{<t_2}(S_{>t_1}, S'_{>t_1}) \wedge R_{>t_2}(S_{>t_1}, S'_{>t_1}) \end{aligned}$$

In the last line, the first condition can be simplified further by observing that q can be only true on defined values, and since $S_{>t_1}$ and $S'_{>t_1}$ return defined values only for time points greater than t_1, q can be true only for time points $t_2 > t_1$. Moreover, the second and third conditions can be simplified by applying Lemma 4.2, that is, $Q_{<t_2}(S_{>t_1}, S'_{>t_1}) = Q|_{]t_1,t_2[}(S, S')$ and $R_{>t_2}(S_{>t_1}, S'_{>t_1}) = R_{>t_2}(S, S')$. (The latter equation is due to the fact that $t_2 > t_1 \Rightarrow]t_1, \infty[\cap]t_2, \infty[=]t_2, \infty[$.)

Next, the condition $p(S(t_1), S'(t_1))$ is equivalent to $p(S_{<t_2}(t_1), S'_{<t_2}(t_1))$, since $t_1 < t_2$, and $P_{<t_1}(S, S')$ implies that $P_{<t_1}(S_{<t_2}, S'_{<t_2})$ is true. Finally, $Q|_{]t_1,t_2[}(S, S')$ can be also written as $Q_{>t_1}(S_{<t_2}, S'_{<t_2})$. Thus, we can derive:

$$\begin{aligned}
&\exists t_1 : p(S_{<t_2}(t_1), S'_{<t_2}(t_1)) \wedge P_{<t_1}(S_{<t_2}, S'_{<t_2}) \wedge Q_{>t_1}(S_{<t_2}, S'_{<t_2}) \\
=\ &(P \textbf{ until } p \textbf{ then } Q)(S_{<t_2}, S(P \rhd p \rhd Q)^{\leftarrow} (S_1, S_2)_{<t_2}) \\
=\ &(P \textbf{ until } p \textbf{ then } Q)_{<t_2}(S, S')
\end{aligned}$$

The last condition, together with the conditions $q(S(t_2), S'(t_2))$ and $R_{>t_2}(S, S')$, show that the right-hand side also holds for S and S'. The other direction is proved analogously. ■

In order to be able to denote developments concisely, we use some syntactic sugar in writing down cascades of compositions. Compositions are denoted simply by a sequence of predicates linked together by an infix operator $\rhd$. More precisely, we allow only (satisfiable and uninterrupted) alternating sequences of spatial and spatio-temporal predicates of length ≥ 2. This means, the *development language* Π of predicate sequences is given by the following regular expression (we use the abbreviation X^c for denoting the nonempty sequences of Xs separated by cs; brackets denote optional components):

$$\Pi = (p \rhd P)^{\rhd} [\rhd p] \mid (P \rhd p)^{\rhd} [\rhd P]$$

This makes it, for example, impossible that two continuously moving spatio-temporal objects satisfy **Inside** immediately followed by **Disjoint**. In contrast, **Inside** first followed by **meet** (or **Meet**) and then followed by **Disjoint** can be satisfied.

The translation into (nested) temporal compositions is done by the mapping C defined in the following equation. Note that the first case is needed to capture some recursive calls of C (e.g., in the translation of $P \rhd p \rhd Q$).

$$\begin{aligned}
C(P) &= P \\
C(P \rhd p) &= P \textbf{ until } p \\
C(P \rhd p \rhd \Pi) &= P \textbf{ until } p \textbf{ then } C(\Pi) \\
C(p \rhd P) &= p \textbf{ then } P \\
C(p \rhd P \rhd \Pi) &= p \textbf{ then } C(P \rhd \Pi)
\end{aligned}$$

Now, by the term *development* we specifically mean a sequence of predicates combined by $\triangleright$. As an example consider the development:

Disjoint $\triangleright$ **meet** $\triangleright$ **Inside** $\triangleright$ **meet** $\triangleright$ **Disjoint**

This is an abbreviation for (i.e., is translated by C into):

Disjoint ***until*** **meet** ***then*** (**Inside** ***until*** **meet** ***then*** **Disjoint**)

Since composition is an associative operation, the chosen nesting does not matter.

We have defined $\triangleright$ in a way that only alternating sequences of spatio-temporal and spatial predicates can be built. However, sometimes it is convenient to be able to omit a spatial predicate next to its corresponding instant spatio-temporal predicate (e.g., we would like to write **Disjoint** $\triangleright$ **Meet** instead of **Disjoint** $\triangleright$ **meet** $\triangleright$ **Meet**). We therefore allow a corresponding shortcut in our notation which is justified by the fact that whenever an instant spatio-temporal predicate holds immediately before or after another spatio-temporal predicate, then there are precisely defined time points where the predicate holds the first and the last time. Let i be an instant spatial predicate, and let I be its corresponding spatio-temporal predicate. Here, P and Q denote either basic spatio-temporal predicates or predicate sequences that end (in the case of P) or start (in the case of Q) with a basic spatio-temporal predicate. Then we allow the abbreviations presented in Table 4.24.

Finally, we have to describe how existentially quantified predicates fit into the sequencing syntax. In general, we would like to be able to put existentially quantified predicates next to other spatio-temporal predicates *without* having to give a connecting spatial predicate, for example, we would like to express the fact that two disjoint objects meet at some time later simply by writing:

Disjoint $\triangleright$ $\exists$**meet**

Fortunately, we can always expand an existentially quantified predicate into a sequence containing only spatial and universally quantified predicates. This is captured in the following result.

Table 4.24 "Normalized" and "raw" mode of developments.

Abbreviation	*Expands to*
$I \triangleright Q$	$I \triangleright i \triangleright Q$
$P \triangleright I$	$P \triangleright i \triangleright I$
$P \triangleright I \triangleright Q$	$P \triangleright i \triangleright I \triangleright i \triangleright Q$

Lemma 4.6 *Existential expansion.*

$$\exists p = \texttt{True} \rhd p \rhd \texttt{True}$$

Exercise 4.15 Show the correctness of Lemma 4.6.

Thus, the previous example is expanded to:

$$\texttt{Disjoint} \rhd \texttt{True} \rhd \texttt{meet} \rhd \texttt{True}$$

which is then further expanded to:

$$\texttt{Disjoint} \rhd \texttt{true} \rhd \texttt{True} \rhd \texttt{meet} \rhd \texttt{True}$$

which can also be transformed into a nested *until-then* expression.

4.4.8 An Algebra of Spatio-Temporal Predicates

So far, we have constructed developments by *sequential* temporal composition. But there are several other logical connectives that can be defined to combine predicates. These efforts result in an algebra with spatio-temporal predicates as objects and combinators, such as $\rhd$ and others, as operations. One example of such an advanced predicate combinator relates to the ability to express *disjunctions* of spatio-temporal predicates.

Definition 4.39 *Temporal alternative.* Let P and Q be spatio-temporal predicates. The *temporal alternative* between P and Q is then defined as:

$$P \mid Q := \lambda(S_1, S_2).P(S_1, S_2) \vee Q(S_1, S_2)$$

Consider, for example, a moving point on the border of a region. The situations that can arise when the point leaves the border are captured by the alternative:

$$\texttt{Disjoint} \mid \texttt{Inside}$$

It remains to be explained what the meaning of alternatives within developments is. For instance, when we have to describe the situation that a point eventually leaves the border of a region, we would like to be able to simply write (note that we give $\mid$ a higher precedence than $\rhd$):

$$\texttt{Meet} \rhd \texttt{Disjoint} \mid \texttt{Inside}$$

(which is expanded to **Meet** $\triangleright$ **meet** $\triangleright$ **Disjoint** | **Inside**.) Fortunately, $\triangleright$ distributes over | from the left as well as from the right. This is shown in Lemma 4.7.

Lemma 4.7 *Distributivity of composition.* Let P, Q, and R be spatio-temporal predicates, and let p be a spatial predicate. We can then define:

1. $P \triangleright p \triangleright (Q \mid R) = (P \triangleright p \triangleright Q) \mid (P \triangleright p \triangleright R)$
2. $(P \mid Q) \triangleright p \triangleright R = (P \triangleright p \triangleright R) \mid (Q \triangleright p \triangleright R)$

This can be shown as follows. Consider equation 1 in the preceding list. $P \triangleright p \triangleright Q \mid R$ is true for two spatio-temporal objects S and S' if there is some time point t so that (i) $p(S(t), S'(t))$, (ii) $P_{<t}(S, S')$, and (iii) $(Q \mid R)_{>t}(S, S')$ is true. Unrolling the definitions of constriction and alternative, the latter condition is equivalent to $Q(S_{>t}, S'_{>t}) \vee R(S_{>t}, S'_{>t})$. Since $\wedge$ distributes over $\vee$, we can rewrite the whole condition as a disjunction:

$$((\mathrm{i}) \wedge (\mathrm{ii}) \wedge Q(S_{>t}, S'_{>t})) \vee ((\mathrm{i}) \wedge (\mathrm{ii}) \wedge R(S_{>t}, S'_{>t}))$$

The first alternative characterizes the development $P \triangleright p \triangleright Q$, and the second one describes $P \triangleright p \triangleright R$. By folding the definition of temporal alternative we obtain the right-hand side. Equation 2 is proved similarly. ■

This means that we can always convert developments containing alternatives into what we call *development normal form* (i.e., an alternative of developments, each of which does not contain any alternatives; for these the previous syntax rules apply).

Note, however, that | does not distribute over $\triangleright$. To investigate this topic, we first have to syntactically fix what distribution over a composition means. Since temporal alternative is only defined for spatio-temporal predicates, a reasonable view is that the alternative is moved to all spatio-temporal predicates in the composition. Thus, in general, we have:

$$P \mid (Q \triangleright p \triangleright R) \neq (P \mid Q) \triangleright p \triangleright (P \mid R)$$

This can be seen as follows. Let P = **Disjoint**, $Q = R$ = **Inside**, and p = **meet**. Now, a moving point and a moving region that are disjoint certainly fit the predicate on the left hand side (because of the alternative P), but they fail for the right-hand side, because there it is required that they meet.

A further operation on spatio-temporal predicates is negation:

Definition 4.40 *Predicate negation.* Let P be a spatio-temporal predicate. The *temporal negation* of P is defined as:

$$\sim P := \lambda(S_1, S_2).\neg(P(S_1, S_2))$$ ■

Next, we define a "backward" or "reverse" combinator for spatio-temporal predicates. The definition is based on a concept of "reflection" for spatio-temporal objects. This means we define that the reverse of a development P is true for two objects if, and only if, P holds for the reflection of these objects.

The reflection of a single object S can be explained as follows. Imagine S exists in an interval $[t_1, t_2]$ (i.e., $dom(S) = [t_1, t_2]$), and S moves (and possibly changes its shape) from its initial value $S(t_1)$ to $S(t_2)$. Then, the corresponding reflected object *reflect*(S) is given by moving backward in the same interval from $S(t_2)$ to $S(t_1)$. Formally, we can achieve this effect by defining *reflect*(S) to yield at time t the value that S had at time $\sup(dom(S)) - t + \inf(dom(S))$. Here, sup and inf denote the supremum and infimum of a set; their use is required in those cases when the domain of a spatio-temporal object is a (half-) open set.

Now since predicates are defined on pairs of objects, we need a concept of reflection for two objects. The definition is similar to that for a single object, but we have to take into account the dependence and the union of both objects' lifetimes. This means that both objects are not reflected independently of one another but are possibly shifted in time toward an earlier beginning or a later ending of their companion object. This will be illustrated in Figure 4.19. We therefore define a function *reflect* that takes two spatio-temporal objects and returns the pair of reflected objects.

Definition 4.41 *Object reflection.* Let S_1 and S_2 be two spatio-temporal objects. The *reflection* of S_1 and S_2 is defined as:

$$\begin{aligned} reflect(S_1, S_2) := \; & (\lambda t \in D.S_1(t_s - t + t_i), \lambda t \in D.S_2(t_s - t + t_i)) \\ & \text{where } D = dom(S_1) \cup dom(S_2),\ t_s = \sup(D),\ t_i = \inf(D) \end{aligned}$$ ■

Note again that this definition, which reflects both objects with respect to the supremum of both objects' lifetimes, is different from reflecting both objects in isolation and taking the pair of these reflections. To see this, consider a (constant, non-moving) region R existing during an interval $[t_1, t_2]$ and a moving point P existing during the interval $[t_2, t_3]$ that touches R and then moves away. This is shown in the left part of Figure 4.19 (where we show a 2D projection and assume that time increases from bottom to top). Now, *reflect*(R, P) yields the objects shown in the middle, in contrast to the pair of isolated reflected objects that are shown on the right.

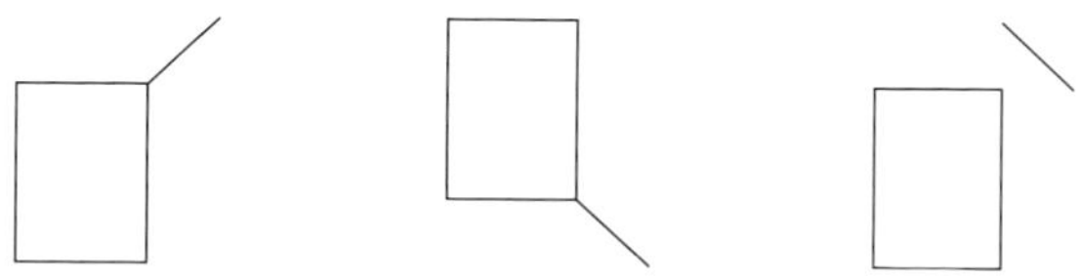

Figure 4.19 Object reflection.

Now we can define the backward combinator based on object reflection. The following definition indicates that the reverse of P holds for two objects S_1 and S_2 if P holds for the reflection of S_1 and S_2. This is much simpler than to define reflection inductively on the construction of predicates.

Definition 4.42 *Predicate reflection.* Let P be a spatio-temporal predicate. The *reflection* of P is defined as:

$$P^{\leftarrow} := \lambda(S_1, S_2).P(reflect(S_1, S_2))$$ ■

Predicate reflection obeys a number of interesting laws. For instance, reflection does not change basic spatio-temporal predicates, nor does it reverse the order of predicates in a composition (see Section 4.4.9).

Finally, we introduce the following predicate combinators, which are useful in the specification of spatio-temporal predicates: P^+ holds if P holds repeatedly, but at least once (i.e., a development given by a nonempty sequence of Ps holds). P^* is similar to P^+ except that P need not hold at all. $P \,\&\, Q$ denotes *spatio-temporal conjunction* of predicates. $P \,\&\, Q$ holds whenever P and Q hold for a pair of objects. Likewise, $P \rightarrow Q$ denotes *spatio-temporal implication.*

Definition 4.43 *Derived combinators.* Let P and Q be arbitrary spatio-temporal predicates. Then:

1. $P^+ := P \rhd P^*$
2. $P^* := \texttt{True} \mid P^+$
3. $P \,\&\, Q := {\sim}({\sim}P \mid {\sim}Q)$
4. $P \rightarrow Q := {\sim}P \mid Q$ ■

The definitions for & and → are based here on the combinators for temporal alternative (Definition 4.39) and predicate negation (Definition 4.40). This is a bit shorter than giving the object-based definitions using logical $\wedge$ and $\Rightarrow$, and, more importantly, it simplifies proofs involving these operators (e.g., Lemma 4.11).

Exercise 4.16 The object-based definitions using logical operators are equivalent to those given in Definition 4.43. For instance, for & we could give the following definition:

$$P \,\&\, Q := \lambda(S_1, S_2).P(S_1, S_2) \wedge Q(S_1, S_2)$$

Show the equivalence to the specification in Definition 4.43. ■

In the following text, we present a collection of useful laws for the algebra defined so far. First, we look at some very elementary relationships between different operators and predicates. For instance, **True** is a unit with respect to | and is a left (right) unit with respect to developments that begin (end) with a spatial predicate. Moreover, **True** is not affected by constriction. Likewise, **False**, which is defined as $\lambda(S_1, S_2).false$, is a zero with respect to | and $\triangleright$. Like **True**, **False** is not affected by constriction.

Lemma 4.8 *Zero & unit.*

1. $\textbf{True} \mid P = \textbf{True} = P \mid \textbf{True}$
2. $\textbf{False} \mid P = P = P \mid \textbf{False}$
3. $\textbf{True} \triangleright p \triangleright P = p \triangleright P$
4. $P \triangleright p \triangleright \textbf{True} = P \triangleright p$
5. $\textbf{False} \triangleright p \triangleright P = \textbf{False} = p \triangleright P \triangleright \textbf{False}$
6. $\textbf{True}|_I = \textbf{True}$
7. $\textbf{False}|_I = \textbf{False}$ ■

Exercise 4.17 Show the correctness of Lemma 4.8. ■

We have already seen in Lemma 4.5 that predicate composition is associative. The same is true for disjunction. Moreover, disjunction is also commutative.

Lemma 4.9 *Associativity and commutativity of alternative.*

1. $P \mid (Q \mid R) = (P \mid Q) \mid R$
2. $P \mid Q = Q \mid P$ ■

Exercise 4.18 Show the correctness of Lemma 4.9. ■

An immediate consequence of the definition of negation is as shown in Lemma 4.10.

Lemma 4.10 *Double negation.*

$$\sim(\sim P) = P$$ ■

The proof is trivial. We also have a correspondence of de Morgan's laws.

Lemma 4.11 *De Morgan's laws.*

1. $\sim(P \mid Q) \quad = \ \sim P \ \& \sim Q$
2. $\sim(P \ \& \ Q) \quad = \ \sim P \mid \sim Q$

Exercise 4.19 Show the correctness of Lemma 4.11.

Predicate reflection leads to several useful laws, which are given in the following Lemma.

Lemma 4.12 *Reflection propagation.*

1. $P^{\leftarrow} \quad = \ P$ if P is a basic spatio-temporal predicate
2. $(P^{\leftarrow})^{\leftarrow} \quad = \ P$
3. $(P \rhd p \rhd Q)^{\leftarrow} \ = \ Q^{\leftarrow} \rhd p \rhd P^{\leftarrow}$

This can be shown as follows. Equation 1 in the preceding list follows directly from the definition of existential and universal quantification, because a systematic temporal reordering of object values as performed by *reflect* does not affect the validity of predicates or the temporal aggregation.

For proving equation 2, we first insert the definition of predicate inflection twice and obtain:

$$(P^{\leftarrow})^{\leftarrow}(S_1, S_2) = (P^{\leftarrow})(reflect(S_1, S_2)) = P(reflect(reflect(S_1, S_2)))$$

Next, we need the property that object reflection is self-inverse. In the following, let D, t_s, and t_i be defined as in Definition 4.41. We show the effect of double reflection on the first argument (S_1); the case for S_2 is analogous.

$$\begin{aligned} reflect(reflect(S_1, S_2)) &= reflect(\lambda t \in D.S_1(t_s - t + t_i), \ldots) \\ &= (\lambda t' \in D'.(\lambda t \in D.S_1(t_s - t + t_i))(t'_s - t' + t'_i), \ldots) \\ &= (\lambda t' \in D'.S_1(t_s - (t'_s - t' + t'_i) + t_i), \ldots) \\ &= (\lambda t' \in D'.S_1(t_s - t'_s + t' - t'_i + t_i), \ldots) \end{aligned}$$

Now, we observe that the union of the domains of S_1 and S_2 is equal to the union of the domains of the corresponding reflected objects. This means that $D' = D$ and, in particular, that $t'_s = t_s$ and $t'_i = t_i$. Hence, the previous expression can be simplified to:

$$(\lambda t' \in D'.S_1(t'), \ldots)$$

which is equal to $(S_1, \ldots)$. Performing the same transformation for the second argument thus yields that *reflect* ∘ *reflect* is the identity function on pairs of spatio-temporal objects. This shows that $P(\mathit{reflect}(\mathit{reflect}(S_1, S_2))) = P(S_1, S_2)$, which completes the proof.

We show equation 3 by unrolling the definition of reflection:

$$(P \rhd p \rhd Q)^{\leftarrow}(S_1, S_2) = (P \rhd p \rhd Q)(\mathit{reflect}(S_1, S_2))$$

Let $(S_1', S_2') = \mathit{reflect}(S_1, S_2)$. Now, the right-hand side is true if there is a time point t such that $p(S_1'(t), S_2'(t))$, $P_{<t}(S_1', S_2')$, and $Q_{>t}(S_1', S_2')$ are true. By the definition of *reflect*, t was mapped from some time point t'. Thus, p holds for the original, unreflected object pair (S_1', S_2') at t', that is:

$$p(S_1(t'), S_2(t'))\ (*)$$

Again, by the definition of *reflect*, all time points $< t$ are mapped from all those time points $> t'$, and all time points $> t$ are mapped from all those time points $< t'$. Hence, we also know that $P_{>t'}(S_1', S_2')$ and $Q_{<t'}(S_1', S_2')$ is true. This is equivalent to $P^{\leftarrow}{}_{>t'}(S_1, S_2)$ and $Q^{\leftarrow}{}_{<t'}(S_1, S_2)$, which together with (*) is nothing but the definition for $Q^{\leftarrow} \rhd p \rhd P^{\leftarrow}$. ■

There are several relationships that can be exploited for optimization or spatio-temporal reasoning in general. Imagine, for example, that predicates are used in a constraint database to enforce certain developments of objects that might often be done by listing alternative developments. From Lemma 4.7 we can derive:

Lemma 4.13 *Development factorization.*

$$(P \rhd p \rhd Q \rhd q \rhd R) \mid (P \rhd p \rhd Q' \rhd q \rhd R) = P \rhd p \rhd Q \mid Q' \rhd q \rhd R$$

This can be shown as follows. We can group subdevelopments explicitly. This means that we write the left-hand side as:

$$(P \rhd p \rhd (Q \rhd q \rhd R)) \mid (P \rhd p \rhd (Q' \rhd q \rhd R))$$

Then, we can apply equation 1 from Lemma 4.7 from right to left and get:

$$P \rhd p \rhd (Q \rhd q \rhd R) \mid (Q' \rhd q \rhd R)$$

Now, we can apply equation 2 from Lemma 4.7 to the alternative within the development and obtain:

$$P \rhd p \rhd (Q \mid Q' \rhd q \rhd R)$$

Finally, ungrouping yields the right-hand side of the Lemma. ■

This result can be used to "factorize" common parts of alternative developments to simplify the enforcement of spatio-temporal constraints.

4.4.9 Examples

After so many conceptual considerations, we now present some examples. The previous mentioned predicates "enter" and "cross" for a moving point and a moving region can now be simply defined by:

Enter := **Disjoint** ▷ **meet** ▷ **Inside**
Cross := **Disjoint** ▷ **meet** ▷ **Inside** ▷ **meet** ▷ **Disjoint**

It seems that predicate specifications become longish very quickly. Consider, for example, the definition of **Cross** for two moving regions:

Cross := **Disjoint** ▷ **meet** ▷ **Overlap** ▷ **coveredBy** ▷ **Inside** ▷ **coveredBy** ▷ **Overlap** ▷ **meet** ▷ **Disjoint**

However, since sequential composition is associative, we can well define complex predicates in a modular way by successively composing simpler predicates. For instance, we can define **Cross** by composing **Enter** and a corresponding predicate **Leave**:

Leave := $\overleftarrow{\textbf{Enter}}$
Cross := **Enter** ▷ **Leave**

To see that this definition is equivalent to the previous one, we have to prove that **Inside** ▷ **Inside** = **Inside** and that for a moving point and a moving region $\overleftarrow{\textbf{Enter}}$ = **Inside** ▷ **meet** ▷ **Disjoint**. We shall consider such laws in the following text.

A note on macros and syntax: The expansion of macro definitions, such as **Enter** or **Leave** in **Cross**, is performed before any other syntactic rule is applied.

By using ∀ predicates, developments of objects are specified very precisely. In contrast, more relaxed specifications can be obtained by *exists* predicates. For example, an alternative specification of **Cross** that does not care about the precise process of entering and leaving can be given by:

Cross := **Disjoint** ▷ ∃**inside** ▷ **Disjoint**

The right-hand side expands to:

Disjoint ▷ **true** ▷ **True** ▷ **inside** ▷ **True** ▷ **true** ▷ **Disjoint**

which demonstrates nicely how **True** works as a wildcard in development specifications.

A point object that is located on the border of a region and that might temporarily leave the border an arbitrary number of times can be specified by:

TempLeave:= (**Meet** ▷ **Disjoint**)* ▷ **Meet**

Examples for & are difficult to find since, for example, two distinct basic spatio-temporal predicates cannot be satisfied at the same time but only in sequence. However, to specify subsequent predicates we do have sequencing available. In fact, ▷ plays the role of a "multiplication operation" with respect to spatio-temporal predicates, and & is just included for completeness. Finally, | is a kind of "summation operation."

As an example for spatio-temporal implication, consider the predicate:

Visitor := (**Enter** ▷ **True**) → (**True** ▷ **Leave**)

This predicate yields true for objects that always leave whenever they enter a region. In particular, the predicate is true for objects that are always inside or disjoint from the moving region. Hence, it is not identical to **Cross**, but rather subsumes it as a special case. An application is traveling: A foreigner who never enters a country does not have to leave it. Likewise, inhabitants of the country do not enter it but may leave it. Only when a foreigner enters the country must he or she leave the country again.

Finally, we list some further examples for two moving regions. We previously discussed the definition for **Cross**.

Enter	:=	**Disjoint** ▷ **meet** ▷ **Overlap** ▷ **coveredBy** ▷ **Inside**
Leave	:=	$\overleftarrow{\textbf{Enter}}$
Cross	:=	**Enter** ▷ **Leave**
Touch	:=	**Disjoint** ▷ **meet** ▷ **Disjoint**
Snap	:=	**Disjoint** ▷ **Meet**
Release	:=	**Meet** ▷ **Disjoint**
Bypass	:=	**Snap** ▷ **Release**
Excurse	:=	**Meet** ▷ **Disjoint** ▷ **Meet**
Into	:=	**meet** ▷ **Overlap** ▷ **coveredBy**
OutOf	:=	$\overleftarrow{\textbf{Into}}$
Enter	:=	**Disjoint** ▷ **Into** ▷ **Inside** (2nd (equivalent) definition)

Melt := **Disjoint** ▷ **meet** ▷ **Overlap** ▷ **Equal**
Separate := $\textbf{Melt}^{\leftarrow}$
Spring := **equal** ▷ **Overlap** ▷ **meet** ▷ **Disjoint**
Graze := **Disjoint** ▷ **meet** ▷ **Overlap** ▷ **meet** ▷ **Disjoint**
Graze2 := **Disjoint** ▷ **meet** ▷ **Overlap** ▷ (**CoveredBy** ▷ **Overlap**)* ▷ **meet** ▷ **Disjoint**

These definitions should be self-explanatory. Of course, the chosen names depend on the applications using them. On the other hand, they allow as to define nuances such as the two predicates **Separate** and **Spring**, which only differ in the first elements of their sequences.

An interesting observation is that the definition for **Leave** and **Cross** is the same in both the moving point/moving region and in the moving region/moving region case. Only the definition of the **Enter** predicates, which in both cases rest on the basic spatio-temporal predicates, is different, due to different object types such as operands and different underlying topological predicates. Hence, the assembling of basic spatio-temporal predicates to more complex ones, and giving these a name, introduces some kind of abstraction mechanism.

4.4.10 A Canonical Collection of Spatio-Temporal Predicates

In this section, we search for a canonical collection of spatio-temporal predicates from which more complex ones can be composed. Based on the conceptual neighborhood graph described in Section 4.4.2, we can construct the related, so-called *development graph* which expresses possible topological changes of spatio-temporal objects *over time*. Each vertex is labeled either with a spatial, that is, an instant, predicate (such as **meet**), or with an elementary spatio-temporal predicate (such as **Disjoint**). Hence, each vertex models a time point or a temporal duration in which this predicate is valid. An edge represents the sequence operator ▷, that is, (v, w) stands for $v \triangleright w$. A path $(v_1, v_2, \ldots, v_n)$ within the graph describes a possible temporal development $v_1 \triangleright v_2 \triangleright \ldots \triangleright v_n$ of topological relationships between two spatio-temporal objects.

Before we consider the temporal evolution of two moving regions (the region/region case), we will first deal with an easier case and look at the temporal evolution of a moving point and a moving region (the point/region case); we will also shortly mention the point/point case. We start with a definition of the development graph.

Definition 4.44 The point/region *development graph* is defined as $DG = (V, E)$ such that:

1. $V = V_{ID} \cup V_{mM}$ where $V_{ID} = \{$**Inside**, **Disjoint**$\}$, $V_{mM} = \{$**meet**, **Meet**$\}$
2. $E = V_{ID} \times V_{mM} \cup V_{mM} \times V_{ID}$ ■

In summary, we obtain four symmetrical, bidirectional relationships. We are not interested in all of the paths in the development graph. The reasons are that there are infinitely many paths due to cycles and that we are searching for a canonical collection of spatio-temporal predicates. Hence, we have to appropriately restrict the set of all possible paths.

A first restriction is to forbid infinite cycles, since we are only interested in paths of finite length. Moreover, we tighten this condition according to the following observation. If a path properly contains an instant predicate (such as **`meet`**), together with its corresponding basic spatio-temporal predicate (such as **`Meet`**), we can regard this situation as a reoccurrence of a topological relationship. The only difference relates to the temporal duration of the topological relationship. This leads to the definition of a *quasi-cycle*.

Definition 4.45 A *quasi-cycle* of a development graph $DG = (V, E)$ is a path $v = (v_1, v_2, \ldots, v_n)$ in DG such that v is a cycle or such that v_1 is a spatial predicate and v_n is its corresponding spatio-temporal predicate, or vice versa. ■

Definition 4.46 A *development path* of a development graph DG is a path in DG that does not *properly* contain any quasi-cycles. ■

In the point/region case, quasi-cycles can only occur between **`meet`** and **`Meet`**. Figure 4.20 shows the development graph for the point/region case on the left side and the seven possible development paths starting with **`Inside`** on the right side.

Since the development graph is symmetric in the point/region case (i.e., each of the four vertices can be selected as the start vertex of a path and we obtain the same isomorphic graph), we obtain a total of 28 paths. This means that there are 28 distinct temporal evolutions of topological relationships between a moving point and an evolving region without repetitions. For each alternative we could define our

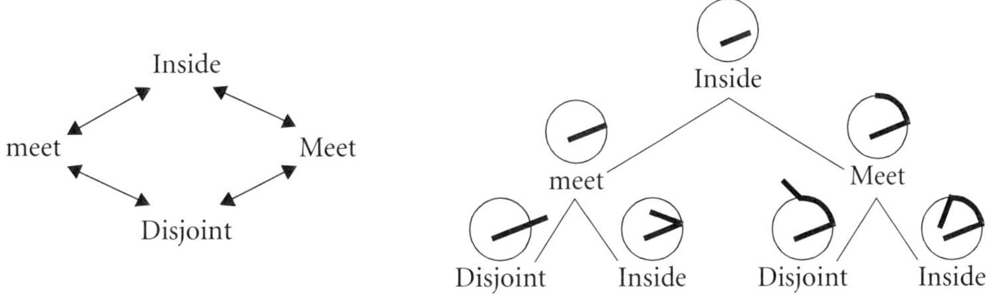

Figure 4.20 Development graph for a moving point and a moving region.

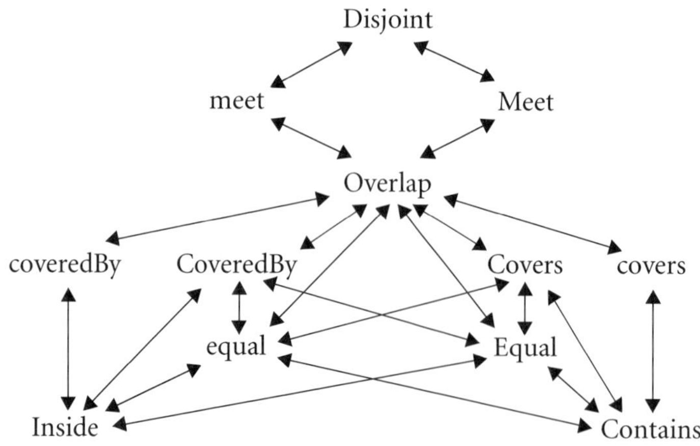

Figure 4.21 Development graph for two moving regions.

own spatio-temporal predicate. In the point/point case, we obtain 13 possible development paths.

We now consider the region/region case, where the development graph is as shown in Figure 4.21. In this case, the number of development paths amounts to 2,198. The large numbers of possible predicates (13 in the point/point case, 28 in the point/region case, and 2,198 in the region/region case) impedes an arrangement of a canonical collection of spatio-temporal predicates. Hence, either the user is furnished with an appropriate, small, application-specific set of predicates, or the user is allowed to use spatial and spatio-temporal predicates as a language and construct new predicates according to his or her needs.

To support the user, at least two solutions to these problems are conceivable—namely, either an extension of the well-known query language SQL to a *spatio-temporal query language* introduced in this chapter or the design of a *visual query language*. In Section 4.4.11, we will see how our query language extension enables us to textually formulate spatio-temporal queries that relate to developments of spatial objects over time and that are hence based on spatio-temporal predicates. Moreover, a *macro definition* mechanism allows the user to assemble more complex spatio-temporal predicates from more elementary ones. In a convenient and intuitive manner, a visual language, which is not described here, can be proposed that allows the graphical specification of a development. This specification is then translated into a sequence of spatio-temporal and spatial predicates. The main idea is to represent spatio-temporal objects in a two-dimensional way by their trace. The intersections of these traces with other objects are then interpreted and translated into the corresponding predicate sequences.

4.4.11 Querying Developments in STQL

We now extend the description of our SQL-like spatio-temporal query language and demonstrate the integration of spatio-temporal predicates and the querying of developments. We will consider queries from three (simplified) application scenarios. The first scenario refers to a flight/weather information system. Flight and weather conditions play a central role for the feasibility of flights and the safety of passengers. Here, we use the following relations:

```
flights(id: string, Route: mpoint)
weather(kind: string, Extent: mregion)
```

Again, `mpoint` and `mregion` denote the two types for moving points and moving regions, respectively. The attribute `id` identifies a flight, and `Route` records the route of a flight over time. The attribute `kind` classifies different weather events, such as hurricanes, high-pressure areas, or snowfall; `Extent` yields the evolving extent of each weather event.

The second scenario is related to forest fire control management which pursues the important goal of learning from past fires and their evolution. We assume a database containing relations with schemata:

```
forest(forestname: string, Territory: mregion)
forest_fire(firename: string, Extent: mregion)
fire_fighter(fightername: string, Location: mpoint)
```

The relation `forest` records the location and the development of different forests (attribute `Territory`) growing and shrinking over time (e.g., through clearing, cultivation, and destruction processes. The relation `forest_fire` documents the evolution of different fires from their ignition up to their extinction (attribute `Extent`). The relation `fire_fighter` describes the motion of fire fighters being on duty from their start at the fire station up to their return (attribute `Location`).

The third scenario relates to a database about the migration of birds in order to explore their behavior patterns over the years:

```
birds (swarm: string, Movement: mpoint)
```

Before we have a look at some queries, we first motivate the necessity of spatio-temporal predicates especially for temporal developments and ask: Determine the flights entering a hurricane. The problem here is that for each plane/hurricane combination we have to check the validity of different spatial predicates during a series of events and periods in a given temporal order. This means that we have to examine whether there has been a constellation when the plane and the hurricane were disjoint for a while, when afterward they met at one point in time, and when finally the plane was inside the hurricane for a while. The development of entering a hurricane is only true if each of the three subqueries can be answered in the affirmative and if they have occurred one after the other. The series is like a specification that has to be matched at least once by each plane/hurricane combination. Without use of spatio-temporal predicates, we can express this query by the following statement:

```
SELECT id
FROM flights, weather
WHERE kind = "hurricane" AND
  not(val(atinstant(Route, start(deftime(Route)))) inside
    val(atinstant(Extent, start(deftime(Route)))))
      AND
  val(atinstant(Route, end(deftime(Route)))) inside
  val(atinstant(Extent, end(deftime(Route))))
```

Obviously, this query is rather complicated. It works as follows: After the computation of the departure time of the flight (**start(deftime(Route))**), the (time, point)-pair is computed at this instant by the operation **atinstant**, and the point is returned by applying the *val* function. In a similar way, the extent of the hurricane at the same instant is determined as a region. Using the spatial predicate **inside**, we check whether the point lies inside the region. If this is not true, we know that at the departure time of the flight the plane was outside of the hurricane. Similarly, we compute the arrival time of the flight (**end(deftime(Route))**) and determine the point and the region, respectively, at this instant. Again, we check whether the point lies inside the region, and, if this is true, we know that the plane must have entered the hurricane. This, in particular, implies that they met at the border of the hurricane. A limitation of this query is that we cannot determine whether plane and hurricane met only for one moment (straight entering) or whether the plane ran along the border for a while and then entered the hurricane (delayed entering). Hence, the evaluation of entering is more a matter of conclusion than a matter of computation. We will see how to express queries such as these more concisely in the following text.

For integrating spatio-temporal predicates and developments into our query language, we extend it by the set of eight basic spatio-temporal predicates and by a facility to assemble new complex predicates from more elementary ones.

We again consider the flight-weather information system. Let us first reconsider the example query of finding all planes that ran into a hurricane. With a predicate combinator >> that has the semantics of temporal composition $\triangleright$ we can formulate the query as:

```
SELECT id FROM flights, weather
WHERE kind = "hurricane" AND
Route Disjoint>>meet>>Inside Extent
```

Since some compound predicates will be needed more frequently and since some of them have quite longish specifications, we introduce a *macro definition* facility as part of the data definition language to introduce new predicates. The syntax is given in the following display. As basic predicates (*p-basic*), we allow all the basic spatio-temporal predicates introduced in Section 4.4.5.

p-def	→	DEFINE *p-name* AS *p-expr*
p-expr	→	*p-basic*
	|	*p-name*
	|	*p-expr* >> *p-expr*
	|	*p-expr* | *p-expr*
	|	*rev*(*p-expr*)

We use the convention that | binds stronger than >>, and that combinators >> and | bind stronger than predicate application. This is the reason why we were able to omit the brackets around the spatio-temporal predicate in the preceding example query.

Now, we can define a predicate **Enters** as follows:

```
DEFINE Enters AS Disjoint>>meet>>Inside
```

Hence, we can formulate the query asking for planes entering a hurricane also as:

```
SELECT * FROM flights, weather
WHERE kind = "hurricane" AND
  Route Enters Extent
```

As further examples, consider the definition of the predicates **Leaves**, **Crosses**, and **Bypass**:

```
DEFINE Leaves AS rev(Enters)
DEFINE Crosses AS Enters>>Leaves
DEFINE Bypass AS Disjoint>>Meet>>Disjoint
```

Note that the predicate **Crosses** is equal to the definition:

```
DEFINE Crosses
  AS Disjoint>>meet>>Inside>>meet>>Disjoint
```

because $\textbf{Enters}^{\leftarrow}$ = **Inside** ▷ **meet** ▷ **Disjoint** and **Inside** ▷ **Inside** = **Inside**.

The following example illustrates the construct of alternative. The query is to find all planes that either crossed or bypassed a snowstorm.

```
SELECT id FROM flights, weather
WHERE kind = "snowstorm" AND
  Route Crosses|Bypasses Extent
```

We can use development predicates also within GROUP BY clauses (*spatio-temporal grouping*). For example, we might be interested in the number of planes that were, respectively, not entering snowstorms or fog areas:

```
SELECT COUNT(*) FROM flights, weather
WHERE kind = "snowstorm" OR kind = "fog"
GROUPBY Route Enters Extent
```

To demonstrate the use of developments on two moving regions, we switch to the forest-fire control management scenario. We could be interested, for example, in all forests that were completely destroyed by a particular fire. The fact that a forest is destroyed means that it is, at least from some time on, completely inside of (or equal to) the fire region (i.e., after the fire is over, the forest does not exist anymore). But before these, many different relationships between the fire and the forest are possible (e.g., the fire ignition can happen within the forest, at its border, or outside). Since we do not care about all these possibilities, we can use the known predicate **True**, which we denote by _ as a wildcard preceding the final condition. This leads to the following query:

```
SELECT name FROM forest, fire
WHERE Territory _>>Inside|Equal Extent
```

This means that for a certain period of time we do not care at all about the relationship between the forest and the fire, which is expressed by _ that constantly yields true; we only require the existence of a time point after which **Inside** or **Equal** holds.

Finally, as an example for querying spatio-temporal developments of two moving points, consider the relation recording the migration of birds. We might be interested in swarms that fly together, then take different routes for some time, and finally meet again. This can be expressed by the following query:

```
DEFINE Remeets
  AS _>>Meet>>Disjoint>>Meet>>_

SELECT A.swarm, B.swarm
FROM birds AS A, birds AS B
WHERE A.Movement Remeets B.Movement
```

4.5 Further Exercises

Exercise 4.20 Queries and Lifting

We want to derive new binary predicates *east*, *south*, *west*, and *north*, with the semantics that the first argument is the center of a coordinate system, and the points of the open half planes correspond to the four directions; the half plane right of the *y-axis* defines the direction east, thus:

```
LET north-east = FUN (p: point, q: point)
  north(p,q) AND east(p,q);
```

yields TRUE for every point of the first quadrant without points of the *x*- or *y*-axis.

1. Use the LET mechanism to define the four predicates with signatures `point` × `point` → `bool`. Furthermore, we define a predicate *east_of_points* with signature `point` × `points` → `bool`.

   ```
   LET east_of_points = FUN (p: point, q: points)
     LET prel1 = SET(pts, q) decompose[pts, pt];
     LET prel2 = SELECT east(pt,p) AS is_east FROM prel1;
     ELEMENT( SELECT all(is_east) FROM prel2 );
   ```

   As a reminder: `LET all = AGGREGATE(and, TRUE)`

2. Argue why it is possible to *lift* this predicate, and similarly predicates for the other three directions, to a signature `mpoint` × `points` → `mbool`.
3. The following figure shows the trajectory of a ship *S* modeled as a moving point and a minefield *F*. Write queries answering the following questions and use results of part (1) or (2) when needed:

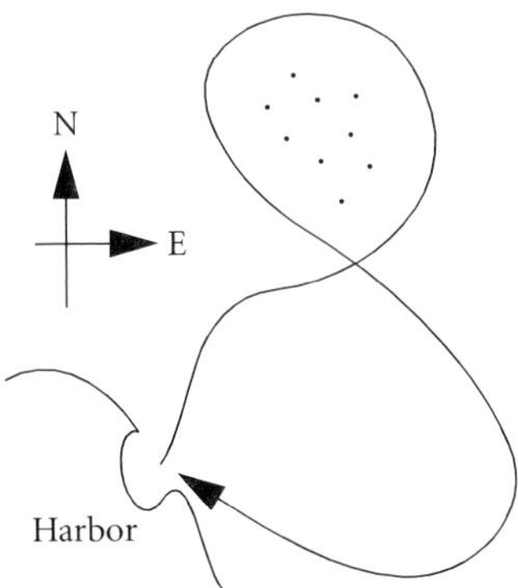

a. Restrict S to the times when the ship was northeast of the minefield.

b. When and where does S move toward west and south, including movements parallel to the west or south axis?

c. Assume you do not have the graphical representation of the scene. How can you determine the direction at the start of the cruise?

Exercise 4.21 Algorithms for Lifted Operations

Describe an algorithm that determines the area of a moving region over its whole lifespan as a moving real.

Hint: It may be helpful to start with finding an algorithm for the computation of the area of simple polygons (cycles).

Exercise 4.22 Representation of Moving Reals

In the previous exercise, it was shown that our representation of moving reals suffices for representing the lifted area of a moving region. In this exercise, we extend that result slightly. Show that our representation suffices for representing:

1. The lifted perimeter of a moving region
2. The lifted distance between two moving points

Exercise 4.23 Flowers and Bees

In this exercise, we try to model the habits of swarms of bees using spatio-temporal predicates and developments. The scenario is as follows: A beekeeper places the hives of several swarms in a park. In the surrounding area there are a lot of flowerbeds with different types of flowers. Each bed has only one kind of flowers (e.g., only orchids). We assume that all of the flowers are currently blooming, so that the bees can collect the nectar from all flowerbeds. The swarms of bees are modeled as moving regions. The flowerbeds are also modeled as moving regions, since we actually don't consider the flowerbeds themselves but those parts of the beds that weren't already harvested by the bees. Hence, if a flowerbed is completely harvested, the moving region disappears. We assume that the bees are so kind as not to make holes in the flowerbeds but harvest the beds from the outside to the inside (see figure). This means that a swarm always has contact with the bed's border when harvesting a bed. The maximal area harvested by a swarm is the area of the swarm itself.

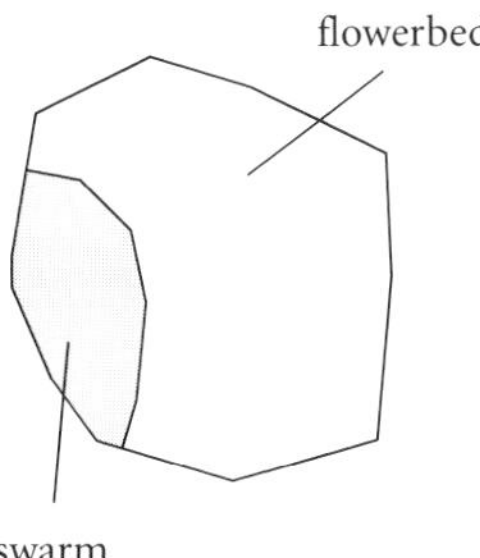

1. Formulate the following predicates. You may use the already existing predicates described in the course text.

   `Orientate`: The swarm is just flying around, searching for a flowerbed to harvest, (i.e., it crosses or meets one flowerbed during the search).

   `HarvestOneBed`: The swarm enters a flowerbed and collects nectar. The bed may or may not be completely harvested in the end.

   `CompletelyHarvested`: The swarm enters the flowerbed and collects all available nectar.

2. We use the relations:

```
swarms (id: string; route: mregion)
unharvestedFlowerbeds (flowers: string; extent: mregion)
```

   Formulate the following queries using STQL:

   a. Find all the swarms that harvested in flowerbed "orchids."

   b. How many flowerbeds were completely harvested?

   c. Find all the swarms that first orientated and then began to collect nectar.

Exercise 4.24 Spatio-Temporal Predicates

1. Define a predicate that holds for the trajectory of a moving point and a (static) region which is presented in the following figure. It should be applicable to

similar developments (e.g., with more or less border crossings) and written as compactly as possible; moreover, it has to be composed of basic predicates.

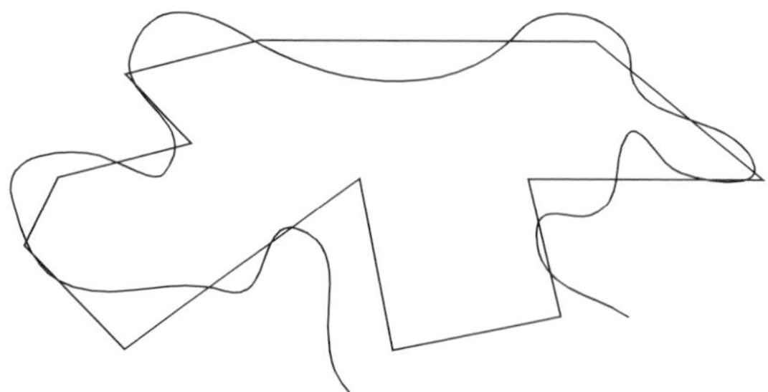

2. The following figure shows three moving regions A, B, and C at time points $t_1, \ldots, t_5$; t_1 is the initial state and t_5 is the final state. Their movement of position and extent is considered to be continuous. However, before the initial and after the final state the topological relationship of the regions does not change. Define predicates p_1, p_2, and p_3 such that $A\ p_1\ B$, $A\ p_2\ C$, and $B\ p_3\ C$ hold whatever the movements between the snapshots are.

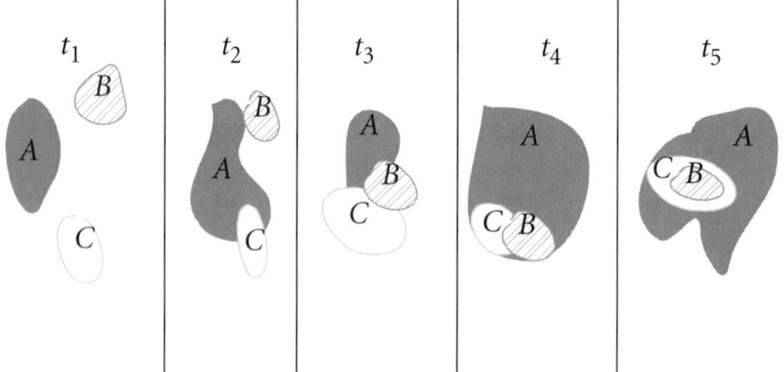

Exercise 4.25 Point/Point Development Graph

Define the point/point development graph and argue that there are 13 possible development paths.

4.6 Bibliographic Notes

The presentation in this chapter is based on the articles by Erwig et al., 1999; Güting et al., 2000; Forlizzi et al., 2000. The first of these articles (Erwig et al., 1999) describes the idea of spatio-temporal data types and in particular discusses the distinction between abstract and discrete models. This is underlying Section

4.1; some of the material has already been presented in Section 1.4. The second article (Güting et al., 2000) then offers a precise design of spatio-temporal types and operations; this is the abstract model of Section 4.2. The third article (Forlizzi et al., 2000) defines a discrete model for the abstract model of Güting et al., 2000, which is presented in Section 4.3.

A detailed study of algorithms for the operations using the representations of the discrete model is given in Cotelo Lema et al., 2003. Algorithms for constructing moving region representations of the discrete model from a given series of snapshots of regions (e.g., from observations such as aerial photographs or satellite images) are described in Tøssebro and Güting, 2001.

An extension of the model presented in this chapter to handle network constrained movement is provided in Güting et al., 2005. See Section 8.3 for a more detailed discussion of network-based moving objects and the related literature.

Another extension of this model to address uncertainty was developed by Tøssebro and Nygård, 2002; Tøssebro and Nygård, 2003; see also Tøssebro's thesis (Tøssebro, 2002). Basically, they develop a system of uncertain data types corresponding to the "crisp" types presented in this chapter.

A recent project aims at developing a spatio-temporal model and query language explicitly—not for moving objects but for supporting discrete changes (Griffiths et al., 2001b; Griffiths et al., 2001a).

A data model for time-dependent partitions of the plane is given in Erwig and Schneider, 1999b. Another such model that supports only discrete changes can be found in Onofrio and Pourrabas, 2003.

Topological relationships between two-dimensional spatial objects serve as an important foundation of spatio-temporal predicates. For a long time they have been a focus of research in disciplines such as spatial databases, geographical information systems, CAD/CAM systems, image databases, spatial analysis, computer vision, artificial intelligence, cognitive science, psychology, and linguistics. A number of models have been devised to characterize topological relationships. A well-known approach, which is taken in this chapter, is the *9-intersection model* (Egenhofer et al., 1989; Egenhofer and Herring, 1990; Egenhofer and Franzosa, 1991), identifying the eight topological relationships between two *simple* regions. A generalization to *complex* regions can be found in Behr and Schneider, 2001.

The concept of spatio-temporal predicates has been formally developed in Erwig and Schneider, 2002. An integration of these predicates into an SQL-like query language called STQL can be found in Erwig and Schneider, 1999a. A visual query language for the graphical specification of spatio-temporal predicates and the translation process of a query specification into a development are described in Erwig and Schneider, 2000; Erwig and Schneider, 2003.

Further work that builds on the idea of spatio-temporal developments is from Djafri et al., 2002.

5 Data Structures and Algorithms for Moving Objects Types

In this chapter, based on the discrete model described in Section 4.3, we develop data structures for its data types as well as algorithms for a selected collection of its operations. In the design of operations in the abstract model (Section 4.2), all operations have been defined to be applicable to all combinations of argument types for which they could make any sense for the user (i.e., they are overloaded). This leads to a very large set of functionalities for operations. At the implementation level, the number of algorithms for the operations increases, since it is not always the case that different argument types for one overloaded operation can be handled by the same algorithm. Hence, we reduce the scope of our study; the kind of reduction will be described in Section 5.2.1.

Section 5.1 describes the employed data structures in detail. This is the basis for describing and analyzing algorithms. Section 5.2 introduces algorithms for operations on temporal data types, and Section 5.3 investigates algorithms for lifted operations.

5.1 Data Structures

5.1.1 General Requirements and Strategy

Data structures designed for use as attribute data types in a database environment must satisfy some requirements. Values are placed into memory under the control of the DBMS, which in turn, implies that one should not use pointers, and representations should consist of a small number of memory blocks that can be moved efficiently between secondary and main memory.

One way to satisfy these requirements is described in the following text. Data types are generally represented by a record (called the *root record*), which contains some fixed-size components and possibly one or more references to arrays. Arrays are used to represent the varying size components of a data type value and are allocated to the required size. All pointers are expressed as array indexes.

Another aspect is that many of the data types are set valued. Sets will be represented in arrays. We always define a unique order on the set domains and store elements in the array in that order. In this way, we can enforce that two set values are equal if, and only if, their array representations are equal; this makes efficient comparisons possible. Further, all implemented algorithms must run on these block-based data structures.

A final aspect is that different algorithms processing the same kind of objects usually prefer different internal object representations. In contrast to traditional work on algorithms, the focus here is not on finding the most efficient algorithm for one single problem (operation), together with a sophisticated data structure, but rather on considering our algebra as a whole and on reconciling the various requirements posed by different algorithms within a single data structure for each data type. In addition, it is our goal to identify algorithmic schemes that can be applied to a large number of operations.

5.1.2 Nontemporal Data Types

The base types `int`, `real`, `string`, `bool`, and `instant` are represented by a record, which consists of a corresponding programming language value together with a Boolean flag indicating whether the value is defined. For `string`, the value is a character array of fixed length. For `instant`, the value is of an auxiliary data type *coordinate*, which is a rational number of a certain precision. Two predefined constants *mininstant* and *maxinstant* describe the first and last representable instants in the past and the future, respectively. This means we assume a bounded and not an infinite time domain at the discrete level.

Next, we look at the spatial data types, which all use the type *coordinate* for representing coordinates. A `point` value is represented by a record with two values x and y of the *coordinate* type and a *defined* flag. A `points` value is a finite set of points in the plane. It is represented by a (root) record containing a reference to an array. Each element of the array represents one point by its two coordinates. Points are in (x, y)-lexicographic order.

A `line` value, shown in Figure 4.11(b), at the discrete level is a finite set of line segments that are intersection free.[1] It is represented as a root record with one array of *halfsegments*. The idea of halfsegments is to store each segment twice: once for

[1] The reason is that we can then reuse the so-called *ROSE algebra* implementation (see Section 5.5), which has this requirement. Of course, it is also possible to allow intersections of segments which lead to different algorithms if lines are involved.

the left (i.e., smaller) end point and once for the right end point. These are called the *left* and *right halfsegments*, respectively, and the relevant point in the halfsegment is called the *dominating* point. The purpose of this is to support *plane-sweep* algorithms, which traverse a set of segments from left to right and have to perform an action (e.g., insertion into a sweep status structure) on encountering the left and another action on meeting the right end point of a segment. Each halfsegment is represented as a pair of `point` values for the end points plus a flag to indicate the dominating end point. Halfsegments are ordered in the array following a lexicographic order extended by an angle criterion to treat halfsegments with the same dominating point.

A `region` value (Figure 4.12) is given by the set of line segments forming its boundary. At a higher structural level, it is a finite set of edge-disjoint faces. A `region` value is represented by a root record with three arrays. The first array (segments array) contains a sequence of records, where each record contains a halfsegment plus an additional field *next-in-cycle*, which links the segments belonging to a cycle (in clockwise order for outer cycles, counterclockwise for hole cycles, so the area of the face is always to the right). Therefore, one can traverse cycles efficiently. The second and third arrays (cycles and faces arrays) represent the list of cycles and the list of faces, respectively, belonging to the `region` value. They are also suitably linked together so that one can traverse the list of cycles belonging to a face, for example.

Exercise 5.1 Let us have a closer look at the halfsegment representation of the types `line` and `region`.

1. Let $N \in \{\mathbb{I}, \mathbb{Q}, \mathbb{R}\}$ (i.e., N is either the set of integer numbers, rational numbers, or real numbers). Let $P = N \times N$ be the set of points based on N. Define the lexicographical order relation $<_P$ on P.
2. Let H be the set of halfsegments defined over P. Define an order relation $<_H$ on H. Take into account the possible topological configurations of two halfsegments. Assume the ROSE algebra case in which two halfsegments are intersection free (i.e., either they are disjoint or they share exactly one common end point).
3. Draw a region consisting of two triangles, one inside the other, and name the segments $s_1, \ldots, s_6$. Determine the halfsegment sequence of the region. To each halfsegment attach a flag indicating on which side the interior of the region is located.

■

For the three data types `points`, `line`, and `region` we also introduce several *summary fields* stored in the respective root records. Their goal is to provide certain data about the object in constant time instead of executing an expensive algorithm for their computation. Values for these fields can be easily calculated during the construction of a spatial object. The minimum bounding box of an object, which is an axis-parallel rectangle, is given by the field *object_mbb*. The field *no_components* keeps the number of points for a `points` value, the number of connected components for a `line` value, and the number of faces for a `region` value. For `line` values the field *length* returns the total length of line segments as a real number. The fields *perimeter* and *area* store corresponding real numbers for a *region* value. In addition, for all the arrays used in the representation there is a field giving their actual length. Hence, one can determine the number of segments or faces for a `region` value, for example.

The range data types `rint`, `rreal`, `rstring`, `rbool`, and `periods` are represented by a root record containing an array whose entries are interval records ordered by value (all intervals must be disjoint and nonadjacent—hence, there is a total order). An interval record contains four components (s, e, lc, rc), where s and e are the start and end value of the interval, respectively (therefore of type `int`, `real`, etc.), and *lc* and *rc* are Booleans indicating whether the interval is left closed or right closed, respectively. Summary fields are also defined for range types. The number of intervals is stored in the field *no_components* as an integer. The minimal and maximal values assumed in a set of intervals are given in the fields *min* and *max*, respectively, of the corresponding data types. For `periods` values, the sum of the lengths of all intervals is kept in the field *duration*.

An `intime` value of type `iint`, `ireal`, `istring`, `ibool`, `ipoint`, or `iregion` is represented by a corresponding record (*instant*, *value*), where *value* is of the corresponding data type.

5.1.3 Temporal Data Types

All temporal data types are represented by the so-called *sliced representation* (Section 4.3.1). It describes a value of a temporal (moving) data type as a set of units (Figure 4.17). A unit is represented by a record containing a pair of values (*interval, unit function*). The *interval* defines the time interval for which the unit is valid; it has the same form (s, e, lc, rc) as intervals in the range types. The *unit function* represents a "simple" function from time to the corresponding nontemporal type α, which returns a valid α value for each time instant in *interval.* For each temporal type there will be a corresponding *unit function* data structure. The time intervals of any two distinct units are disjoint; hence units can be totally ordered by time.

Units for the discretely changing types `const(int)`, `const(string)`, and `const(bool)` use as a unit function a value of the corresponding nontemporal type. Hence, for a unit (i, v), the function is $f(t) = v$.

The `ureal` unit function is represented by a record (a, b, c, r), where a, b, c are real numbers and r is a boolean value. The function represented by this 4-tuple is

$$f(t) = at^2 + bt + c \text{ if } r \text{ is } \textit{false}, \text{ and } f(t) = \sqrt{at^2 + bt + c} \text{ if } r \text{ is } \textit{true}.$$

Hence, we can represent (piecewise) quadratic polynomials and square roots thereof.

A `upoint` unit function is represented by a record (x_0, x_1, y_0, y_1), representing the function $f(t) = (x_0 + x_1\, t, y_0 + y_1\, t)$. Such functions describe a linearly moving point. We also call the tuple (x_0, x_1, y_0, y_1) an *mpoint* ("moving point").

A `uregion` unit function is represented by a record containing three arrays: an *msegments* array, a *cycles* array, and a *faces* array. The *msegments* ("moving segments") array stores the "msegments" of the unit, using lexicographic order on the tuples defining the msegment. As for `region`, each msegment record has an additional field *next-in-cycle*, and msegments of a cycle are linked in cyclic order, always having the interior of the face at their right. The *cycles* and *faces* arrays are managed the same as `region`. The *cycles* array keeps a record for each cycle in the `uregion` unit, containing a pointer (represented by an array index) to the *first-mseg-in-cycle* and a pointer to the *next-cycle-in-face*. The *faces* array stores one record per face, with a pointer to the *first-cycle-in-face*.

A value of a temporal data type incorporates a collection of units and is represented as a root record containing an array of units ordered by their time interval.

Summary fields, which are later used in various algorithms, are added to the root record of the moving object or to the record representing the unit, respectively. At the object level, for all temporal types, the field *no_units* keeps the number of units as an integer, and the field *deftime* stores a `periods` value representing the set of time intervals for which the moving object is defined. The value for *deftime* is obtained from merging the definition time intervals of the units. We also call this the *deftime index*. The information in the root record of the `periods` value is integrated into the root record of the moving object, which now contains a *deftime* array as well as its *units* array. For the nonspatial temporal types `mint`, `mreal`, `mstring`, and `mbool`, the fields *min* and *max* contain the minimum and maximum values of the respective data type that the object takes in all its definition time. For the spatio-temporal types `mpoint` and `mregion`, the field *object_pbb* comprises the *projection bounding box*, which represents the minimum rectangle of all points in the 2D space that at some time instant belong to the spatio-temporal object.

At the unit level, for the `ureal` type, the fields *unit_min* and *unit_max* hold real numbers for the minimum and maximum values, respectively, assumed by the unit function. For the types `upoint` and `uregion`, the field *unit_pbb* contains the *unit projection bounding box* for the spatial projection of the unit. For the `uregion` type, the field *unit_no_components* contains the number of moving faces of the unit as an integer; the fields *unit_perimeter* and *unit_area* represent `ureal` unit functions describing the development of the perimeter and the area during the unit interval; and the field *unit_ibb* includes the *unit interpolation bounding box*, which is a "moving rectangle" and a more precise filter than the unit projection bounding box. It connects the bounding box of the `uregion` projection at the start time of the unit with the bounding box of the projection at the end time. It is stored as a record $(a_{xmin}, b_{xmin}, a_{xmax}, b_{xmax}, a_{ymin}, b_{ymin}, a_{ymax}, b_{ymax})$, representing one linear function f_i for each bounding box coordinate (*xmin*, *xmax*, *ymin*, and *ymax*), with the value $f_i = a_i t + b_i$. The various projection bounding boxes are later used for a sequence of filter steps.

5.2 Algorithms for Operations on Temporal Data Types

In this section, we give algorithmic descriptions of operations on temporal data types for projection into domain and range (Section 5.2.2), for interaction with values from domain and range (Section 5.2.3), and for rate of change (Section 5.2.4).

5.2.1 Common Considerations

Selecting a subset of algorithms

The abstract model described in Section 4.2 puts the emphasis on consistency, closure, and genericity; in particular, all operations have been defined to be applicable to all combinations of argument types for which they could make any sense. The result is a very large set of functionalities for operations. This set is even enlarged by the fact that it is not always the case that different argument types for one operation can be handled by the same algorithm. To make it manageable, we reduce the scope of our algorithm descriptions as follows. First, we do not study algorithms for operations on nontemporal types as such; this type of algorithm on static objects has been studied before in the computational geometry and spatial database literature. An example would be an algorithm for testing whether a *point* value is located in a *region* value. However, we will study the lifted versions of these operations that involve moving objects. Second, we do not consider the types *mpoints* and *mline* or any signature of an operation involving these types. These types have been added to the abstract model mainly for reasons of closure and consistency; they are by far not as important as the types *mpoint* and *mregion*, which are in the focus of interest. Third, we do not consider predicates based on topology; these are the predicates **touches**, **attached**, **overlaps**, **on_border**, and **in_interior**. They are, of course, useful, but we limit the scope of our considerations here. Fourth, we do not deal with the *mregion* × *mregion* case, since its treatment follows a rather complex algorithmic scheme. You are referred to the original literature (see Section 5.5).

Together with the restrictions just mentioned, it is not so easy to figure out which functionalities remain. Therefore, in the following sections, we list explicitly which signatures remain to be considered for each operation.

Notations

From now on, we denote the first and second operand of a binary operation by *a* and *b*, respectively. We denote the argument of unary operations by *a*. In com-

Table 5.1 Notations.

Symbol	*Meaning*
a, b	first and second argument
m, n, r	numbers of units of first and second arguments and of the result
M, N, R	sizes of arguments and of result
u, v, w	sizes of two argument units and of a result unit
$u_{max}, v_{max}, w_{max}$	maximal sizes of units for the two arguments and for the result
d	size of a *deftime* index

plexity analysis, m and n are the numbers of units (or intervals) of, respectively, a and b, while r is the number of units in the result. If a is a type having a variable size, we denote by M the number of "components" of a. That is, for example, if a is of type *points*, then M is the number of points contained in a; but if a is of type *mregion*, then M is the number of moving segments comprising a. In any case, the size of a is $O(M)$. For the second argument b and for the result of an operation, we use the same meaning N and R, respectively. If a (respectively b, or the result) is of type *mregion*, we denote by u (respectively v, w) the number of moving segments comprising one of its units and by u_{max} (respectively v_{max}, w_{max}) the maximum number of moving segments contained in a unit. Finally, let d denote the size of the *deftime* index of a moving object. For easy lookup, these notations are summarized in Table 5.1.

All complexity analyses done in this chapter consider CPU time only. So this assumes that the arguments are already in main memory and does not address the problem of whether they need to be loaded entirely or if this can be avoided.

Most of the operations are polymorphic (i.e., allow for several combinations of argument and result types). To avoid long listings of signatures, but still to be precise about which signatures are admitted, we use the following abbreviation scheme, illustrated here for the **rangevalues** operator: For $\alpha \in$ {*int*, *bool*, *string*, *real*}:

rangevalues	$m\alpha$	$\rightarrow r\alpha$

Here, α is a type variable ranging over the types mentioned; each binding of α results in a valid signature. Hence, this specification expands into the list:

rangevalues	*mint*	$\rightarrow$ *rint*
	mbool	$\rightarrow$ *rbool*
	mstring	$\rightarrow$ *rstring*
	mreal	$\rightarrow$ *rreal*

Refinement partitions

We now describe an algorithmic scheme that is common to many operations. In the following text, we call an argument of a temporal type a *moving argument.* Every binary operation whose arguments are moving ones requires a preliminary step, where a *refinement partition* of the units of the two arguments is computed. A refinement partition is obtained by breaking units into other units (Figure 5.1) that have the same value but are defined on smaller time intervals, so that a resulting unit of the first argument and one of the second argument are defined either on the same time interval or on two disjoint time intervals. We denote the number of units in the refinement partition of both arguments by p. Note that $p = O(n + m)$. We use M' (respectively N') with the same meaning as M (respectively N), referring to the size of the refined partition of the units of a (respectively b). We compute the refinement partition by a parallel scan of the two lists of units with a complexity of $O(p)$. This complexity is obvious for all types that have units of a fixed size—hence, for all types but `mregion`. Even for the latter type, this complexity can be achieved if region units are not copied, but pointers to the original units are passed to the subalgorithm processing a pair of units for a given interval of the refinement partition. If the refinement partition for two `mregion` arguments is computed explicitly (copying units), the complexity is $O(M' + N')$.

For many operations, whose result is one of the temporal types, a postprocessing step is needed to merge adjacent units having the same value. This requires time $O(r)$.

Filtering approach

Even if not stated, each algorithm *filters* its arguments using the auxiliary information (i.e., the summary fields) provided by them, which varies according to argument types (see Section 5.1). The term *filter* is widely used in geometric query processing to describe a prechecking on approximations. For example, a spatial join on two sets of regions may be implemented by first finding pairs of overlapping bounding boxes (also called MBRs, minimal bounding rectangles) and then performing a precise check of the geometries of the qualifying pairs. The first is then

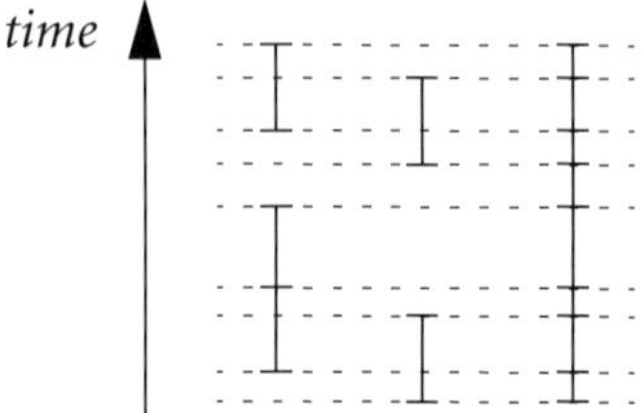

Figure 5.1 Two sets of time intervals are on the left; their refinement partition is on the right.

called the *filter step* and the latter the *refinement step*. In this book and elsewhere, the term is also used to describe prechecking on approximations of two single spatial data type values, before running a more expensive precise algorithm.

For filtering, minimum and maximum values (stored in the *min* and *max* fields of the root record) for moving nonspatial types as well as bounding boxes for nontemporal spatial types are used. For *mpoint* and *mregion*, filtering is performed using projection bounding boxes. Moreover, for *mregion*, two more filtering steps, with increased selectivity, are performed using first projection bounding boxes and then interpolation bounding boxes of individual units.

5.2.2 Projection to Domain and Range

The operations described in this section get a *moving* or *intime* value as operand and compute different kinds of projections either with respect to the temporal component (i.e., the domain) or the function component (i.e., the range) of a moving value.

deftime. This operation returns all times for which a moving object is defined. The signatures for all $\alpha \in$ {*int*, *bool*, *string*, *real*, *point*, *region*} are:

deftime $m\alpha \rightarrow$ *periods*

The algorithmic scheme for all operations is to read the intervals from the *deftime* index incorporated into each argument object. The time complexity is $O(r) = O(d)$.

rangevalues. This operation is defined for one-dimensional argument types only and returns all unit values assumed over time as a set of intervals. We obtain the following signatures for $\alpha \in$ {*int*, *bool*, *string*, *real*}:

rangevalues $m\alpha \rightarrow r\alpha$

For the type *mbool*, in $O(1)$ time we look up the minimal range value *min* and the maximal range value *max* of the moving Boolean. The result is one of the interval sets {[*false*, *false*]}, {[*true*, *true*]}, or {[*false*, *true*]}. For the types *mint* and *mstring*, we scan the mapping (i.e., the unit function values), insert the range values into a binary search tree, and finally traverse the tree and report the ordered sequence of disjoint intervals. This takes $O(m + m \log k)$ time if k is the number of different values in the range. For the type *mreal*, we use the summary fields *unit_min* and *unit_max* of each real unit. As each unit function is continuous, it is guaranteed that all values in the range [*unit_min*, *unit_max*] are assumed so that we obtain an interval of values. The task is to compute the union of all these intervals as a set of disjoint intervals. This can be done by sorting the end points of intervals and then sweeping along this one-dimensional space, maintaining a counter to keep track of whether the current position is covered or not, in $O(m \log m)$ time.

The projection of a moving point into the plane may consist of points and of lines; these can be obtained separately by the operations **`locations`** and **`trajectory`**.

`locations`. This operation returns the isolated points in the projection of an *`mpoint`* as a *`points`* value. This kind of projection is especially useful when a moving point never changes its position or does it in discrete steps only. Thus, its signature is:

`locations` *`mpoint`* $\rightarrow$ *`points`*

In the first step, we scan all units of the *`mpoint`* value and compute for each unit the projection of its three-dimensional segment into the plane. As a result, we obtain a collection of line segments and points (the latter given as degenerate line segments with equal end points). This computation takes $O(m)$ time. From this result, only the points have to be returned, and only those points that do not lie on one of the line segments. Therefore, in the second step, we perform a segment intersection algorithm with plane sweep, where we traverse the collection from left to right and only insert line segments into the sweep status structure. For each point, we test whether there is a segment in the current sweep status structure containing the point. If this is the case, we ignore the point; otherwise, the point belongs to the result and is stored (automatically in lexicographical order) in a *`points`* value. This step and also the total time takes $O((m + k) \log m)$, if k is the number of intersections of the projected segments.

`trajectory`. This operation computes the more natural projection of a continuously moving point as a *`line`* value. Its signature is:

`trajectory` *`mpoint`* $\rightarrow$ *`line`*

In the first step, we scan all units of the *`mpoint`* value, ignore those units with three-dimensional segments vertical to the xy-plane, and compute for each remaining unit the projection of its three-dimensional segment into the plane. This takes $O(m)$ time. In the second step, we perform a plane sweep algorithm to find all pairs of intersecting, collinear, or touching line segments, and we return a list of intersection-free segments. This needs $O(m' \log m)$ where $m' = m + k$ and k is the number of intersections in the projection. Note that $k = O(m^2)$. In the third step, we insert the resulting segments into a *line* value. Since sorting is needed for this, $O(m' \log m')$ time is required; this is also the total time needed for this algorithm, which can be as bad as $O(m^2 \log m^2)$ in terms of parameter m.

traversed. This operation computes the projection of a moving region into the plane.

traversed *mregion* $\rightarrow$ *region*

Let us first consider how to compute the projection of a single region unit into the plane. We use the observation that each point of the projection in the plane either lies within the region unit at its start time or is traversed by a boundary segment during the movement. Consequently, the projection is the geometric union of the start value of the region unit and all projections of moving segments of the region unit into the plane.

The algorithm has four steps. In the first step, all region units are projected into the plane. In the second step, the resulting set of segments is sorted, to prepare a plane sweep. In the third step, a plane sweep is performed on the projections in order to compute the segments forming the contour of the covered area of the plane. In the fourth step, a *region* value has to be constructed from these segments. In a bit more detail, the algorithm is as shown in Figure 5.2.

The time complexity of the first step is $O(M)$. The second step needs $O(M \log M)$; the third step needs $O(M' \log M)$, where $M' = M + K$ and K is the number of intersections of segments in the projection. The final step takes $O(R \log R)$, where R is the number of segments in the contour of the covered area. In the worst case, we may have $R = \Theta(M')$. Hence, the total time complexity is $O(M' \log M')$.

inst, **val**. For values of *intime* types, these two trivial projection operations yield their first and second component, respectively, in $O(1)$. For $\alpha \in$ {*int*, *bool*, *string*, *real*, *point*, *region*} we obtain the signatures:

inst $i\alpha \rightarrow$ *instant*

val $i\alpha \rightarrow \alpha$

5.2.3 Interaction with Domain/Range

atinstant. This operation restricts the moving entity given as an argument to a specified time instant. For $\alpha \in$ {*int*, *bool*, *string*, *real*, *point*, *region*} we obtain the signatures:

atinstant $m\alpha \times$ *instant* $\rightarrow i\alpha$

The algorithmic scheme, which is the same for all types, first performs a binary search on the array containing the units to determine the unit containing the argument time instant t and then to evaluate the moving entity at time t. For types *mint*, *mbool*, and *mstring*, this is trivial. For types *mpoint* and *mreal*, it is simply

Algorithm *traversed(mr)*

Input: a moving region *mr*

Output: a region representing the trajectory of *mr*

Method:

Step 1: Let L be a list of line segments, initially empty;

for each region unit **do**
compute the region value r at start time;
put each line segment of r together with a flag indicating whether it is a *left* or *right* segment into L (it is a left segment if the interior of the region is to its right);
project each moving segment of the unit into the plane and put these also with a left/right flag into L
endfor

Step 2: Sort the (half)segments of L in x, y-lexicographical order;

Step 3: Perform a plane sweep algorithm over the segments in L, keep track in the sweep status structure of how often each part of the plane is covered by projection areas, and write segments belonging to the boundary (i.e., segments that separate 0-areas from c-areas with $c > 0$) into a list L'

Step 4: Sort the segments of L' in lexicographical order, and insert them into a `region` value

end.

Figure 5.2 Algorithm *traversed.*

the evaluation of low-degree polynomial(s) at t. For all these types the time needed is $O(\log m)$. For type `mregion`, each moving segment in the appropriate region unit is evaluated at time t to get a line segment. A proper region data structure is then constructed, after a lexicographical sort of halfsegments, in time $O(R \log R)$. The total complexity is $O(\log m + R \log R)$.

atperiods. This operation restricts the moving entity given as an argument to a specified set of time intervals. For $\alpha \in$ {*int*, *bool*, *string*, *real*, *point*, *region*} we obtain:

atperiods $m\alpha \times periods \rightarrow m\alpha$

For all types, it is essentially required to form an intersection of two ordered lists of intervals, where in each list binary search is possible. There are three kinds of strategies. The first strategy is to perform a parallel scan on both lists returning those units of a (or parts thereof) whose time interval is contained in time intervals of b. The complexity is $O(m + n)$. The second strategy performs for each unit in a a binary search on b for its start time. Then it scans along b to determine intersection time intervals and produce corresponding copies of this unit. The complexity is $O(m \log n + r)$. A variant is to switch the role of the two lists and hence obtain complexity $O(n \log m + r)$. The third strategy is more sophisticated. For the first interval in b, we perform a binary search for the unit s in a containing (or otherwise following) its start time. For the last interval in b, we perform a binary search for the unit e in a containing (or otherwise preceding) its end time. Compute q as the number of units between s and e (using the indexes of s and e). This has taken $O(\log m)$ time so far. Now, if $q < n \log m$ then do a parallel scan of b and the range of a between s and e computing result units. Otherwise, first for each interval in b perform a binary search on a for its start time, and afterward scan along a to determine intersection time intervals and produce corresponding copies of this unit. The time required is either $O(\log m + n + q)$, if $q < n \log m$, or $O(n \log m + r)$, if $q \geq n \log m$. The total time required is $O(\log m + n + \min(q, n \log m) + r)$, since if $q < n \log m$, then $q = \min(q, n \log m)$, while otherwise $n \log m = \min(q, n \log m)$.

We expect that often m will be relatively large and n and r be small. For example, let $n = 1$ and $r = 0$. In this case, the complexity reduces to $O(\log m)$. On the other hand, if $n \log m$ is large, then the complexity is still bounded by $O(\log m + n + q)$ (note that $r \leq q$), which is in turn bounded by $O(m + n)$ (because $q \leq m$). Hence, this strategy gracefully adapts to various situations, is output sensitive, and never more expensive than the simple parallel scan of both lists of intervals.

For type `mregion` copying into result units is more expensive and requires a complexity of $O(\log m + n + \min(q, n \log m) + R)$, where R is the total number of *msegments* in the result.

`initial`, **`final`**. These operations provide the value of the operand at the first and last instant of its definition time, respectively, together with the value of the time itself. For $\alpha \in$ {*int*, *bool*, *string*, *real*, *point*, *region*} we obtain the signatures:

`initial`, **`final`** $\quad m\alpha \rightarrow i\alpha$

For all types the first (last) unit is accessed and the argument is evaluated at the start (end) time instant of the unit. The complexity is $O(1)$, but for type `mregion` it is $O(R \log R)$ required to build the `region` value.

`present`. This operation allows us to check whether the moving value exists at a specified instant or is ever present during a specified set of time intervals. For $\alpha \in$ {*int*, *bool*, *string*, *real*, *point*, *region*} we obtain the signatures:

present	*mα* × *instant*	→ *bool*
	mα × *periods*	→ *bool*

When the second parameter is an instant, for all types the approach is to perform a binary search on the *deftime* array for the time interval containing the specified instant. Time complexity is $O(\log d)$. When the second parameter is a period, for all types the approach is similar to the one used for **atperiods**. Differences are: Instead of using the list of units of the first parameter, its *deftime* array is used; as soon as the result becomes *true*, the computation can be stopped (*early stop*); and no result units need to be reported. Time complexity is, depending on the strategy followed: $O(d + n)$, $O(d \log n)$ or $O(n \log d)$, $O(\log d + n + \min(q, n \log d))$. An overall strategy could be to determine q in $O(\log d)$ time and then—since all parameters are known – to select the cheapest among these strategies.

at. The purpose of this operation is the restriction of the moving entity to a specified value or range of values. For $\alpha \in$ {*int*, *bool*, *string*, *real*} and $\beta \in$ {*point*, *points*, *line*, *region*} we obtain the signatures:

at	*mα*	× α	→ *mα*
	mα	× *rα*	→ *mα*
	mpoint	× β	→ *mpoint*
	mregion	× *point*	→ *mpoint*
	mregion	× *region*	→ *mregion*

The general approach for the restriction to a specified value is based on a scan of each unit of the first argument, which is checked for equality with the second argument. For *mbool*, *mint*, and *mstring*, the equality check for units is trivial, while for *mreal* and *mpoint* we need to solve equations, produce a corresponding number of units in the output, and possibly merge adjacent result units with the same value. In any of the previous cases complexity is $O(m)$.

For *mregion* × *point*, we use the algorithm for the more general case of the operation **inside**(*mpoint* × *mregion*) (see Section 5.3). The kernel of this algorithm is the intersection between a line in 3D, which corresponds to a (moving) point, and a set of trapeziums in 3D, which corresponds to a set of (moving) segments. In the increasing order of time, with each intersection the (moving) point alternates between entering and leaving the (moving) region represented by trapeziums, and the list of resulting units is correspondingly produced. In this particular case, point b corresponds to a vertical line in 3D (assuming an (x, y, t)-coordinate system, and the complexity is $O(M + K \log k_{max})$, where K is the overall number of intersections between moving segments of a and (the line of) point b, and k_{max} is the maximum number of intersections between b and the moving segments of a unit of a.

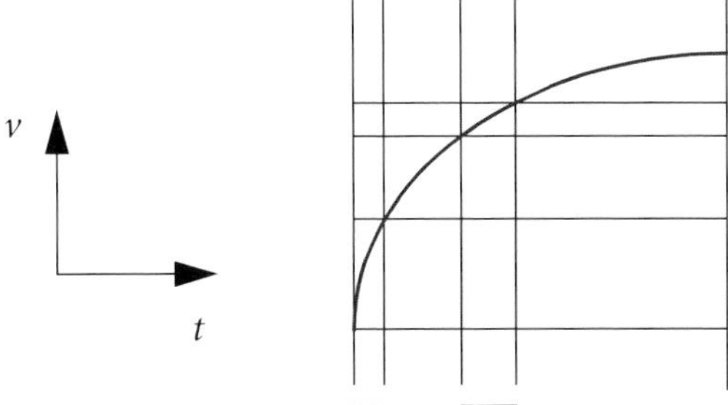

Figure 5.3 The **at** operation on a real unit and a set of real intervals. Two units with the same unit function and the time intervals shown at the bottom are returned.

For the restriction to a specified range of values different approaches are used. For `mbool` it is simply a scan of *a*'s units, with $O(m)$ complexity. For `mint` and `mstring`, a binary search on *b*'s range is performed for each unit of *a*, with an $O(m \log n)$ complexity.

For `mreal`, the problem is illustrated in Figure 5.3. For each unit of *a* we have to find parts of the unit function intersecting *b* by means of a binary search on the intervals of *b* (using the lowest value of *a* given by the *min* field in the current unit) plus a scan along *b*. For each intersection of the unit function of *a* with an interval of *b*, we return a unit with the same unit function and an appropriately restricted time interval. The complexity is $O(m \log n + r)$.

For `mpoint` × `points`, for each unit of *a*, we do a binary search on *b* with the *x*-interval of the *unit_pbb* to find the first point of *b* that is inside that *x*-interval. Starting from the found point, we scan the points of *b* checking each of them first to see if they are in the *unit_pbb* and then whether they intersect the moving point. Then, we sort the resulting units. The complexity is $O(m \log N + K' + r \log r)$, where K' is the sum, over all units, of the number of points of *b* that are inside the *x*-interval of the respective *unit_pbb*. An alternative approach is to compute for each unit of *a* the intersection of the *unit_pbb* and of the *object_pbb* of *b* as a filter. If the bounding boxes intersect, we compute the intersection of the moving point with each point of *b* and then sort the resulting units. The complexity is $O(mN + r \log r)$.

For `mpoint` × `line`, for each unit of *a*, we prefilter by intersecting its *unit_pbb* with *b*'s *object_mbb* and process intersecting pairs by computing the intersection between the `mpoint` value of *a*'s current unit (a line segment in 3D) and each line segment of *b* (which is a vertical rectangle in 3D), producing result units corresponding to intersections. Afterward, we sort the result units. The complexity is $O(mN + r \log r)$.

For `mpoint` × `region`, we use the algorithm for the more general case of operation **`inside`**(`mpoint` × `mregion`). This means, that initially we convert the `region` value into a `uregion` unit, replacing segments by corresponding (vertical) msegments. The complexity is $O(mN + K \log k_{max})$, where K is the total number of intersections of mpoints (3D segments) in a with msegments in b, and k_{max} is the maximal number of msegments of b intersected by a single `mpoint` value.

For `mregion` × `region`, we use the algorithm for **`intersection`** in the more general case, `mregion` × `mregion` (see Section 5.3).

`atmin`, `atmax`. These operations restrict the moving value to the time when it is minimal or maximal. For $\alpha \in$ {`int`, `bool`, `string`, `real`} we obtain the following signatures:

`atmin`, `atmax` $m\alpha \rightarrow m\alpha$

For all types we scan the units to see if their value is the minimum (respectively maximum) as given by the *min* (respectively *max*) field of the moving object. For `mreal` the comparison is done with the *unit_min* or *unit_max* summary field. If the unit qualifies, its time interval is reduced to the corresponding instant or interval. The complexity is $O(m)$.

`passes`. This allows us to check whether the moving value ever assumed (one of) the value(s) given as a second argument. For $\alpha \in$ {`int`, `bool`, `string`, `real`} and $\beta \in$ {`point`, `points`, `line`, `region`} we obtain the signatures:

`passes`	$m\alpha$	× α	→	`bool`
	`mpoint`	× β	→	`bool`
	`mregion`	× β	→	`bool`

For `mbool`, compare b with index *min* or *max*, with a complexity of $O(1)$. For `mint`, `mstring`, and `mreal`, we scan each unit (in the latter case use *unit_min* and *unit_max* values as a filter) and stop when a matching value is found. The complexity is $O(m)$.

For `mpoint` × β and `mregion` × β, we proceed as for the **`at`** operation, but stop and return *true* as soon as an intersection is discovered. In the worst case, complexities are the same as for the **`at`** operation.

5.2.4 Rate of Change

The following operations deal with an important property of any time-dependent value—namely, its rate of change.

derivative	*mreal*	→	*mreal*
derivable	*mreal*	→	*mbool*
speed	*mpoint*	→	*mreal*
velocity	*mpoint*	→	*mpoint*
mdirection	*mpoint*	→	*mreal*

They all have the same global algorithmic scheme and scan the mapping of the units of the argument moving object a, computing in constant time for each unit of a a corresponding result unit, possibly merging adjacent result units with the same value. The total time needed is $O(m)$. In the following text, we briefly discuss the meaning of an operation and how the result unit is computed from the argument unit.

derivative. This operation has the obvious meaning (i.e., it returns the derivative of a moving real as a moving real). Unfortunately, in this discrete model it cannot be implemented completely. Recall that a real unit is represented as $u = (i, (a, b, c, r))$, which, in turn, represents the real function:

$$at^2 + bt + c,$$

if $r = false$, and the function:

$$\sqrt{at^2 + bt + c},$$

if r = true, both defined over the interval i. Only in the first case is it possible to represent the derivative again as a real unit—namely, the derivative is $2at + b$—which can be represented as a unit $u' = (i, (0, 2a, b, false))$. In the second case, $r = true$, we assume that the result unit function is undefined. Since for any moving object units exist only for time intervals with a defined value, we return no result unit at all.

This partial definition is problematic, but it seems to be better than not offering the operation at all. On the other hand, the user must be careful when applying this function. To alleviate the problem, we introduce next an additional operation: **derivable** (not present and not needed in the abstract model).

derivable. This new operation checks for each unit of a moving real whether or not it describes a quadratic polynomial whose derivative is representable by a real unit. It returns a corresponding Boolean unit.

speed. This operation computes the speed of a moving point as a real function. Since each *upoint* unit describes a linear movement, the resulting *ureal* unit contains just a real constant, whose computation is trivial.

velocity. This operation computes the velocity of a moving point as a vector function. Again, due to the linear movement within a *upoint* unit, the velocity is constant at all times of the unit's interval $[t_0, t_1]$. Hence, each result unit contains a constant moving point representing the vector function:

$$\mathbf{velocity}(u, t) = \left(\frac{x(t_1) - x(t_0)}{t_1 - t_0}, \frac{y(t_1) - y(t_0)}{t_1 - t_0}\right)$$

mdirection. For all times of the lifespan of a moving point, it returns the angle between the x-axis and the tangent (i.e., the direction) of a moving point at time t. Due to the linear movement within a *upoint* unit, the direction is also constant within the unit's interval. A special case arises if, for two temporally consecutive units u and v, two end points coincide—that is, if, $x_u(t_1) = x_v(t_0)$ and $y_u(\mathrm{t}_1) = y_v(t_0)$. Then, **mdirection**$(v, t)$ is assigned to this common end point, in agreement with the formal definition of semantics from the abstract model.

Exercise 5.2 Let v be a *upoint* unit and t be a time instant. Give the precise formula for **mdirection**(v, t). ■

turn. This operation computes the change of direction of a moving point at all times of its lifespan. Within a *upoint* unit u, there is no change of the direction, since the unit function is linear. Hence (also in the end points), **turn**$(u, t) = 0$ holds for all times of the unit's interval and for all *upoint* units. This is not an interesting result; hence, this operation need not be implemented within this particular discrete model.

5.3 Algorithms for Lifted Operations

In this section, we give algorithmic descriptions of *lifted operations*. Recall that these are operations originally defined for nontemporal objects that are now applied to "moving" variants of the arguments. We consider predicates (Section 5.3.1), set operations (Section 5.3.2), aggregation (Section 5.3.3), numeric properties (Section 5.3.4), distance and direction (Section 5.3.5), and Boolean operations (Section 5.3.6).

5.3.1 Predicates

isempty. This predicate checks, for each time instant, whether the argument is defined. For $\alpha \in$ {*int*, *bool*, *string*, *real*, *point*, *region*} we obtain the signatures:

isempty $m\alpha \rightarrow$ *mbool*

The result is defined from *mininstant* to *maxinstant* (the "bounds" of time introduced in Section 5.1.2). We scan the *deftime* index returning units with value *true* for intervals where a is defined and units with value *false* in the other case. The complexity is $O(d)$.

=, ≠. These predicates check for equality of the arguments over time. For $\alpha \in$ {*int*, *bool*, *string*, *real*, *point*, *region*} we obtain the signatures:

1. $m\alpha \times \alpha \rightarrow$ *mbool*
2. $m\alpha \times m\alpha \rightarrow$ *mbool*

The general approach for operations of group 1 is based on a scan of each unit of the first argument, which is checked for equality with the second argument. The equality check for all cases but *mregion* is done as in the corresponding cases for the **at** operation (see Section 5.2.3), except that a Boolean unit is returned, and so complexities are the same. For *mregion* the equality check for units is done as follows. First, check whether u and N are equal numbers. If not, we report a single unit (i, *false*), where i is the time interval of the argument unit. Otherwise, we proceed as follows: We consecutively take each moving segment s of the current unit of a. If s is *static* (i.e., does not change in time), we search for a matching segment in b (*). If this search fails, we return (i, *false*). Otherwise, we continue this procedure, until s is not static or s is the last segment. If s is the last segment and static, we return (i, *true*) (i.e., the projection of the unit is equal to b). Otherwise, s is not static, and we compare s with all segments of b, finding k intersections at the instants $t_1, \ldots, t_k$ such that s is equal to a segment in b. If $k = 0$, we return (i, *false*). Otherwise, for each intersection at time t_i, we do the following: For each moving segment s of the current unit, we evaluate s at time t_i and take this segment to search for a matching segment in b (*). If the search succeeds for all s, we have found a matching region and return (i, *true*). Otherwise, we continue with t_{i+1}. If for all t_i no matching regions have been found, we return (i, *false*).

This algorithm is based on the observation that if the *uregion* unit has only a single moving segment, then it can be equal to a static region only in a single instant of time. Steps labeled (*) take time $O(\log N)$, because halfsegments in the *region* representation are ordered lexicographically. The worst-case complexity per unit is $O(kN \log N)$. In the worst case, $k = O(N)$, but in most practical cases, k is a small constant. Assuming the latter, the total complexity is $O(mN \log N)$. In fact, in practice, in almost all cases during the evaluation of a unit an early stop will occur so that most units will be evaluated in $O(1)$ time, and if the moving region is never equal to the static region, this can be determined in $O(m)$ time.

The general approach for the operations of group 2 is based on a parallel scan of units of the refinement partition. Each pair of units is checked for equality. For `mbool`, `mint`, and `mstring`, such a check is trivial. For `mreal` and `mpoint` we first check whether coefficients are the same: if so, we produce the output unit; otherwise, we intersect the curves and produce the output units (at most a small constant number). In any of the previous cases, the complexity is $O(p)$.

For `mregion` we process each pair of units with time interval i of the refinement partition as follows: If u and v are different, then we return (i, *false*). Otherwise, we perform a parallel scan of the lists of moving segments to find a pair (s_1, s_2) of different segments. If no pair of different segments is discovered, we return (i, *true*). Otherwise, let s' be the smaller segment among s_1 and s_2 (this segment is guaranteed not to appear in the other list) and compare s' with the remaining segments of the other list, finding k intersections at times $t_1, \ldots, t_k$ such that s' finds an equal counterpart. If $k = 0$, we return (i, *false*). Otherwise, for each time t_i we evaluate both units, sort the obtained segments, and perform a parallel scan to check for equality. We can stop early if a nonmatching pair of segments is found. Otherwise, we return an appropriate result unit (*).

Noting that a step labeled (*) requires time $O(u \log u)$, the per-unit time complexity is $O(ku \log u)$. In the worst case $k = O(u)$, but in most practical cases, k is a small constant. Assuming the latter, the total complexity is $O(p\ u_{max} \log u_{max})$. Again, if the two moving regions are never equal, then a pair of units will almost always be handled in $O(1)$ time, and the total time will be $O(p)$.

`intersects`. This predicate checks whether the arguments intersect. Signatures considered are:

intersects	*points*	×	*mregion*	→	*mbool*
	region	×	*mregion*	→	*mbool*
	line	×	*mregion*	→	*mbool*
	mregion	×	*mregion*	→	*mbool*

For *points* × *mregion* we use the corresponding algorithm for the **inside** predicate (see the following text). The *mregion* × *mregion* case for a number of operations is rather complex and not described here (see Section 5.5). This scheme can be specialized to the cases *region* × *mregion* and *line* × *mregion*.

inside. This predicate checks if a is contained in b. Signatures considered are:

inside	*mregion* × *points*	→ *mbool*
	mregion × *line*	→ *mbool*
	mpoint × *region*	→ *mbool*
	point × *mregion*	→ *mbool*
	mpoint × *mregion*	→ *mbool*
	points × *mregion*	→ *mbool*
	mpoint × *points*	→ *mbool*
	mpoint × *line*	→ *mbool*
	line × *mregion*	→ *mbool*
	region × *mregion*	→ *mbool*
	mregion × *region*	→ *mbool*
	mregion × *mregion*	→ *mbool*

In the first two cases, the result of the operation is always *false*. For *mpoint* × *region* and *point* × *mregion* we use the more general algorithm for case *mpoint* × *mregion* (briefly described in Section 5.2.3). For each unit, the *upoint* value is a line segment in 3D that may stab some of the moving segments of the *uregion* value, which are trapeziums in 3D. In the order of time, with each intersection the *upoint* value alternates between entering and leaving the *uregion* value. Hence, a list of Boolean units is produced that alternates between *true* and *false*. In case no intersections are found, we need to check whether, at the start time of the unit interval, the point was inside the region. This can be implemented by a well-known technique in computational geometry—the "plumbline" algorithm—which counts how many segments in 2D are above the point in 2D. The complexity is $O(N' + K \log k_{max})$.

Exercise 5.3 Let us assume a *upoint* unit *up* and a *uregion* unit *ur* with the same unit interval $i = (s, e, lc, rc)$ after the refinement partition. According to the description just given, formulate an algorithm *upoint_inside_uregion*(*up*, *ur*) that computes a mapping (sequence) of constant Boolean units expressing when *up* was and was not inside *ur* during *i*. For simplicity, we assume that *i* is closed. It is straightforward but a bit lengthy to treat the other cases. ■

In case of *points* × *mregion*, for each of the points of a we use the algorithm for the case *point* × *mregion*. The complexity is $O(M(N + K \log k_{max}))$. For *mpoint* × *points* we consider each unit of a, and for each point of b we check whether the moving point passes through the considered point. If so, we produce a unit with a *true* value at the right time instant. Afterward we sort all produced units by time and then add remaining units with a *false* value. The complexity is $O(mN + r \log r)$. The case `mpoint` × `line` is similar to the previous one, but we also have to consider that, if the projection of a moving segment overlaps with a segment of *b*, the corresponding result unit is defined on a time interval rather than a single instant. For `line` × `mregion`, `region` × `mregion`, and `mregion` × `region` we proceed as in the more general case `mregion` × `mregion` (see Section 5.5).

$<, \leq, \geq, >$. These predicates check the order of the two arguments. For $\alpha \in$ {`int`, `bool`, `string`, `real`} we obtain the signatures:

$<, \leq, \geq, >$	α	×	$m\alpha$	→	`mbool`
	$m\alpha$	×	α	→	`mbool`
	$m\alpha$	×	$m\alpha$	→	`mbool`

Algorithms are analogous to those for operation =.

5.3.2 Set Operations

We recall that for set operations regularized set semantics are adopted. For example, forming the union of a `region` and a `points` value yields the same `region` value, because a region cannot contain isolated points.

`intersection`. This predicate computes the intersection of the arguments. For $\alpha \in$ {`int`, `bool`, `string`, `real`, `point`} and $\beta \in$ {`points`, `line`, `region`} we obtain the signatures:

1.	$m\alpha$	×	α	→	$m\alpha$
	`mpoint`	×	β	→	`mpoint`
	`mregion`	×	`point`	→	`mpoint`
	`mregion`	×	`region`	→	`mregion`
2.	$m\alpha$	×	$m\alpha$	→	$m\alpha$
	`mpoint`	×	`mregion`	→	`mpoint`
	`mregion`	×	`mregion`	→	`mregion`

For all signatures of group 1, we use the corresponding algorithms for operation **`at`** (see Section 5.2.3).

For the signatures of group 2 (both arguments are moving ones and belong to the same point type), we do a parallel scan of the refinement partition units; for time intervals where the values of the argument are the same, we produce a result unit with such a value. For the cases `mpoint` and `mreal` this requires solving equation(s). In any case, the complexity is $O(p)$.

The algorithm for case *mpoint* × *mregion* is analogous to the corresponding one for the **inside** operation (see Section 5.3.1), but it reports *upoint* units with the same value as *a* instead of Boolean units with a *true* value and no unit instead of Boolean units with a *false* value. The *mregion* × *mregion* case is not treated here (see Section 5.5).

union. This operation computes the union of the arguments. Signatures considered are:

union	*mpoint*	×	*region*	→	*mregion*
	mpoint	×	*mregion*	→	*mregion*
	point	×	*mregion*	→	*mregion*
	mregion	×	*region*	→	*mregion*
	mregion	×	*mregion*	→	*mregion*

For *mpoint* × *region*, the result is region *b* for all times for which *a* is defined (due to the regularized set semantics). Hence, *d* corresponding *uregion* units have to be constructed, getting time intervals from scanning the *deftime* index of *a*. Since sorting is required once to put msegments in the *uregion* units into the right order, the complexity is $O(dN + N \log N)$. For *mpoint* × *mregion* and *point* × *mregion* we simply return *b* as the result. For *mregion* × *region* we use the more general algorithm for the case *mregion* × *mregion* (see Section 5.5).

minus. This operation computes the difference of *a* and *b*. For $\alpha \in$ {*int*, *bool*, *string*, *real*, *point*} and $\beta \in$ {*points*, *line*, *region*} we obtain the signatures:

1.	$m\alpha$	×	α	→	$m\alpha$
	α	×	$m\alpha$	→	$m\alpha$
	$m\alpha$	×	$m\alpha$	→	$m\alpha$
	mpoint	×	β	→	*mpoint*
	point	×	*mregion*	→	*mpoint*
	mpoint	×	*mregion*	→	*mpoint*
2.	*region*	×	*mpoint*	→	*mregion*
	mregion	×	*point*	→	*mregion*
	mregion	×	*mpoint*	→	*mregion*
	mregion	×	*points*	→	*mregion*
	mregion	×	*line*	→	*mregion*
3.	*mregion*	×	*region*	→	*mregion*
	region	×	*mregion*	→	*mregion*
	mregion	×	*mregion*	→	*mregion*

For all cases where the type of a is a point type (group 1), algorithms are similar to those for **intersection**, except for the production of result units. The complexities are the same as for the corresponding algorithms for **intersection**. Algorithms for the cases in group 2 are trivial due to the regularized set semantics. For *region* × *mpoint* we simply transform *a* into a moving region defined on the same definition time as *b*, with a complexity $O(dM + M \log M)$ (as discussed previously for **union**(*mpoint* × *region*)), while for other type combinations of group 2 we simply return *a* as the result. For *mregion* × *region* and *region* × *mregion* we use the algorithm for the more general case *mregion* × *mregion* (see Section 5.5).

5.3.3 Aggregation

Aggregation in the unlifted mode reduces sets of points to points. In the lifted mode it does this for all times of the lifespan of a moving object. In our reduced type system we only have to consider moving regions.

center. This operation computes the center of gravity of a moving region over its whole lifespan as a moving point. The signature is:

center *mregion* → *mpoint*

The algorithm scans the mapping of *uregion* units. Because a *uregion* unit develops linearly during the unit interval $i = [t_0, t_1]$, the center of gravity also evolves linearly and can be described as a *upoint* unit. It is, therefore, sufficient to compute the centers of the regions at times t_0 and t_1 and to determine the pertaining linear function afterward. For computing the center of a region we first triangulate all faces of the region. This can be done in time $O(u \log u)$ and results in $O(u)$ triangles (see Section 5.5). For each triangle in constant time we compute its center viewed as a vector and multiply this vector by the area of the triangle. For all triangles we sum up these weighted products and divide this sum by the sum of all weights (i.e., the areas of all triangles). The resulting vector is the center of the region. Please note that the center of gravity can lie outside of all faces of the region. Altogether, the time complexity for computing the center is $O(u \log u)$. For a *uregion* unit, by interpolation between the centers at its start and end times, a corresponding *upoint* unit is determined. The total time for the center operation on a moving region is $O(M \log u_{max})$.

Exercise 5.4 Let *ur* be a *uregion* unit and *t* be a time instant. Give the precise formula for **center**(*ur*, *t*). ■

5.3.4 Numeric Properties

These operations compute some lifted numeric properties for moving regions.

no_components	*mregion* → *mint*	
perimeter	*mregion* → *mreal*	
area	*mregion* → *mreal*	

Here, **no_components** returns the time-dependent number of components (i.e., faces) of a moving region as a moving integer, and **perimeter** and **area** yield the respective quantities as moving reals. The algorithmic scheme is the same for all three operations and very simple. We scan the sequence of units and return the value stored in the respective summary field *unit_no_components*, *unit_perimeter*, or *unit_area*, possibly merging adjacent units with the same unit function. This requires $O(m)$ time for m units.

The values for the summary fields are computed when their *uregion* unit is constructed. The *unit_no_components* is determined as a by-product when the structure of faces within the unit is set up (see Section 5.1). For the *unit_perimeter* function we have to consider that the boundary of a *uregion* unit consists of moving segments; for each of them the length evolves by a linear function. Hence, the perimeter, being the sum of these lengths, also evolves by a linear function. The perimeter function can be computed either by summing up the coefficients of all moving segments' length functions or by a linear interpolation between the start and end time perimeter of the unit.

For the *unit_area* function the computation is slightly more complex. The area of a simple static polygon (a cycle) c consisting of the segments $s_0, \ldots, s_{n-1}$ with $s_i = ((x_i, y_i), (x_{(i+1) \bmod n}, y_{(i+1) \bmod n}))$ may be determined by calculating the areas of the trapeziums under each segment s_i down to the x-axis[2] and subtracting the areas of the trapeziums under the segments at the bottom of the cycle from the areas of the trapeziums under the segments at the top of the cycle. We can express this by the formula:

$$area(c) = \sum_{i=0}^{n-1} (x_{(i+1) \bmod n} - x_i) \cdot \frac{y_{(i+1) \bmod n} + y_i}{2}$$

Note that if cycles are connected clockwise, then in this formula top segments will yield positive area contributions and bottom segments negative ones, as desired. Hence, the formula computes correctly a positive area value for outer cycles

[2] This assumes that y-values are positive. If they are not, we can instead form trapeziums by subtracting a sufficiently negative y-value.

(see Section 5.1.2). Indeed, for hole cycles (represented in counterclockwise order), it computes a negative value, which is also correct, since the areas of hole cycles need to be subtracted from the region area. This means that we can simply compute for all cycles of a region their area according to the previous formula and form the sum of these area contributions to determine the area of the region.

In a `uregion` unit, where we have moving segments, we can replace each x_i and each y_i by a linear function. For a moving unit cycle c we therefore have:

$$area(c, t) = \sum_{i=0}^{n-1} (x_{(i+1) \bmod n}(t) - x_i(t)) \cdot \frac{y_{(i+1) \bmod n}(t) + y_i(t)}{2}$$

Each factor in the sum is the difference, respectively, sum of two linear functions. Hence, it is a linear function again, and therefore the product is a quadratic polynomial. The sum of all quadratic polynomials is a quadratic polynomial as well. Again, we can sum up the area function contributions over all moving cycles of a `uregion` unit to get the area function for the unit. The cost of computing the *unit_perimeter* and *unit_area* fields is clearly linear in the size of the unit—that is, $O(u)$ time. In all cases, it is dominated by the remaining cost for constructing the `uregion` unit.

5.3.5 Distance and Direction

In this section, we discuss lifted distance and direction operations.

distance. The distance function determines the minimum distance between its two argument objects for each instant of their common lifespan. The pertaining signatures are for $\alpha, \beta \in$ {*point*, *region*}:

distance	*mreal*	× *real*	→	*mreal*
	mreal	× *mreal*	→	*mreal*
	*m*α	× β	→	*mreal*
	*m*α	× *m*β	→	*mreal*

For all function instances the algorithm scans the mapping of the units of the moving object(s) and returns one or more `ureal` units for each argument unit. The computation of the distance between an `mreal` value and a `real` value s leads to several cases. If $ur = (i, (a, b, c, r)) \in$ `ureal` with $i = [t_0, t_1]$, $t_0 < t_1$, and $r = false$, the unit function of ur describes the quadratic polynomial $at^2 + bt + c$. The distance between ur and s is then given by the function $f(t) = at^2 + bt + c - s$, which is a quadratic polynomial, too. Unfortunately, this function usually does not always yield a positive value for all $t \in i$, as required in the definition of distance. Therefore, it is necessary to determine the instants of time when $f(t) = 0$ and to invert the value of the function in those time intervals when it is negative. To program this, we need to distinguish various cases, which is a bit tedious. In any case, we obtain as a result either one, two, or three new `ureal` units. If $r = true$, the function of ur describes the square root polynomial:

$$\sqrt{at^2 + bt + c}.$$

The distance between ur and s is then given by the function:

$$\sqrt{at^2 + bt + c} - s.$$

Unfortunately, this term is not expressible by a square root polynomial and thus not by a `ureal` unit. Hence, this operation is not implementable within this discrete model. Similarly as discussed previously for the **`derivative`** operation, we believe it is better to offer a partial implementation than none. Hence, for square root polynomial units, we consider the result as undefined and return no unit at all (again, as for derivative). The **`derivative`** operation can also be used here to check for which part of the argument the result could be computed. In both cases, the time complexity is $O(1)$ per unit and $O(m)$ for a moving real.

The algorithm for computing the distance between two `mreal` values is similar to the previous one, because a `real` value in the previous context can be regarded as a "static" moving real. The difference is that first a refinement partition of both moving reals has to be computed, which takes $O(m + n)$. If $ur = (i, (a, b, c, r))$ and $vr = (i, (d, e, f, s))$ are corresponding `ureal` units of both refined moving reals with $r = s = false$, their distance is given by the quadratic polynomial $(a - d)t^2 + (b - e)t + (c - f)$, which has to be processed as in the previous algorithm. If $r = true$ or $s = true$, no unit is returned. The time complexity of this algorithm is $O(m + n)$.

We now consider the case of an `mpoint` value and a `point` value $p = (x', y')$ with $x', y' \in$ `real`. If $up = (i, (x_0, x_1, y_0, y_1)) \in$ `upoint` with $x_0, x_1, y_0, y_1 \in$ `real`, the evaluation of the linearly moving point at time t is given by $(x(t), y(t)) = (x_1 t + x_0, y_1 t + y_0)$. Then, the distance is:

$$\begin{aligned} distance((up, p), t) &= \sqrt{(x(t) - x')^2 + (y(t) - y')^2} \\ &= \sqrt{(x_1 t + x_0 - x')^2 + (y_1 t + y_0 - y')^2} \end{aligned}$$

Further evaluation of this term leads to a square root of a quadratic polynomial in t, which is returned as a `ureal` unit. The time complexity for a moving point and a point is $O(m)$. The distance calculation between two *mpoint* values requires first the computation of the refinement partition in $O(m + n)$ time. The distance of two corresponding *upoint* units *up* and *vp* is then determined similarly to the previous case and results again in a square root of a quadratic polynomial in *t*, which is returned as a *ureal* unit. This algorithm requires $O(m + n)$ time.

The remaining operation instances can be grouped according to two algorithmic schemes. The first algorithmic scheme relates to the distance computation between a moving point and a region, between a moving point and a moving region, and between a moving region and a point. The second algorithmic scheme refers to the distance computation between a moving region and a region as well as between two moving regions. The grouping is possible because the spatial argument objects can be regarded as "static" spatio-temporal objects. Therefore, the first algorithmic scheme deals with the distance between a moving point and a moving region, and the second algorithmic scheme deals with the distance between two moving regions. Both algorithmic schemes are rather complex and not dealt with here (see Section 5.5).

direction. This operation returns the angle of the line from the first to the second point at each instant of the common lifespan of the argument objects.

direction	*mpoint* × *point*	→ *mreal*
	point × *mpoint*	→ *mreal*
	mpoint × *mpoint*	→ *mreal*

Unfortunately, the results of these operation instances cannot be represented as a moving real, because their computation requires the use of the arc tangent function. This can be shown as follows: Given two points $p = (x_1, y_1)$ and $q = (x_2, y_2)$, the slope between the horizontal axis and the line through p and q can be determined by:

$$\tan \alpha = \frac{y_2 - y_1}{x_2 - x_1}. \text{ Thus, } \alpha = \arctan \frac{y_2 - y_1}{x_2 - x_1} \text{ holds.}$$

We can continue this to the temporal case. For two *upoint* units (after the calculation of the refinement partition), as well as for a *upoint* unit and a *point* value, this leads to:

$$\alpha(t) = \arctan \frac{y_2(t) - y_1(t)}{x_2(t) - x_1(t)} \text{ and } \alpha(t) = \arctan \frac{y_2(t) - y_1}{x_2(t) - x_1}, \text{ respectively.}$$

Consequently, this operation is not implementable in this discrete model.

5.3.6 Boolean Operations

Boolean operations are included in the scope of operations to be temporally lifted.

and, **or**. These operators represent the lifted logical conjunction disjunction connectives, respectively. Their signatures are:

and, **or**	*mbool*	×	*bool*	→	*mbool*
	mbool	×	*mbool*	→	*mbool*

For the first operator instance we scan all Boolean units in a and evaluate for each unit the unlifted logical connective applied to its Boolean value and to b, returning a corresponding unit. Time complexity is $O(m)$. For the second operator instance we compute the refinement partition and then proceed in the same way for pairs of units. Time complexity is $O(p)$.

not. This operation is the lifted logical negation operator. Its signature is:

not	*mbool*	→	*mbool*

Here, we just scan the units, negating their values, in $O(m)$ time.

5.4 Further Exercises

Exercise 5.5 Implementation of the *region* type

Let `HalfSegment` be a Java class representing the halfsegments in the course. This class provides a method `compare` with the same return value as the `compareTo` method of the class `String`.

1. Implement a class `LinkedHalfSegment` based on `HalfSegment`, which can be used in a region to represent cycles of halfsegments.
2. Implement the data type *region* as Java class `Region`. In this class, implement a method `sortHalfSegments` that sorts the contained halfsegments not destroying the cycles.
3. Draw an instance of your data type representing the region on the following page.

Notes:

- Use the order on points and halfsegments described in Exercise 5.1.
- Use the abbreviation x_L (x_R) to designate the segment x, where the smaller (greater) point is the dominating point of this halfsegment.

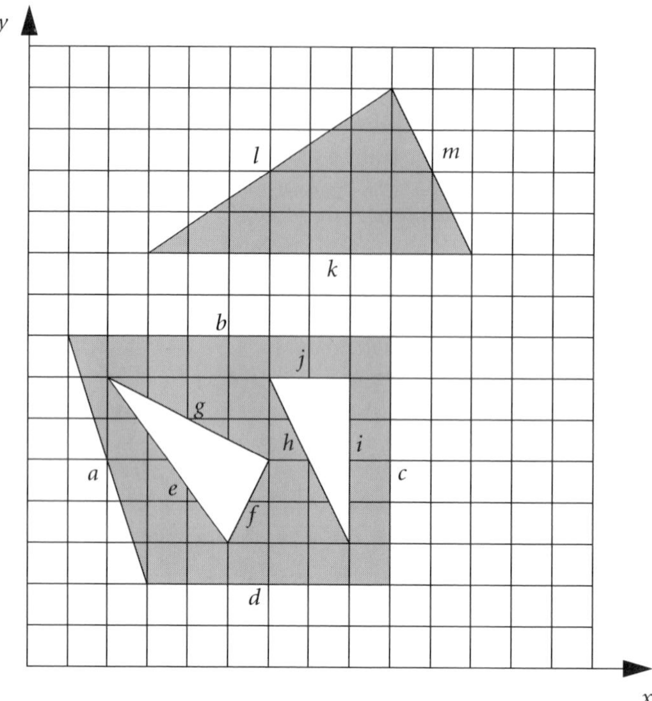

5.5 Bibliographic Notes

The presentation in this chapter is based on the article by Cotelo Lema et al., 2003 which gives a detailed study of algorithms for the operations using the representations of the discrete model in Forlizzi et al., 2000. The article by Cotelo Lema et al., 2003, especially deals with the `mregion` × `mregion` case for the set operations **`intersection`**, **`union`**, and **`difference`** and for the predicates **`intersects`** and **`inside`**, as well as with distance operations between two moving spatial objects. These more complicated algorithms have been omitted in this book. That article also considers data structures for spatial data types, which are similar to those in Güting et al., 1995, for the *ROSE* algebra. Other literature about spatial data structures and algorithms can be found in the computational geometry literature (Preparata and Shamos, 1991; de Berg et al., 2000) and in the spatial database literature (Rigaux et al., 2002; Shekhar and Chawla, 2003). The plane sweep paradigm is explained in Bentley and Ottmann, 1979. Triangulation of a region, needed for the center operation, is described in Garey et al., 1978. We also discuss triangulation algorithms in some detail in Section 6.3.3.

6 The Constraint Database Approach

In this chapter, we consider a radically different approach to the modeling and manipulation of spatial or spatio-temporal values or moving objects: the constraint database approach. There are two main ideas, which are very simple:

- Spatial objects are point sets in a k-dimensional space. This is nothing other than a relation with k attributes, one for each dimension. Hence, represent spatial objects simply as relations and manipulate them with the very well established tools for this purpose, such as first-order logic or relational algebra or, in fact, any kind of relational query language. Don't be frightened by the fact that these point sets and hence these relations usually are infinite.
- Infinite relations cannot be stored or manipulated in a computer; hence, we must find finite representations for them. As a finite representation, use simple formulas from first-order logic based on *constraints*, which are equations of a certain form. For example, the infinite point set in two dimensions forming a rectangle $(x_{left}, x_{right}, y_{bottom}, y_{top})$ can be described by the formula:

  $$x \geq x_{left} \wedge x \leq x_{right} \wedge y \geq y_{bottom} \wedge y \leq y_{top}$$

  Such a formula is assumed to represent the relation:

  $$\{(x, y) \in \mathbb{R}^2 \mid x \geq x_{left} \wedge x \leq x_{right} \wedge y \geq y_{bottom} \wedge y \leq y_{top}\}$$

  Map operations on infinite relations to corresponding operations on these finite representations.

Incidentally, this is exactly the same idea of distinguishing between abstract and discrete models explained in Chapter 4. Use a conceptual model that is allowed to define types in terms of infinite sets, and then define a discrete model that offers finite representations for all the types of the abstract model. Here, we have only a single abstract type, namely, *infinite relation*, and a class of discrete models, *constraint relations*, that differ in the precise form of constraints they admit.

In the following text, we first consider in Section 6.1 the data model of infinite relations from a purely conceptual point of view. In particular, we study how spatial and spatio-temporal objects could be represented and queries formulated, reusing our examples from earlier chapters. Then, in Section 6.2, we introduce a discrete model, constraint relations, able to represent the infinite relations of the conceptual model. In particular, relational algebra can be defined on the constraint representations. Implementation aspects for the constraint model and algebra are discussed in Section 6.3.

6.1 An Abstract Model: Infinite Relations

Suppose we are allowed to use potentially infinite relations as a conceptual model. Let us reconsider some of the examples of earlier chapters dealing with spatial values or moving objects.

A first obvious approach is to use just regular relations and allow them to be infinite. However, a set of spatial objects can also be viewed as a finite set of shapes, each of which is an infinite set of points. In other words, the infinite set of points belonging to all spatial objects is grouped by objects into subsets. This leads naturally to a concept of either nested relations or an abstract data type "geometry," where a value of type geometry is an infinite relation that can be manipulated by a relational query language. We consider the flat case and then the nested/ADT case in the following sections.

6.1.1 Flat Relations

In Section 1.2.2, we introduced relations for a simple geographical application:[1]

```
city (name: string, pop: int, center: point)
country (name: string, area: region)
river (name: string, route: line)
highway (name: string, route: line)
```

[1] We use here the slightly modified schemata from Example 4.5, to be later consistent with examples from Chapter 4.

Let us remodel them in terms of infinite relations. Spatial types are not needed anymore; we just represent entities in terms of their *x*- and *y*-coordinates:

```
city (name: string, pop: int, x: real, y: real)
country (name: string, x: real, y: real)
river (name: string, x: real, y: real)
highway (name: string, x: real, y: real)
```

In this representation, a city is represented as a single tuple, since we have assumed that the location is represented by a (center) point only. A river, highway, or country, however, is represented by an infinite number of tuples that all have the same *name* value but contain distinct (x, y) pairs. Observe that the relation schema does not tell us anything about the respective geometric shape, since there are no spatial data types; a city might as well be represented by a region according to that schema.

The queries from Section 1.2.2 now look as follows:

Example 6.1 What is the total population of cities in France?

```
SELECT SUM(c.pop)
FROM city AS c, country AS s
WHERE c.x = s.x AND c.y = s.y AND s.name = 'France'
```

This works well. If a city is inside France, then it will join with one of the infinitely many tuples of France. ■

Example 6.2 Return the part of the river Rhine that is within Germany.

```
SELECT r.x, r.y
FROM river AS r, country AS s
WHERE r.name = 'Rhine' AND s.name = 'Germany' AND
  r.x = s.x AND r.y = s.y
```

Again, this works nicely. A point of the river Rhine will be in the result if it finds a matching point within a Germany tuple. As with the underlying relations, the result is infinite, but we don't care. ■

Example 6.3 Make a list, showing for each country the number of its neighbor countries.

```
LET neighbors =
  SELECT c1.name AS country1, c2.name AS country2
  FROM country AS c1, country AS c2
  WHERE c1.x = c2.x AND c1.y = c2.y AND c1.name # c2.name
  GROUP BY c1.name, c2.name;
```

```
SELECT country1, COUNT(*)
FROM neighbors
GROUP BY country1
```

Here, we need two different grouping steps; therefore, it is necessary to first compute an intermediate relation. If we group in the first step by only one country, then there is no way to find out how many distinct countries appear in such a group with infinitely many tuples. ▪

In any case, we were able to formulate all these examples easily, so the model looks quite promising and attractive. We could just work with comparisons of coordinates; no knowledge about spatial types or operations was required.

Let us continue our little study with examples from Chapter 4.

Example 6.4 (Example 4.6) Compute the region of Europe from the regions of its countries.

```
LET Europe = SELECT x, y FROM country
```

We just had to project out the country name. Indeed, this is remarkably simple. The result is a relation containing all the points of Europe. ▪

Example 6.5 (Example 4.7) Find the point where the highway A1 crosses the river Rhine.

```
LET RhineA1 =
  SELECT r.x, r.y
  FROM river AS r, highway AS h
  WHERE r.name = 'Rhine' AND h.name = 'A1' AND
    r.x = h.x AND r.y = h.y
```

No problem. ▪

Example 6.6 (Example 4.8) How long is the common border of France and Germany?

We can get the common border of France and Germany as follows:

```
SELECT c1.x, c1.y
FROM country AS c1, country AS c2
WHERE c1.name = 'France' AND c2.name = 'Germany'
  AND c1.x = c2.x AND c1.y = c2.y
```

However, then there is no way to compute the "measure" of the resulting infinite relation, at least not with the basic model of infinite relations without extension. For a finite relation we could count the tuples, but that is not possible here.

Let us assume that we have a new kind of aggregate function that works on infinite relations. It is called MEASURE and is applicable to one or more real-valued columns. Then, we can formulate the query completely as:

```
SELECT MEASURE(c1.x, c1.y)
FROM country AS c1, country AS c2
WHERE c1.name = 'France' AND c2.name = 'Germany'
  AND c1.x = c2.x AND c1.y = c2.y
```

Example 6.7 (Example 4.9) Find the cities north and within 200 kilometers of Munich.

We assume that the environment permits user-defined functions.

```
LET distance = fun (x1, y1, x2, y2: real) ...;
LET direction = fun (x1, y1, x2, y2: real) ...;
```

These should be defined as in Chapter 4. The rest is then just an ordinary query on a finite relation.

We now consider the modeling of moving objects. In Chapters 1 and 4, we had example relations (Example 4.10):

```
flight (id: string, from: string, to: string, route: mpoint)
weather (id: string, kind: string, area: mregion)
```

These moving objects are embedded in a 3D space with coordinates x, y, and t. We can also model them as infinite relations:

```
flight (id: string, from: string, to: string,
  t: real, x:real, y:real)
weather (id: string, kind: string, t: real, x:real, y:real)
```

Let us first consider the queries from Section 1.4.6.

Example 6.8 Find all flights from Düsseldorf that are longer than 5000 kilometers.

```
LET flightDistanceFromDUS =
  SELECT f.id, MEASURE(f.x, f.y) AS length
  FROM flight as f
  WHERE f.from = 'DUS'
  GROUP BY f.id;
```

```
SELECT f.id, f.length
FROM flightDistanceFromDUS as f
WHERE f.length > 5000
```

We first need to group in order to recover the set of points belonging to each flight separately and determine each flight's length. ■

Example 6.9 Retrieve any pair of airplanes that during their flight came closer to each other than 500 meters.

```
SELECT f1.id, f2.id
FROM flight AS f1, flight AS f2
WHERE f1.id # f2.id AND f1.t = f2.t AND
  DISTANCE(f1.x, f1.y, f2.x, f2.y) < 0.5
```

We introduced `distance` as a user-defined function in Example 6.7. There, it was no problem, since it was only evaluated on finite instances. Here, distance needs to be evaluated on infinitely many instances. Whether this is implementable remains to be seen. At least it may be necessary to view it as a system function. To indicate this, it was written in capitals. ■

Example 6.10 At what times was flight BA488 within the snow storm with id S16?

```
SELECT f.t
FROM flight AS f, weather AS w
WHERE f.id = 'BA488' AND w.id = 'S16' AND
  f.t = w.t AND f.x = w.x AND f.y = w.y
```

Here, after performing the intersection between flight and snowstorm, we have projected on the time dimension. ■

Example 6.11 (Example 4.11) How large was the area within France affected by hurricane Lizzy?

```
SELECT MEASURE(c.x, c.y)
FROM country AS c, weather AS w
WHERE c.name = 'France' AND w.id = 'Lizzy' AND
  c.x = w.x AND c.y = w.y
```

Observe how, by ignoring the t coordinate of the hurricane, we get the **`traversed`** operation for free. ■

Example 6.12 (Example 4.11) At what time did hurricane Lizzy start?

```
SELECT MIN(t)
FROM weather
WHERE id = 'Lizzy'
```

Once more, this is remarkably easy. ■

Example 6.13 (Example 4.12) How long was hurricane Lizzy over France?

```
SELECT MEASURE(w.t)
FROM country AS c, weather AS w
WHERE c.name = 'France' AND w.id = 'Lizzy' AND
  c.x = w.x AND c.y = w.y
```
■

Example 6.14 (Example 4.12) Where was flight KLM066 while Lizzy was over France?

```
LET period =
  SELECT w.t
  FROM country AS c, weather AS w
  WHERE c.name = 'France' AND w.id = 'Lizzy' AND
    c.x = w.x AND c.y = w.y;

SELECT f.x, f.y
FROM flight AS f, period AS p
WHERE f.id = 'KLM066' AND f.t = p.t
```
■

6.1.2 Nested Relations

Modeling a set of spatial entities as a flat infinite relation loses the grouping of points into objects. Alternatively, we can choose to represent the spatial information as a subrelation within an attribute. This corresponds to a nested relational model with just one level of nesting. In this case, our spatial example relations are as follows:

```
city (name: string, pop: int, x: real, y: real)
country (name: string, area: (x: real, y: real))
river (name: string, route: (x: real, y: real))
highway (name: string, route: (x: real, y: real))
```

In this model, we assume that the top-level relation is a finite, ordinary relation. We have left the city relation as it was, since there is only a single point for each city tuple. We consider once more the first two queries:

Example 6.15 What is the total population of cities in France?

```
SELECT SUM(c.pop)
FROM city AS c, country AS s, s.area AS a
WHERE c.x = a.x AND c.y = a.y AND s.name = 'France'
```

Now, the variable *a* ranges over the subrelation *area* of each country tuple *s*. Each city tuple in France finds a matching tuple in the *area* subrelation of France. ■

Example 6.16 Return the part of the river Rhine that is within Germany.

```
SELECT [ra.x, ra.y] AS part
FROM river AS r, r.route AS ra, country AS s, s.area AS sa
WHERE r.name = 'Rhine' AND s.name = 'Germany' AND
  ra.x = sa.x AND ra.y = sa.y
```

The query gets a little bit more complicated than in Example 6.2, since we need extra variables for the subrelations. The result is again a finite relation with an infinite subrelation. In this case, the result will have a single tuple with an attribute *part* containing the subrelation. Hence, it has the schema:

```
(part: (x: real, y: real))
```
■

Using nested relations we gain some flexibility, since the result can also be structured into objects.

Example 6.17 Return for each river its part within Germany.

```
SELECT r.name, [ra.x, ra.y] AS part
FROM river AS r, r.route AS ra, country AS s, s.area AS sa
WHERE s.name = 'Germany' AND ra.x = sa.x AND ra.y = sa.y
```
■

Let us also model moving objects in nested relations.

```
flight (id: string, from: string, to: string,
  route: (t: real, x:real, y:real))
weather (id: string, kind: string, area: (t: real, x:real,
  y:real))
```

The query from Example 6.8 can then be formulated in a single step.

Example 6.18 Find all flights from Düsseldorf that are longer than 5000 kilometers.

```
SELECT f.id
FROM flight AS f
WHERE f.from = 'DUS' AND
  ELEMENT(SELECT MEASURE(r.x, r.y) FROM f.route AS r) > 5000
```

6.1.3 Conclusion

We have seen that many queries on spatial data or on moving objects can be formulated easily and naturally in the conceptual model of infinite relations. We have just used standard relational query languages with very few extensions (MEASURE and DISTANCE). Major advantages of such a model—if it were implementable—would be the following:

- The user does not need to learn lots of different operations to deal with specific data types.
- The model is dimension independent; hence, it can work with spatial data in any dimension.

Therefore, this model is certainly very attractive. Let us now see to which extent it can be implemented.

6.2 A Discrete Model: Constraint Relations

6.2.1 Spatial Modeling with Constraints

The basic idea of the constraint approach for the modeling of infinite relations (k-dimensional point sets) is to describe a relation as a logical formula over certain atomic constraints. Hence, a k-ary relation is defined as:

$$\{ (x_1, \ldots, x_k) \in \mathbb{R}^k \mid \Phi(x_1, \ldots, x_k) \}$$

where $\Phi(x_1, \ldots, x_k)$ is a formula over variables $x_1, \ldots, x_k$. The relation contains exactly the points that make the formula true. Some examples of atomic constraints are:

$$x = 7.2$$
$$3x + 5.6y \leq 2$$
$$x^2 + y^2 + z^2 \leq 1$$

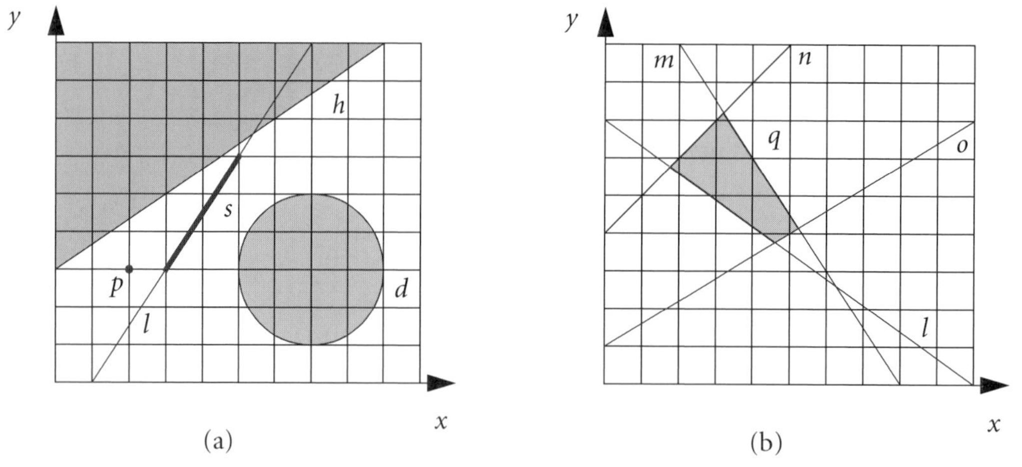

Figure 6.1 Constraint representation of simple geometric shapes (a); a convex polygon (b).

We will later discuss the precise form of constraints admitted. Formulas are built, as usual, by the logical connectives $\wedge$, $\vee$, $\neg$ and quantifiers $\exists$, $\forall$.

Simple geometric shapes can be represented by constraint formulas as follows; see also Figure 6.1(a).

- A point *p*: $x = 2 \wedge y = 3$
- A line *l*: $1.5x - y = 1.5$
- A line segment *s*: $1.5x - y = 1.5 \wedge x \geq 3 \wedge x \leq 5$
- A half-plane *h*: $2x - 3y \leq -9$
- A disk *d*: $x^2 - 14x + y^2 - 6y \leq -54$

A conjunction of constraints corresponds to an intersection of the respective geometric shapes. Hence, a conjunction of half-plane constraints describes a convex polygon; see Figure 6.1(b).

- A convex polygon *q*:

$$
\begin{array}{lll}
 & 7x + 10y \geq 70 & \text{(half-plane } l\text{)} \\
\wedge & 3x + 2y \leq 24 & \text{(half-plane } m\text{)} \\
\wedge & -x + y \leq 4 & \text{(half-plane } n\text{)} \\
\wedge & -3x + 5y \geq 5 & \text{(half-plane } o\text{)}
\end{array}
$$

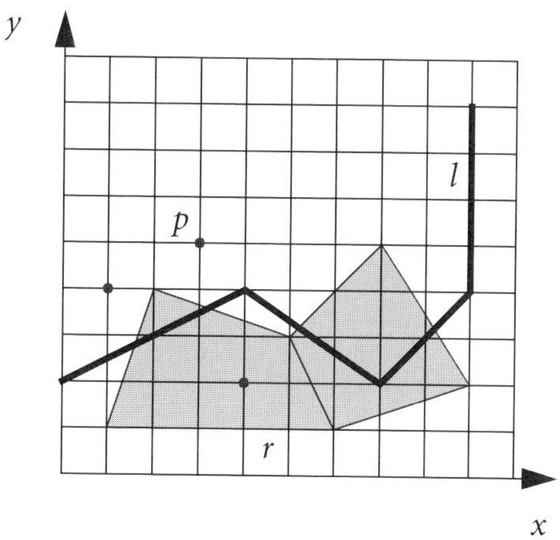

Figure 6.2 Constraint representation of spatial data types.

A conjunction of constraints is also called a *symbolic tuple*. Such a symbolic tuple describes in general a convex shape in *k* dimensions.

More complex shapes can be described by a set of symbolic tuples connected in a *disjunction*, also called a *symbolic relation*. Figure 6.2 shows a `points` value *p*, a `line` value *l*, and a `region` value *r* represented by symbolic relations.

- `points` value *p*:

$$\begin{aligned} & (x = 1 \wedge y = 4) \\ \vee \quad & (x = 3 \wedge y = 5) \\ \vee \quad & (x = 4 \wedge y = 2) \end{aligned}$$

- `line` value *l*:

$$\begin{aligned} & (-x + 2y = 4 \wedge x \geq 0 \wedge x \leq 4) \\ \vee \quad & (2x + 3y = 20 \wedge x \geq 4 \wedge x \leq 7) \\ \vee \quad & (x - y = 5 \wedge x \geq 7 \wedge x \leq 9) \\ \vee \quad & (x = 9 \wedge y \geq 4 \wedge y \leq 8) \end{aligned}$$

- `region` value r:

$$\begin{aligned} & (y \geq 1 \wedge 3x - y \geq 2 \wedge x + 3y \leq 14 \wedge 2x + y \leq 13) \\ \vee \quad & (2x + y \geq 13 \wedge x - y \geq 2 \wedge 3x + 2y \leq 31 \wedge x - 3y \leq 3) \end{aligned}$$

Note that the constraint model is really a generalization of the classical relational model. The classical model allows only equality constraints involving a single variable of the form *Attribute* = *Value*. For example, the relation shown in Table 6.1 could be represented as a constraint relation:

(Author = "Rigaux" ∧ Title = "Spatial Databases" ∧
  Publisher = "Morgan Kaufmann")
∨ (Author = "Scholl" ∧ Title = "Spatial Databases" ∧
  Publisher = "Morgan Kaufmann")
∨ (Author = "Voisard" ∧ Title = "Spatial Databases" ∧
  Publisher = "Morgan Kaufmann")
∨ (Author = "Revesz" ∧ Title = "Introduction to Constraint Databases" ∧
  Publisher = "Springer")

In this case, a symbolic tuple represents a classical tuple, and a symbolic relation represents a standard relation.

The precise form of atomic constraints determines which geometric shapes can be represented. Two important classes are:

- Polynomial constraints of the form:

$$p(x_1, \ldots, x_k) \; \theta \; b$$

  where $p(x_1, \ldots, x_k)$ is a polynomial over the variables $x_1, \ldots, x_k$ (any valid expression involving constants, variables, addition, and multiplication), θ is a comparison operator, and b is a constant. Polynomial constraints can represent disks, for example; see Figure 6.1(a).

- Linear constraints of the form:

$$a_1x_1 + \ldots + a_kx_k \; \theta \; b$$

  Linear constraints can represent only linear shapes, such as straight lines, polygons, hyperplanes, or polytopes.

Polynomial constraints are obviously much more expressive in the shapes they can describe. On the other hand, implementation of such a model gets much harder than for a model with linear constraints. In the following text, we restrict

Table 6.1 A standard relation.

Author	*Title*	*Publisher*
Rigaux	Spatial Databases	Morgan Kaufmann
Scholl	Spatial Databases	Morgan Kaufmann
Voisard	Spatial Databases	Morgan Kaufmann
Revesz	Introduction to Constraint Databases	Springer

attention to linear constraints, which, as we have seen, correspond to the representations of spatial types and moving objects used elsewhere in this book.[2]

6.2.2 The Linear Constraint Data Model

Let us now define the data model more precisely.

Definition 6.1 A *linear constraint* is a predicate of the form:

$$a_1x_1 + \ldots + a_kx_k \; \theta \; b$$

where the a_i and b are integer constants, the x_i denotes variables, and θ is a comparison operator in the set $\{\leq, =\}$. ■

Note that we can use rational coefficients, since it is always possible to replace them by integers. Furthermore, the term a_ix_i represents the sum $x_i + \ldots + x_i$ (a_i times). The predicate $\geq$ may be used, as the inequality can be rewritten into a form using the $\leq$ predicate. Hence atomic formulas need only constants and variables over $\mathbb{R}$, integers, addition, and the predicates $=$ and $\leq$.

Given linear constraints, we can plug them as atomic formulas into first-order logic and get the language of constraint formulas defined in the standard way.

Definition 6.2 The language $\mathcal{L}$ of *linear constraint formulas* is defined as follows:

1. A linear constraint is a linear constraint formula.
2. If f and g are linear constraint formulas, then $f \wedge g$, $f \vee g$, and $\neg f$ are linear constraint formulas.
3. If f is a linear constraint formula with a free variable x, then $(\exists x) f$ and $(\forall x) f$ are linear constraint formulas. ■

Definition 6.3 Let $S \subseteq \mathbb{R}^k$ be a potentially infinite k-ary relation. S is a *linear constraint relation* if there exists a linear constraint formula $\varphi(x_1, \ldots, x_k)$ with k distinct free variables $x_1, \ldots, x_k$ such that:

$$(x_1, \ldots, x_k) \in S \;\Leftrightarrow\; \varphi(x_1, \ldots, x_k) \text{ is true}$$

Then φ is called a *constraint representation of* S, and S is the *interpretation of* φ. ■

[2] However, the representation of moving reals in Section 4.3 and in Chapter 5 goes beyond linear representations.

For a given set S there are many possible representations as a linear constraint formula. We adopt a specific normal form with the following properties:

- The formula is quantifier free.
- The formula is in disjunctive normal form (DNF).

It is possible to put any formula into this form[3] due to the fact that there is an algorithm for existential quantifier elimination. Universal quantifiers can be eliminated due to the identity $(\forall x)\ f \equiv \neg\ (\exists x)\ \neg\ f$. De Morgan's laws can be used to achieve disjunctive normal form, which is:

$$f_1 \vee f_2 \vee \ldots \vee f_n$$

where each f_i is a conjunction of atomic linear constraints, of the form:

$$g_1 \wedge g_2 \wedge \ldots \wedge g_m$$

This normal form leads to the view of symbolic tuples and relations already mentioned.

Definition 6.4 A *symbolic tuple* is a conjunction of linear constraints. A *symbolic relation* is a finite set of symbolic tuples R representing the disjunction of all tuples in R. ■

6.2.3 Relational Algebra for Constraint Relations

Relational query languages such as SQL, for example, are founded on first-order logic, called the relational calculus in this context, or relational algebra. For evaluation, usually the query language is translated to relational algebra, which is then mapped to specific evaluation techniques. Hence, if we are able to define a version of the relational algebra that manipulates linear constraint relations, we get close to an implementation of the desired query language for infinite relations.

A linear constraint relation is a possibly infinite set $S \subseteq \mathbb{R}^k$ represented finitely by a symbolic relation e_S. Operations on infinite linear constraint relations are implemented by corresponding operations on the representing symbolic relations.

[3] It is possible if the full set of comparison operators $\{<, >, \leq, \geq, =, \neq\}$ is available. We follow the original literature (see Section 6.5, "Bibliographic Notes") in allowing only $\{\leq, =\}$ in linear constraints. This leads to a model where only closed shapes can be represented; see a related discussion for spatial data types in Section 4.2.2. The motivation is probably that the implementation is simplified if only closed shapes need to be represented.

The operations of the relational algebra are well known. Let R_1 and R_2 be two relations.

- $R_1 \cup R_2$, $R_1 \cap R_2$, $R_1 - R_2$, the classical set operations. R_1 and R_2 must have the same schema (set of variables).
- $\sigma_F(R_1)$, selection. In the classical case, F is a predicate involving attributes of R_1 and comparison operators such as $=$, $<$, and so on. On constraint relations, we assume that F is a linear constraint.
- $\pi_{[x1, ..., xm]}(R_1)$, projection.
- $R_1 \times R_2$, Cartesian product. R_1 and R_2 must have disjoint schemata (sets of variables).
- $R_1 |\times| R_2$, the natural join. R_1 and R_2 have some common attributes (variables).

The operations are defined on symbolic relations as follows. Let e_1 and e_2 be the symbolic relations representing R_1 and R_2, respectively.

- $R_1 \cup R_2 \equiv e_1 \cup e_2$
- $R_1 \cap R_2 \equiv \{ t_1 \wedge t_2 \mid t_1 \in e_1, t_2 \in e_2 \}$
- $R_1 - R_2 \equiv \{ t_1 \wedge t_2 \mid t_1 \in e_1, t_2 \in C(e_2) \}$, where $C(e_2)$ is the set of tuples of a linear constraint formula in DNF corresponding to the formula $\neg e_2$.
- $\sigma_F(R_1) \equiv \{ t \wedge F \mid t \in e_1 \}$
- $\pi_{[x1, ..., xm]}(R_1) \equiv \{ \pi_{[x1, ..., xm]}(t) \mid t \in e_1 \}$ where $\pi_{[x1, ..., xm]}(t)$ denotes the projection of a symbolic tuple on the variables $x_1, \ldots, x_m$.
- $R_1 \times R_2 \equiv \{ t_1 \wedge t_2 \mid t_1 \in e_1, t_2 \in e_2 \}$
- $R_1 |\times| R_2 \equiv \{ t_1 \wedge t_2 \mid t_1 \in e_1, t_2 \in e_2 \}$

We can see that the expressions for $R_1 \cap R_2$, $R_1 \times R_2$, and $R_1 |\times| R_2$ are the same. Nevertheless, these are distinct operations depending on the sets of variables of the two arguments, which can be equal (intersection), disjoint (product), or overlapping (join).

Computing the complement symbolic relation $C(e)$ for a symbolic relation e is a rather difficult operation. An algorithm for this is given in Section 6.3.5.

Projection of a symbolic tuple on some of its variables means projecting a convex polyhedron into a lower-dimensional space. Algorithms for this are also discussed in the following text.

We can see that the symbolic evaluation behaves a bit strangely. It defines a correct result, but the representation is surely not a minimal one. For example, selection in the classical case generally reduces the number of tuples (often very much). Here, the number of symbolic tuples remains exactly the same; these are even larger, since they have an additional constraint. Similarly, the result of intersection in the classical case is not greater than any of the argument relations; here it has the size of the Cartesian product.

The reason is that the conjunction of two symbolic tuples (or a tuple and a selection constraint F) may very well yield a formula that is unsatisfiable (i.e., defines the empty relation). A kind of clean-up is needed that removes "empty" symbolic tuples from the result. This clean-up might be done immediately, together with each operation, or it could be postponed to a later stage.

Even if a result tuple is nonempty, it may have redundant constraints. For example, if we put together constraints $x \leq 7$ and $x \leq 4$, the resulting symbolic tuple $x \leq 7 \wedge x \leq 4$ can be simplified to $x \leq 4$. The clean-up should include removing redundancies.

In the following text, we illustrate the evaluation of relation operations on constraint relations for selection, intersection, and projection operations.

Selection

Example 6.19 We first consider a simple selection query on the line value l from Figure 6.2. The query is: Find the part of l east of position $x = 5$. In the relational algebra this corresponds to a selection:

$$\sigma_{x \geq 5}(l)$$

The query is illustrated in Figure 6.3. We represent the symbolic relations for line l and region r as shown in Figure 6.4. Each symbolic tuple is represented in a separate

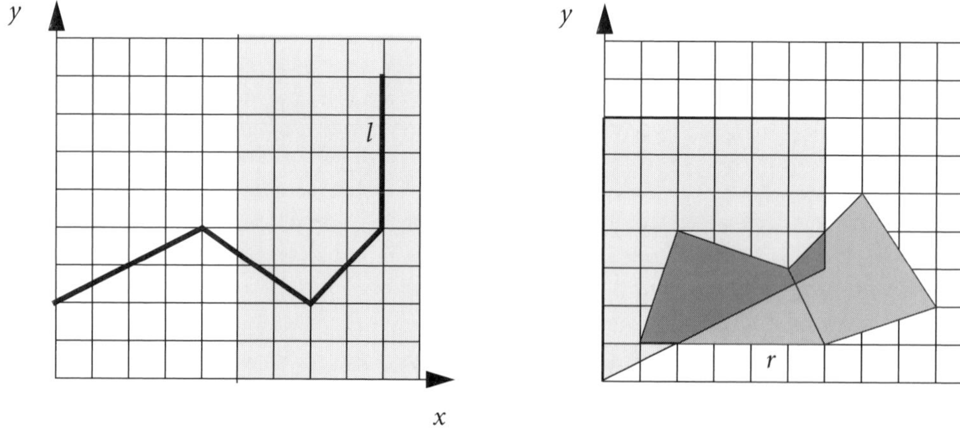

Figure 6.3 $\sigma_{x \geq 5}(l)$ (a); $\sigma_{x - 2y \leq 0 \wedge x \leq 6 \wedge y \leq 7}(r)$ (b).

$-x$	$+2y$	$=$	4
x		$\geq$	0
x		$\leq$	4
$2x$	$+3y$	$=$	20
x		$\geq$	4
x		$\leq$	7
x	$-y$	$=$	5
x		$\geq$	7
x		$\leq$	9
x		$=$	9
	y	$\geq$	4
	y	$\leq$	8

(a)

	y	$\geq$	1
$3x$	$-y$	$\geq$	2
x	$+3y$	$\leq$	14
$2x$	$+y$	$\leq$	13
$2x$	$+y$	$\geq$	13
x	$-y$	$\geq$	2
$3x$	$+2y$	$\leq$	31
x	$-3y$	$\leq$	3

(b)

Figure 6.4 Symbolic relations for line l (a); for region r (b).

box. The $\wedge$ symbol within a symbolic tuple, as well as the $\vee$ between symbolic tuples, is omitted in this representation.

The evaluation of $\sigma_{x \geq 5}(l)$ is shown in Figure 6.5. The result is obtained by simply adding the constraint $x \geq 5$ to each symbolic tuple of l; see Figure 6.5(b).

As mentioned previously, a "real" evaluation happens only when each of the resulting symbolic tuples is checked for inconsistencies and redundancies. Figure 6.5(c) illustrates this step. In this case, we discover that the first tuple in (b) is inconsistent (i.e., defines an empty point set), since $x \leq 4$ and $x \geq 5$ cannot be simultaneously fulfilled for any x value. In the second tuple, we can remove a redundancy, since $x \geq 4$ and $x \geq 5$ reduce to $x \geq 5$. In the third tuple, $x \geq 7$ and $x \geq 5$ reduce to $x \geq 7$. Finally, in the fourth tuple, $x \geq 5$ is redundant due to $x = 9$.

Observe that each of the resulting tuples in Figure 6.5(c) corresponds to one solution line segment in Figure 6.3(a). ■

Example 6.20 As a second selection example, consider $\sigma_{x - 2y \leq 0 \wedge x \leq 6 \wedge y \leq 7}(r)$. This query is illustrated in Figure 6.3(b).

Here, in the simplification step (Figure 6.6), constraints $x \leq 6$ and $y \leq 7$ are redundant for the first tuple, and constraints $3x + 2y \leq 31$, $x - 3y \leq 3$, and $y \leq 7$ are redundant for the second tuple. How do we know this? As a human, you can see it with the naked eye in Figure 6.3(b): The redundant constraints do not contribute to

(a)

$-x$	$+2y$	$=$	4
x		$\geq$	0
x		$\leq$	4
$2x$	$+3y$	$=$	20
x		$\geq$	4
x		$\leq$	7
x	$-y$	$=$	5
x		$\geq$	7
x		$\leq$	9
x		$=$	9
	y	$\geq$	4
	y	$\leq$	8

(b)

$-x$	$+2y$	$=$	4
x		$\geq$	0
x		$\leq$	4
x		$\geq$	5
$2x$	$+3y$	$=$	20
x		$\geq$	4
x		$\leq$	7
x		$\geq$	5
x	$-y$	$=$	5
x		$\geq$	7
x		$\leq$	9
x		$\geq$	5
x		$=$	9
	y	$\geq$	4
	y	$\leq$	8
x		$\geq$	5

(c)

$2x$	$+3y$	$=$	20
x		$\geq$	5
x		$\leq$	7
x	$-y$	$=$	5
x		$\geq$	7
x		$\leq$	9
x		$=$	9
	y	$\geq$	4
	y	$\leq$	8

Figure 6.5 Symbolic relations for line l (a); for $\sigma_{x \geq 5}(l)$ (b); for $\sigma_{x \geq 5}(l)$ after simplification (c).

the convex polygon resulting from intersecting all constraints. A constraint database system can determine this using an algorithm that we describe in Section 6.3.4. ■

Intersection

The evaluation method for intersection is the same as for Cartesian product and join. All pairs of symbolic tuples from the two argument relations are formed.

Example 6.21 We consider the intersection of line l and region r, illustrated in Figure 6.7(a). The resulting symbolic relation is shown in Figure 6.8. ■

Exercise 6.1 Apply simplification to the relation in Figure 6.8. ■

$$
\begin{array}{rrcr}
\hline
 & y & \geq & 1 \\
3x & -y & \geq & 2 \\
x & +3y & \leq & 14 \\
2x & +y & \leq & 13 \\
\hline
2x & +y & \geq & 13 \\
x & -y & \geq & 2 \\
3x & +2y & \leq & 31 \\
x & -3y & \leq & 3 \\
\hline
\end{array}
$$

(a)

$$
\begin{array}{rrcr}
\hline
 & y & \geq & 1 \\
3x & -y & \geq & 2 \\
x & +3y & \leq & 14 \\
2x & +y & \leq & 13 \\
x & -2y & \leq & 0 \\
x & & \leq & 6 \\
y & & \leq & 7 \\
\hline
2x & +y & \geq & 13 \\
x & -y & \geq & 2 \\
3x & +2y & \leq & 31 \\
x & -3y & \leq & 3 \\
x & -2y & \leq & 0 \\
x & & \leq & 6 \\
y & & \leq & 7 \\
\hline
\end{array}
$$

(b)

$$
\begin{array}{rrcr}
\hline
 & y & \geq & 1 \\
3x & -y & \geq & 2 \\
x & +3y & \leq & 14 \\
2x & +y & \leq & 13 \\
x & -2y & \leq & 0 \\
\hline
2x & +y & \geq & 13 \\
x & -y & \geq & 2 \\
x & -2y & \leq & 0 \\
x & & \leq & 6 \\
\hline
\end{array}
$$

(c)

Figure 6.6 Symbolic relations for region r (a); for $\sigma_{x-2y \leq 0 \wedge x \leq 6 \wedge y \leq 7}(r)$ (b); for $\sigma_{x-2y \leq 0 \wedge x \leq 6 \wedge y \leq 7}(r)$ after simplification (c).

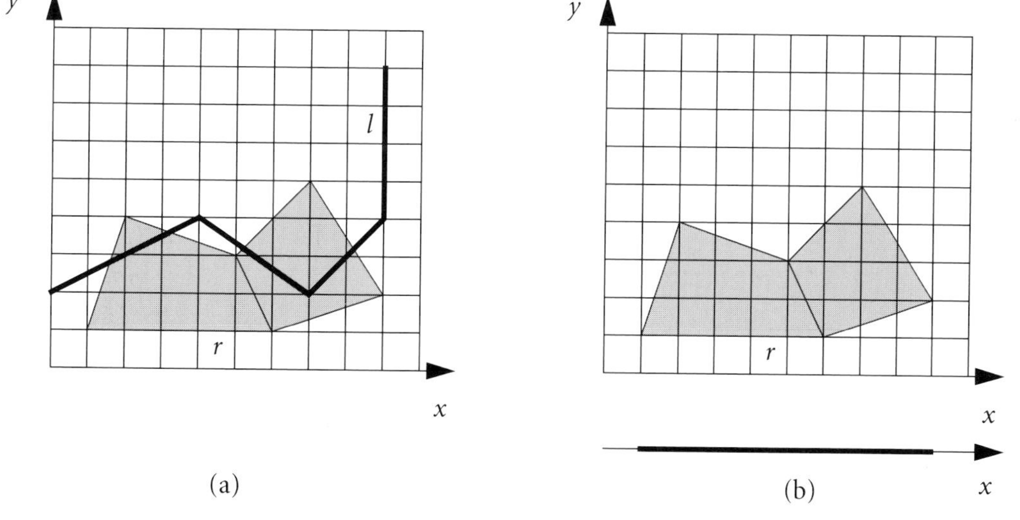

Figure 6.7 $l \cap r$ (a); $\pi_x(r)$ (b).

$$\begin{array}{rrcr}
-x & +2y & = & 4 \\
x & & \geq & 0 \\
x & & \leq & 4 \\
 & y & \geq & 1 \\
3x & -y & \geq & 2 \\
x & +3y & \leq & 14 \\
2x & +y & \leq & 13
\end{array}$$

$$\begin{array}{rrcr}
2x & +3y & = & 20 \\
x & & \geq & 4 \\
x & & \leq & 7 \\
 & y & \geq & 1 \\
3x & -y & \geq & 2 \\
x & +3y & \leq & 14 \\
2x & +y & \leq & 13
\end{array}$$

$$\begin{array}{rrcr}
x & -y & = & 5 \\
x & & \geq & 7 \\
x & & \leq & 9 \\
 & y & \geq & 1 \\
3x & -y & \geq & 2 \\
x & +3y & \leq & 14 \\
2x & +y & \leq & 13
\end{array}$$

$$\begin{array}{rrcr}
x & & = & 9 \\
 & y & \geq & 4 \\
 & y & \leq & 8 \\
 & y & \geq & 1 \\
3x & -y & \geq & 2 \\
x & +3y & \leq & 14 \\
2x & +y & \leq & 13
\end{array}$$

$$\begin{array}{rrcr}
-x & +2y & = & 4 \\
x & & \geq & 0 \\
x & & \leq & 4 \\
2x & +y & \geq & 13 \\
x & -y & \geq & 2 \\
3x & +2y & \leq & 31 \\
x & -3y & \leq & 3
\end{array}$$

$$\begin{array}{rrcr}
2x & +3y & = & 20 \\
x & & \geq & 4 \\
x & & \leq & 7 \\
2x & +y & \geq & 13 \\
x & -y & \geq & 2 \\
3x & +2y & \leq & 31 \\
x & -3y & \leq & 3
\end{array}$$

$$\begin{array}{rrcr}
x & -y & = & 5 \\
x & & \geq & 7 \\
x & & \leq & 9 \\
2x & +y & \geq & 13 \\
x & -y & \geq & 2 \\
3x & +2y & \leq & 31 \\
x & -3y & \leq & 3
\end{array}$$

$$\begin{array}{rrcr}
x & & = & 9 \\
 & y & \geq & 4 \\
 & y & \leq & 8 \\
2x & +y & \geq & 13 \\
x & -y & \geq & 2 \\
3x & +2y & \leq & 31 \\
x & -3y & \leq & 3
\end{array}$$

Figure 6.8 Symbolic relation for $l \cap r$.

Projection

Projection is a bit more complex; it can be done using the so-called Fourier-Motzkin elimination method, which allows us to eliminate one variable from a conjunction of constraints C. This corresponds to projecting a k-dimensional polyhedron into a k–1-dimensional space. It is assumed that each constraint in C is an inequality involving variable y. The technique uses two steps:

1. Within each constraint in C, isolate y. This partitions C into two subsets:
   —Constraints of the form $y \geq \alpha_i$, $i = 1, \ldots l$
   —Constraints of the form $y \leq \beta_j$, $j = 1, \ldots m$
2. Replace C by the set of constraints $\{\alpha_i \leq \beta_j \mid i = 1, \ldots l, j = 1, \ldots m\}$.

The second step is justified, since for any point $(x_1, \ldots, x_{k-1}, y)$ fulfilling all constraints in C, all the lower bounds α_i on y must be less than or equal to all upper bounds β_j on y.

In projecting a symbolic tuple, constraints not containing variable y are left unchanged. If there is an equality constraint involving y, it can be transformed into $y = \gamma$. Then, we can project by simply replacing y by γ everywhere.

Example 6.22 We project region r on the x-axis, as shown in Figure 6.7(b); hence, compute $\pi_x(r)$. Step 1 is illustrated in Figure 6.9; step 2 is shown in Figure 6.10.

(a)

	y	$\geq$	1
$3x$	$-y$	$\geq$	2
x	$+3y$	$\leq$	14
$2x$	$+y$	$\leq$	13
$2x$	$+y$	$\geq$	13
x	$-y$	$\geq$	2
$3x$	$+2y$	$\leq$	31
x	$-3y$	$\leq$	3

(b)

y	$\geq$	1	
y	$\leq$	$3x$	-2
y	$\leq$	$-1/3\,x$	$+14/3$
y	$\leq$	$-2x$	$+13$
y	$\geq$	$-2x$	$+13$
y	$\leq$	x	-2
y	$\leq$	$-3/2\,x$	$+31/2$
y	$\geq$	$1/3\,x$	-1

Figure 6.9 Symbolic relation for region r (a); variable y isolated (step 1) (b).

(a)

	1	$\leq$	$3x$	-2
	1	$\leq$	$-1/3\,x$	$+14/3$
	1	$\leq$	$-2x$	$+13$
$-2x$	$+13$	$\leq$	x	-2
$-2x$	$+13$	$\leq$	$-3/2\,x$	$+31/2$
$1/3\,x$	-1	$\leq$	x	-2
$1/3\,x$	-1	$\leq$	$-3/2\,x$	$+31/2$

(b)

1	$\leq$	x
x	$\leq$	11
x	$\leq$	6
5	$\leq$	x
-5	$\leq$	x
3/2	$\leq$	x
x	$\leq$	9

Figure 6.10 Result of step 2 (a); constraints evaluated (b).

Finally, the resulting symbolic tuples can still be simplified, and we get the relation shown in Figure 6.11. We can observe that this is the correct projection on the x-axis for each of the two convex components of region r. Note also that the convex regions (intervals) of the two symbolic tuples in Figure 6.11 overlap. There might be another simplification step applied, not to each symbolic tuple but to a symbolic relation as a whole, which would merge the two symbolic tuples into one with the two constraints $1 \leq x$ and $x \leq 9$. ■

Exercise 6.2 Consider the symbolic tuple $t \equiv$

$$2x + 3y + 5z \leq 30 \wedge x \geq 0 \wedge y \geq 1 \wedge z \geq 2$$

Eliminate variable z; that is, compute $\pi_{x,\,y}(\{t\})$. ■

1	$\leq$	x
x	$\leq$	6
5	$\leq$	x
x	$\leq$	9

Figure 6.11 Final result of $\pi_x(r)$.

6.3 Implementation of the Constraint Model

In this section, we consider the implementation of a model similar to the one in Section 6.2. The strategies described are roughly those of the Dedale prototype (for references, see the Bibliographic Notes). This prototype deals, first of all, with spatial values in two dimensions. There are additional concepts to handle higher-dimensional values that have a *key* in a space of two or less dimensions. This allows us to represent values such as a moving point in a (x, y, z, t) 4D-space, because it is a function from t (1D) into a 3D space. It is also possible to represent digital terrain models, which reside in a 3D space (x, y, z) but are functions from xy into z.

6.3.1 Representation of Relations

The top-level relations are finite and are the same as in any other relational or object-relational system; they can be implemented using standard techniques. For example, a relation can be represented as a set of records within a file, where the record and file abstractions are offered by a storage manager component dealing with transactions, logging, locking, recovery, and so forth.

The symbolic subrelations or constraint formulas representing infinite nested relations can be stored like other nonstandard attributes: as a binary storage object of varying size. The DBMS will offer a mechanism to deal with attribute values of varying and possibly large size. These are the same requirements as already discussed for the implementation of spatial or spatio-temporal data types in Section 5.1.1.

6.3.2 Representation of Symbolic Relations (Constraint Formulas)

We assume that the symbolic relation is in a normal form, described in the following text.

A linear constraint $a_1x_1 + \ldots + a_kx_k \ \theta \ b$ is represented in a simple data structure containing the coefficients $a_1, \ldots, a_k, b$ and the type of the constraint ($\leq$ or $=$). The result is a compact storage block, a sequence of bytes, called a *constraint byte block*.

A constraint tuple is represented as a sequence of the byte blocks of its constraints. Depending on whether the constraint byte blocks have a variable or a fixed size, a more or less complex management is needed to keep the positions of the individual constraints. Again, the result is a byte block, called a *tuple byte block*.

A constraint relation is represented as a sequence of tuple byte blocks, again with some additional bookkeeping to keep track of the positions of the tuple byte blocks. The result is a *relation byte block*.

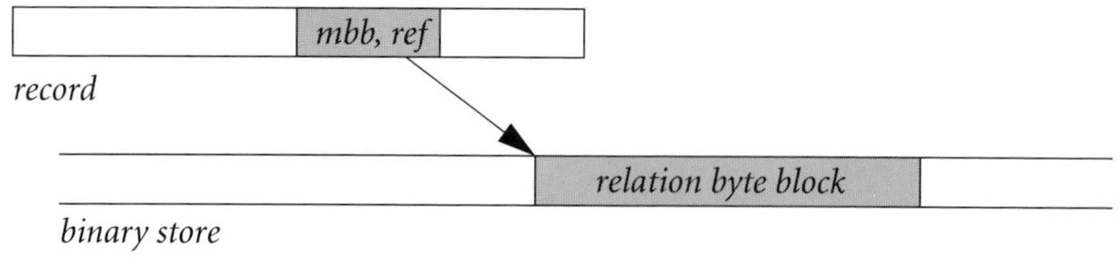

Figure 6.12 Storage of symbolic relations.

In addition, a minimal bounding box (*mbb*) for the points of the k-dimensional space satisfying the constraint relation is stored; hence, a tuple of the form $((min_1, \ldots, min_k), (max_1, \ldots, max_k))$. The bounding box is used to speed up computations, as was done in Sections 5.1.3 and 5.2.1.

A symbolic relation is stored in *normal form*, which means the following:

1. It is in disjunctive normal form. This means geometrically that spatial entities have been decomposed into convex components.
2. There are no redundant constraints in a conjunct. For example, $x \leq 3$ and $x \leq 5$ cannot both occur in a conjunct.
3. There are no inconsistent constraints in a conjunct (i.e., each conjunct is satisfiable). For example, $x \leq 3$ and $x \geq 5$ cannot occur in the same conjunct.
4. The constraints within a tuple are stored in a certain order, which allows for an efficient conversion to a vector mode representation. This is needed, for example, for displaying the value at the user interface (see the next section).

In total, a symbolic relation is stored as a pair (*mbb*, *ref*), where *mbb* is the minimal bounding box, and *ref* is a reference to the position where the relation byte block can be found. In the Dedale prototype, relation byte blocks of different top-level tuples are put sequentially into some binary store, as illustrated in Figure 6.12.

6.3.3 Data Loading and Conversion

We now consider how spatial data in a 2D space, which are usually given in vector format (or boundary representation), can be converted to constraint relations in normal form. The essential requirement is that a decomposition into convex shapes is performed.

Spatial data in 2D usually come as points, polylines, or polygons. A point (x_0, y_0) is represented as a constraint tuple:

$$x = x_0 \land y = y_0$$

A polyline is represented as a symbolic relation with one tuple per line segment. That tuple consists of five constraints, namely, one constraint for the supporting line and four constraints describing the bounding box of the line segment. For example, the first segment of `line` value l (Section 6.2.1) would be represented as:

$$-x + 2y = 4 \wedge x \geq 0 \wedge x \leq 4 \wedge y \geq 2 \wedge y \leq 4$$

Each line segment is a convex component. Using four constraints to describe the complete bounding box (rather than only two for an x-range or y-range) allows for a simple treatment of special cases such as horizontal and vertical segments. Hence, converting points or polylines to the constraint representation is no problem. The only more difficult issue is the decomposition of polygons into convex components.

A simple idea would be to decompose a polygon into triangles, assuming an algorithm for triangulation is given. However, this would result in a representation with a very large number of convex components (= symbolic tuples). For efficient processing, it is desirable to represent polygons by a minimal number of convex components.

There is an algorithm computing a decomposition into an optimal number of convex components. However, on the one hand, it is complex and on the other hand, it has a rather large time complexity—namely, $O(r^2 n \log n)$, where r is the number of so-called *notches*. A notch is a vertex of the polygon with an interior angle greater than π.

In the following text, we describe a few relatively simple algorithms, which, together, allow us to compute a decomposition into a nonoptimal but also not too large number of convex components. We proceed in three steps by describing algorithms for:

- Decomposing a polygon into monotone polygons
- Triangulating a monotone polygon
- Building convex polygons from a triangulation

Decomposing a polygon into monotone polygons

First, we are interested in so-called *monotone* polygons, because for them there exists a simple algorithm for triangulation. A polygon is monotone with respect to the x-axis, if it consists of a lower and an upper boundary, each of which is a monotone polygonal chain.

Definition 6.5 A *polygonal chain* is a sequence $<p_0, \ldots, p_n>$ of points in the plane ($p_i \in \mathbb{R}^2$) representing the sequence of edges $<(p_0, p_1), (p_1, p_2), \ldots, (p_{n-1}, p_n)>$. ■

Definition 6.6 A polygonal chain $<p_0, \ldots, p_n>$ is called *monotone with respect to the x axis* (*monotone*, for short) if $p_{i+1}.x > p_i.x \; \forall i \in \{0, \ldots, n-1\}$. ■

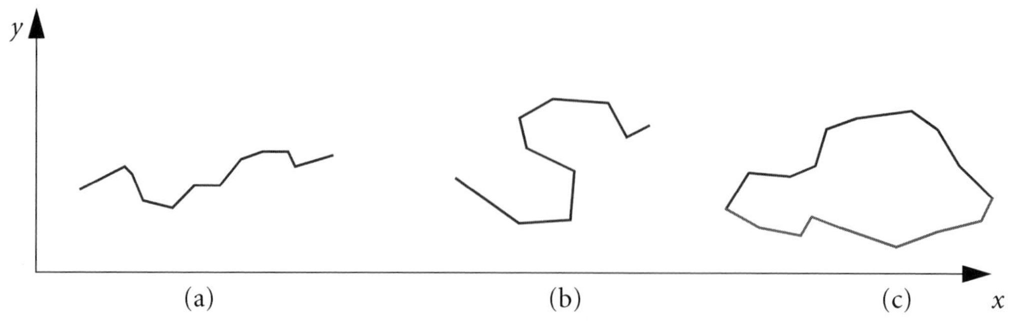

Figure 6.13 A monotone polygonal chain (a); a chain that is not monotone (b); a monotone polygon (c).

This is equivalent to saying that a monotone chain intersects any vertical line in at most one point.

Definition 6.7 A simple polygon is called *monotone* (with respect to the x-axis), if its boundary can be represented by two polygonal chains that are both monotone. ■

These concepts are illustrated in Figure 6.13.

The problem now is to decompose an arbitrary simple polygon into a set of monotone polygons. Consider the polygon in Figure 6.14(a). By adding the thick lines shown in Figure 6.14(b) it can be split into monotone polygons.

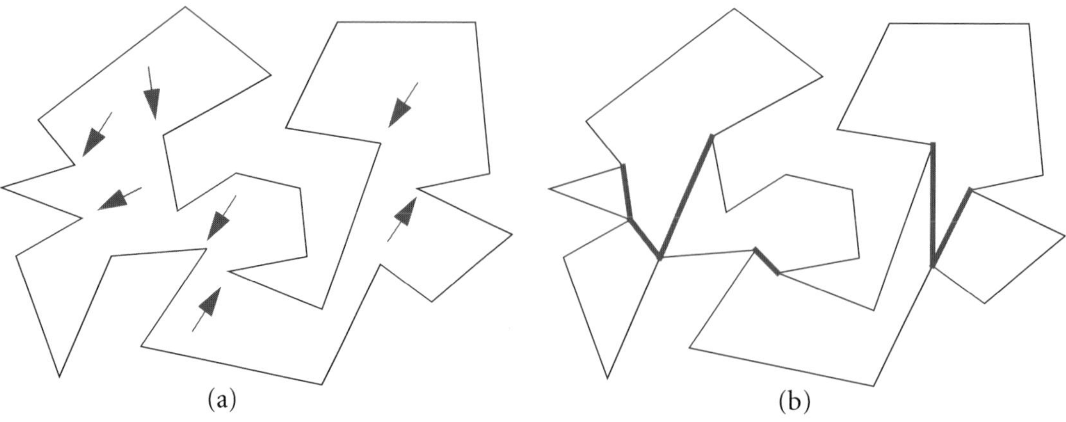

Figure 6.14 A simple polygon and its interior cusps (a); split edges added by the decomposition algorithm (b).

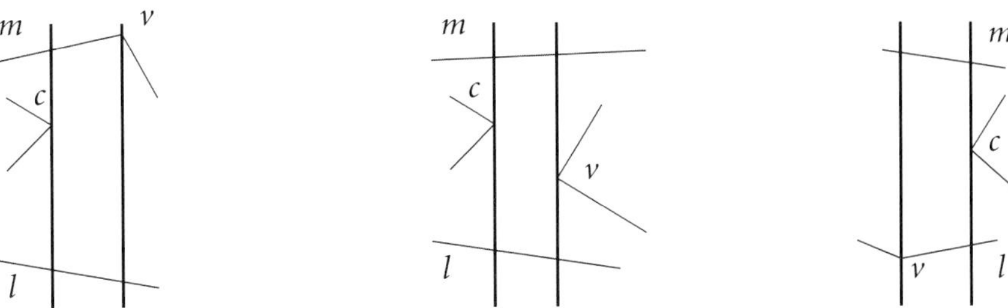

Figure 6.15 Cusp regions.

There are certain vertices in a simple polygon that make it nonmonotone—namely, notches (vertices with an interior angle greater than π) for which both incident edges of the polygon are on the same side of a vertical line through the vertex. We call these *interior cusps*. An interior cusp is called a *left* (*right*) *cusp* if its incident edges are both on the *left* (*right*) *side* of the vertical line. The interior cusps are indicated by arrows in Figure 6.14(a).

To create monotone polygons, each interior cusp needs to be connected by a line segment (called a *split edge*) to some other vertex of the polygon. Split edges are used to separate distinct monotone polygons. They are shown in Figure 6.14(b).

The split edges can be computed in a plane-sweep algorithm along the x-axis. A cusp c is connected to another vertex v selected according to the following rules. Let l and m be the two edges of the polygon immediately below and above c. Let the *cusp region* of c be the trapezium formed by a vertical line through c, the edges l and m, and a vertical line through the closest vertex in x-direction between l and m. This closest vertex is v. It may either be an end point of l or m or another cusp. This is illustrated in Figure 6.15.

The plane-sweep needs to handle various types of transitions when passing a vertex; these are shown in Figure 6.16. Shaded areas indicate where the polygon is.

The sweep status structure is a y-ordered list of edges currently intersecting the sweep line. In addition, it contains entries for left cusps that are yet unresolved, that is, for which the cusp region has not been passed completely by the sweep line. Each

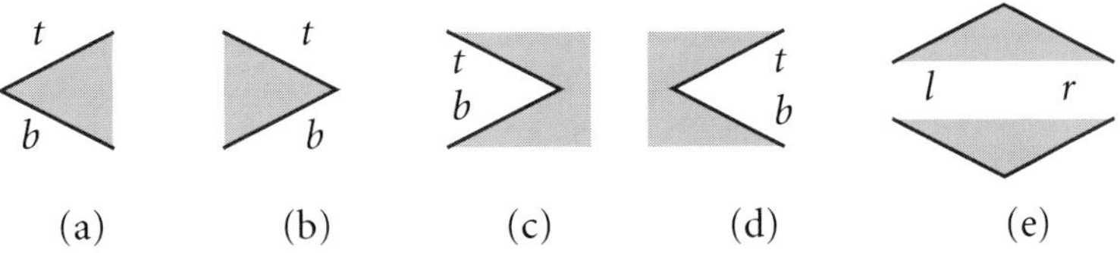

Figure 6.16 Five possible transitions in the plane-sweep.

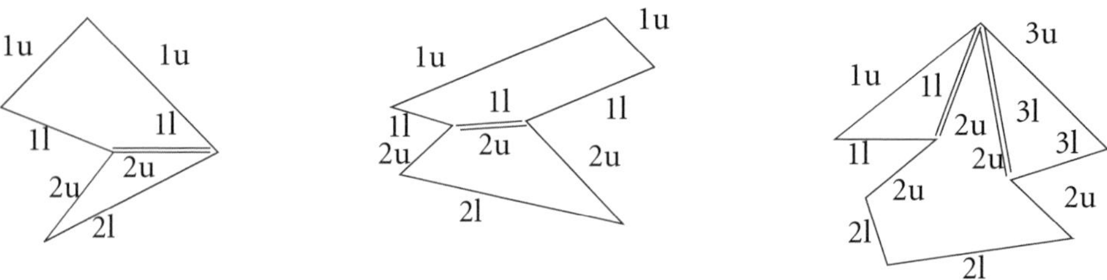

Figure 6.17 Numbering edges of monotone polygons.

edge in the sweep status structure is additionally marked with a polygon identifier (for the monotone polygon to be returned) and a flag from the set $\{l, u\}$ indicating whether it belongs to the lower or upper boundary of that polygon. Figure 6.17 illustrates this numbering scheme, which allows us to return separate monotone polygons. Observe that a split edge created by the algorithm actually corresponds to two edges of distinct monotone polygons.

Algorithm 6.1 Decomposition into Monotone Polygons

Input: A simple polygon P given by its set of edges S.

Output: A set of monotone polygons $M_1, \ldots, M_n$, whose union is P. Each monotone polygon M_i is returned as a pair (L_i, U_i), where L_i and U_i are sequences of edges forming the lower and upper boundary of M_i, respectively.

Method:

Step 1: Prepare the plane-sweep by representing each edge in S by its left and right end point (or halfsegment). Sort all halfsegments by x-coordinate. Let this be the sweep event structure *SE*.

Step 2: Let *SS* be the sweep status structure, initially empty. Scan the halfsegments in *SE* and handle the five types of transitions shown in Figure 6.16. In all transitions, let b and t be the bottom and top segment, respectively, or l and r the left and right segment, and let v be the vertex involved.

Case (a)—a left end: Get a new polygon identifier i. Enter edge entries (b, i, l) and (t, i, u) into *SS*.

Case (b)—a right end: Find the entries (b, i, l) and (t, j, u) in *SS*.
if there is a cusp (w, m, n) between (b, i, l) and (t, j, u) **then** create split edges $(w\text{-}v, m, u)$ and $(w\text{-}v, n, l)$ and output them. Remove the cusp from *SS*.
endif

Output (b, i, l) and (t, j, u) and remove them from *SS*.
Case (c)—a left cusp: Find the entries (b, i, u) and (t, j, l) in *SS* and output them. Delete them from *SS* and enter a cusp entry (v, i, j) at that position.
Case (d)—a right cusp: Find the edges $(bottom, i, l)$ and (top, j, u) immediately below and above v in *SS*.
if there is a cusp (w, m, n) between these edges in *SS* **then** create split edges $(w\text{-}v, m, u)$ and $(w\text{-}v, n, l)$ and output them. Remove the cusp from *SS*.
lower := *m*; *higher* := *n*;
else let w.l.o.g. (top, j, u) be the edge whose left end point has the larger x-coordinate among $(bottom, i, l)$ and (top, j, u), and let w be that end point. Get a new polygon identifier k. Create split edges $(w\text{-}v, j, u)$ and $(w\text{-}v, k, l)$ and output them. Replace the entry (top, j, u) by an entry (top, k, u) in *SS*. (A new monotone polygon numbered k has been started and the edge *top* now belongs to that polygon, see the rightmost example in Figure 6.17.)
lower := *j*; *higher* := *k*;
(treat the case that edge *bottom* has the larger end point analogously.)
endif;
enter entries $(b, lower, u)$ and $(t, higher, l)$ into *SS*.
Case (e)—a bend: W.l.o.g. let l and r be upper edges. Find the entry (l, j, u) in *SS*.
higher := *j*;
if there is a cusp (w, m, n) immediately below (l, j, u) in *SS* **then** create split edges $(w\text{-}v, m, u)$ and $(w\text{-}v, n, l)$ and output them. Remove the cusp from *SS*.
higher := *m*;
endif;
Output edge (l, j, u) and delete it from *SS*. Enter entry (r, higher, u) into *SS*.
(treat the case that l and r are lower edges analogously.)

end.

Step 1 of the algorithm requires $O(n \log n)$ time due to the sorting of left and right end points. In step 2, if a balanced tree structure is used to represent the y-ordered sequence of edges, each transition can be handled in $O(\log n)$ time. Hence, the time required for step 2 as well as the whole algorithm is $O(n \log n)$.

Triangulating a monotone polygon

Triangulating a monotone polygon consists of adding *diagonals*, edges between vertices that lie entirely inside the polygon and do not intersect other diagonals. The algorithm scans the vertices of the x-monotone polygon in increasing x-order. Whenever possible, it adds a diagonal, which splits off a triangle, thereby reducing the polygon yet to be triangulated, called the *remaining polygon*. An example polygon with diagonals added by the algorithm is shown in Figure 6.18.

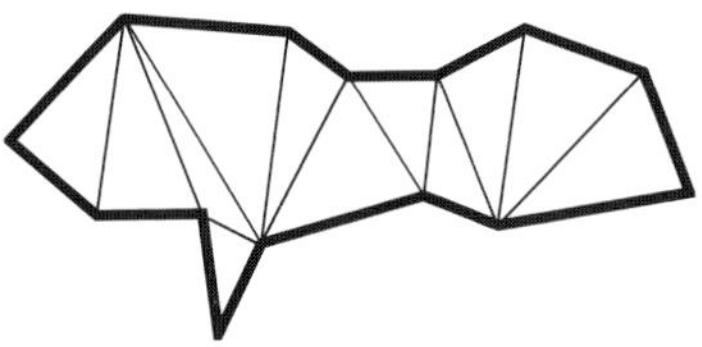

Figure 6.18 Monotone polygon with diagonals added.

The algorithm maintains a stack <$q_1, \ldots, q_i$> of vertices that have been processed but for which diagonals could not yet be created. The stack contents <$q_1, \ldots, q_i$> have the following properties:

1. <$q_1, \ldots, q_i$> are in increasing x-order.
2. <$q_1, \ldots, q_i$> form a chain on the boundary of the remaining polygon.
3. The interior angles of the boundary of the remaining polygon at <$q_2, \ldots, q_{i-1}$> are at least π.
4. The next vertex to be processed is adjacent to either q_1 or q_i (or both).

Here is the algorithm.

Algorithm 6.2 Triangulating a Monotone Polygon

Input: A monotone polygon P given by its lower boundary L and upper boundary R each given as an x-ordered sequence of edges.

Output: A triangulation of P (i.e., a set of triangles whose union is P).

Method:

Step 1: In a parallel scan of L and R, compute the x-ordered sequence of vertices $p_1, \ldots, p_n$ of P.

Step 2: Initialize the stack as <p_1, p_2>. Scan $p_3, \ldots, p_n$:

Let <$q_1, \ldots, q_i$> denote the stack contents and q the next vertex to be processed.
Case (a): q is adjacent to q_1 but not to q_i (Figure 6.19[a])
    Add diagonals $(q, q_2), (q, q_3), \ldots, (q, q_i)$, reporting the corresponding triangles.
    Replace the stack contents by <q_i, q>.
Case (b): q is adjacent to q_i but not to q_1 (Figure 6.19[b])
    $j := i;$

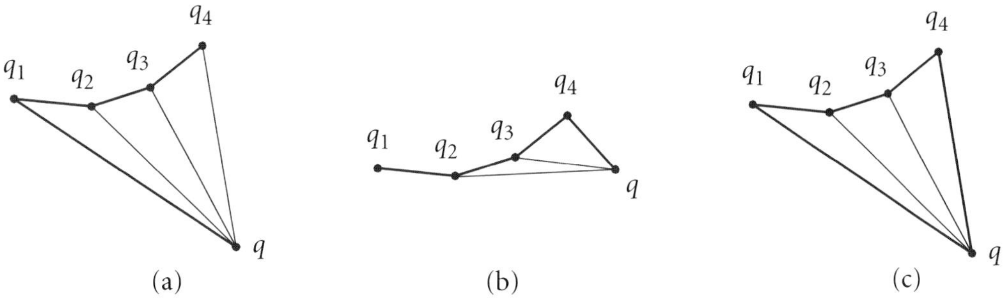

Figure 6.19 Three cases in Algorithm 6.2.

> **while** $j > 1$ and the internal angle (q_{j-1}, q_j, q) is less than π **do**
> add diagonal (q, q_{j-1});
> report the corresponding triangle (q, q_{j-1}, q_j);
> remove q_j from the stack;
> $j := j - 1$;
> **endwhile;**
> add q to the stack.
> Case (c): q is adjacent to both q_1 and q_i (Figure 6.19[c])
> Add diagonals $(q, q_2), (q, q_3), \ldots, (q, q_{i-1})$ and report the corresponding triangles including the triangle (q, q_{i-1}, q_i). q is the final vertex p_n of the polygon.

end.

For the correctness of the algorithm it is crucial that all added diagonals lie inside the polygon. This is easy to check. In cases (a) and (c), vertex q lies on one side and the vertices $q_2, \ldots, q_3$ on the other side of a line through q_1 and q_2. All other vertices of the remaining polygon have larger x-coordinates than q. Therefore, it is correct to add the diagonals as done by the algorithm. In case (b) similar arguments apply.

For the analysis of the time complexity, it is important to know that the number of triangles of a triangulation is linear in the number of vertices of the polygon.

Exercise 6.3 Show that the number of triangles of any triangulation of a simple polygon with n vertices has exactly $n - 2$ triangles and $n - 3$ diagonals.

Hint: Use the fact that a diagonal splits the polygon into two polygons with smaller numbers of vertices. ■

We can now analyze the time complexity of Algorithm 6.2. Step 1 needs only $O(n)$ time for merging two ordered sequences. In step 2, each vertex processed in one of the cases, (a) through (c), requires only constant time except for the diagonals created and triangles reported. However, we have just seen in Exercise 6.3 that the total number of diagonals and triangles is $O(n)$. Therefore, the time complexity of the whole algorithm is $O(n)$.

Together with Algorithm 6.1 we now have a complete algorithm for triangulating a simple polygon in $O(n \log n)$ time.

Building convex polygons from a triangulation

Given a triangulation of a simple polygon *P*, computing a decomposition of *P* into convex components is rather easy.

Algorithm 6.3 Decomposing a Simple Polygon into Convex Components

Input: A monotone polygon *P* and a triangulation *T* of *P*.

Output: A set of convex polygons whose union is *P*.

Method:

Let *D* be the set of diagonals in triangulation *T*, that is, edges of triangles that are not edges of *P*.
Consider the edges of *D* in any order.
for each edge (q, r) of *D* **do**
  if removing (q, r) from *D* leaves interior angles smaller than π at both q and r
  then remove (q, r) from *D* **endif**;
endfor;
report the remaining polygons;

end.

The algorithm correctly creates convex polygons, because it starts with triangles (which are convex polygons) and then by removing an edge merges two adjacent convex polygons only if the resulting polygon is still convex.

For a polygon with n vertices, the number of triangles and diagonals is $O(n)$. The algorithm can be implemented in such a way that each diagonal can be checked in constant time (this will be done in the exercises); hence, the running time is $O(n)$.

The remaining question is how good the decomposition is—that is, how many convex components it creates relative to the optimal number of such components.

Theorem 6.1 Algorithm 6.3 creates a decomposition of polygon P into less than four times the optimal number of convex components.

Proof: Let OPT be the optimal number of convex components, and let c be the number of convex components created by the algorithm. Let r be the number of notches (vertices with interior angle greater than π) in P. Let D' be the diagonals remaining after applying the algorithm (i.e., the diagonals separating convex components). Observe that for each notch one partitioning edge in D' is needed. Two notches might share the same diagonal; therefore, we have a lower bound on OPT:

$$OPT \geq 1 + \lceil r/2 \rceil$$

Now, assign each edge in D' to one of its end points—namely, the end point p which prevented its removal. We claim that each notch can get assigned no more than two edges in this way.

This can be shown as follows. Assume by contradiction that a notch gets assigned three edges, and let them, together with the edges of P forming the notch, be numbered clockwise e_1, e_2, e_3, e_4, e_5 (Figure 6.20).

Now, the angle between e_1 and e_3 must be greater than π to justify e_2, and the angle between e_3 and e_5 must be greater than π to justify e_4. But this means that the angle between e_1 and e_5 is greater than 2π, a contradiction. Therefore, no more than two edges can be assigned to any notch. This leads to an upper bound on the number d of diagonals:

$$d \leq 2r$$

Since $c = d + 1$, we also have a bound on the number of convex components c:

$$c \leq 2r + 1 = (2r + 4) - 3 \leq 4\,OPT - 3$$

This completes the proof. ■

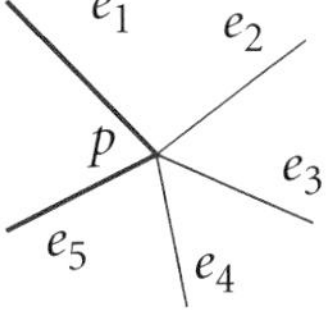

Figure 6.20 Edges around a notch.

On the whole, we have obtained an efficient algorithm to decompose a simple polygon into a not too large number of convex components.

Each convex polygon is now represented as a conjunction of the constraints defining its boundary edges as half-planes. In the tuple byte block these constraints are stored in counterclockwise order. This allows us to rebuild the polygon from the constraint tuple by a linear scan, for example, to draw the polygon on the screen.

So we have achieved our goal of converting given polygon data to constraint representation.

6.3.4 Normalization of Symbolic Tuples

An important task in query processing is the normalization of symbolic tuples. The goal is to transform a conjunction of constraints into the normal form described in Section 6.3.2. In particular, satisfiability should be checked, and redundant constraints should be removed.

The algorithm for normalization roughly works as follows. First, the given constraints are scanned and the number of constraints with an "=" operator is determined. Except for degenerate cases, if this number is greater than two, the tuple is not satisfiable; if it is two, the tuple describes a point; if it is one, the tuple describes a line segment; otherwise, it describes a polygon. In the latter case, an algorithm for half-plane intersection is called, which, in turn, uses an algorithm for intersecting convex polygons. We describe the algorithms bottom-up, hence in the sequel algorithms for:

- Computing the intersection of two convex polygons
- Computing the intersection of a set of half-planes
- Normalization

Computing the intersection of two convex polygons

The intersection of two convex polygons is a convex polygon. The idea of the intersection algorithm is illustrated in Figure 6.21. By drawing a vertical line through each vertex of the two polygons, we divide the plane into vertical stripes, or *slabs*. The intersection of each of the convex polygons with a slab is a trapezium (which may degenerate into a triangle). The result polygon is the union over all slabs of the intersection of two trapeziums within each slab. The latter can be computed in constant time.

Algorithm 6.4 *CPI(P, Q)* (Convex Polygon Intersection)

Input: Convex polygons P and Q, each given as a sequence of vertices in clockwise order.

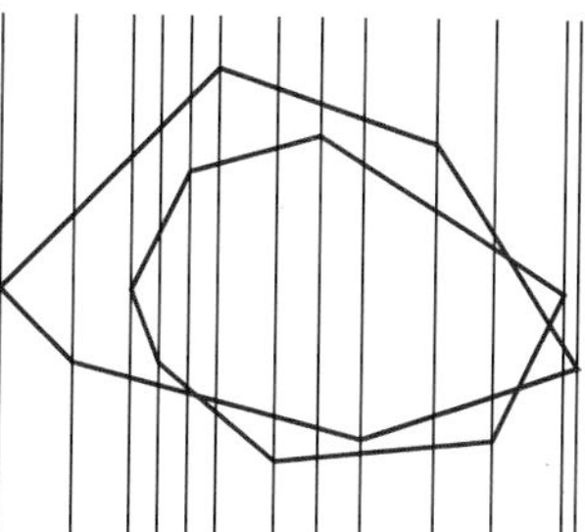

Figure 6.21 Intersecting two convex polygons.

Output: The polygon $P \cap Q$.

Method:

1. Compute an x-ordered sequence of slabs for the vertices of P's upper boundary, P's lower boundary, Q's upper boundary, and Q's lower boundary, respectively. Lower boundaries can be recognized by decreasing x-coordinates in the list of vertices. The order for lower boundaries can be inverted in linear time using a stack, for example. Each slab has an associated bottom or top edge of one of the polygons.
2. Merge the four sequences of slabs into one refined sequence. Now, each slab has associated one or two trapeziums.
3. For each slab, compute the intersection of its trapeziums (if there is only one, the intersection is empty).
4. Scan the sequence of intersection polygons for each slab and merge them into a result polygon. Return this polygon.

end.

Step 1 can be implemented in linear time, scanning along the vertices of P or Q in clockwise order. Step 2 consists of merging ordered sequences, which can also be done in linear time. Step 3 requires constant time per slab; hence, it is also linear in the number of slabs or vertices. Step 4 is also linear. Hence, for two convex polygons with m and n vertices, respectively, the total time required by Algorithm 6.4 is $O(m + n)$.

Computing the intersection of a set of half-planes

Here the idea is quite simple: We convert each half-plane into a convex polygon by intersecting it with a sufficiently large rectangle. In a divide-and-conquer algorithm, we merge bottom-up subsets of constraints by computing the intersection of the convex polygons resulting from each recursive call.

Algorithm 6.5 *HPI*(C) (Half-Plane Intersection)

Input: A set C of inequality constraints defining half-planes.

Output: A convex polygon, representing the nonredundant constraints in C.

Method:

Let $C = \{C_1, \ldots, C_n\}$. Let *RECT* be a sufficiently large rectangle.
if $|C| = 1$
then return $C_1 \cap RECT$
else return $CPI(HPI(\{C_1, \ldots, C_{\lceil n/2 \rceil}\}), HPI(\{C_{\lceil n/2 \rceil + 1}, \ldots, C_n\})$
endif

end.

This is a balanced divide-and-conquer algorithm for which the merge step—intersecting two convex polygons—takes $O(n)$ time. It is well known that the overall cost is $O(n \log n)$.

Normalization

We are now ready to describe the algorithm for normalization. To simplify description, degenerated cases (e.g., two constraints representing parallel lines, or unbounded objects), are not treated here. The algorithm takes as input and returns a data structure representing a symbolic tuple, with the following fields:

- *constraints*: the set of linear constraints forming this tuple
- *type*: a type description from the set {*Unknown*, *Point*, *Segment*, *Polygon*}
- *mbb*: the bounding box of the point set described by constraints
- *normal*: a Boolean indicating whether this tuple is normalized

The algorithm uses two auxiliary functions: *MBB*, which returns for a given polygon its bounding box, and *ToConstraints*, which transforms a convex polygon to constraint representation. The algorithm is shown in Figure 6.22.

When the algorithm treats the case $|CEQ| = 1$ (the tuple describes a line segment), the equality constraint for the line is converted into an inequality constraint defining a half-plane to be able to compute the intersection of the line with the polygon defined by the other constraints, using the half-plane intersection algorithm. The normalized tuple then contains the line constraint, together with the constraints for the bounding box of the intersection of the half-planes.

The time complexity is dominated by the calls to *HPI*, hence is $O(n \log n)$.

Algorithm 6.6 Normalization of Symbolic Tuples

Input: A symbolic tuple *t*.

Output: A normalized symbolic tuple *t*'.

Method:

```
t'.constraints := ∅; t'.type := Unknown; t'.mbb := ∅; t'.normal := true;
let CEQ be the subset of equality constraints (lines) of t.constraints and let
   CNE = t.constraints\CEQ (half-planes);
if |CEQ| > 2 then                  // tuple is unsatisfiable, don't change t'
elsif |CEQ| = 2 then               // a point p
   if every constraint in CNE contains p
   then t'.constraints := (x = p.x ∧ y = p.y);
      t'.type := Point;
      t'.mbb := MBB(p);
   endif
elsif |CEQ| = 1 then               // a line segment
   let c be the constraint in CEQ converted into a half-plane constraint;
   if HPI(CNE ∪ {c}) is not empty
   then t'.constraints := CEQ ∪ ToConstraints(MBB(HPI(CNE ∪ {c})));
      t'.type := Segment;
      t'.mbb := MBB(HPI(CNE ∪ {c}));
   endif
else                               // |CEQ| = 0, a convex polygon
   if HPI(CNE) is not empty
   then t'.constraints := ToConstraints(HPI(CNE));
      t'.type := Polygon;
      t'.mbb := MBB(HPI(CNE));
   endif
endif;
return t'

end.
```

Figure 6.22 Algorithm for normalization of symbolic tuples.

6.3.5 Implementation of Algebra Operations

We now consider the implementation of the operations of the relational algebra for constraint relations (Section 6.2.3). Here again is the definition of these operations:

- $R_1 \cup R_2 \equiv e_1 \cup e_2$
- $R_1 \cap R_2 \equiv \{ t_1 \wedge t_2 \mid t_1 \in e_1, t_2 \in e_2 \}$
- $R_1 - R_2 \equiv \{ t_1 \wedge t_2 \mid t_1 \in e_1, t_2 \in C(e_2) \}$, where $C(e_2)$ is the set of tuples of a linear constraint formula in DNF corresponding to the formula $\neg e_2$.
- $\sigma_F(R_1) \equiv \{ t \wedge F \mid t \in e_1 \}$
- $\pi_{[x1, ..., xm]}(R_1) \equiv \{ \pi_{[x1, ..., xm]}(t) \mid t \in e_1 \}$ where $\pi_{[x1, ..., xm]}(t)$ denotes the projection of a symbolic tuple on the variables $x_1, \ldots, x_m$
- $R_1 \times R_2 \equiv \{ t_1 \wedge t_2 \mid t_1 \in e_1, t_2 \in e_2 \}$
- $R_1 |\times| R_2 \equiv \{ t_1 \wedge t_2 \mid t_1 \in e_1, t_2 \in e_2 \}$

Three auxiliary operations on relations are useful; they are *NORMALIZE*, *SATISFY*, and *OVERLAP*.

Operation *NORMALIZE* scans the symbolic tuples and normalizes each of them, omitting empty tuples in the result.

Operation *SATISFY* checks whether a symbolic relation is satisfiable. It also processes sequentially the symbolic tuples, normalizes each tuple, and stops as soon as a non-empty tuple is found, returning *true*. If there is no such tuple, *false* is returned.

Operation *OVERLAP* processes two symbolic relations and forms for each pair of symbolic tuples their conjunction if the bounding boxes overlap. Note that the resulting tuples are not in normal form.

The relation algebra operations are then processed as follows.

Union, ∪

The two lists of symbolic tuples are concatenated. This requires only O(1) time.

Intersection, ∩; product, ×; and join, |×|

These operations all have the same definition and are all implemented by a call to *OVERLAP*. The complexity is $O(mn)$ for two arguments of size m and n, respectively. The result is not normalized.

Selection, σ

The selection $\sigma_F(R)$ is implemented as $OVERLAP(R, \{F\})$. This requires $O(n)$ time for a relation R of size n. The result is not normalized.

Projection, π

In the general k-dimensional case, the Fourier-Motzkin method described in Section 6.2.3 can be used. In the two-dimensional case discussed here, a simpler implementation is possible: Each tuple is normalized; this includes the computation of the bounding box for the tuple, as we have seen (Algorithm 6.6). Then, the bounding box can simply be projected on the x- or y-axis. For a symbolic relation with n tuples this requires $O(n)$ time (assuming each tuple is processed in constant time).

Difference, –

The only operator that has a more involved implementation is difference. We only discuss difference of polygonal objects.[4]

The idea for implementing the difference $R_1 - R_2$ in two dimensions is illustrated in Figure 6.23. First, a *cell decomposition* of the plane is computed as follows. Trans-

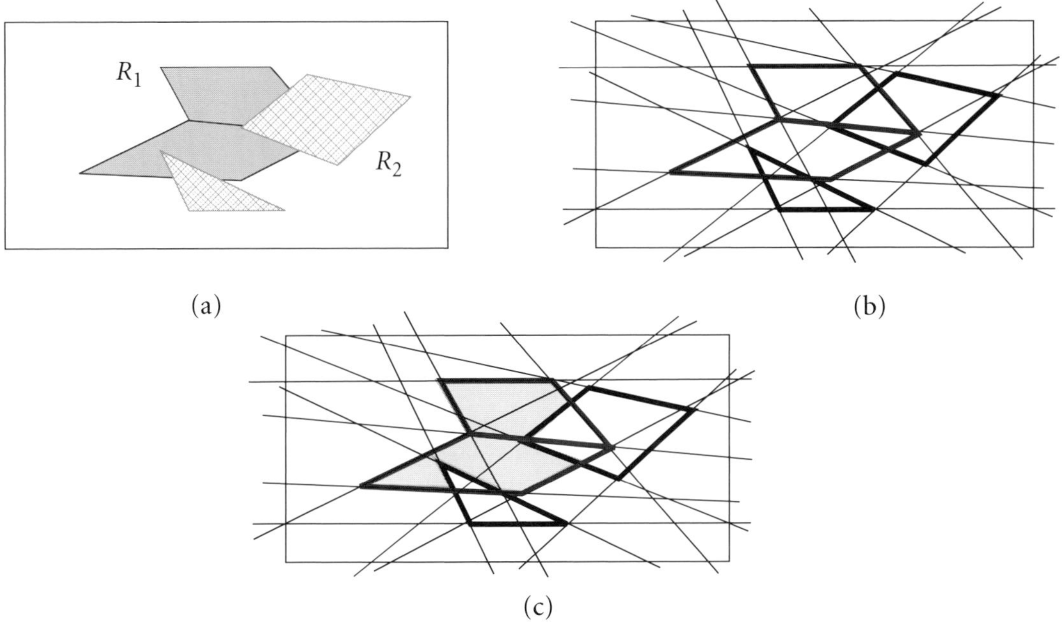

Figure 6.23 Relations R_1 and R_2 (a); the corresponding cell decomposition (b); the result is the set of cells belonging to R_1 but not R_2 (c).

[4] Forming the difference of other types of data, such as subtracting polygons from line segments or vice versa, and the related issues of closure, are not discussed in the original literature.

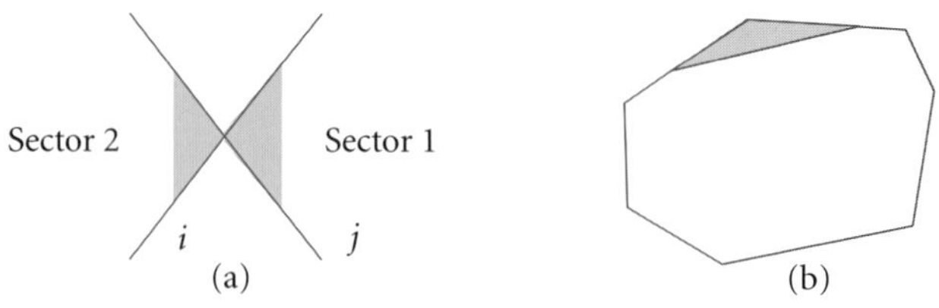

Figure 6.24 The sectors of an intersection (a); a sector belonging to a cell (b).

Algorithm 6.7 Computing a Cell Decomposition

Input A set C of inequality constraints defining half-planes.

Output: A set of symbolic tuples, representing the cell decomposition induced by C.

Method:

1. Let $L = \{l_1, \ldots, l_n\}$ be the set of lines bounding the half-planes in C.
2. Compute an $n \times n$ matrix M as follows: $M_{ij} := (i, j, p_{ij})$, where p_{ij} is the intersection of lines l_i and l_j.
3. For each row i of M, sort its entries, which are intersections with other lines, along the line l_i (e.g., by increasing x-coordinates $p_{ij}.x$).
4. Compute a second $n \times n$ matrix N as follows: Scan each row of M. When processing an entry (i, j, p_{ij}) in field M_{ik}, set :

$$N_{ij} := (k, \mathit{false}, \mathit{false})$$

   This means that the entry for the intersection of lines l_i and l_j can be found in matrix M in field M_{ik} and that none of the sectors of that intersection has been used for a cell. The two *false* entries represent the sectors 1 and 2 (Figure 6.24).
5. Scan all entries in matrix N. For each sector of an intersection not yet processed (marked *false*) do:

   start a new cell;
   visit in clockwise order the vertices of the cell. For each vertex do:
      add the corresponding constraint to the cell description;
      mark the sector of the intersection belonging to the current cell as visited (*true*)
   output the cell description.

end.

Figure 6.25 Algorithm for computing a cell decomposition.

form all the half-plane constraints of the two relations into line equations. These lines decompose the 2D plane into convex cells. Since a cell is not intersected by any constraint (line), each cell is either entirely inside or entirely outside of any of the regions R_1 and R_2. This means that both R_1 and R_2 are unions of cells. Second, check for each cell whether it belongs to R_1 and/or R_2, and return the cells belonging to R_1 but not R_2.

An algorithm for computing a cell decomposition is shown in Figure 6.25. For a set of n lines, it first sets up in two $n \times n$ matrices a data structure that allows us to find for a given intersection on any line its neighbor intersections in constant time. It then builds cell descriptions by walking in clockwise direction along the boundary of a cell. Each vertex of a cell that is passed consumes one sector of an intersection (see Figure 6.24). An intersection between two lines has four sectors (ignoring degenerate cases such as multiple lines intersecting in the same point). For an intersection between lines l_i and l_j, the two sectors given by sweeping from l_i to l_j in clockwise direction are maintained at matrix entry N_{ij}, the other two at N_{ji}. A sector consumed at a cell is marked (*visited* = *true*) at its matrix entry. The algorithm terminates when all sectors have been marked visited and hence, been consumed at cells.

The time complexity of Algorithm 6.7 is as follows. Step 1 takes $O(n)$ time; step 2 takes $O(n^2)$ time. Due to the sorting, step 3 needs $O(n^2 \log n)$ time. Step 4 again requires $O(n^2)$ time. Step 5 needs constant time per sector processed, hence, also $O(n^2)$. Thus, the total time complexity is $O(n^2 \log n)$, and the algorithm requires $O(n^2)$ space.

Once the cell decomposition is given, computing the difference is easy (but costly). For each cell, check whether an interior point is contained in any of the symbolic tuples of R_1 and/or R_2. Since there are $O(n^2)$ cells that need to be checked against n constraints in R_1 and R_2, the total time complexity for computing the difference is $O(n^3)$.

6.4 Further Exercises

Exercise 6.4 Infinite Relations

In this assignment we model a public transport network with bus and train routes using nested relations. Buses and trains are moving points on a network of bus stops and train stations.

1. Define the relations `station` and `vehicle` containing the needed spatial or spatio-temporal information as nested relations and some string attributes identifying lines, vehicles and stations.
2. Formulate a query to create a new relation `transit(name: string, line1: string, line2: string)`. In other words, find all places where you can

change from one line to another. Keep in mind that some time is needed for this transit. Hence, we will search for connections with more than 5 minutes but less than 10 minutes between arrival and departure.

3. Find all connections between St. Paul's and Victoria Station starting at 5:00 P.M. with exactly one change of vehicles and order them by the time used for the trip.

Exercise 6.5 Linear Constraints

1. In the following figure, a line l and a region r consisting of three parts are displayed. Write down the symbolic relations for both l and r.

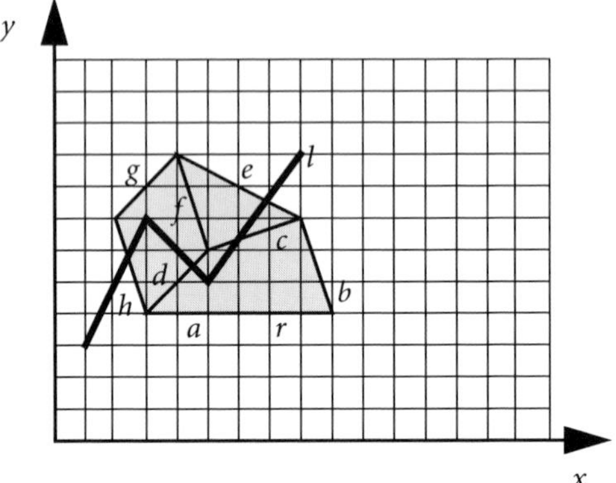

2. The intersection of l and r is computed by $l \cap r$. In a first step, write down the symbolic relation for $l \cap r$. Afterward simplify the tuples. Finally, a simplification should be done on the tuples among each other.

3. The following figure shows a 3D object. Determine the symbolic relation for the object.

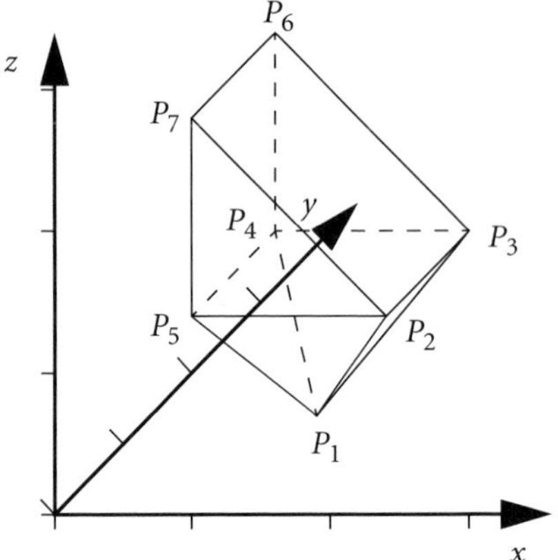

$P_1 = (6, 2.5, 0), P_2 = (9, 2, 5), P_3 = (9, 5, 5), P_4 = (3, 5, 5),$
$P_5 = (3, 2, 5), P_6 = (3, 5, 12), P_7 = (3, 2, 12)$

Exercise 6.6 Monotone Polygons

Decompose the following simple polygon into monotone polygons using Algorithm 6.4 and insert the split edges and the polygon identifiers for the resulting decomposition.

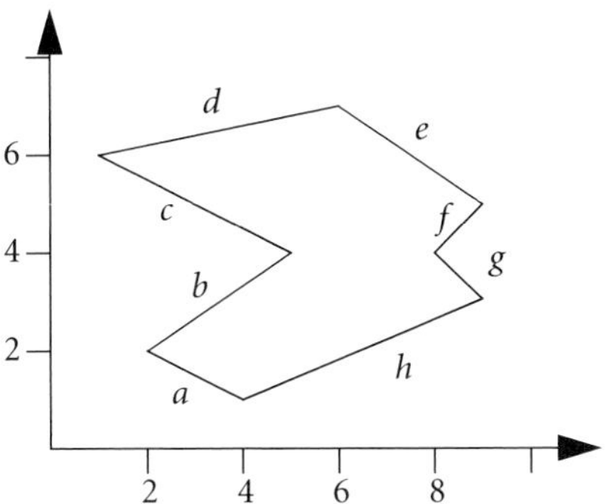

6.5 Bibliographic Notes

The concept of constraint databases was proposed in articles by Kanellakis et al., 1990; Kanellakis et al., 1995. A book covering the subject has been written by Revesz, 2002. Many branches of research on constraint databases are described in Kuper et al., 2000.

Our description in Chapter 6 is mostly based on the articles by Grumbach and colleagues, the team developing the Dedale prototype (Grumbach et al., 1997, 1998, 2000, 2001; and Rigaux et al., 2003). Grumbach et al., 1997, 1998, provide the basic model and implementation design; Grumbach et al., 2001, focus on spatio-temporal applications; and Grumbach et al., 2000, show how interpolated data can be handled in the constraint framework in a generic way. The concept covers such diverse applications as modeling and querying elevation data and moving objects. A nice overview of the research of this group is given in Rigaux et al., 2003. The linear constraint model is also described in Chapter 4 of the book by Rigaux et al., 2002. Some of the relevant algorithms (our Section 6.3) are described in Chapter 5 of that book.

Infinite relations as a conceptual model, similar in spirit to Section 6.1, are described in Chapter 1 of Revesz, 2002. A nested relational model with one level of nesting, similar to the one presented in Section 6.1.2, is used in Dedale. A similar nested relational model is used in Belussi et al., 1997.

The Fourier-Motzkin variable elimination technique for inequalities is described, for example, in Schrijver, 1986.

The original model of Kanellakis et al., 1990, 1995, uses polynomial constraints. A study on the advantages and drawbacks of restricting to linear constraints is given in Vandeurzen et al., 1995. A deep study of what is and is not expressible in the linear constraint model with first-order logic as a query language is given in Vandeurzen's Ph.D. thesis (1999); see also Vandeurzen et al., 2001.

Further work on constraint databases addressing specifically spatio-temporal or moving objects applications includes Chomicki and Revesz, 1997; Chomicki and Revesz, 1999; Su et al., 2001; and Mokhtar et al., 2002. Chomicki and Revesz, 1997, briefly mention a model that has polygons whose vertices move linearly with time. Chomicki and Revesz, 1999, consider simple geometric entities whose temporal development can be described by affine mappings and study closure properties of such structures under operations. Moving point objects with a focus on modeling concepts such as speed and acceleration are discussed in Su et al., 2001. Mokhtar et al., 2002, develop a general distance-based query language and an efficient evaluation technique by plane-sweep.

The description of the implementation of the constraint model in Section 6.3 is generally based on the work of the Dedale group; the implementation aspects are described in Grumbach et al., 1997; Rigaux et al., 2003. The storage of constraint relations (Sections 6.3.1 and 6.3.2) is described in Rigaux et al., 2003, Section 5.2. The algorithm for decomposing into an optimal number of convex polygons, with running time $O(r^2 n \log n)$, can be found in Keil, 1985.

The algorithm for decomposing into monotone polygons is due to Lee and Preparata, 1977, Section 5. It was worked out in a little more detail here. Based on this, Garey et al., 1978, proposed the algorithm for triangulating monotone polygons. Alternative algorithms for triangulation were described by Hertel and Mehlhorn, 1983; Mehlhorn, 1984, Section VIII.4.2; and Chazelle, 1991, who finally discovered an optimal algorithm running in $O(n)$ time. The technique for building convex polygons from a triangulation and Theorem 6.1 are described in Hertel and Mehlhorn, 1983; Mehlhorn, 1984, Section VIII.4.2.

The algorithm for intersection of convex polygons is due to Shamos and Hoey, 1976, and is also described in Preparata and Shamos, 1991, Section 7.2.1. The reduction of half-plane intersection to intersection of convex polygons (algorithm *HPI*) and algorithm *NORMALIZE* are described in Rigaux et al., 2003, Section 5.3. The implementation of algebra operations, Section 6.3.5, is also taken from Rigaux et al., 2003, Section 5.3. The algorithm for difference is described in more detail in Grumbach et al., 1997, Section 5.

7 Spatio-Temporal Indexing

The design and construction of *index structures* has always been an intensive and extensive research topic in the database field. The main task of an index structure is to ensure fast access to single or several records in a database on the basis of a search key and thus avoid an otherwise necessary sequential scan through a file. For this purpose, index structures provide some particular operations to support special query types: *exact match queries*, *range queries*, and *sequential access*. These query types play an important role in query processing. For standard, alphanumeric data, a number of index structures have been proposed, including the indexed sequential method (ISAM), tree-based index structures (e.g., B-tree, B^+-tree, B^*-tree), and hash-based index structures (e.g., external static, dynamic, extensible, or linear hashing).

Emerging nonstandard applications, such as multimedia, medical, weather, environmental, bioinformatics, and astrophysics applications, are based on more and more complex data and algorithms and require new, sophisticated indexing techniques. As we have seen in previous chapters, spatial and spatio-temporal data also belong to this category. For spatial data, many *geometric index structures* have been devised as multidimensional *spatial access methods* (SAMs). These structures do not include the time aspect. For temporal (standard) data, *temporal index structures* have been proposed to index valid and/or transaction times. These structures do not consider any spatial aspect. They mainly deal with stepwise constant (i.e., discretely changing data). For example, the salary of an employee changes from time to time at certain instants but remains constant in between. Both kinds of index structures form the basis for the current approaches on *spatio-temporal index structures*, which are the topic of this chapter. Their goal is, in particular, to index continuous movements of spatial objects. The advancements in this area are very rapid, and it is difficult to keep pace with new developments in a book.

In Section 7.1, we give an overview of some needed geometric concepts that form the basis of the spatio-temporal index structures described in this chapter. Section 7.2 describes the specific requirements of moving objects index structures that have to cope with the motion of spatial objects. It also summarizes some of the earlier, limited approaches for indexing spatio-temporal data. Section 7.3 then focuses on recent proposals for indexing current and near-future movement. Finally, Section 7.4 deals with recent approaches for indexing trajectories in the past.

7.1 Geometric Preliminaries

To make this chapter self-contained and to be able to understand the approaches of spatio-temporal index structures described in this chapter, we present some purely geometric concepts as their basis. These concepts include the R-tree family (Section 7.1.1), the technique of duality transformation (Section 7.1.2), external partition trees (Section 7.1.3), catalog structures (Section 7.1.4), external priority search trees (Section 7.1.5), and external range trees (Section 7.1.6).

7.1.1 Indexing Multidimensional Space with the R-tree Family

One of the first, most important, and most popular SAMs designed to support extended spatial objects is the R-tree. The R-tree and its later variants, the R^*-tree and the R^+-tree, are height-balanced trees and natural extensions of the B-tree for k dimensions. Spatial objects are represented by their *minimum bounding box* (MBB), also called *minimum bounding rectangle* (MBR). The MBB of a spatial object s is the smallest, axis-parallel rectangle (in k dimensions) enclosing s; hence, it forms an approximation of s. The SAMs of the R-tree family are data driven (i.e., their structure adapts itself to the MBB distribution in k dimensions). As with the B-tree, each tree node, whether internal or leaf, is mapped onto a disk page. But while B-trees are built on keys upon which a total order is defined, R-trees organize their MBBs according to a topological containment relation. Each node is associated with a k-dimensional box, which represents the MBB of all MBBs of its child nodes.

The R-tree

R-trees are characterized by the following properties:

- Every node contains between m and M entries. The two parameters are chosen in such a way that $0 < m \leq M/2$ holds.
- For each entry (*mbb*, *nodeid*) of a nonleaf node, *mbb* is the MBB that spatially contains the MBBs in the child node pointed to by the node identifier *nodeid*.

- For each entry (*mbb*, *oid*) of a leaf node, *mbb* is the MBB that spatially contains the *k*-dimensional object pointed to by the object identifier *oid*.
- The root node has at least two entries and thus children, unless it is a leaf node.
- All leaves are at the same level.

An object identifier *oid* and a node identifier *nodeid* contain the addresses of the object and the tree node, respectively, in the database. Figure 7.1 shows a collection of 14 spatial objects indexed by their MBBs as well as the corresponding R-tree with $m = 2$ and $M = 4$. The MBBs of the leaf nodes *a*, *b*, *c*, and *d* are represented by a dashed line. We see that MBBs at the same level of the R-tree may overlap; they do not constitute an exact partition of the space. Each MBB of a node (except the root node) must be properly contained in and assigned to a unique MBB of a parent node.

The maximal number *M* of entries in a node depends on the entry length *e* and the *disk page capacity*, *p* (i.e., $M = \lfloor p/e \rfloor$). The maximum number of levels (i.e., the depth) of an R-tree indexing a collection of *N* spatial objects is at most $\lfloor log_m(N) \rfloor - 1$ and at least $\lfloor log_M(N) \rfloor - 1$. In the worst case, there will be a node-space utilization of m/M, except for the root.

Search operations such as point and range queries are processed in a top-down recursive manner. The query point or query region is first tested against each entry (*mbb*, *nodeid*) in the root node. If the query point is located inside *mbb* or if the query region overlaps with *mbb*, the search algorithm is applied recursively to the entries pointed to by the child node identifiers. This process stops after reaching the leaves of the R-tree. The entries in the determined leaf nodes are used to retrieve the corresponding objects. Due to overlapping MBBs at each level of an R-tree, a query

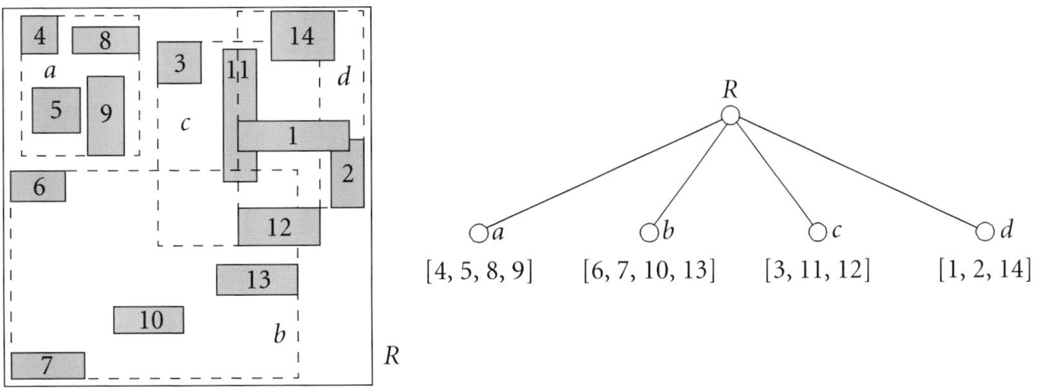

Figure 7.1 A collection of spatial objects and its R-tree representation.

point can lie in several of them and a query region can overlap several of them. This means that the search path is not unique and that the search algorithm usually has to follow several search paths in the R-tree.

Search performance depends on two parameters: coverage and overlap. The *coverage* of a level of the tree is the total area covered by all MBBs of all nodes at that level. Hence, the coverage is an indirect measure of the dead or empty space area covered by the tree if we relate it to the sum of the areas of the indexed spatial objects. The *overlap* of a level of the tree is the total space area covered by more than one bounding box associated with the nodes at that level. Overlapping bounding boxes may necessitate a visit of more than one path of the tree to find an object. Hence, a minimization of the degree of overlap is a worthwhile goal. However, the overlap problem in the R-tree implies that a worst-case performance of search operations cannot be determined, even if we aim at minimizing the overlap.

For inserting an object, the tree is first traversed top-down, beginning at the root and ending at a leaf. At each level of the R-tree, we either find one or several nodes whose MBB contains the object's MBB, or we find that there is no such node. In the former case, if several nodes can be selected, we take one of them; otherwise, we take the only one. In the latter case, we choose a node such that the enlargement of its MBB is minimal. In both cases, we repeat this process recursively until a leaf is reached. If the leaf node is not full, a new entry (*mbb*, *oid*) is added to the node associated with the leaf. If the MBB of the leaf has to be enlarged, the MBB of the parent node must be updated too. It can happen that such an enlargement of the MBB of a leaf has to be propagated up the tree, in the worst case up to its root. If the leaf node is full, a split occurs. The node-split algorithm is rather complex and is not described here.

The R^*-tree

We have described a minimization of the coverage and the overlap as worthwhile goals to improve the performance of the R-tree. The overlap minimization is even more critical than the coverage minimization. The R^*-tree is a variant of the R-tree that provides several improvements to the insertion algorithm. In the two-dimensional space it relies on a combined parameter optimization of node overlapping, the area covered by a node, and the perimeter of a node's MBB. The latter parameter considers the shape of the MBB, since, given a fixed area, the shape that minimizes the rectangle perimeter is the square. There are no well-founded techniques to simultaneously minimize all three parameters. Instead, experiments with several heuristics are performed.

The R^+-tree

In the R^+-tree, the MBBs at a given level do not overlap but are disjoint. Consequently, for a point query a single, unique path is followed from the root to a leaf. To achieve nonoverlapping MBBs for areal spatial objects, their MBBs may be split by several MBBs in nonleaf nodes of the tree. If an object MBB is split by two or more MBBs in higher-level nodes of the R$^+$-tree, each of the entries associated with those inner node MBBs will have a descendant leaf node that points to that object. Unlike the previous variants, the run-time complexity of this operation is bounded by the height of this tree. The properties of an R$^+$-tree are as follows:

- The MBB of each nonleaf node contains all MBBs of its subtrees.
- An MBB of a spatial object to be indexed is assigned to all leaf nodes whose MMBs it overlaps or to the leaf node in whose MBB it is contained.
- The MBBs of two nodes at the same level do not overlap.
- The root has at least two entries, unless it is a leaf.
- All leaves are at the same level.

Figure 7.2 depicts an R$^+$-tree. We observe that both at the nonleaf level and at the leaf level, the MBBs of nodes are not overlapping. MBB 1 is overlapping the leaves *p* and *q*, and the MBBs of *p* and *q* are (and have to be) disjoint. Because MBBs can be duplicated, an R$^+$-tree can be significantly larger than the R*-tree constructed on the same data set. The construction and maintenance of the R$^+$-tree are algorithmically considerably more complex than that of the R-tree and the R*-tree. To insert a spatial object, its MBB is inserted in all nodes of the MBBs it overlaps. Nonoverlapping MBBs at the same level are achieved by *clipping*. When an MBB *mbb* to be inserted overlaps several node MBBs $\{mbb_1, \ldots, mbb_n\}$, *mbb* is split into a collection of MBBs, one for each mbb_i it overlaps, and it is recursively inserted along each of the paths starting at these mbb_is. Consequently, the same MBB will be kept in several

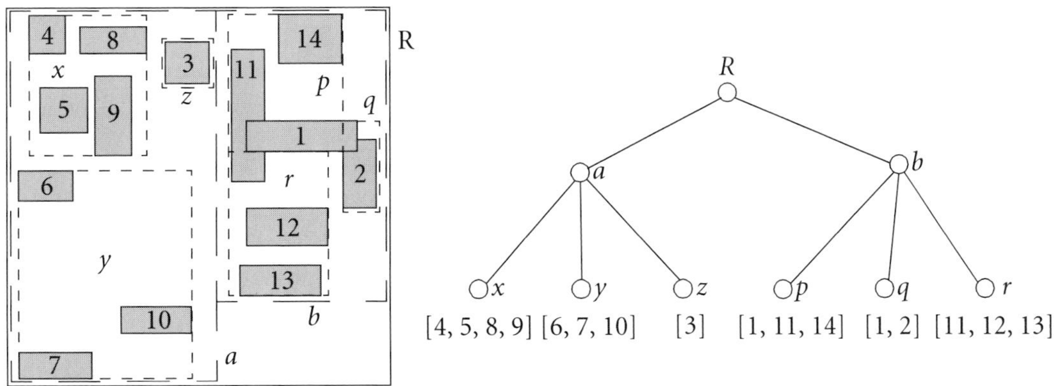

Figure 7.2 A collection of spatial objects and its R$^+$-tree representation.

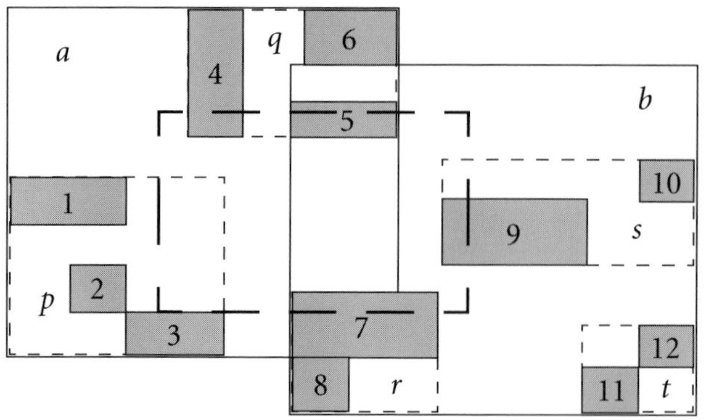

Figure 7.3 A collection of spatial objects to be indexed.

leaf nodes of the tree. This may increase the height of the tree, but search operations will be performed more efficiently.

Exercise 7.1 For the set of leaf and nonleaf nodes in Figure 7.3, determine to which member of the R-tree family this diagram belongs, draw the corresponding tree representation, and list the nodes searched by the bold dashed query rectangle. First-level nodes are *a* and *b*. Second-level nodes are *p*, *q*, *r*, *s*, and *t*. Leaf nodes include 1, 2, ..., 12. ■

7.1.2 Duality

Duality is a powerful technique used in geometric algorithms. It leverages the fact that in the plane both a point and a line can be described by two parameters. A point is given by its *x*- and *y*-coordinates; a line has a slope and an intercept with the *y*-axis. Therefore, we can map a set of points to a set of lines, and vice versa, in a one-to-one manner. Such a mapping is called a *duality transform(ation)*. It is not defined for vertical lines. This case can be handled separately and is usually not a problem. The image of an object (point or line) σ under a duality transform is called the *dual* σ^* of the object. For example, the dual p^* of a point $p := (a, b) \in \mathbb{R}^2$ can be defined as the line $p^* := (y = ax - b)$, and the dual l^* of the line l with $y = ax + b$ is then the point p such that $p^* = l$ (i.e., $l^* := (a, -b) \in \mathbb{R}^2$).

We also say that a duality transform maps objects from the *primal plane* to the *dual plane*. This mapping can even be defined in such a way that certain properties of a set of points in the primal plane translate to certain other (e.g., equal) properties for a set of lines in the dual plane. Let p be a point in the plane, and let l be a nonvertical line in the plane. A duality transform $o \rightarrow o^*$ is then *incidence preserving* (i.e., $p \in l$ if, and only if, $l^* \in p^*$) and it is *order preserving* (i.e., p lies above [respectively below, on] l if, and only if, l^* lies above [respectively below, on] p^*). The dual of a strip σ is a vertical line segment σ^* in the sense that a point p lies

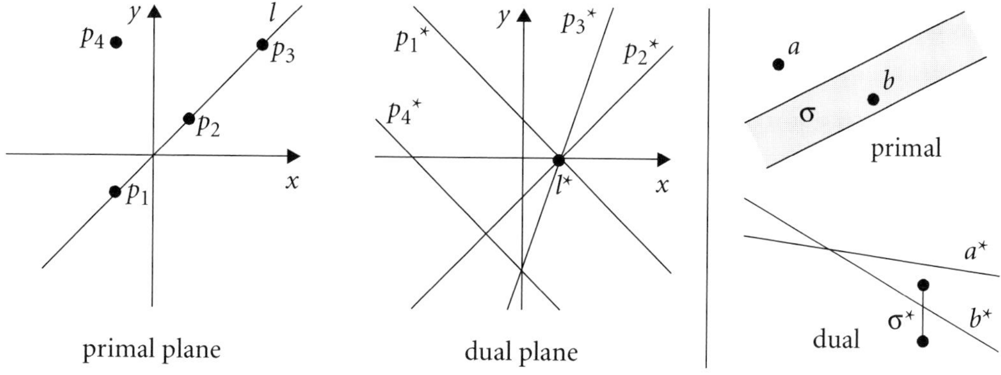

Figure 7.4 The duality transformation.

inside σ if, and only if, the dual line p^* intersects σ^*. Figure 7.4 illustrates these properties. The three points p_1, p_2, and p_3 lie on the line l in the primal plane, and the three lines $p_1{}^*$, $p_2{}^*$, and $p_3{}^*$ go through the point l^* in the dual plane. The point p_4 is located above the line l in the primal plane, and the point l^* lies above the line $p_4{}^*$ in the dual plane. The point b is situated in the strip σ, and the dual line b^* intersects σ^*.

Now that we have seen how the principle of duality works, the question remains how it can be useful. In order to solve a problem in the primal plane, we can solve it in the dual plane, in particular, if it is easier to compute there, and mimic the solution to the dual problem in the primal plane. The reason is that the primal and dual problems are essentially the same. Another advantage is that transforming a problem to the dual plane can provide a new perspective from a different angle and give the insight needed to solve it.

Exercise 7.2 The duality transform can also be applied to objects other than points and lines. Consider a segment $s = (p, q)$, where p and q are the end points of s. What is the dual s^* of s? Assume a line l intersecting s. Where is its dual l^* located with respect to s^*?

7.1.3 External Partition Tree

Partition trees are a popular data structure for geometric range searching and exist both in an internal and an external memory setting. They are based on the concept of simplicial partitions. For a set S of N points in the Euclidean plane $\mathbb{R}^2$, a *simplicial partition* of S is a set $\Pi = \{(S_1, \Delta_1), \ldots, (S_r, \Delta_r)\}$ where $\{S_1, \ldots, S_r\}$ is a partitioning of S into disjoint subsets, and Δ_i is a triangle that contains all the points in S_i.

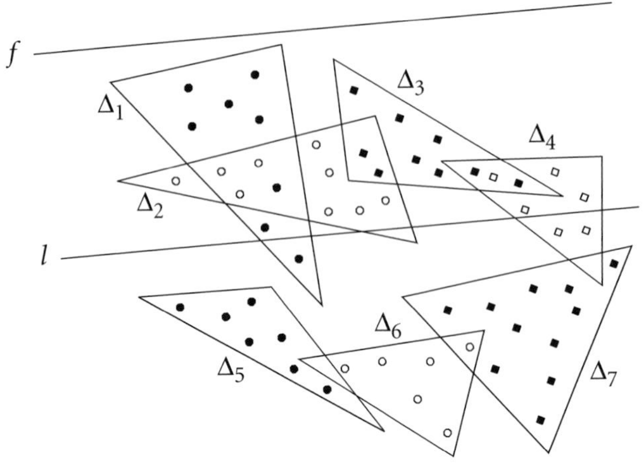

Figure 7.5 A simplicial partition.

A point of S may lie in many triangles, but it is assigned to only one subset S_i (Figure 7.5). The *size* r of Π is the number of subset-triangle pairs. A simplicial partition is called *balanced* if each subset S_i contains not more than $2N/r$ points (i.e., $|S_i| \leq 2N/r$). In other words, in balanced simplicial partitions, none of the triangles contains more than twice the average number of points of the triangles. The *crossing number* of a simplicial partition is the maximum number of triangles that can be crossed by a single line.

Exercise 7.3 What is the size of the simplicial partition in Figure 7.5? Is this simplicial partition balanced? What is its crossing number? ■

The question remains regarding how simplicial partitions and crossing numbers can be used. A possible application is to answer half-plane queries. If a triangle Δ_i of the partition is not crossed by the bounding line of a query half-plane h, then its associated point set S_i either lies completely in h or is completely disjoint from h. Hence, we only have to check those point sets S_i, for which Δ_i is crossed by the bounding line of h. For example, if we queried with the half-plane lying above l in Figure 7.5, we would have to investigate three of the seven point sets. The efficiency of the query processing therefore depends on the crossing number of the simplicial partition. The lower the crossing number is, the better the query response time is. It has been shown that for a given set S of N points in the plane, a parameter $s = O(B)$, and $n = N/B$, one can construct in time $O(ns)$ a balanced simplicial partition Π of size $O(s)$ for S such that the crossing number of Π is $O(\sqrt{s})$.

For building a partition tree T for S, we apply a recursive construction scheme. We associate each node v in a partition tree with a subset $S_v \subseteq S$ of points and a triangle Δ_v. Hence, the root of the tree contains the whole set $S_{root} = S$ and a triangle Δ_{root} that contains all $N_{root} = N$ points of S. Let $N_v = |S_v|$ and $n_v = \lceil N_v/B \rceil$, where B is the block size (i.e., the number of points that fit into a disk block). Hence, $n_{root} = n = \lceil N/B \rceil$. The subtree rooted at v can be constructed as follows. If $N_v \leq B$, then S_v fits into a single block, and v becomes a leaf node. Otherwise, v becomes an internal node of degree $r_v = \min(cB, 2n_v)$ for some constant $c \geq 1$. We compute a balanced simplicial partition $\Pi_v = \{(S_1, \Delta_1), \ldots, (S_{r_v}, \Delta_{r_v})\}$ for S_v with crossing number $O(\sqrt{r_v})$, and then recursively construct a partition tree T_i for each subset S_i and triangle Δ_i. For each i, we store the vertices of triangle Δ_i and a pointer to T_i in v; the root of T_i is the ith child of v and is associated with S_i and Δ_i. We need $O(c) = O(1)$ blocks to store any node v. The choice of r_v assures that every leaf node contains $\Theta(B)$ points. Hence, the height of the partition tree is $O(\log_B n)$, and, since the tree contains $O(n)$ nodes, it uses $O(n)$ disk blocks. The total construction time requires $O(N \log_B n)$ disk accesses.

For querying, the following question is of interest: Find all points inside a query strip σ. For this, we visit T in a top-down manner, assuming we are at node v. If v is a leaf, we report all points of S_v that lie inside σ. Otherwise, we test each triangle Δ_i of Π_v. If Δ_i lies completely outside σ, we ignore it. If Δ_i lies completely inside σ, we traverse the ith subtree of v and report all points in S_i. Finally, if σ crosses Δ_i, we recursively visit the ith child of v. Each point in σ is reported exactly once. We can show that, given a set S of N points in $\mathbb{R}^2$ and a parameter $\varepsilon > 0$, S can be preprocessed into an index of size $O(n)$ blocks so that the points inside a query strip can be found in $O(n_v^{1/2+\varepsilon} + k)$ disk accesses, where k is the number of points found.

Exercise 7.4 Construct the first two levels of the partition tree given by the simplicial partition in Figure 7.5. Find all points inside the query strip bounded by the lines f and l. Mark the nodes of the partition tree depending on whether a node is selected, visited, or not visited. Indicate which nodes of the second level are recursively visited. ■

Insertions and deletions are treated by the technique of *partial rebuilding*. At each node v in the tree, we store the number N_v of points in its subtree. To insert a new point p into the subtree rooted at v, we first increment N_v. If v is a leaf, we add p to S_v. Otherwise, there is a triangle d in the simplicial partition Π_v so that p is located in d, and p is recursively inserted into the corresponding subtree. In case more than one triangle in Π_v contains p, we choose the one whose subtree is smallest. The deletion process is similar. The difference is that it has to know the leaf of the tree that stores the point to be deleted. This can be achieved by maintaining a separate dictionary, which, for each point p, records the index of the leaf containing p. It can be shown that the index can be constructed in $O(N \log_B n)$ disk accesses, and points can be inserted or deleted at an amortized cost of $O(\log^2_B n)$ disk accesses each.

Occasionally, in order to ensure the same query time as in the static case, we have to rebuild parts of the partition tree after an update and balance them. A node u is *unbalanced* if it has a child v such that either $N_v < N_u/2r_u$ or $N_v > 4N_u/r_u$; in particular, the parent of a leaf v is unbalanced if either $N_v < B/4$ or $N_v > 2B$. The constants 2 and 4 have been chosen arbitrarily here. Each insertion or deletion of a point is followed by a rebalancing if necessary; we rebuild the subtree rooted at the unbalanced node closest to the root. Rebuilding the subtree rooted at any node v requires $O(N_v \log_B n_v)$ disk accesses, and the counter N_v is incremented or decremented $\Omega(N_v)$ times between rebuilds. Hence, the amortized cost of modifying N_v is $O(\log_B n_v)$ disk accesses. Since each insertion or deletion changes $O(\log_B n)$ counters, the overall amortized cost of an insertion or deletion is $O(\log_B^2 n)$ disk accesses

7.1.4 Catalog Structure

A *catalog structure* can be used to answer three-sided range queries on a set S of B^2 points[1] using $O(1 + k)$ disk accesses. Let the points (x_i, y_i) in S be sorted in increasing x-coordinate order. The catalog structure C consists of $2B - 1$ blocks $b_1, b_2, \ldots, b_{2B-1}$ storing the points. In addition, it includes a constant number of *catalog blocks*. With each block b_i we associate a rectangle $[x_{l_i}, x_{r_i}] \times [y_{d_i}, y_{u_i}]$. The catalog blocks store these $2B - 1$ rectangles. Block b_i contains a point $(x_j, y_j) \in S$ if, and only if, the point lies inside or directly above the block's rectangle (i.e., $x_{l_i} \leq x_j \leq x_{r_i}$ and $y_{d_i} \leq y_j$).

The construction of the blocks b_i begins with the initial creation of B blocks $b_1, b_2, \ldots, b_B$. For each $1 \leq i \leq B$, the rectangle associated with b_i has left x-coordinate $x_{(i-1)B+1}$, right x-coordinate x_{iB}, and bottom y-coordinate $-\infty$. This means that b_i comprises the points $(x_{(i-1)B+1}, y_{(i-1)B+1}), \ldots, (x_{iB}, y_{iB})$. In the next step, we sweep a horizontal line upward from $y = -\infty$, and for each block b_i we simultaneously count the number of points in b_i lying above the sweep line. When the sweep line reaches a point (x_j, y_j) such that two consecutive blocks b_i and b_{i+1} both have fewer than $B/2$ points lying above the line $y = y_j$, the upper y-coordinate of the rectangles associated with b_i and b_{i+1} is set to y_j. The blocks b_i and b_{i+1} are then not considered anymore during the sweep, but a new block b_r is created whose rectangle has left x-coordinate x_{l_i}, right x-coordinate $x_{r_{i+1}}$, and bottom y-coordinate y_j. Consequently, b_r contains the most B points that lie above the line $y = y_j$. The sweep proceeds in this manner until the line reaches $y = +\infty$. At that point, at most $B + (B - 1) = 2B - 1$ blocks have been created. Figure 7.6(a) gives an example. The construction of the entire catalog structure takes $O(B)$ disk accesses.

For answering a three-sided query of the form $[a, b] \times [c, \infty[$, first the catalog blocks are loaded into main memory in constant time. Then all blocks are determined whose associated rectangle intersects the bottom edge $[a, b] \times c$ of the query

[1] The catalog structure will be used as a component of another data structure described in Section 7.1.5. Then it will become clear why it makes sense to have a data structure that stores exactly B^2 points.

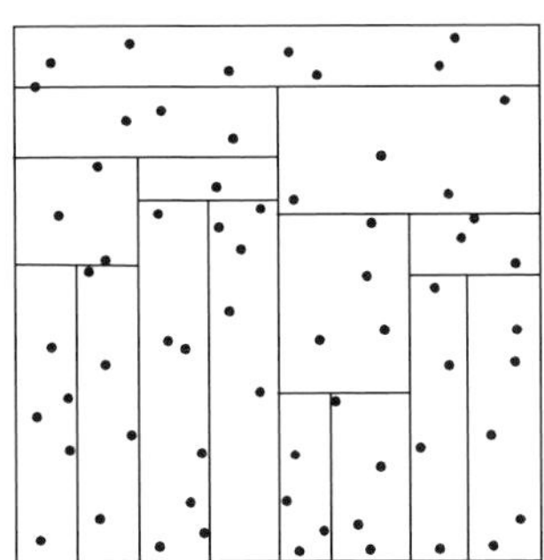

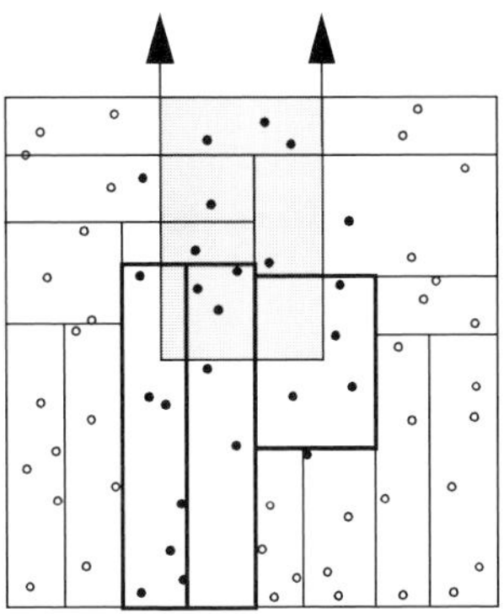

Figure 7.6 An example catalog structure with $B = 8$. Each block contains the points inside or above its rectangle (a); the blocks loaded during the query process are shown by the bold rectangles and contain the solid points (b).

range. These blocks are loaded into main memory one at a time, and the relevant points are reported. The query requires $O(1 + k)$ disk accesses, since every consecutive pair of blocks, except possibly for the blocks containing a and b, contributes at least $B/2$ points to the result. Figure 7.6(b) illustrates this.

The structure can be made dynamic by the concept of *global rebuilding*. The strategy is to log updates in an additional block U. After B updates U is full, and the complete structure is reconstructed from scratch in $O(B)$ disk accesses. Hence, the amortized cost of any insertion or deletion is $O(1)$ disk accesses. For each query we spend an extra disk access and check U to ensure that query results are consistent with recorded updates.

7.1.5 External Priority Search Tree

We discuss the linear space *external priority search tree* and focus on answering three-sided queries of the form $[a, b] \times [c, \infty[$ on a set S of N points in $O(\log_B n + k)$ disk accesses, where $n = \lceil N/B \rceil$. The structure uses a base B-tree on the x-coordinates of the points in S. The fanout of the tree is assumed to be B. Each internal node v stores an x-range X_v, which is subdivided into *slabs* by the x-ranges of its children. The highest B points of each child (slab) v_i of v, which have not been stored in ancestors of v, are stored in an auxiliary catalog structure C_v (Section 7.1.4); it uses $O(B)$ blocks and supports three-sided queries and updates in $O(1 + k)$ disk accesses. Hence, we store $O(B^2)$ points in C_v. Since every point is stored in exactly one catalog structure, the external priority search tree requires $O(n)$ blocks.

Given a three-sided query of the form $q = [a, b] \times [c, \infty[$, we answer it by starting at the root of the external priority search tree and traversing the tree recursively to

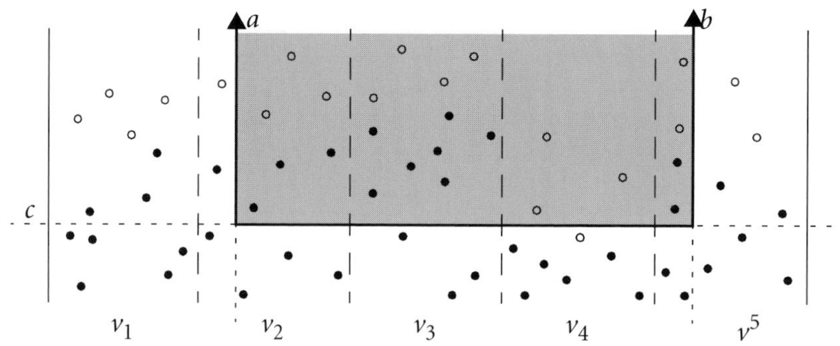

Figure 7.7 Shown are the slabs $v_1, \ldots, v_5$ corresponding to a node v in the external priority search tree. The highest B points in each slab (shown in white) are stored in C_v; the other (black) points are stored recursively. To answer the query, we search in C_v for the relevant marked white points and then recursively search in the slabs v_2, v_3, and v_5 for the relevant black points.

the appropriate subtree. At each node v, we query the catalog structure C_v to find the points of $C_v \cap q$. If a or b lies in X_{v_i} or if the x-coordinates of at least B points of $C_v \cap q$ lie in X_{v_i}, we recursively proceed at v_i. Figure 7.7 gives an example. During the query only $O(\log_B n)$ nodes v are visited because a or b lies in X_v. For every other node v, the query procedure reports at least B points at the parent of v whose x-coordinates lie in X_v. Consequently, it reports all K points in q in $O(\log_B n + k)$ disk accesses. Since a catalog structure can be updated in $O(1)$ disk accesses, it can be shown that the external priority search tree can be updated in $O(\log_B n)$ disk accesses.

7.1.6 External Range Tree

The *external range tree* R is a three-level structure. Let S be a set of N points in the plane $\mathbb{R}^2$. The primary structure belonging to R is a tree over the x-coordinates of the N points in S, which is organized similar to a B-tree and has a fanout r chosen to be $r = \log_B n$. In a natural way each node v represents an x-range X_v. The children $v_1, v_2, \ldots, v_r$ of v subdivide this range into $\log_B n$ slabs. The x-coordinates of slab boundaries are stored in a B-tree so that the slab containing a query point can be found in $O(\log_B \log_B n)$ disk accesses. Let $S_v \subseteq S$ be the set of N_v points whose x-coordinates lie in the x-range X_v. S_v is stored in four secondary data structures associated with v. One of these structures is a B-tree B_v on S_v; it uses the y-coordinates of its points as the keys. The three other structures are external priority search trees (Section 7.1.5).

An external priority search tree is employed to answer three-sided range queries in $O(\log_B n + k)$ disk accesses (i.e., it can report the points lying in a rectangle of the form $[a, b] \times [c, \infty[)$. The first two priority search trees, denoted by $P^]{(v)}$ and $P^[(v)$, store the points in S_v such that range queries of the forms $]-\infty, a] \times [b, c]$ and $[a, \infty[\times [b, c]$ can be answered in $O(\log_B n + k)$ disk accesses. The third priority search tree $P^{\div}(v)$ stores points with respect to the y-coordinates of the points in S_v as follows. Assume that $p = (x_p, y_p) \in S_v$ is a point lying in the jth slab (i.e., $p \in S_{v_j}$). If p is not the point with the maximum y-coordinate in S_{v_j}, let $q = (x_q, y_q) \in S_{v_j}$ be the successor of p in the positive y-direction. Next, we map point p to the point $p^* = (y_p, y_q)$. Let S_v^* be the resulting set of points for all points $p \in S_v$. $P^{\div}(v)$ is constructed in such a way that all t points lying in a range of the form $]-\infty, a] \times [a, \infty[$ can be reported in $O(\log_B n + t/B)$ disk accesses. A point $p^* = (y_p, y_q)$ lies in such a range if, and only if, the y-interval $[y_p, y_q]$ intersects the horizontal line $y = c$ (see Figure 7.8). Because only one such interval exists within each slab, we can conclude that $t = \log_B n$. In addition to each point p^* stored in $P^{\div}(v)$, we also store a pointer to the leaf of B_{v_j}, which stores the corresponding point p of S_{v_j}. Since external priority search trees and B-trees use linear space, and since each point p is stored in secondary structures of all the $O(\log_{\log_B n} n) = O(\log_B n/(\log_B \log_B n))$ nodes on the path from the root to the leaf node storing the x-coordinate of p, the structures use $O(n \log_B n/(\log_B \log_B n))$ blocks in total.

External range trees can be used to find the points inside a query rectangle $q = (a, b, c, d)$ in $O(\log_B n + k)$ disk accesses as follows. In $O(\log_B n/(\log_B \log_B n)) \times O(\log_B \log_B n) = O(\log_B n)$ disk accesses the highest node v in R is found so that a and b lie in different slabs of v. Let us assume that a lies in the x-range of v_i and b in the x-range of v_j. The query rectangle q can be decomposed into three parts: $q^[= ([a, b] \cap X_{v_i}) \times [c, d]$, $q^] = ([a, b] \cap X_{v_j}) \times [c, d]$, and $q^{\div} = q \backslash (q^[\cup q^])$ (compare to Figure 7.8). The points contained in $q^[$ and $q^]$ can be reported in $O(\log_B n + k)$ disk accesses using $P^[(v_i)$ and $P^](v_j)$, respectively. To determine the points in $q^{\div}$, we first investigate $P^{\div}(v)$ with $]-\infty, c] \times [c, \infty[$ to find in each S_{v_l} for $i < l < j$ the lowest point that lies in $q^{\div}$ (and thus the pointer to the corresponding point in B_{v_l}). The B-trees B_{v_l} enable the report of all points of $S_{v_l} \cap q^{\div}$. The total number of needed disk accesses is $O(\log_B n + k)$.

An update on the external range tree requires $O(1)$ updates on the secondary structures on each of the $O(\log_B n/(\log_B \log_B n))$ levels of the base tree. Each update requires $O(\log_B N)$ disk accesses, because the external priority search tree can be updated in $O(\log_B n)$ disk accesses. We also need to update the primary structure. As an improvement, it can be shown that insertion or deletion of points can also be performed in $O(\log^2{}_B n/(\log_B \log_B n))$ disk accesses each.

7.2 Requirements for Indexing Moving Objects

What is special with spatio-temporal indexing and especially with indexing of moving objects? Are spatial index structures capable of indexing moving objects? These are the questions we try to answer in this section. Our goal is also to constitute a specification and classification scheme for *spatio-temporal access methods* (STAMs).

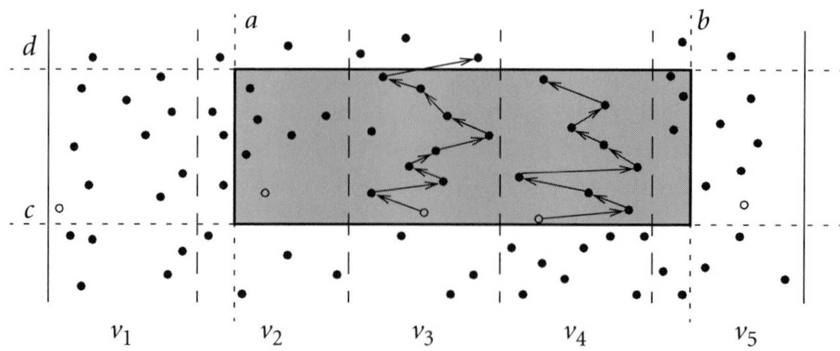

Figure 7.8 Shown are the slabs $v_1, \ldots, v_5$ corresponding to a node v in the primary tree. To find the points in the shaded rectangle, three-sided queries are answered by using $P^{\lceil}(v_2)$ and $P^{\rceil}(v_5)$. They allow us to find the lowest point in each slab above the bottom of the rectangle by using $P^{\mp}(v)$. Starting with the lowest point, we walk upward through the points inside slabs v_3 and v_4.

For that purpose, we assume an alternative but equivalent definition of a spatio-temporal object.

A *spatio-temporal object o* (denoted by its identification number *o_id*) is a time-evolving spatial object—that is, its evolution or history is represented by a set of triplets (o_id, s_i, t_i), where s_i (also called *spacestamp*) is the location of object *o_id* at instant t_i (also called *timestamp*). Hence, a point (nonpoint) time-evolving object can be represented by a line (volume) in the three-dimensional space and corresponds to a moving point (moving region).

7.2.1 Specifics of Spatio-Temporal Index Structures

As an obvious solution to indexing moving objects data, we could employ an off-the-shelf access method for spatial data, such as the R-tree or the quadtree.[2] But

[2] The quadtree is another popular data structure for organizing spatial objects in two dimensions; there are also *k*-dimensional variants. The basic idea is to build a tree, where each node has an associated rectangle, as follows: The root of the tree has an associated rectangle (say, a square) that covers the entire space of interest. Divide this square into four equal-sized parts ("quadrants"). Recursively construct quadtrees for the four quadrants and make them sons of the root. We can, for example, store points in a quadtree and then construct the tree to such a depth that each leaf contains only a limited number of points and hence can be stored as an external memory bucket. A book covering quadtrees in detail has been written by Samet, 1990. Remarks about the quadtree in this section are only relevant if you happen to know the structure from elsewhere; we do not cover it in this book.

several issues arise when we attempt to equate spatio-temporal objects with three-dimensional objects and to manipulate them by simply employing methods from the purely spatial domain. These issues, which prevent a simple use of geometric index structures, are as follows.

Data set supported. The nature of the advanced data must be investigated from a broad spectrum of applications of the application field considered and must be known beforehand. This knowledge usually has an essential influence on the design and construction of pertaining index structures. In the spatio-temporal case, we have identified moving points, moving regions, and, with minor importance, moving lines as the essential time-evolving spatial object classes.

Valid versus transaction time. As we have learned in Section 1.3, the temporal database literature has identified a number of time models that partially can coexist. In particular, *transaction time* (i.e., the time when a fact is current in the database and may be retrieved) and *valid time* (i.e., the time when a fact is true in the modeled reality) have been identified. This leads to (at least) three known kinds of *spatio-temporal database management systems (STDBMS)*: *valid-time* (also called *historical*), *transaction-time* (also called *rollback*), and *bitemporal* databases. In the same manner, indexing techniques can also be classified according to this taxonomy.

Database dynamics. Another way of characterizing the requirements of spatio-temporal index structures is to take into account the degree of dynamics of a spatio-temporal database. The first case is that the cardinality of a database (i.e., the number of moving objects) is static over time, but moving objects may change their location. An example is a military application where the positions of ships must be monitored over time. The second case is the reverse (i.e., the cardinality changes over time, but the locations of all spatial objects in the database remain static). An example here is a sequence of maps using points to show the seismic acticity of a region. The third case allows both the database cardinality and the objects' locations to vary over time. An example here is a forest fire outbreak at different locations. The fourth and remaining case relates to a database consisting of a fixed number of nontemporal spatial objects; they can be manipulated with spatial database approaches. Spatio-temporal index structures can be tailored to the corresponding case and provide specialized support for accelerated data access.

Loading of data. Another issue refers to bulk (batch) or dynamic loading of data into the database. That is, we distinguish between applications whose data are bulk loaded with a timestamp t_i in the database and where an update of past instants is not allowed, and applications with dynamic insertions and updates of objects' timestamps (not applicable to transaction-time databases). The design of an efficient STAM also depends on this distinction.

Approximations of moving objects. As we have seen in Section 7.1, R-trees and their variants approximate spatial objects by their *minimum bounding boxes* (MBBs) in order to construct the spatial index. Transfering this approach to spatio-temporal objects turns out to be an inefficient solution due to the dynamic nature of moving objects. Since these objects are moving around, their MBBs usually

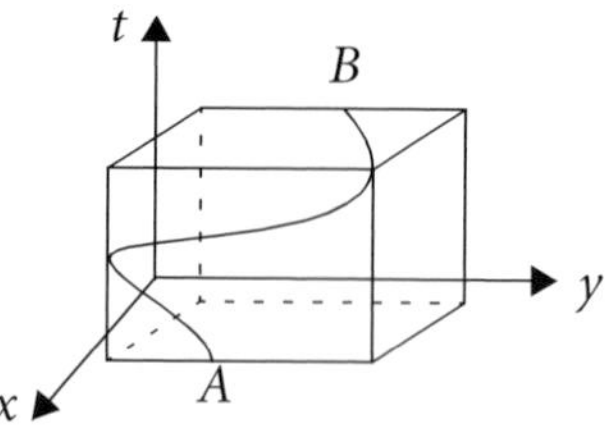

Figure 7.9 The MBB of a moving point occupies a large portion of the data space.

include a vast amount of dead, nonvisited space. This undoubtedly leads to extremely large and overlapping data rectangles, which, in turn, lead to an inefficient indexing performance. Figure 7.9 shows as an example the trajectory of a point object moving from location *A* to location *B*. It is obvious that the corresponding MBB comprises a large portion of the data space, thus leading to high overlap and therefore to small discrimination capability of the index structure. Consequently, alternative representations have to be considered or devised.

Alternatively, if we store a moving object in a linear quadtree, we have to decompose it into a number of maximal blocks. Dynamically evolving spatial objects can be assumed to consist of a great number of maximal blocks. Hence, a large number of quadcodes will have to be inserted into the quadtree structure.

Peculiarity of the time dimension. In a moving object, time is not just another third dimension, since it takes monotonically increasing values. This special feature should be taken into account for the construction of STAMs. More precisely, for each two consecutive triplets (o_id, s_i, t_i) and (o_id, s_{i+1}, t_{i+1}) of an object o_id, $t_{i+1} > t_i$ always holds. This feature also causes a side effect, because all objects' instances with t_i lower than a threshold could be considered as obsolete. This means that a large portion of a STAM could be packed in order to reduce index space, since no updates are permitted for the corresponding data. Alternatively or additionally, a purging process could be employed to move obsolete data to tertiary storage, or even delete them.

Exercise 7.5 Take the coordinate system from Figure 7.9 and draw a three-dimensional object that represents a three-dimensional curve but does not correspond to the trajectory of a moving point. Argue for the correctness of your drawing. ■

Support of specific spatio-temporal queries. The ultimate objective of indexing techniques is the efficient retrieval of data that satisfy the constraints of a user-defined query. Each application domain gives rise to specialized queries. For example, in the spatial domain, operations such as *spatial selection*, *spatial join*, and *nearest-neighborhood* queries are of interest. But, in the spatio-temporal domain, users could be interested in other kinds of queries. An example is *timeslice queries*, where a timeslice can be an instant or an interval. A series of timeslices allow the visualization of a spatio-temporal database within a time interval. Another example is *history queries*, which, for example, retrieve all instances of a specified object identified by *o_id*. Hence, the definition of a widely accepted and rather comprehensive collection of spatio-temporal queries is obviously necessary, not only for the purposes of an appropriate index design, but also for the design of spatio-temporal data models, query languages, benchmarks, and so on.

The aforementioned issues, and possibly several others not mentioned here, exert a decisive influence on the design of STAMs and show that STAMs are different from purely spatial indexes. This means that we cannot simply treat the time dimension as an extra dimension in multidimensional space.

7.2.2 Specification Criteria for Spatio-Temporal Index Structures

In the following text, we present specification criteria that should be supported by an efficient spatio-temporal index technique. According to the discussion in Section 7.2.1, we distinguish three types of specification issues: issues on data types and data sets supported, issues on index construction, and issues on query processing.

Data types and data sets supported

We have already seen that both point (moving points) and nonpoint (moving regions, moving lines) spatial objects evolving over time have to be efficiently supported by appropriate STAMs. With respect to the time dimensions supported, we have to distinguish transaction-time, valid-time, and bitemporal index structures. With respect to the dynamics of a data set, we differentiate *growing* index structures, where the number of still objects changes over time; *evolving* index structures, where spatial objects move over time but their number remains constant; and *full-dynamic* index structures, where spatial objects move over time and the cardinality of moving objects varies in the database. With respect to the timestamp update issue, we distinguish index structures on *bulk loaded* or *batch inserted static* data, where the assumption is that all objects' instances are known in advance and no insertion or update is allowed; on *chronological* or *append-only* data, where only current instances are dynamically inserted or updated, or on *dynamic* data, where insertions or updates of any object instance, referred to any timestamp (not meaningful in transaction-time databases), is allowed. In the spatial domain, only the static and the dynamic classes are meaningful.

Index construction

Due to the specific nature of spatio-temporal data and the previously mentioned peculiarity of the time dimension, an efficient STAM should take several issues into account during its construction that extend the relevant concepts for purely spatial indexes. In the following text, we consider efficient handling of new entries, obsolete entries, and granularity change. Our focus is on hierarchical tree structures and not, for example, on hashing methods, which do not seem to be appropriate for multidimensional indexing purposes.

Insert and split operations. Each time a new triplet (o_id, s_i, t_i) of an object o is inserted into the database, the root entries are checked to select the one that "fits" the new entry. This procedure is repeated recursively at deeper levels until the leaf level is reached. The entry is then inserted into one of the leaf pages. The insertion is based on the spatial and temporal coordinates and keeps the peculiarity of the time axis in mind. In case of a page overflow, an appropriate handling of overflow entries could lead either to a split operation, a forced reinsertion procedure, or even to using overflow pages. Total (e.g., similar to the R^+-tree split operation) or partial (i.e., according to space or time coordinates) disjointedness criteria can be considered to efficiently handle page overflow.

Pack and purge operations to handle obsolete entries. Index pages consisting of or containing obsolete entries could be packed or purged in order to reduce disk space. These reorganization and cleansing techniques could be part of the design of a STAM due to the nature of the data involved. Regarding packing, we can leverage the experimental result that the average page capacity of dynamic tree indexes is about 67 percent. This leads, for example, to the 3-to-2 merge technique, which means that three consecutive obsolete pages, each being around 67 percent full, are merged into two full pages. Regarding purging, pages consisting of obsolete entries are removed from the index organization. In both cases, a remarkable space saving could be achieved.

Change timestamp granularity. When the timestamp granularity (i.e., the unit of measure in the time dimension) is coarsened (e.g., from an hour to a day), the underlying index should be reorganized in order to express the objects' timestamps with respect to the new time measure.

Query processing

The major objective of a STAM is to efficiently support query processing. The broader the set of supported queries is, the more applicable and useful the access method becomes. In the following text, we discuss a set of fundamental query types.

Selection queries. Queries of the form, "Find all objects that have been located within a specific area (or at a specific point) and/or during a specific time interval (or at a specific time instant)" are the most common spatio-temporal questions addressed by STDBMS users. Under the assumption of a hierarchical tree structure, the retrieval procedure is obvious: starting from the root node(s), a downward traversal of the index is performed by applying the criterion of intersected intervals (for time) and ranges (for space) between the query window and each node approximation. In the "or" case of this query type, we ask for a *temporal* or *spatial projection* of the moving object.

Join queries. Queries of the form, "Find all objects that have been located spatially close (i.e., with distance *d*) and during a specific time interval (or at a specific time instant)" fall under this category. An application is accident detection by comparing vehicle trajectories. The retrieval procedure is as follows: Starting from the two root nodes, a downward traversal of the two indexes is performed in parallel, by comparing the entries of each visited node according to the *overlap* operator.

Nearest-neighbor queries. Queries of the form, "Find the *k*-closest objects with respect to an area or location in a time interval *I*" are also of interest.

We have only mentioned three important query types. Other query types include the *timeslice* (which can be transformed into partially-point or range queries) and the *history* (which could be supported by the maintenance of appropriate *to-next* pointers) operations. Spatio-temporal indexing should also support spatio-temporal predicates used as spatio-temporal selection or spatio-temporal join conditions. The problem here is that the number of possible predicates is infinite.

7.2.3 A Survey of STAMs in the Past

Until recently, attempts to design spatio-temporal indexing techniques have been exclusively restricted to purely spatial indexing supporting multidimensional data or temporal indexing for standard data types (e.g., numbers, strings). In the following text, we will describe some of these approaches and, in particular, show their shortcomings. These approaches can be classified into the following categories:

- Methods that treat time as another dimension
- Methods that incorporate the time information into the nodes of the index structure but without assuming another dimension
- Methods that use overlapping index structures in order to represent the state of the database in different (valid or transaction) time instants

The first category represents the obvious idea to treat time simply as another dimension, since the tools to handle multidimensional data are already available. An example is the 3D R-tree, which considers time as an extra dimension on top of the original two-dimensional space and which transforms two-dimensional regions into three-dimensional boxes (MBBs). The retrieval of objects that fulfill a spatio-temporal range constraint (e.g., "Find all objects that overlap object *X* both in space and time") is implemented by a typical three-dimensional range query in the R-tree structure. The intended application scope of the 3D R-tree involves objects that do not change their location through time. Hence, no dead space is introduced by their three-dimensional representation, which is different in the case of moving objects (see Figure 7.9).

The second category incorporates time information as time intervals into the structure. This leads to the RT-tree, which is the spatio-temporal version of the

R-tree. Spatial and temporal information are kept and maintained separately. Each entry, either in a leaf or nonleaf node, contains entries of the form (S, T, P), where S is the spatial information (MBB), T is the temporal information (interval), and P is a pointer to a subtree or the detailed description of the object. Let $T = (t_i, t_j)$, $i \leq j$, t_j be the current timestamp and t_{j+1} be the consecutive one. In case a spatial object does not change from t_j to t_{j+1}, T is updated to $T' = (t_i, t_{j+1})$. As soon as an object changes its spatial location, let us say at time t_j, a new entry with the temporal information $T = (t_j, t_j)$ is created and inserted into the RT-tree. The approach has the following limitations: If the number of objects that change is large, the RT-tree grows considerably. Since all instances of the objects with their respective timestamps are kept in a single tree, queries that focus on a specific timestamp face the overhead of the remaining ones. When a node overflows, a split strategy is needed. The spatial, temporal, or both characteristics can be used, but no proposal has been made on when to use each approach.

The third category includes the MR-tree and the HR-tree. Both approaches pursue the concept of creating different index instances for different transaction timestamps. But in order to save disk space, common paths are maintained only once, since they are shared among the index instances. Hence, links between different index instances are created so that the collection of all index instances forms an acyclic graph. The concept of overlapping tree structures is simple to understand and implement. When the objects that have changed their location in space are relatively few, this approach is very space efficient. However, if the number of moving objects from one instant to another is large, this approach degenerates to independent tree structures, since no common paths are likely to be found. Figure 7.10 shows an example of overlapping trees for two different time instants t_0 and t_1. The dashed lines represent links to common paths.

Table 7.1 classifies the proposed approaches for spatio-temporal indexing purposes according to the specification criteria in Section 7.2.2. All approaches considered are able to index regions (including points as a special degenerate case), and three out of four approaches support transaction time. Except for the 3D R-tree, the approaches are classified as full-dynamic (with respect to the data set dynamics) and chronological (with respect to timestamp updates). The 3D R-tree handles growing and static databases, since objects are accompanied by a valid-time lifespan

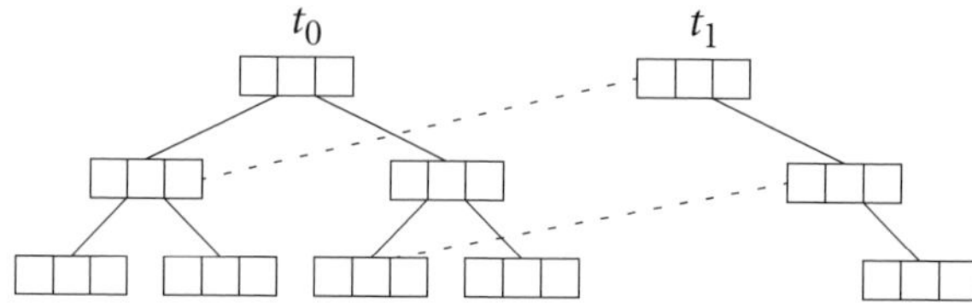

Figure 7.10 Overlapping trees for two different time instants t_0 and t_1.

Table 7.1 : Evaluation of STAMs in the past.

STAM Specification	*MR-tree*	*RT-tree*	*3D R-tree*	*HR-tree*
Data types supported	region	region	region	region
Types of time supported	transaction time	transaction time	valid time	transaction time
Data set dynamics	full-dynamic	full-dynamic	growing	full-dynamic
Timestamp update	chronological	chronological	static	chronological
Specific object approximation	yes	yes	no	yes
Handling obsolete entries	no	no	no	no
Specific query processing algorithms	yes (timeslice)	no	yes (timeslice)	yes (timeslice)

without changing their location in space; all objects' instances are known in advance. Regarding the remaining specifications, the 3D R-tree does not take into account specific approximations, since each object is represented by its MBB, but it implements a specific timeslice operation. Overlapping trees such as the MR-tree and the HR-tree maintain a set of MBBs per object, although with no links to each other, and efficiently handle specific variants of timeslice operations.

In summary, a limited support of specific spatio-temporal operations or the lack of specific object approximations other than MBBs is the general rule. Although all approaches support static or chronological databases, no special handling of obsolete object instances is considered. Consequently, besides extending and improving existing approaches, new proposals are needed. Some of them will be described in the next two sections.

7.3 Indexing Current and Near-Future Movement

In this section, we deal with the indexing of the current and anticipated future positions of moving objects. We have already discussed a data model for this case in Chapter 3. Section 7.3.1 discusses some general strategies and concepts that are common to all indexing techniques discussed afterward. Section 7.3.2 introduces the time-parameterized R-tree (TPR-tree). Section 7.3.3 explains the dual data transformation approach. In Section 7.3.4 we deal with the idea of time-oblivious indexing. Kinetic B-trees for one-dimensional chronological queries are introduced in Section 7.3.5, and in Section 7.3.6 we employ kinetic external range trees for two-dimensional chronological queries. Section 7.3.7 deals with time-responsive indexing based on multiversion kinetic B-trees, and Section 7.3.8 discusses time-responsive indexing based on multiversion external kinetic range trees.

7.3.1 General Strategies

Continuous movement poses new challenges to database technology. In conventional index structures, the data to be stored are static and remain constant unless these data are explicitly modified from time to time. Capturing and indexing continuous movement with this assumption entails either performing frequent updates or recording outdated, inaccurate data, neither of which is an attractive, efficient, or feasible alternative.

By analogy with the modeling approaches presented in Chapters 3 and 4, a solution is to capture the continuous movement in a way so that the mere advance of time does not necessitate frequent, explicit updates. That is, rather than storing explicit positions and their changes, functions of time that express the moving objects' positions are stored. Updates are then only necessary when the parameters of the functions (e.g., velocity, direction) change. Using temporal functions, the probable location of a moving object can be easily computed for any time in the future. While this minimizes the update overhead, in Chapter 3 we saw some novel problems introduced by this approach.

The index structures discussed here are restricted to moving points, which are represented by linear approximations. In general, several conceptual distinctions may be made regarding approaches to the indexing of future linear trajectories of moving points.

First, approaches may be different with respect to the space that they index. If objects move in the d-dimensional space, their future trajectories may be indexed as lines in $(d + 1)$-dimensional space. We have already used this view as a visualization of moving points. If a point moves in the two-dimensional space, it can be regarded as a three-dimensional line. Alternatively, trajectories may be mapped to points in a higher-dimensional space and then indexed (Section 7.3.3). Another alternative is to index data in its native d-dimensional space, which can be done by parameterizing the index structure using velocity vectors and thus enabling the index to be viewed at any future time (Section 7.3.2).

Second, a distinction can be made as to whether the index partitions the data (e.g., as do R-trees) or the embedding space (e.g., as do quadtrees). When indexing data in its native space, an index based on data partitioning seems to be more appropriate. But if trajectories are indexed as lines in the $(d + 1)$-dimensional space, this method may introduce substantial overlap if clipping is not used.

Third, indexes may differ in the degrees of data replication they imply. Replication may improve query performance but may also adversely affect update performance.

Fourth, approaches can require periodic index rebuilding. Some approaches use single indexes that are only working and valid for a certain time period. In these approaches, a new index must be created before its predecessor is no longer functional. Other approaches may employ an index, which, in principle, remains working indefinitely (Section 7.3.2). It may be the case that from time to time it is recommendable to optimize the index, since the index deteriorates as time goes on.

7.3.2 The TPR-tree

The first indexing technique to be discussed is the *time-parameterized R-tree* (*TPR-tree*, for short). It naturally extends the R*-tree and employs a linear function per moving point being indexed. The parameters of a function are the position and the velocity vector of the object at the time the function is reported to the database. The bounding boxes in the tree are functions of time, too. The strategy is to continuously follow the enclosed moving points (or other rectangles) as these move. As with the R-trees, the new index is able to index points in one-, two-, and three-dimensional space. The TPR-tree indexes data in its native space, does not employ replication, and does not require periodic index rebuilding.

Problem description

The position of an object in the d-dimensional space at some time t now or in the future is given by $x(t) = (x_1(t), x_2(t), \ldots, x_d(t))$ and modeled as a linear function of time. Such a function is specified by two parameters. The first one is a position $x(t_{ref})$ for the object at some specified time t_{ref}; it is called the *reference position*. The second parameter is a *velocity vector* $v = (v_1, v_2, \ldots, v_d)$ for the object. Hence, $x(t) = x(t_{ref}) + v(t - t_{ref})$. If an object's position is observed at some time t_{obs}, the first parameter $x(t_{ref})$ may be the object's position at this time, or it may be the position the object would have at some other, chosen reference time, given the velocity vector v observed at t_{obs} and the position $x(t_{obs})$ observed at t_{obs}. This kind of modeling has two advantages: It enables us to make tentative future predictions of the objects' positions, and it solves the problem of frequent updates. Objects may report their positions and velocity vectors only when their actual positions deviate from what they have previously reported by some given threshold. The problem of an appropriate balance between update frequency and desired accuracy has been discussed in Chapter 3.

In the TPR-tree, the reference position and the velocity are also employed for representing the coordinates of the bounding boxes in the index as a function of time. This is illustrated in Figure 7.10. Figure 7.11(a) shows the positions and velocity vectors at time 0. Figure 7.11(b) shows one possible assignment of the objects to MBBs in an R-tree at time 0 and assumes a maximum of three objects per node. Previous work has shown that minimizing the quantities such as overlap, dead space, and perimeter leads to an index with good query performance. Thus, the assignment seems to be well chosen. However, although queries are well supported at time 0, the movement of the objects may adversely affect this assignment. Figure 7.11(c) yields the positions of objects and MBBs at time 3. The MBBs have grown to stay valid; two of them are overlapping and the degree of dead space has increased, too. The reason is that originally objects belonging to the same MBB (e.g., objects 4 and 5) were close, but the different directions of their movement cause their positions to diverge fast and hence the MBBs to grow. Queries at time 3 will probably have a worse query performance, and an assignment of objects to MBBs according

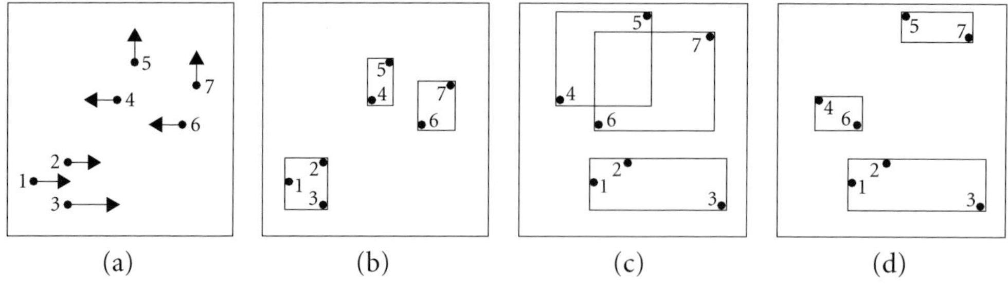

Figure 7.11 Moving points and resulting leaf-level MBBs in an R-tree.

to the Figure 7.11(d) would be more preferable for them. Otherwise, at time 0, this assignment would have yielded worse query performance than the original assignment. Consequently, the assignment of objects to MBBs must take into account when most queries will arrive.

Query types

The queries supported by the TPR-tree retrieve all points with positions within specified regions. In the following text, let a d-dimensional rectangle R be specified by its d projections $[a_1^s, a_1^e], \ldots, [a_d^s, a_d^e]$ into the d coordinate axes, where $a_i^s \leq a_i^e$ for $1 \leq i \leq d$. Further, let R, R_1, and R_2 be three d-dimensional rectangles, and let t, t^s, and t^e with $t^s \leq t^e$ be three time values that are not less than the current time. We distinguish between three query types, based on the regions they specify:

- *Timeslice query* (type 1). $Q = (R, t)$ specifies a hyper-rectangle R located at time point t.
- *Window query* (type 2). $Q = (R, t^s, t^e)$ defines a hyper-rectangle R that covers the interval $[t^s, t^e]$. In other words, this query retrieves points with trajectories in (x, t)-space crossing the $(d + 1)$-dimensional hyper-rectangle $([a_1^s, a_1^e], \ldots, [a_d^s, a_d^e], [t^s, t^e])$.
- *Moving query* (type 3). $Q = (R_1, R_2, t^s, t^e)$ specifies the $(d + 1)$-dimensional trapezoid obtained by connecting R_1 at time t^s and R_2 at time t^e.

The second query type is a generalization of the first one and is itself a specialization of the third type. Figure 7.12 illustrates the query types on a one-dimensional data set $\{o_1, o_2, o_3, o_4\}$ representing temperatures measured at different locations. Queries Q_0 and Q_1 are timeslice queries. Q_2 is a window query, and Q_3 is a moving query.

Let *iss*(Q) denote the time when a query Q is issued. The two parameters, reference position and velocity vector, of the trajectory of a moving object as seen by a

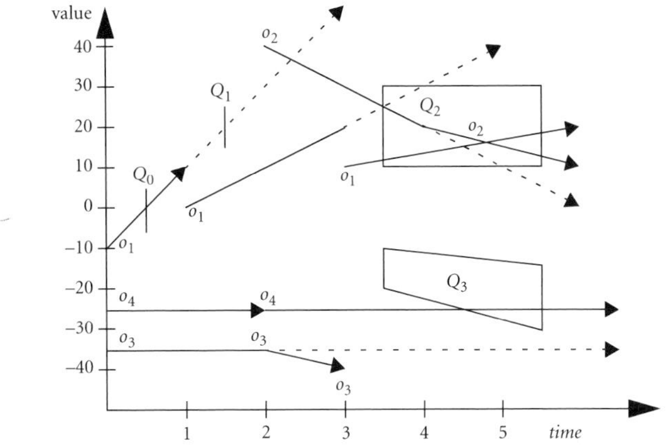

Figure 7.12 Query examples for one-dimensional data.

query Q depend on $iss(Q)$, since objects update their parameters as time elapses. A look at object o_1 in Figure 7.12 reveals this. Its movement is described by one trajectory for queries with $iss(Q) < 1$, another trajectory for queries with $1 \leq iss(Q) \leq 3$, and a third trajectory for queries with $3 \leq iss(Q)$. For example, the answer to query Q_1 is o_1, if $iss(Q) < 1$, otherwise, it is empty if $iss(Q) \geq 1$.

Figure 7.12 shows that depending on $iss(Q)$, the result of a query Q can be different and that queries far in the future are probably of little value, because the positions predicted at query time become more and more imprecise as queries move into the future and because updates not known at query time may happen. Hence, the main benefit in real-world applications will be achieved if queries relate to the "near future," which is some limited time window extending from the current time.

Problem parameters

Three parameters affect the indexing problem and the qualities of a TPR-tree (Figure 7.12):

- *Querying window* (W). It describes how far queries can look into the future. Thus, $iss(Q) \leq t \leq iss(Q) + W$, for type 1 queries, and $iss(Q) \leq t^s \leq t^e \leq iss(Q) + W$ for queries of types 2 and 3.
- *Index usage time* (U). It denotes the time interval during which an index will be used for querying. Thus, $t_l \leq iss(Q) \leq t_l + U$, where t_l is the time when an index is created or loaded.
- *Time horizon* (H). This is the length of the time interval from which the times t, t^s, and t^e addressed in queries are taken. The time horizon for an index is considered as the index usage plus the querying window.

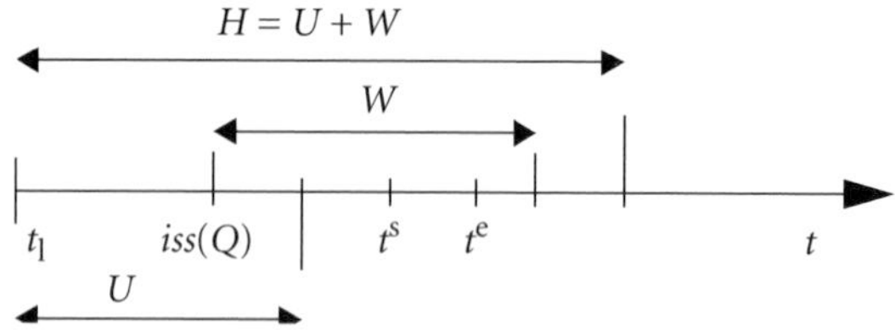

Figure 7.13 The problem parameters: time horizon H, index usage time U, and querying window W.

Therefore, a newly created index must support queries that reach H time units into the future. Later we will see that parameter U is not only useful for static data sets and bulk loading but also in a dynamic setting where index updates are permitted. Although a TPR-tree is functional at all times after its creation, a change of the parameter U during insertion can increase the search performance of the tree.

Structure of the TPR-tree

A TPR-tree is a balanced, multiway tree and has the structure of an R-tree. Leaf nodes contain the position of a moving point and a pointer to the moving point object in the database. Internal nodes comprise a pointer to a subtree and a rectangle that bounds the positions of all moving points or other bounding boxes in that subtree. As said before, the position of a moving point is represented by a reference position and a velocity vector (x, v) in the one-dimensional case, where $x = x(t_{ref})$. We assume that $t_{ref} = t_l$, the index creation time. We could also set t_{ref} to some constant value (e.g., 0) or use different t_{ref} values in different nodes.

To bound a group of d-dimensional moving points, we use d-dimensional bounding boxes, which are also time parameterized (i.e., their coordinates are functions of time). A d-dimensional, *time-parameterized bounding box* bounds a group of d-dimensional moving points or bounding boxes of subtrees at all times not earlier than the current time. An issue is to find a balance between how precise a bounding box bounds the enclosed moving points or subordinate bounding boxes over time and the storage required to capture the bounding box. An obvious solution could be to use time-parameterized bounding boxes that are always minimal, but the storage cost appears to be excessive. In the general case, this leads to checking all the enclosed moving objects. Figure 7.14 shows an example where a node consists of two one-dimensional points A and B moving toward each other (an extension to any number of points is straightforward). At each time, each of these points plays the role of the lower or upper bound of the minimum bounding interval. Instead of using these always minimum bounding boxes or intervals, the TPR-tree employs so-called *conservative* bounding boxes, which are minimal at some time instant but possibly and most likely not at later times. In the one-dimensional case, the lower/upper bound of a conservative interval is set to move with the mini-

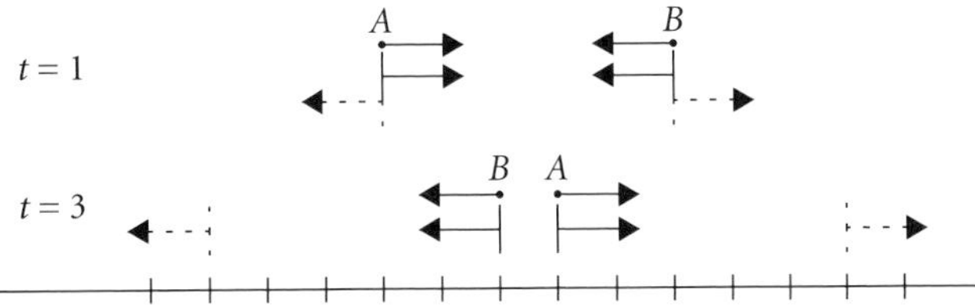

Figure 7.14 Conservative (dashed) versus always-minimum (solid) bounding intervals.

mum/maximum speed of the enclosed points (speeds are negative or positive depending on the direction). This practice ensures that the moving points are bounded by the conservative bounding interval at all times considered. In Figure 7.14, the left or right border of the conservative interval starts at the position of object A or B at time 0 and moves in left or right direction at the speed of object B or A. Hence, conservative bounding intervals never shrink.

Based on our assumption that $t_{ref} = t_l$, a one-dimensional time-parameterized bounding interval $[x^s(t), x^e(t)] = [x^s(t_l) + v^s(t - t_l), x^e(t_l) + v^e(t - t_l)]$ and is represented as (x^s, x^e, v^s, v^e), where $x^s = x^s(t_l) = min\{o_i.x^s(t_l) \mid 1 \leq i \leq n\}$, $x^e = x^e(t_l) = max\{o_i.x^e(t_l) \mid 1 \leq i \leq n\}$, $v^s = min\{o_i.v^s \mid 1 \leq i \leq n\}$, and $v^e = max\{o_i.v^e \mid 1 \leq i \leq n\}$. The o_i ranges over the n bounding intervals to be enclosed. In case the o_i range over n moving points is enclosed, $o_i.x^s(t_l)$ and $o_i.x^e(t_l)$ are replaced by $o_i.x(t_l)$, and $o_i.v^s$ and $o_i.v^e$ are replaced by $o_i.v$. We call these intervals and rectangles, which bound for all times not before t_l, *load-time bounding intervals* and *boxes*. These intervals and boxes never shrink; they may even grow too much, so it is favorable to be able to adjust them occasionally. In particular, it can be necessary to adjust the bounding boxes every time any of the enclosed moving points or bounding boxes are updated. The following adjustments may be made during updates to the bounding boxes: $x^s = min\{o_i.x^s(t_{upd}) \mid 1 \leq i \leq n\} - v^s(t_{upd} - t_l)$ and $x^e = max\{o_i.x^e(t_{upd}) \mid 1 \leq i \leq n\} - v^e(t_{upd} - t_l)$. Here, t_{upd} is the time of the update, and for moving points the formulas must be changed as before. We call these intervals and rectangles *update-time bounding intervals* and *boxes*. Figure 7.15 illustrates the two types of bounding boxes.

The solid top and bottom lines show the load-time, time-parameterized bounding interval for the four moving points represented by the four straight lines. At time t_{upd}, a more narrow and thus better update-time bounding interval is given that is bounding from t_{upd} and onward (until the next update).

Querying

With these definitions of bounding intervals and boxes, we show how the three query types can be answered by using the TPR-tree. To answer a timeslice query is similar to the process for the regular R-tree. The only difference is that all bounding boxes are computed for the time t^q asked for in the query before intersection is

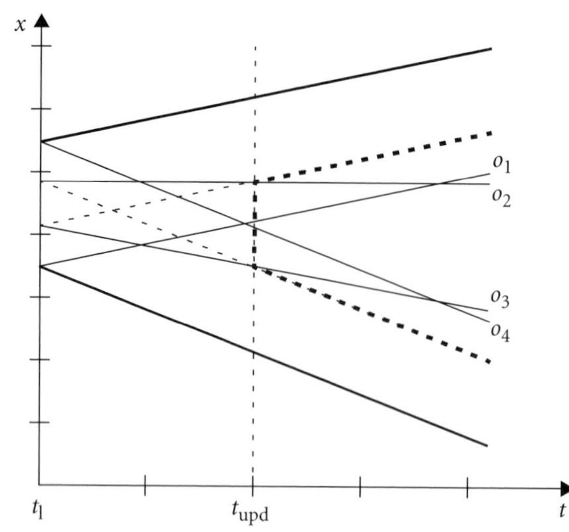

Figure 7.15 Load-time (solid) and update-time (dashed) bounding intervals for four moving points.

checked. Hence, a bounding interval given by (x^s, x^e, v^s, v^e) satisfies a query $((a^s, a^e), t^q)$ if, and only if, $a^s \leq x^e + v^e(t_q - t_l) \wedge a^e \geq x^s + v^s(t_q - t_l)$. For answering window queries and moving queries, we need to be able to check whether, in (x, t)-space, the trapezoid of a query (Figure 7.16) intersects with the trapezoid formed by the part of the trajectory of a bounding box that is between the start and end times of the query. For one spatial dimension this is relatively simple. For more dimensions we may employ generic polyhedron-polyhedron intersection tests (not discussed here). In our simpler case, a more efficient algorithm may be devised.

In particular, we need an algorithm for checking whether a d-dimensional time-parameterized bounding box R given by the parameters $(x_1^s, x_1^e, x_2^s, x_2^e, \ldots, x_d^s, x_d^e, v_1^s, v_1^e, v_2^s, v_2^e, \ldots, v_d^s, v_d^e)$ intersects a moving query $Q = (([a_1^s, a_1^e], [a_2^s, a_2^e], \ldots, [a_d^s, a_d^e], [w_1^s, w_1^e], [w_2^s, w_2^e], \ldots, [w_d^s, w_d^e]), [t^s, t^e])$. For reasons of convenience, we have slightly modified the definition of a moving query (type 3) from that given previously, which specifies the $(d + 1)$-dimensional trapezoid by connecting the bounding box R_1 at time t^s to the bounding box R_2 at time t^e. Instead of rectangle R_2, we use velocity vectors. The velocities w_i are obtained by subtracting R_2 from R_1 and then normalizing them with the length of the interval $[t^s, t^e]$. The algorithm is based on the observation that two moving bounding boxes intersect if there is a time point when they intersect in each dimension. Hence, for each dimension j with $1 \leq j \leq d$, the algorithm determines the time interval $I_j = [t_j^s, t_j^e] \subseteq [t^s, t^e]$ when the time-parameterized bounding box and the time-parameterized query rectangle intersect in that dimension. If $I = \bigcap_{j=1}^{d} I_j = \varnothing$, the moving rectangles do not intersect and an empty result is returned; otherwise the time interval I is pro-

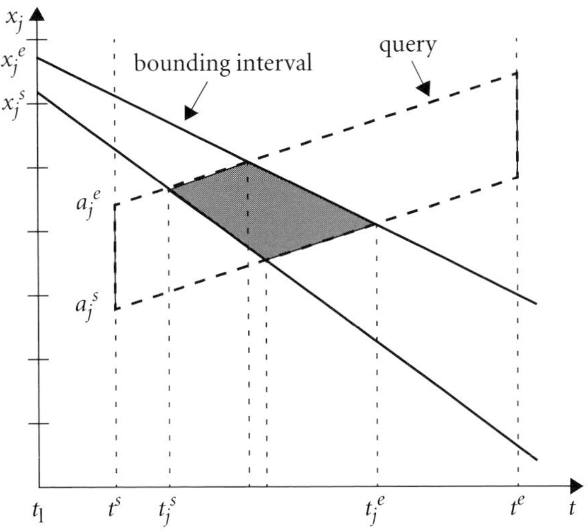

Figure 7.16 Intersection of a moving bounding box and a moving query.

vided when the rectangles intersect. The intervals for each dimension j are computed as follows:

$$I_j = \begin{cases} \varnothing & \text{if } (a_j^S(t^S) > x_j^e(t^S) \wedge a_j^S(t^e) > x_j^e(t^e)) \vee \\ & \quad (a_j^e(t^S) < x_j^S(t^S) \wedge a_j^e(t^e) < x_j^S(t^e)) \\ [t_j^S, t_j^e] & \text{otherwise} \end{cases}$$

The first (second) term of the disjunction expresses that Q is above (below) R. The value t_j^s is defined as follows:

$$t_j^S = \begin{cases} t^S + (x_j^e(t^S) - a_j^S(t^S))/(w_j^S - v_j^e) & \text{if } a_j^S(t^S) > x_j^e(t^S) \\ t^S + (x_j^S(t^S) - a_j^e(t^S))/(w_j^e - v_j^S) & \text{if } a_j^e(t^S) < x_j^S(t^S) \\ t^S & \text{otherwise} \end{cases}$$

The first (second) condition expresses that Q is above (below) R at t^s. For t_j^e we obtain:

$$t_j^e = \begin{cases} t^s + (x_j^e(t^s) - a_j^s(t^s))/(w_j^s - v_j^e) & \text{if } a_j^s(t^e) > x_j^e(t^e) \\ t^s + (x_j^s(t^s) - a_j^e(t^s))/(w_j^e - v_j^s) & \text{if } a_j^e(t^e) < x_j^s(t^e) \\ t^e & \text{otherwise} \end{cases}$$

Here, the first (second) condition expresses that Q is above (below) R at t^e.

As an example of how t_j^s and t_j^e are calculated, let us assume the case where Q is below R at t^e. Consequently, Q must not be below R at t^s, because then Q is always below R and there is no intersection. Therefore, the line $a_j^e(t^s) + w_j^e(t - t^s)$ and the line $x_j^s(t^s) + v_j^s(t - t^s)$ intersect within the time interval $[t^s, t^e]$. Solving for t yields the intersection time t_j^e. Figure 7.16 shows a moving query, a bounding box, and their intersection time interval in one dimension.

Exercise 7.6 We have defined a velocity vector v as a tuple $v = (v_1, v_2, \ldots, v_d)$ in d dimensions. Let $d = 2$. (1) If the position p of a moving point at a time t is given by a known function of time—that is, $p(t) = (x(t), y(t))$—how can we in general characterize v, v_1, and v_2 over time? Explain your answer for the two cases where the moving point shows a linear or polynomial behavior. (2) Devise an alternative definition of the velocity vector $v = (v_1, v_2)$. ■

Heuristics for tree organization

An important issue is how to group moving objects into nodes so that the tree most efficiently supports timeslice queries when assuming a time horizon H. Hence, the objective is to find principles, or heuristics, that are appropriate both for dynamic insertions and bulk loading. When H is close to zero, the tree can simply employ existing R-tree insertion and bulk-loading algorithms. The movement of the point objects and the bounding boxes becomes unimportant; only their initial positions and extent matter. However, when H is large, grouping the moving points according to their velocity vector is of importance. The bounding boxes should be as small as possible at all times in $[t_l, t_l + H]$, which is the time interval during which the result of the insertion or bulk-loading operation may be visible to queries. Hence, t_l is the time of an insertion or the index creation time. To achieve the minimization of bounding boxes, their growth rates, and hence the values of their velocity extents, must be kept low. In the one-dimensional space, the velocity extent of a bounding interval is equal to $v^e - v^s$.

The insertion and bulk-loading algorithms of the R*-tree, which are to be extended to moving points, aim at minimizing objective functions, such as the areas of the bounding boxes, their perimeters, and the degree of overlapping among the bounding boxes. In our setting, where these functions are time dependent, we have to consider their development in the interval $[t_l, t_l + H]$. For that purpose, given an objective function $A(t)$, the integral

$$\int_{t_l}^{t_l+H} A(t)\,dt$$

should be minimized. If $A(t)$ is the area function, the integral calculates the area (volume) of the trapezoid that represents part of the trajectory of a bounding box in (x, t)-space (see Figure 7.16).

Insertion and deletion

The insertion algorithm of the R*-tree uses functions for computing the area of a bounding box, the intersection of two bounding boxes, the margin of a bounding box (when splitting a node), and the distance between the centers of two bounding boxes (used when performing forced reinsertions). The insertion algorithm of the TPR-tree is the same as that of the R*-tree but with the exception that instead of the functions just mentioned, their integrals are deployed. Computing the integrals of the area, the perimeter, and the distance is relatively straightforward. Computing the integral of the intersection of two time-parameterized bounding boxes is an extension of the algorithm for checking whether such bounding boxes overlap. At each time of the bounding box intersection, the intersection region is again a bounding box, and in each dimension the upper (lower) bound of this bounding box is the upper (lower) bound of one of the two intersecting bounding boxes. Hence, the time interval returned by the overlap-checking algorithm is divided into consecutive time intervals so that during each of these, the intersection is defined by a time-parameterized bounding box. The intersection area integral is then calculated as a sum of area integrals. For the one-dimensional case, Figure 7.16 shows the splitting of the intersection time interval into three smaller intervals.

In a dynamic setting, the querying window W remains part of the time horizon H and is the length of the time period where integrals are computed in the insertion algorithm. The length of the other part of H depends on the update frequency. If it is high, the effect of an insertion will not last long, and H should not exceed W by too much.

Another modification is necessary regarding the split algorithm. The R*-tree split algorithm takes one distribution of entries between two nodes from a set of candidate distributions, which are created based on sortings of point positions along each of the coordinate axes. In the TPR-tree split algorithm, moving point (or bounding box) positions at different time points are employed when sorting. Regarding load-time bounding boxes, positions at t_l are used, and regarding update-time bounding boxes, positions at the current time are used. In addition to the sortings along the spatial dimensions, sortings along the velocity dimensions are also considered. That is, sortings are obtained by sorting the coordinates of the velocity vectors. The reason for this is that distributing the moving points based on the velocity dimensions may lead to bounding boxes with smaller "velocity extents," which thus grow more slowly.

Deletions in the TPR-tree are the same as in the R*-tree. An underflow in a node leads to its elimination and to a reinsertion of its entries.

7.3.3 The Dual Data Transformation Approach

In this section, we describe the *dual data transformation approach* to index moving objects. Duality, a concept widely used in the computational geometry literature, in general maps a hyperplane in $\mathbb{R}^d$ to a point in $\mathbb{R}^d$ and vice versa. The goal is to allow a more intuitive formulation of a problem and to find an easier solution for it.

The dual space-time representation in one dimension

We assume that originally the trajectories of moving points are given as lines in the time-location (t, y) plane. The equation of each line is $y(t) = vt + a$, where the velocity v is the slope and a is the intercept. More precisely, the trajectory is not a line but a semiline starting from some point (x_i, y_i). However, since we ask queries related to the present or to the future, the assumption of a trajectory as a line does not have any affect on the correctness of the answer. The minimum and maximum velocities are denoted as v_{min} and v_{max}, respectively. The motion of moving points on the y-axis is supposed to be limited between 0 and a constant y_{max}.

In particular, we are interested in proximity queries, which are window queries and report all objects that reside inside the spatial interval $[y_{1q}, y_{2q}]$ during the time interval $[t_{1q}, t_{2q}]$, where $t_{now} \leq t_{1q} \leq t_{2q}$. Figure 7.17 shows a number of trajectories and a query in the (t, y) plane. The query is expressed as a 2D interval $[y_{1q}, y_{2q}] \times [t_{1q}, t_{2q}]$.

In the context here, the idea is to map a line from the *primal* plane (t, y) to a point in the *dual* plane. The dual plane is defined in a way so that one axis represents the slope of an object's trajectory and the other axis represents its intercept. Hence, the line with the equation $y(t) = vt + a$ is represented by the point (v, a) in the dual space (this is also called the *Hough-X transform*). The values of v are bounded by $-v_{max}$ and v_{max}, whereas the values of the intercept depend on the current time t_{now}. The range for a is then $[-v_{max} \times t_{now}, y_{max} + v_{max} \times t_{now}]$.

Of course, the window query Q also has to be transformed into the dual space. It can be expressed as a polygon by using linear constraints as follows:

For $v > 0$, we obtain: $Q = v \geq v_{min} \wedge v \leq v_{max} \wedge a + t_{2q}\, v \geq y_{1q} \wedge a + t_{1q}\, v \leq y_{2q}$.

For $v < 0$, we obtain: $Q = v \leq -v_{min} \wedge v \geq -v_{max} \wedge a + t_{1q}\, v \geq y_{1q} \wedge a + t_{2q}\, v \leq y_{2q}$.

Exercise 7.7 Prove the correctness of these constraints. Assume that $a \leq y_{2q}$ and use Figure 7.18 as a guide. ■

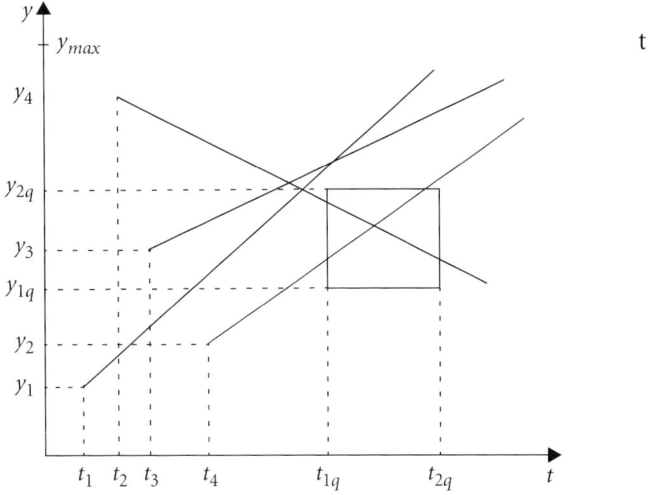

Figure 7.17 Trajectories and query in the (t, y) plane.

Since the query is different for positive and negative slopes, we can use two structures to store the dual points. The range of the *a*'s values is now $[-v_{max} \times t_{now}, y_{max} - v_{min} \times t_{now}]$. But because the time is monotonically increasing, the values of the intercept are not bounded. If the value of the maximum velocity is important, the values of the intercept can become very large and this potentially can be a problem.

A solution is to work with two indexes. The idea is to start a new index after $T_{period} = y_{max} / v_{min}$ time instants. At each time instant a given point is stored in one of the two indexes. Initially, all points inserted from time $t = 0$ to T_{period} have their intercept at $t = 0$ and are stored in the first index. After time T_{period} points have their intercept at $t = T_{period}$ and are stored in the second index. Points of the first index that are updated after time T_{period} are deleted from this index and inserted in the second index. Hence, after T_{period} time instants we can be sure that there is no object that has not updated its motion information. After $t = T_{period}$ the first index is removed and the next index starts at time $2 \cdot T_{period}$. This approach ensures that the absolute values of intercept are always between 0 and $v_{max} \times T_{period}$. The queries are directed to both indexes.

Lower bounds

The dual space-time representation transforms the problem of indexing moving objects on a line to the problem of so-called *simplex range searching* in two dimensions. Given a set *S* of 2D points, we are interested in efficiently answering queries

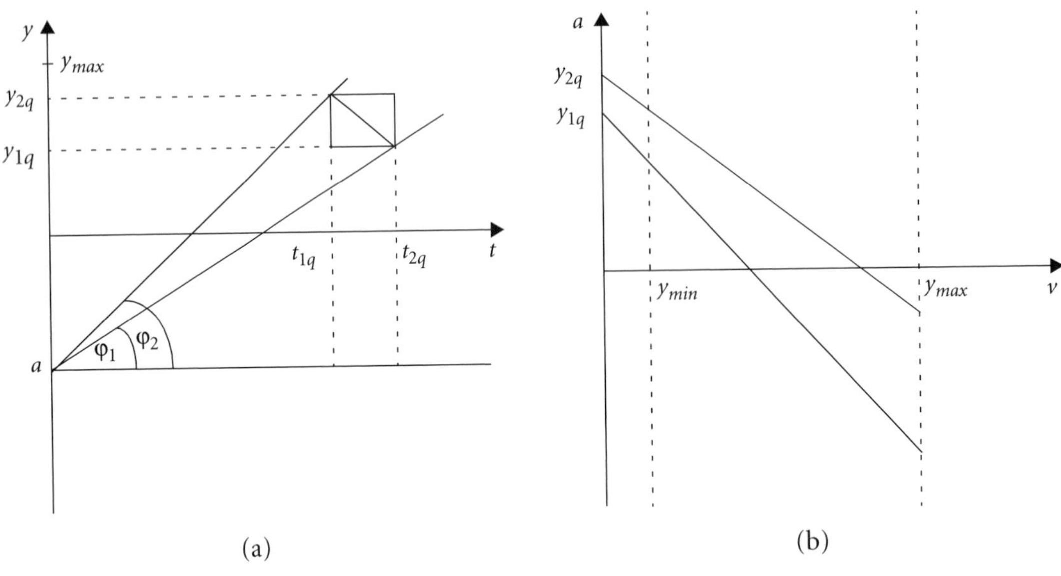

Figure 7.18 A query in the primal (t, y) plane (a); a query in the dual (v, a) plane (b).

of the form: Given a set of linear constraints (inequalities) $ax \leq b$, find all points in S that satisfy all the constraints. Geometrically speaking, the constraints form a polygon in the plane, and the task is to find all points in the interior of the polygon. This problem has been extensively studied previously in the static, main memory setting. Simplex reporting in d dimensions (i.e., reporting all the points that are located within a query region) can be performed in time $O(N^{\delta} + K)$, where N is the number of points, K is the number of the reported points, and $0 < \delta \leq 1$. It requires space $\Omega(N^{d(1-\delta)-\varepsilon})$ for any fixed ε.

Assume that a disk access transmits B units of data in a single operation (i.e., B is the page capacity). Then the minimum number of pages needed is $n = \lceil N/B \rceil$ and the minimum number of disk accesses to report the answer is $k = \lceil K/B \rceil$. It can be shown (although it is not done here) that simplex reporting in d dimensions can be performed in time $O(n^{\delta} + k)$ with $0 < \delta \leq 1$ and space $\Omega(n^{d(1-\delta)-\varepsilon})$ for any fixed ε.

An almost optimal solution

An almost optimal main memory algorithm for simplex range searching on a given static set of points is based on the idea of *partition trees* and *simplicial partitions* presented in Section 7.1.3. The answering process for a range query is as follows. Each of the triangles in the simplicial partition at the root is checked to see if it is inside the query region, outside the query region, or intersects one of the lines that define the query. In the first case, all points located in the triangle are reported, and in the second case, the triangle is discarded. In the third case, we must have a closer look and consider the children of the triangle. It can be shown that the query time is $O(N^{1/2+\varepsilon} + K)$, where ε is a small positive constant and K is the number of reported points.

A corresponding external memory algorithm of static partition trees answers queries in $O(n^{1/2+\varepsilon} + k)$ disk accesses with $n = \lceil N/B \rceil$ and $k = \lceil K/B \rceil$. For our purposes, this structure has to be made dynamic. In Section 7.1.3, we saw how points can be inserted or deleted in a partition tree. These operations require $O(\log_B^2 n)$ disk accesses each.

Improving the average time

A problem with these results is that partition trees turn out not to be very useful in practice, since the query time is $O(n^{1/2+\varepsilon} + k)$ for every query, and the hidden constant factor becomes large if we choose a small ε. We present two different approaches to improve the average query time. A first approach leverages the many available access methods for indexing point data. All these index structures have been designed to address *orthogonal* range queries (e.g., queries expressed as a multidimensional hyper-rectangle). Most of them can be easily modified to be applicable to nonorthogonal queries such as simplex queries. One of these solutions answers simplex range queries on the basis of R-trees by changing the search procedure of the tree and providing simple methods to test whether a linear constraint query region and a hyper-rectangle overlap. For answering a range query in the dual space, it is unclear which index structure is the more appropriate one, given the highly skewed distribution of points in the dual space. Index structures based on *kd*-trees seem to be more promising than R-trees. The reason is that R-trees will split using only one dimension (the intercept), since they tend to cluster data points into squarish regions. But *kd*-tree-based methods will use both dimensions for splitting. Hence, they are expected to have a better performance for the range query.

The second approach is based on a different representation of a line. The equation $y(t) = vt + a$ of a line is now written as

$$t = \frac{1}{v} y - \frac{a}{v}.$$

The mapping of this line representation into the dual plane leads to a point with coordinates

$$n = \frac{1}{v} \text{ and } b = -\frac{a}{v}$$

(also called the *Hough-Y transform*). The value b is the point where the given line intersects the line $y = 0$. Note that this transform cannot represent horizontal lines (similar to the fact that the Hough-X transform cannot represent vertical lines). But this is not a problem, since the lines considered here have a minimum and a maximum slope. Based on the Hough-Y transform, the second approach pursues the goal of query approximation (Figure 7.19). In general, the b-coordinate can be calculated at different horizontal lines $y = y_r$. The query region is given by the intersection of two half-space queries. The first line intersects the line

$$n = \frac{1}{v_{max}} \text{ at the point } (t_{1q} - \frac{v_{2q} - y_r}{v_{max}}, \frac{1}{v_{max}})$$

and the line

$$n = \frac{1}{v_{min}} \text{ at the point } (t_{1q} - \frac{v_{2q} - y_r}{v_{min}}, \frac{1}{v_{min}}).$$

Similarly, the other line intersects the horizontal lines at

$$(t_{2q} - \frac{v_{1q} - y_r}{v_{max}}, \frac{1}{v_{max}}) \text{ and } (t_{2q} - \frac{v_{1q} - y_r}{v_{min}}, \frac{1}{v_{min}}).$$

As a next step, we approximate the simplex query with the rectangle query

$$[(t_{1q} - \frac{v_{2q} - y_r}{v_{min}}, t_{2q} - \frac{v_{1q} - y_r}{v_{max}}), (\frac{1}{v_{max}}, \frac{1}{v_{min}})].$$

The query area is now enlarged by the area $E = E_1 + E_2$, and its size is:

$$E = \frac{1}{2}\left(\frac{v_{max} - v_{min}}{v_{min} \times v_{max}}\right)^2 (|y_{2q} - y_r| + |y_{1q} - y_r|)$$

We only take into account the points with positive speed and assume that they are kept in a fixed number c of data structures. Each data structure stores exactly the same points but with their b-coordinate computed at different lines $y = y_r$. This means that the ith data structure stores the b-coordinates using the line

$$y = \frac{y_{max}}{c} \times i \; (i = 0, \ldots, c - 1).$$

To answer a query, the data structure minimizing the area E is taken. Since one side of the query rectangle is

$$\left(\frac{1}{v_{max}}, \frac{1}{v_{min}}\right),$$

we can employ a B^+-tree and store only the b-coordinate of the points. This means that the original, enlarged query is mapped to a simple range query on a B^+-tree. If, for the query interval $[y_{1q}, y_{2q}]$, the inequality

$$y_{2q} - y_{1q} \leq \frac{y_{max}}{c}$$

holds, we obtain it by using one of the c data structures (the one that minimizes the value for $|y_{2q} - y_r| + |y_{1q} - y_r|$):

$$E \leq \frac{1}{2}\left(\frac{v_{max} - v_{min}}{v_{min} \times v_{max}}\right)^2 \frac{y_{max}}{c}$$

If

$$y_{2q} - y_{1q} \geq \frac{y_{max}}{c},$$

we subdivide the range $[0, y_{max}]$ into c subranges P_i with $0 \leq i \leq c - 1$, where the subrange P_i is the interval

$$\left[\frac{y_{max}}{c} \times i, \frac{y_{max}}{c} \times i + 1\right].$$

Then we deploy for each P_i an external memory interval tree IT_i, and for each object, we store the time interval for which this object was inside the subrange P_i. Next, we split the original query into a number of queries of the form $[P_j, (t_{1q}, t_{2q})]$ and two more queries when the v_{1q} and v_{2q} are not end points of a subrange. For answering the query $[P_i, (t_{1q}, t_{2q})]$ we have to perform a range query $[(t_{1q}, t_{2q})]$ on IT_i. It can be answered in optimal time $O(\log_B(n) + K_i/B)$ where K_i is the size of the partial answer set. An object can appear in many answers, but we can report it only once, because all needed information such as speed and direction is available. To answer the two queries referring to the end points, we can select two of the c B-trees

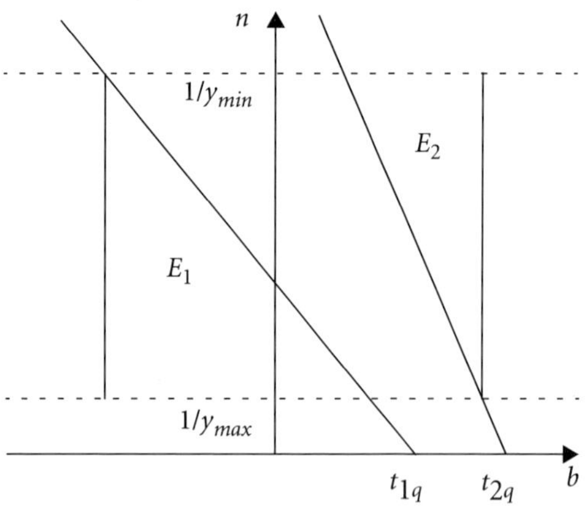

Figure 7.19 A query in the dual plane based on the Hough-Y transform.

such that the previous inequality holds. In a similar way, this procedure can be deployed for the objects with negative speed. In total, we find that the range query can be answered in time $O(\log_B(n) + (K + K')/B)$, where K' is the approximation error. This requires space $O(cn)$, where c is a parameter. The update time is $O(c \log_B(n))$. If we assume that the points are distributed uniformly over the b axis, then the approximation error is bounded by $1/c$. This means that then $K' = O(1/c)$.

Indexing in two dimensions

In the following text, we consider the problem of moving objects in the plane. We assume that these objects move with a velocity between v_{min} and v_{max} and that in the (x, y) plane their motion is restricted to the area $[(0, x_{max}), (0, y_{max})]$.

As a special but very important case, called the 1.5-dimensional problem, we first look at moving objects in the plane whose movement is restricted by a given network of specific routes (e.g., cars on roads, trains on railway lines). If we represent each route of such a network as a sequence of connected, straight segments (polyline), this problem can be reduced to a number of one-dimensional queries. The segments can then be indexed by a standard SAM, which does not lead to a large overhead since usually the number of routes is much smaller than the number of objects moving on them; each route can be approximated by a small number of segments; and updates can be expected to occur rarely. Indexing the points moving on a given route is a one-dimensional problem and can be treated by the methods introduced previously. For a window query, the SAM determines the intersection of the routes with the spatial query rectangle $[x_{1q}, x_{2q}] \times [y_{1q}, y_{2q}]$. The result of this intersection is a set of possibly disconnected line segments.

The general two-dimensional problem allowing free object movement in the restricted area of the plane is more difficult. In the space-time (2D + 1D) representation, the trajectories of moving objects can be viewed as 3D lines. A window query is a cube in the 3D (x, y, t)-space, and the answer is a set of 3D lines crossing the query cube. Unfortunately, it is impossible to directly apply the dual transformation approach for lines in the primal plane (t, y) to lines in the primal (x, y, t)-space, since lines in 3D space have four degrees of freedom. The reason is that the development of each coordinate x or y can be described independently as a linear function over time, each of which requires two parameters. To achieve a dual transformation, we project the 3D lines on the (x, t)- and (y, t)-planes and then take the dual transformations for the two lines of these planes. Hence, a 3D line can be represented by a 4D point (v_x, a_x, v_y, a_y), where the v_x and v_y are the slopes of the lines on the (x, t)- and (y, t)-planes and the a_x and a_y are the intercepts, respectively. The window query is mapped to a simplex query in the dual space. This query is the intersection of four 3D hyperplanes, and the projection of the query to the the (t, x)- and to the (t, y)-plane is a wedge, as in the one-dimensional case. Therefore, we can employ a 4D partition tree and answer the window query in $O(n^{0.75 + \varepsilon} + t)$ disk accesses that almost match the lower bound for four dimensions. A simpler approach to solve the 4D problem is to use an index based on the *kd*-tree. Another approach is to use the independent motions in the x- and y-directions. For each direction the method for the 1D case is applied and two 1D window queries are answered. The intersection of the two answers leads to the answer of the initial query.

7.3.4 Time-Oblivious Indexing with Multilevel Partition Trees

The concept described in Section 7.3.3 proposes to map each line to a point in $\mathbb{R}^4$ and to use four-dimensional partition trees to answer range queries. The problem is that the resulting query time is quite large. An improvement can be achieved if we use a *multilevel partition tree* instead. The general idea of multilevel data structures is to answer complex queries by decomposing them into several simpler components and designing a separate data structure for each component.

Let S be a set of N linearly moving points in a three-dimensional space-time setting. We know that we can interpret S geometrically as a set of 3D lines. The timeslice query asks which moving points intersect a given rectangle R on the xy-plane at time $t = t_q$. A 3D line l intersects R if, and only if, their projections onto the xt- and yt-planes both intersect. We apply a duality transformation to the xt- and yt-planes, as described in Section 7.1.2. Hence, each moving point in the xy-plane induces two static points p^x and p^y in the dual xt-plane and the dual yt-plane, respectively. For any subset $P \subseteq S$ let P^x and P^y, respectively, denote the corresponding points in the dual xt-plane and the dual yt-plane. Any query rectangle, which is projected to query segments in the xt- and yt-planes, induces two query strips σ^x and σ^y and the result of a query is the set of points $p \in S$ such that $p^x \in \sigma^x$ and $p^y \in \sigma^y$.

A multilevel partition tree can now be constructed as follows. Let $\delta < 1/2$ be an arbitrarily small positive constant. We build a *primary* partition tree T^x for the points P^x, where the fanout of each node v is $r_v = \min\{n^\delta, cB, 2n_v\}$. The idea now is that at certain nodes v of T^x, we attach a *secondary* partition tree T_v^y for the points S_v^y. Especially, if $n^\delta > cB$, we attach secondary trees to every node whose depth is a multiple of $\delta \log_{cb} n$; otherwise, we attach secondary trees to *every* node of T^x. In either case, we attach secondary trees to $O(1/\delta) = O(1)$ levels of T^x. Each secondary tree T_v^y requires $O(n_v)$ blocks so that the total size of all the secondary trees is $O(n/\delta) = O(n)$ blocks. Further, we can construct all the secondary trees in $O(N \log_B n)$ expected disk accesses, and by using the partial rebuilding technique, we can insert or delete a point in $O(\log^2{}_B\, n)$ (amortized) expected disk accesses. See Figure 7.20 for an example of a multilevel partition tree.

We obtain a similar algorithm for answering a range query as for the basic partition tree. Given two query strips σ^x and σ, we first search through the primary partition tree for the points in $P^x \cap \sigma^x$. For a triangle Δ_i that lies completely in σ^x, we do not perform a complete depth-first search of the corresponding subtree. Instead, we only search at the next level where secondary trees are available, and for each node v at that level, we use the secondary tree T_v^y to report all points of $P_v^y \cap \sigma^y$.

The following results can be shown: The number of disk accesses required to answer a query at the multilevel data structure T_v^x over N_v points, excluding the $O(K_v/B)$ disk accesses to report the K_v points inside the query range, is $O(n^\delta n_v^{1/2+\varepsilon})$. Further, given a set S of N points in $\mathbb{R}^2$, each moving linearly, we can preprocess S into an index of size $O(n)$ blocks so that both a timeslice query and a window query can be answered in $O(n^{1/2+\varepsilon} + k)$ disk accesses, where $\varepsilon > 0$. The index can be constructed in $O(N \log_B n)$ expected disk accesses, and points can be inserted or deleted at an amortized cost of $O(\log^2{}_B\, n)$ expected disk accesses each.

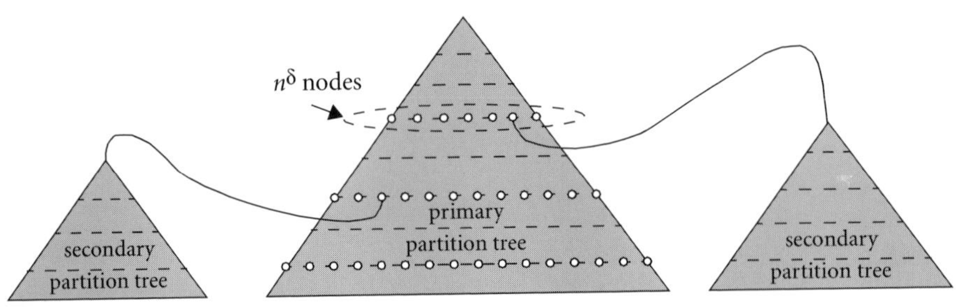

Figure 7.20 Schematic multilevel partition structure. Each node in certain levels of the primary tree points to a secondary structure. Only two secondary trees are shown.

7.3.5 Kinetic B-trees

The approach described now refers to one-dimensional queries, allows the data structure to change over time, and enables a significant improvement of the query time. Queries are only allowed at the current time. The approach can be extended to handle queries in the future as long as they arrive in *chronological order.* The approach is based on the framework of so-called *kinetic data structures,* whose main idea is to store only a "combinatorial snapshot" of the moving points at any time. The data structure only relies on certain combinatorial properties, such as the sorted order of points along x- and y-axes, and changes only at discrete time instants called *events.* When such an event occurs, a *kinetic update* is performed on the data structure. Since the movement of points over time is known, we can predict when any event will occur. A global *event queue,* which is a priority queue, includes all future events and governs the evolution of the data structure.

Let $S = \{p_1, \ldots, p_N\}$ be a set of N points in $\mathbb{R}$, each moving with a fixed velocity. Let $S(t)$ denote the point set at time t. We employ a B-tree T for storing S. T is updated periodically so that $T(t)$ is a valid B-tree for $S(t)$ at all times t. If T is valid at time t, it remains valid as long as the ordering of points in S does not change. Therefore, we specify the events as time instants t_{ij}, at which $p_i(t_{ij}) = p_j(t_{ij})$. We use an external priority queue Q to store the time t_{ij} for every adjacent pair of points p_i, p_j in $S(t)$. The operations *insert, delete,* and *delete-min* can be performed in time $O(\log_B n)$. Let $t^* = t_{ij}$ be the minimum value in Q. At time $now = t^*$, we delete t^* from Q and swap p_i and p_j in T. If the ordering of S before the swap was $\ldots, p_a, p_i, p_j, p_b, \ldots$, then after the swap the pairs (p_a, p_i) and (p_j, p_b) are no longer adjacent and, consequently, t_{ai} and t_{jb} are deleted from Q. Instead, we insert t_{aj} and t_{ib}, since (p_a, p_j) and (p_i, p_b) now become adjacent pairs. We hence spend $O(\log_B n)$ disk accesses at each event. To answer a query at current time we need $O(\log_B n + k)$ disk accesses. S can be stored in a B-tree index of size $O(n)$ blocks.

7.3.6 Kinetic External Range Trees

For two-dimensional chronological queries involving moving points in the plane $\mathbb{R}^2$, so-called *kinetic external range trees* can be employed that are based on the external range trees described in Section 7.1.6. For this purpose, it is necessary to *kinetize* the external range tree so that it can store moving points and efficiently answer range queries at the current time. This necessitates modifications through all participating data structures from the bottom up (i.e., first for the catalog structure C, then for the external priority search tree P, and finally for the the external range tree R).

We start with considering the catalog structure C (Section 7.1.4) and recall that the rectangle of each block b_i in C is defined by four points in S. For moving points, we add the temporal aspect by defining the rectangle associated with b_i at time t as $[x_{l_i}(t), x_{r_i}(t)] \times [y_{d_i}(t), y_{u_i}(t)]$. The four coordinate functions are assumed to be continuous, so that the rectangle of each block changes continuously with time. A point $p_j(t) = (x_j(t), y_j(t))$ has to satisfy the condition $c = x_{l_i}(t) \leq x_j(t) \leq x_{r_i}(t)$ and $y_{d_i}(t) \leq y_j(t)$ until some time t is reached for which holds $x_j(t) = x_{l_i}(t)$, $x_j(t) = x_{r_i}(t)$, or $y_j(t) = y_{d_i}(t)$. This enables us to use C for answering queries until time t, at which time we will have to update the structure.

The detection of violations of condition c is supported by two kinetic B-trees B_x and B_y (Section 7.3.5) over the x- and y-coordinates of the points in S, respectively, together with a common event queue Q. We have to take into account that a kinetic B-tree undergoes a swap event when two of its values become equal. That is, a swap event is given whenever two points $p_j(t)$ and $p_{j'}(t)$ have the same x- or y-coordinate. At each swap event we check to see if condition c still holds for $p_j(t)$ and $p_{j'}(t)$; if not, we simply remove the offending point from C and reinsert it in $O(1)$ disk accesses. In total, the treatment of a swap event requires $O(\log_B B^2) = O(1)$ disk accesses. The change of a trajectory of a point p can be performed in $O(1)$ disk accesses. First, p is deleted from C, B_x, and B_y. Then, the $O(1)$ event times in Q involving p are removed, and finally p and the $O(1)$ new event times are reinserted. In case the trajectories of the points never change, we have $O(B^2)$ events.

A three-sided query $q = [a, b] \times [c, \infty[$ at time t_q is answered exactly as was done on the nonkinetic catalog structure. The only exceptions are the rectangles stored in the catalog blocks as well as the points in the loaded blocks b_i. Then, we calculate the relevant x- and y-coordinates at time t. As previously, the query procedure requires $O(1 + k)$ disk accesses.

At the next higher structure level, we need a dynamic version of an external priority search tree P discussed in Section 7.1.5. We remember that such a tree on a set S of N points consists of an x-coordinate–based B-tree with points stored in auxiliary catalog structures of the internal nodes based on y-coordinates. Due to the definition of the structure on the basis of the x- and y-coordinates of the points in S, the validity of P for a set of moving points at time t is maintained until the next swap event. As with the catalog structure, P can be updated after a swap event by performing two deletions and two insertions in $O(\log_B B)$ disk accesses. To determine the kinetic event times, we maintain the coordinate B-trees B_x and B_y on S, as well as an event queue B-tree Q. Similar to the catalog structure, these structures can all be maintained in $O(\log_B n)$ disk accesses per event. In fact, it is possible to maintain one global version of each of the three structures for the base priority tree and all its auxiliary catalog structures C_v. As previously, we can change the trajectory of a point in $O(\log_B n)$ disk accesses. If the trajectories of the points remain unchanged, there are $O(N^2)$ events. Since S is stored in a kinetic external priority search tree of size $O(n)$ blocks, a three-sided query can be answered in $O(\log_B n + k)$ disk accesses.

As with the external priority search tree, the primary structure of the external range tree (Section 7.1.6) also deals with the x- and y-coordinates of the N points. Again, as previously, the structure remains valid until the x- or y-coordinates of two points become equal. When such a kinetic event happens, the structure is updated by performing two deletions and two insertions in $O(\log^2{}_B n / \log_B \log_B n)$ disk accesses. As previously, we use three global B-trees to determine the kinetic event times in $O(\log_B n)$ disk accesses.

In total, we obtain the following result: A set S of N linearly moving points in $\mathbb{R}^2$ can be stored in a kinetic external range tree of size $O(n \log_B n / \log_B \log_B n)$ blocks. The query to report all points of S that lie inside a given rectangle at a particular time can be answered in $O(\log_B n + k)$ disk accesses. The amortized cost of a kinetic event or trajectory change is $O(\log^2{}_B n / \log_B \log_B n)$ disk accesses. The total number of events is $O(N^2)$, if there is no change of the trajectories.

7.3.7 Time-Responsive Indexing with Multiversion Kinetic B-trees

In retrospect, partition trees are able to answer an arbitrary sequence of times range queries, but the cost of answering each query is high. Kinetic range trees enable a quick answer of queries, with the restriction that the queries must arrive in chronological order. We now deal with an indexing scheme that combines the advantages of both schemes so that queries can be answered quickly and in any order. The number of disk accesses needed to answer a query is small if the query's timestamp t_q is close to the current time. First, we show how to report all points of a set that lie inside a rectangle at time t_q in near future or in near past in $O(\log_B n + k)$ disk accesses. Then, we extend this approach to arbitrary query times.

We have seen that a kinetic data structure K remains fixed until there is an event. For kinetic B-trees, we obtain an event when two points have the same value. For kinetic range trees, an event occurs when some pair of points shares a common x- or y-coordinate. At some of these event times, given by a sequence $t_1, \ldots, t_n$, K is updated. Let K_i be the version of K at time t_i. Assuming that the current time is between t_{i-1} and t_i, we maintain the versions $K_{i-\mu}, K_{i-\mu+1}, \ldots, K_{i+\mu}$ of K for a small $\mu \in \mathbb{N}$. That is, we maintain μ past versions and μ future versions of K. The future versions are, of course, tentative. They are determined by anticipating future events based on the current trajectories of the points. Between K_{i-1} and K_i we only store the "differences." Since μ is assumed to be a small number, we only store a few past versions, and we delete a past version when it becomes too old. A change of a point trajectory between t_{i-1} and t_i may lead to an update of the future versions.

In case of one-dimensional moving points, we can employ a *multiversion kinetic B-tree*. This means that each data element is associated with a lifespan keeping the time at which the element was inserted and possibly the time at which it was deleted. Similarly, a lifespan is attached to each node in the B-tree. We use the phrase that an element or a lifespan is *alive* in its lifespan. Besides the usual B-tree properties (e.g., maximum number of elements in a node), we also require that a node contains $\Theta(B)$ alive elements (or children) in its lifespan. Hence, for a given time t the nodes with a lifespan containing t form a B-tree on the elements alive at that time. An insertion into such a modified B-tree is similar to a normal insertion. First, we traverse the tree from its root to a leaf node z and insert the elements if there is space for them. Otherwise, we have an overflow situation. In this case, we copy all alive elements in z, and the current time becomes the *death time* of z. Thus, z is deactivated. The number of copied alive elements determines the further strategy. Either we split them into two new leaf nodes with an equal number of elements, we construct one new leaf from them, or we copy the alive elements from one of the siblings of z and construct one of two leaves out of all the copied elements. In all cases, we must ensure that there is space for $\Theta(B)$ future updates in each of the new leaves. Then, the new element is inserted into the corresponding leaf, and the *birth time* of all new leaves is set to the current time. Finally, the parents of z are linked by pointers to the new leaves and the pointer to z is deleted. This may lead to cascading overflows on a path to the root of the tree, which are handled in a similar way. This procedure is called *persistent node copying* or *pointer updating*. The deletion of an element is performed similarly. It can be shown that each update operation takes $O(\log_B n)$ disk accesses and that d update operations require $O(d/B)$ additional disk blocks.

If we want to keep $\mu = N$ past and future versions of the tree, we store the death times of all nodes in a global priority tree. At time t_i of the ith event, we delete all nodes of the tree whose death times are in the range $[t_{i-N}, t_{i-N+1}]$. The number of such nodes is $O(\log_B n)$, so that $O(\log_B n)$ disk accesses are needed. It can be shown that the total size of the structure remains $O(n)$ disk blocks. A simpler, alternative method assumes a multiversion B-tree for the time interval $[t_{i-N}, t_{i+N}]$. During the time interval $[t_i, t_{i+N}]$ we build a new, separate multiversion B-tree for the time interval $[t_i, t_{i+2N}]$, using $O(\log_B n)$ disk accesses per event. We can then disregard the older structure at time t_{i+N+1} and use the new one during the interval $[t_{i+N}, t_{i+2N}]$. The advantage of this approach is the avoidance of the global event queue for storing the death times, so that $O(\log_B n)$ processing time at each event is ensured. On the other hand, the disadvantage is that we have to maintain two multiversion B-trees. We will refer to this method of keeping a partial multiversion B-tree as the *replication method*.

If S is a set of N linearly moving points in $\mathbb{R}$, we can store S in an index of size $O(n)$ blocks, so that reporting all points of S that lie inside an axis-aligned rectangle R at time t_q needs $O(\log_B n + k)$ disk accesses, provided that there are at most N events between t_q and the current time. The amortized cost of a kinetic event is $O(\log_B n)$ disk accesses. If a point p is stored at T places in the index, we can update the trajectory of p using $O((1 + T) \log_B n)$ disk accesses.

7.3.8 Time-Responsive Indexing with Multiversion External Kinetic Range Trees

As we know, an external kinetic range tree has three levels. The primary and secondary structures are special versions of B-trees, and the third level structure is the catalog structure A_v (Section 7.1.4) stored at each node v of a priority search tree. This structure is able to answer a three-sided range query on a set of $O(B^2)$ points.

A_v maintains an extra update block U for recording updates (kinetic events). After B kinetic events have occurred, A_v is rebuilt and the old version of A_v is discarded.

To keep multiple versions of A_v, we change the update and query procedures as follows. Whenever a point enters or leaves a block, we record the time of this event in the update block U together with the identity of the point. At the time A_v is rebuilt, we do not discard the old version but instead store its *death time* (i.e., declare it *inactive*). During T kinetic events we keep a sequence of versions A_v^1, A_v^2, ..., $A_v^{T/B}$ of A_v. Only the last version is active, and for each inactive version A_v^j we store its death time, d_j. For T versions of A_v we need $O(T)$ disk blocks.

In order to determine all points of A_v located in a three-sided rectangle R at time t_q, we first search the version A_v^j that is active at time d_j such that $d_{j-1} \leq t_q < d_j$. Since we store multiple versions of the primary and secondary structures of the external kinetic range tree, A_v^j can be found in $O(1)$ disk accesses. We then query A_v^j as described in Section 7.3.6. The one exception is that we report only those points from the update block that were inserted but not deleted before t_q. In total we need $O(1 + K_v/B)$ disk accesses, where K_v is the number of reported points.

Next, we show how to keep multiple versions of a priority search tree P. The insertion procedure of a point into P follows a path from the root to a leaf of P and possibly inserts (and/or deletes) a point into (from) the catalog structure A_v at each node v of the path. Whenever a new copy of A_v is constructed at v, we keep the old copy in the persistent manner described previously and attach the new copy to v. The insertion procedure also updates the priority search tree in the same way as the insertion procedure for a multiversion B-tree, as discussed earlier. Inserting a point in P causes a constant number of updates in at most $O(\log_B n)$ catalog structures. We can show that the total size of the structure for maintaining μ versions of P is $O(\mu \log_B n)$. Each query can still be answered using $O(\log_B n + k)$ disk accesses.

The primary tree K is also kept as a multiversion B-tree. Whenever a new copy of the root of one of the priority search trees or the B-tree is made at node v, we copy the new root persistently at v, as described earlier. The primary tree itself is updated using partial rebuilding. If a subtree rooted at a node v is rebuilt, the old copy of the subtree is maintained and the new copy is attached at the parent of v in a persistent manner. The subtree with root v is rebuilt after $\Omega(N_v)$ update operations, and the insertion or deletion of a point inserts or deletes a point in the secondary structures at all nodes along a path from the root to a leaf. Thus, $O(\log_B n/\log_B \log_B n)$ update operations are executed on secondary structures. Preserving $\mu = n/\log_B n$ versions of the overall structures requires $O((n/\log_B n)\ (\log_B n/\log_B \log_B n)\ \log_B n) = O(n \log_B n/\log_B \log_B n)$ disk blocks. We still spend $O(\log^2{}_B\, n)$ amortized disk accesses at each event to update K. A query is answered similarly to the way described in Section 7.1.6, except that at each node we use the method for multiversion B-trees to decide which child or which secondary structure of a node we should visit.

Finally, all death times of all versions of all auxiliary structures are stored in a global priority queue. When the ith kinetic event occurs at time t_i, all the versions of auxiliary structures are deleted whose death times lie in the interval $[t_{i-\mu}, t_{i-\mu+1}[$.

We can also employ the alternative method, which is simpler but requires two structures at any time.

In total, we obtain that, given a set S of N linearly moving points in $\mathbb{R}^2$, we can preprocess S into an index of size $O(n \log_B n / \log_B \log_B n)$ disk blocks, so that reporting all those points of S that lie inside an axis-aligned rectangle R at a time t_q requires $O(\log_B n + k)$ disk accesses, provided there are at most $n \log_B n$ events between t_q and now. The amortized cost per event is $O(\log^2{}_B n)$. If a point p is stored at T places in the index, we can compute the trajectory of p in $O((1 + T) \log_B n)$ disk accesses.

7.4 Indexing Trajectories (History of Movement)

In this section, we turn our attention to temporal evolutions of spatial objects in the past. More precisely, we focus on querying and indexing trajectories of moving point objects. By sampling the movement of a point object, we obtain a polyline representing the trajectory of the moving point object. An object's trajectory can even be treated as 3D spatial data. Also, in the case of analyzing the history of movement, the main challenge is to query and index *continuously* (and not discretely) changing point objects. Indexing past movements requires the *preservation* of trajectories. This is in contrast to methods for indexing current and near-future movement, where the past plays no, or only a restricted, role. Preservation refers to the particularity that spatio-temporal data related to the past are considered to be appended only with respect to time (i.e., data grows mainly in the temporal dimension).

We now introduce two appropriate access methods that capture these particularities of spatio-temporal data and queries. The first access method is the *Spatio-Temporal R-tree* (*STR-tree*), described in Section 7.4.1. It not only organizes line segments according to spatial properties but also strives to group the segments according to the trajectories to which they belong. This property is termed *trajectory preservation*. The second access method, called the *Trajectory-Bundle tree* (*TB-tree*), is described in Section 7.4.2. It focuses exclusively on trajectory *preservation* and leaves other spatial properties alone.

We have already seen in Figure 7.9 that approximating line segments with MBBs introduces large amounts of "dead space." Such an MBB covers a large portion of the space, whereas the actual space occupied by the trajectory is small. This leads to a high overlap and thus to a small discrimination capability of an R-tree.

Exercise 7.8 If we view an MBB in our spatio-temporal setting, how many different line segments can be represented by the same MBB? Show them in a drawing. ■

In addition, R-trees do not have the knowledge about the particular trajectory a line segment belongs to. As a first improvement, the R-tree structure is modified as follows: Since a line segment can only be contained in four different ways in an MBB, we store this special information at the leaf level by changing the entry format to (*mbb*, *oid*, *orientation*), where the orientation's domain is {1, 2, 3, 4}. We also store the trajectory number (e.g., a number from 0 to n) with each entry, so that a leaf node entry is of the form (*mbb*, *oid*, *traj_id*, *orientation*). As we will see, these measures are not sufficient, and query processing is still problematic.

The ideal feature of an index suitable for object trajectories would be to decompose the overall space with respect to time, which is the dominant dimension where growth and change occur, and simultaneously preserve trajectories.

7.4.1 The STR-tree

The *STR-tree* extends the modified R-tree just described and supports efficient query processing of trajectories of moving points. Apart from the leaf node structure, the main difference between both access methods is their insertion/split strategy. The (purely spatial) insertion procedure of the R-tree has already been described in Section 7.1.1 and is based on spatial proximity. But insertion in the STR-tree does not only consider *spatial closeness* but also partial *trajectory preservation*. That is, the goal is to keep segments belonging to the same trajectory together and thus insert a new line segment as close as possible to its predecessor in the trajectory. For this purpose, the insertion procedure employs an algorithm *FindNode* that yields the node containing the predecessor. As for the insertion, if the node found has room, the new line segment is inserted there. Otherwise, a node split strategy is used. Figure 7.21 shows an example of an index in which the node found by *FindNode* is marked with an arrow. The algorithm *Insert* is as follows:

```
algorithm Insert(node, elem)
  node' := FindNode(node, elem);
  if node' ≠ nil then
    if node' has space then insert elem
    else
      if node' has p or more ancestors then
        if the p – 1 ancestors of node' are full then
          leaf := ChooseLeaf(node'', elem) on a tree, pointed to by node'',
            which excludes the current branch;
          insert elem into leaf
        else
          Split(node')
        endif
      else
        leaf := ChooseLeaf(node, elem); insert elem into leaf
      endif
    endif
  else
    leaf := ChooseLeaf(node, elem); insert elem into leaf
  endif
end.
```

The algorithm *FindNode* is as follows:

```
algorithm FindNode(node, elem)
  if node is not a leaf then
    for each elem' of node whose MBB intersects with the MBB of elem do
      node'' := FindNode(node', elem) where node' is the child node of node
          pointed to by elem'.
      if node'' ≠ nil then return node'' endif
    endfor;
    return nil;
  else
    if node contains an entry that is connected to elem
    then return node
    else return nil
    endif
  endif
end.
```

The algorithm *Insert* has an additional parameter, called the *preservation parameter p*, which represents the number of levels we "reserve" for the preservation of trajectories. When a leaf node returned by *FindNode* is full, the algorithm checks whether the $p - 1$ parent nodes are full (in Figure 7.21, for $p = 2$, we only have to check the node shown in bold at nonleaf level 1). If one of the parent nodes is not full, the leaf node is split. If all $p - 1$ parent nodes are full, algorithm *Insert* executes the original R-tree algorithm *ChooseLeaf* on the subtree, including all nodes further to the right of the current insertion path (the gray shaded tree in Figure 7.21).

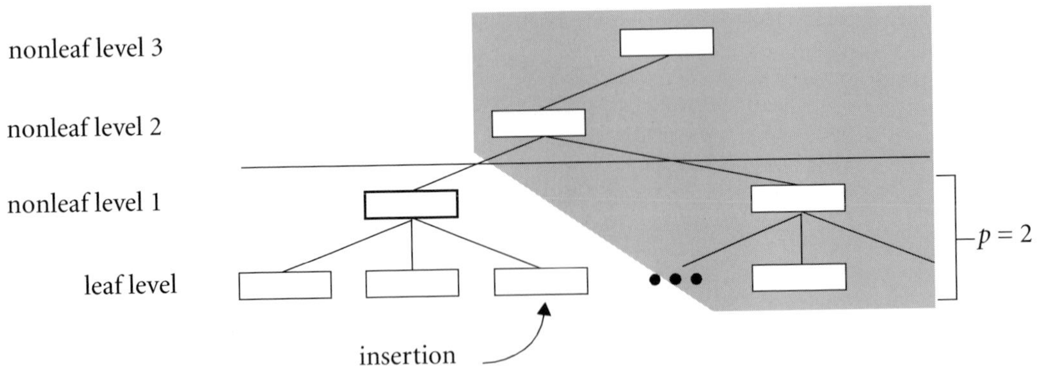

Figure 7.21 Insertion into the STR-tree.

What remains to be discussed is the algorithm *Split*. The splitting strategy has to be designed in a way so that it preserves trajectories in the index. Splitting a leaf node necessitates an analysis of which kinds of segments are represented in a node. Two segments in a leaf node may be part of the same trajectory or not. If they belong to the same trajectory, they may share common end points or not. Hence, a node can have four different kinds of segments. *Disconnected* segments are not connected to any other segment in the node. *Forward-connected* (*backward-connected*) segments have a top (bottom) end point; that is, a more (less) recent end point—that is connected to the bottom (top) end point of another segment of the same trajectory. *Biconnected* segments are both forward connected and backward connected. In the case where all segments are disconnected, the standard R-tree split algorithm *QuadraticSplit* is executed to determine the split. Otherwise, if not all but at least one segment is disconnected, all disconnected segments are moved into the newly created node. Finally, if there are no disconnected segments, the temporally most recent backward-connected segment is placed in the newly created node. This leads to the following algorithm *Split*:

algorithm *Split*(*node*)
    if *node* is a non-leaf node **then**
        execute *SplitNonLeafNode*(*node*)
    else
        execute *SplitLeafNode*(*node*)
    endif
end.

The algorithm *SplitNonLeafNode* is as follows:

algorithm *SplitNonLeafNode*(*node*)
    put the new entry into a new node and keep the old one as it is
end.

The algorithm *SplitLeafNode* is as follows:

algorithm *SplitLeafNode*(*node*)
    if entries in *node* are all disconnected segments **then**
        execute *QuadraticSplit*(*node*)
    elsif *node* contains disconnected and other kinds of segments **then**
        put all disconnected segments in a new node
    elsif *node* does not contain any disconnected segments **then**
        put the newest connected segment in a new node
    endif
end.

This split strategy is more likely to insert newer segments into new nodes than older segments. Splitting nonleaf nodes is simple, since we only create a new node for a new entry. The use of the described insertion and split strategy enables the construction of an index that preserves trajectories and considers time as the dominant dimension when decomposing the occupied space.

7.4.2 The TB-tree

The *TB-tree* has fundamental differences in comparison with the R-tree and the STR-tree. The STR-tree, which is an R-tree-based access method, introduces a new insertion and split strategy to achieve trajectory orientation and does not affect the space discrimination capabilities of the index too much. A central assumption when using the R-tree is that all inserted geometries (i.e., in our case all line segments) are independent. The knowledge that line segments belong to trajectories is only implicitly represented in the R-tree and the STR-tree. The focus of the TB-tree is different in the sense that it strictly preserves trajectories such that a leaf node only incorporates line segments that are part of the same trajectory. Hence, such an index can be regarded as a *trajectory bundle*. Such an approach is only possible if the most important R-tree property of node overlap or spatial discrimination is relaxed. As a drawback, line segments independent from trajectories that lie close will be stored in different nodes. However, by not insisting on space discrimination, we gain on trajectory preservation, which turns out to be important for answering pure spatio-temporal queries.

We have seen that both the R-tree and the STR-tree store entries at the leaf level in the format (*mbb*, *oid*, *traj_id*, *orientation*). Since the TB-tree forbids segments from different trajectories in the same leaf node, the *traj_id* is assigned to the node rather than to each entry. Hence, the format of a leaf node entry is (*mbb*, *oid*, *orientation*).

For insertion, the objective is to "subdivide" the whole trajectory of a moving point into pieces so that each piece includes M line segments. M is the fanout (i.e., a leaf node contains M segments of the trajectory). Figure 7.22 illustrates important stages of the insertion procedure; these are marked with circled numbers from 1 to 6. To insert a new segment, the task is to find the leaf node that contains its predecessor in the trajectory. For this purpose, we traverse the tree from its root and attend every child node that overlaps with the MBB of the new line segment. We choose the leaf node containing a segment connected to the new segment (stage 1 in Figure 7.22). This search process can be summarized by the algorithm *FindNode*, which we already know from the STR-tree. If the leaf node is full, a split strategy is needed. Simply splitting a leaf node would violate the principle of trajectory preservation. Instead, we create a new leaf node. In our example in Figure 7.22, we move upward in the tree until we find a parent node that has space (stages 2 through 4). We select the right-most path (stage 5) to insert the new node. If there is space in the parent node, we insert the new leaf node, as shown in Figure 7.22. If the parent

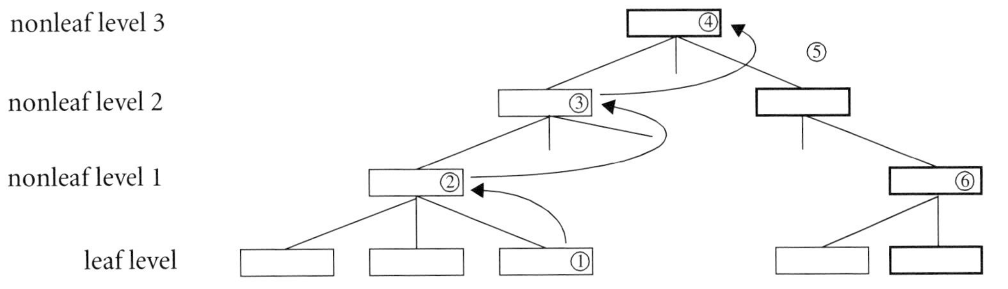

Figure 7.22 Insertion into the TB-tree.

node is full, we split it and create a new node at the nonleaf level 1, which gets the new leaf node as its only child. If necessary, the split is propagated upward. This means that the TB-tree is growing from left to right (i.e., the left-most leaf node is the first node and the right-most node is the last node that was inserted).

Exercise 7.9 Based on the previous explanations, formulate the algorithm *Insert.* ■

We could assume that the pursued strategy results in an index with a high degree of overlap. Indeed, this would be the case if we indexed arbitrary three-dimensional data. But in our case, we only "neglect" two out of three dimensions (namely, the spatial dimensions) with respect to space discrimination. However, the third, temporal, dimension supports space discrimination in the sense that data are inserted in an append-only fashion. Ultimately, the reason is that the motion of spatial objects can be described as a function over increasing time.

The structure of the TB-tree is actually a set of leaf nodes organized in a tree hierarchy. Each leaf node contains a partial trajectory. That is, a complete trajectory is distributed over a set of disconnected leaf nodes. To support efficient query processing, it is necessary to be able to retrieve segments based on their trajectory identifier. A simple solution is to employ a doubly linked list to connect leaf nodes that contain parts of the same trajectory in a way that preserves *trajectory evolution*. Figure 7.23 shows a part of a TB-tree structure and a trajectory illustrating this approach. The trajectory in the example expands over six nodes. In the TB-tree these leaf nodes are connected through a linked list.

By starting from an arbitrary leaf node, these links permit us to retrieve the (partial) trajectory at minimal cost. With the fanout M at a leaf node, the size of the partial trajectory contained in the leaf node is M. We assume $M \geq 3$, and among these M segments we know that by definition $M - 2$ segments are biconnected, one is forward-connected, and one is backward-connected. To find all segments of the same trajectory, we have to follow the pointers of the linked list in both directions to the next and previous leaf nodes.

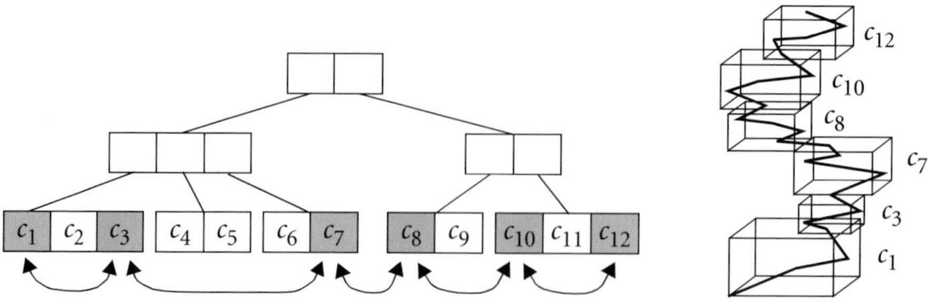

Figure 7.23 The TB-tree structure.

7.4.3 Query Processing

We will here consider three main types of spatio-temporal queries: coordinate-based queries, trajectory-based queries, and combined queries. *Coordinate-based queries* are point, range (window), and nearest-neighbor queries in the resulting 3D space. Examples are queries of the form "Find all objects within a given area (or at a given point) at some time during a given time interval (or at a given time instant)" or "Find the *k*-closest objects with respect to a given point at a given time instant." A special case of a range query is the timeslice query, which determines the positions of moving objects at a given time point in the past.

Trajectory-based queries include *topological queries*, which involve the topology of trajectories, and *navigational queries*, which involve derived information such as speed and heading of objects. Topological queries incorporate *spatio-temporal predicates* (Section 4.4), such as *Disjoint, Meet, Overlap, Enter, Leave, Cross*, and *Bypass*, since they appear in *spatio-temporal selections* and *joins*. Navigational queries derive information from a trajectory, since dynamic information is not explicitly stored. The average or top *speed* of a moving point is determined by the fraction of traveled distance over time. The *heading* of a moving point is given by the vector between two specified positions. The *area* covered by a moving object is calculated by considering the convex hull of its trajectory. Each of these properties is unique, but all depend on the time interval considered. For example, the heading of an object in the last 10 minutes may have been strictly east, but, taking into account the last hour, it may have been northeast. The speed of an object may currently be 100 kilometers/hour, but during the last hour it might have averaged 70 kilometers/hour.

Combined queries include aspects of and connect coordinate-based and topological queries. For example, we can ask: What were the trajectories of objects after they left Tucson between 7:00 A.M. and 8:00 A.M. today in the next hour? This query uses the range "Tucson between 7:00 A.M. and 8:00 A.M. today" to identify the trajectories, while "in the next hour" gives a range to restrict the parts of the trajectories that we want to retrieve. We see that we can construct various query combinations that make sense in the spatio-temporal application context.

In general, to extract information related to trajectories, we have to select the trajectories and the parts of the trajectories we want to return. Trajectories can be selected by their trajectory identifier, by a segment of the trajectory using a spatio-temporal range, by a topological query, and/or by derived information. An example query for spatio-temporal selection is: Find a taxi at the corner of Fifth Avenue and Central Park South between 7:00 A.M. and 7:15 A.M. today.

Next, we discuss how these different query types can be processed by the three access methods of R-tree, STR-tree, and TB-tree. Coordinate-based queries can be processed as a straightforward extension of the classical range query processing using the R-tree. The main idea is to traverse the tree from the root to the bottom according to coordinate constraints until the entries are found in the leaf nodes.

Topological queries can be transformed into and thus reduced to ordinary range queries. We illustrate this with the example query: Which taxis left the Tucson city limits between 7:00 a.m. and 8:00 a.m. today? In Figure 7.24, the cube represents a spatio-temporal range, and t_2 is a trajectory of a moving point leaving the range. The other trajectories t_1, t_3, and t_4 are entering, crossing, or bypassing the specified range, respectively. In order to be able to determine those trajectories leaving a given range we have to check trajectory segments intersecting the four lateral sides of the spatio-temporal range, as shown in Figure 7.24. If a trajectory leaves or enters a range, only one qualifying segment has to be found. By entering (leaving), the starting point or bottom end point of the segment should be outside (inside) the cube. In case a trajectory crosses a range (e.g., t_3), at least two intersections can be found that may result from one, two, or more qualifying segments. In case a trajectory bypasses a range (e.g., t_4), no qualifying segment will be found. Thus, we can employ modified range queries to evaluate spatio-temporal predicates. It must be said that here we have only considered a very simple case. For cases in which complex spatio-temporal predicates are constructed by temporal composition, searching turns out to be much more complicated.

For combined queries, algorithms are different due to the combined search. That is, we not only retrieve all entries contained in a given subspace (range query), we also retrieve entries belonging to the same trajectory. In the following text, we discuss

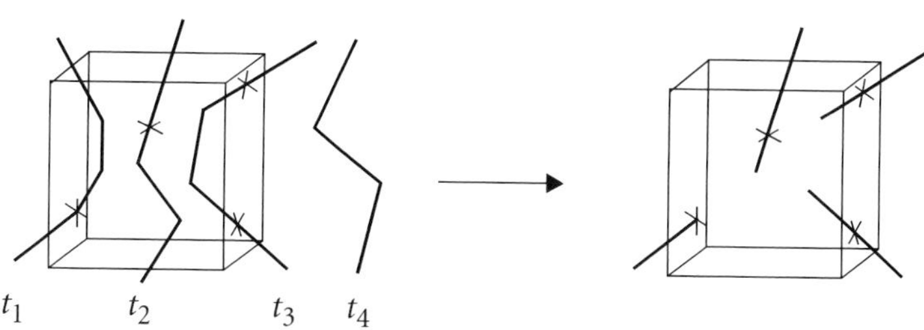

Figure 7.24 Processing topological queries.

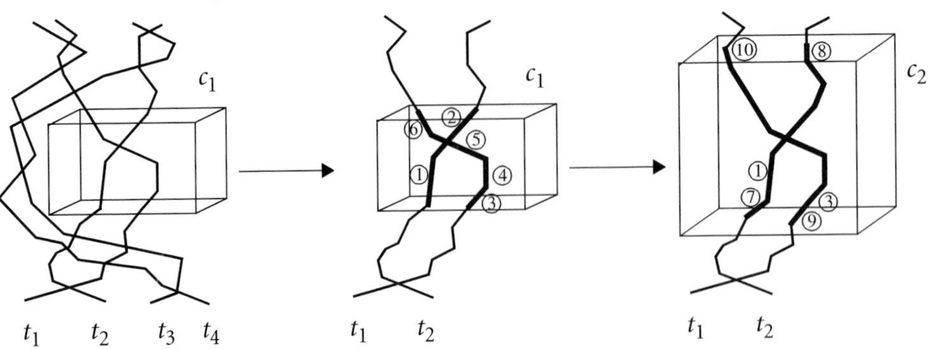

Figure 7.25 Stages in combined search.

separate algorithms for the R-tree and the STR-tree on the one hand and the TB-tree on the other hand. The algorithm for the TB-tree is different, since it leverages the data structure of a linked list between leaf nodes to retrieve partial trajectories.

We start with combined search methods in the R-tree and the STR-tree. The first step is to determine an initial set of segments with respect to a given spatio-temporal range. For that purpose, we apply the range-search algorithm employed in the R-tree. The idea is to descend the tree with respect to intersection properties until the entries are found in the leaf nodes. This is illustrated in Figure 7.25 where we search the tree using the cube c_1 and obtain four segments of trajectory t_1 (labeled 3 to 6) and two segments of trajectory t_2 (labeled 1 and 2). These six segments are emphasized by thick lines.

In the second stage, we extract partial trajectories for an outer range c_2. For each of the found segments we try to find its connecting segment. First, we search in the same leaf node and then in other leaf nodes. For instance, for segment 1 of trajectory t_2 we find two segments, a forward-connected one and a backward-connected one. If we have to search in other leaf nodes, this is done by a range search, with the end point of the segment in question as a predicate. On arrival at the leaf level, the algorithm examines whether a segment is connected to the segment in question. This is performed recursively, and we retrieve more and more segments of the trajectory. The algorithm terminates when a newly found, connected segment is outside cube c_2. The last segments returned for segment 1 are segments 7 and 8. The combined search algorithm is as follows:

algorithm *CombinedSearch*(*node*, *elem*, *range*)
  if *node* is not a leaf **then**
    for each entry *elem* of *node* whose MBB intersects with *range* **do**
      execute *CombinedSearch*(*node*', *elem*, *range*) where *node*' is the child
        node of *node* pointed to by *elem*
    endfor

```
    else
        for each entry elem that satisfies range and
            whose trajectory was not yet retrieved do
                execute DetermineTrajectory(node, elem, range)
        endfor
    endif
end.

algorithm DetermineTrajectory(node, elem, range)
    Loop through node and find segment elem' that is forward connected to elem;
    while found and elem' is within range do
        Add elem' to set of solutions; elem := elem';
        Loop through node and find segment elem' that is forward connected to
            elem;
    endwhile;
    if not found but within range then
        Execute FindConnSegment(root, elem, forward);
        Repeat algorithm from the beginning
    endif;
    The same as above for backward connected
end.

algorithm FindConnSegment(node, elem, direction)
    if node is not a leaf then
        for each entry elem' of node whose MBB intersects the MBB of elem do
            execute FindConnSegment(node', elem, direction) where node' is the
                childnode of node pointed to by elem'
        endfor
    else
        if node contains an entry that is direction connected to elem
        then return node endif
    endif
end.
```

A problem still remaining is that the same trajectory could be retrieved twice. For instance, the initial range search retrieves the two segments 1 and 2 of trajectory t_2. If we use both segments as a starting point, we will obtain the same trajectory twice. We can simply avoid this by keeping the trajectory identifier once it is retrieved and check, before determining a new trajectory, if it had been previously retrieved. In our example, we only use segment 1 or segment 2 but not both to retrieve a partial trajectory t_2 and save retrieving it again for the other segment.

The combined search algorithm of the TB-tree is similar to the one presented previously. The main difference consists in the retrieval of partial trajectories. While the R-tree and the STR-tree provide little help in retrieving trajectories, the linked lists of the TB-tree allow us to obtain connected segments without searching. If, in our example, we want to determine partial trajectories contained in the outer range c_2 for the segments 1 and 2 of t_2 and segments 3 to 6 of t_1, we have the two possibilities that a connected segment can be in the same leaf node or in another leaf node. If it is in the same, finding it is simple. If it is in another leaf node, we have to follow the next (previous) pointer in the linked list to the next (previous) leaf node. Again, we have to take care not to retrieve the same trajectory twice. Thus, we keep the trajectory identifier as soon as a partial trajectory is retrieved. The only algorithmic change relates to the algorithm *FindConnSegment*, which is now as follows:

algorithm *FindConnSegment*(*node, elem, direction*)
  Set *node* to be the node pointed to by the direction pointer
end.

7.5 Further Exercises

Exercise 7.10 Catalog Structure

The catalog structure will be used as an index structure for a set of 100 points. For the variable B we choose the value 10. Use the following illustration for the construction of the catalog structure. Use it directly or make a copy of it. Do *not* redraw it. Mark the points that trigger the construction of a new block.

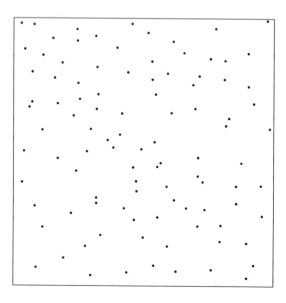

Exercise 7.11 Duality

Prove that the *incidence-preserving* and *order-preserving* properties of the duality transformation, as shown in the book, hold for a pair (point p, line l).

Exercise 7.12 TPR-tree

In contrast to a B-tree, an R*-tree does not partition the domain of the indexing attribute into distinct ranges. As a consequence, at every level L a decision among some possible nodes of the tree must be made to determine a path from the root to a leaf. Along this path the bounding boxes of the inner nodes may be enlarged. In a TPR-tree the bounding boxes are time dependent.

1. Formulate an algorithm *FindLeaf*, which determines a path from the root to a leaf. Call functions for *overlap*, *area*, *coverage*, and *perimeter* and pass the needed information to them; hence, compute the needed information for the function *optimize*, which can be called to determine the best node among several alternatives. Additionally, store the chosen path, since it may be used later to enlarge the MBBs.
2. Outline the *Insert* algorithm. Since the split operation is very complicated and not explained in this book, just call a function *split*. To minimize splits a reinsertion strategy will be used. Hence, the first time an overflow happens in one of the leaf nodes, some objects contained in the leaf will be reinserted (inserted again) into the tree. This will restructure the tree and may avoid splittings. Experiments proved that reinsertion improves performance best when the first $M/3$ objects are reinserted in descending order of the distances measured between their MBB's center and the center of the parent MBB.

Exercise 7.13 Kinetic B-tree

Primarily, a kinetic B-tree is a conventional B-tree together with a global event queue. To create such a tree, in an initial step the event-queue must be created.

Write an algorithm for computing the initial event queue of a kinetic B-tree for a given set of N points in $\mathbb{R}$.

Exercise 7.14 STR-tree

The trajectories of four moving points projected to the x/y plane are displayed in the following figure. Think of the third dimension (time) pointing toward you. All of the moving points start at t_0, meet the first point T_1^i at t_1, and so on.

Exact values for the t_i are not provided, but we know that $t_{i+1} - t_i = 1$.

1. Write down the STR-tree entry for every single segment in the illustration. An MBB should be noted as $(x_{lowerleft}, y_{lowerleft}, t_i, x_{upperright}, y_{upperright}, t_{i+1})$. The first segment of R_1 has *oid* 0 and the last segment of R_4 has *oid* 15.

2. Sequentially, insert all segments into an STR-tree (in *oid* order). The algorithm *ChooseLeaf* mentioned in the book, is as follows:

algorithm *ChooseLeaf* (node N, elem E)
    while N is not a leaf **do**
        Let F be the entry in N whose *mbb* needs least enlargement to include the MBB for E. Resolve ties by choosing the entry with the rectangle of smallest area.
        N := the child pointed to by F
    endwhile;
    return N
end.

For every segment, describe the actions to insert it into the tree. Show the tree after every single split operation. Additionally, show the resulting STR-tree. Choose $m = 1, M = 3, p = 2$.

3. Draw a (2D) picture of the resulting STR-tree partitions.

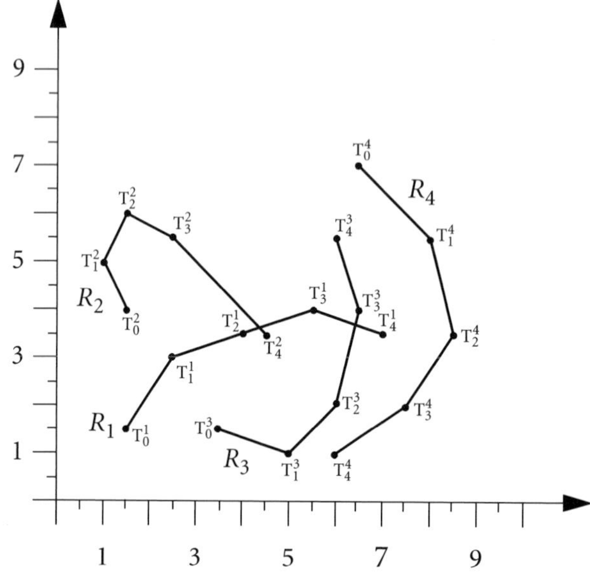

Bibliographic Notes

An enormous amount of literature exists for the geometric concepts described in Section 7.1. The R-tree was first described in Guttman, 1984; the R^*-tree in Beckmann et al., 1990; and the R^+-tree in Sellis et al., 1987. Other descriptions of the R-tree family can be found in Rigaux et al., 2002; Shekhar and Chawla, 2003. The concept of duality is discussed in de Berg et al., 2000. Descriptions of simplicial partitions and partition trees can be found in Matousek, 1992. The partial rebuilding technique was introduced by Overmars, 1983. Priority search trees have been discussed in McCreight, 1985. A description of the catalog structure and the external range tree can be found in Arge et al., 1999.

The presentation in Section 7.2 is based on the article by Theodoridis et al., 1998, describing the specific requirements of spatio-temporal index structures and summarizing some of the earlier, limited approaches for indexing spatio-temporal data. The 3D R-tree is introduced in Theodoridis et al., 1996; the RT-tree in Xu et al., 1990; and the MR-tree as well as the HR-tree in Nascimento and Silva, 1998.

In Section 7.3, the exposition of the TPR-tree is based on Saltenis et al., 2000. The presentation of the dual data transformation approach can be found in Kollios et al., 1999. The discussion of all remaining approaches in this section is based on Agarwal et al., 2003. In particular, kinetic external range trees have been developed as an external extension of kinetic range trees described in Basch et al., 1997.

The description of the STR-tree and the TB-tree for indexing the trajectories of moving points in Section 7.4 is based on Pfoser et al., 2000.

Spatio-temporal indexing is an emerging field, and the amount of literature is growing. In the following paragraphs, we mention a number of works that could not be covered in this book due to space limitations. Regarding indexing current and near-future movement, Tao et al., 2003a, present the TPR^*-tree as an extension of the TPR-tree; it avoids the large update costs of the TPR-tree. The article by Kollios et al., 2005, transforms the problem of indexing moving objects in order to efficiently answer range queries about their current and future positions into a dual space that is easier to index. Another approach has been proposed by Jensen et al., 2004, which employs a B^+-tree-based method to manage moving objects and to ensure fast updating. In Patel et al., 2004, an indexing method, called STRIPES, indexes predicted trajectories in a dual transformed space and uses partitioning instead of a tree method.

Regarding indexing trajectories, Kollios et al., 2001, introduce the use of persistent R-trees for storing trajectory data. The work of Tao and Papadias, 2001, proposes the MV3R-tree, which utilizes the concepts of multi-ersion B-trees and 3D R-trees for timeslice and interval queries about past spatio-temporal data. The articles by Hadjieleftheriou et al., 2002, 2005, deal with the special requirements of index support for spatio-temporal archives.

Indexing for network-based moving objects is addressed in Frentzos, 2003; Pfoser and Jensen, 2003; Almeida and Güting, 2005. A survey on spatio-temporal indexing techniques can be found in Mokbel et al., 2003.

8 Outlook

Moving objects databases have been a very active area of research in recent years. We have tried to cover some of the most fundamental concepts and topics in the book. However, our selection of topics was surely biased by personal interests, and in any case there is a lot of exciting research that has not been addressed. In this short closing chapter, we would like to at least briefly mention some of the remaining issues and a small selection of the relevant literature.

8.1 Data Capture

Our concern in the book has been the management of moving objects data in a database. You may wonder how such data are actually obtained.

For moving point data, the technical background of positioning devices is nicely explained in Roth, 2004. For outdoor movement (e.g., by vehicles), satellite positioning systems such as GPS are adequate. GPS receivers combine signals from several satellites to determine a position, currently with a precision within about 25 meters. Anyone can use these signals (without registering with a service). Major techniques for indoor positioning are infrared beacons and radio beacons. Radio frequency identification (RFID) transponders are a variant of radio beacons; they are small systems with a processor, memory, and an antenna but without a power supply. They take the needed energy from the received signals. RFID tags are used to track goods (e.g., in a production process). A recent development that may have some impact on the use of moving objects technology is the decision by WalMart Corporation to ask their major suppliers to deliver all packages equipped with

RFID tags, so that the company can track its products on the way through the store. This may result in the collection of large volumes of moving point data.

The question of how moving point trajectories can be obtained from sampled positions is addressed in Pfoser and Jensen, 1999. The position of the object between measurements is not known precisely; the authors show that the uncertain trajectory can be viewed as a sequence of overlapping ellipses, if a maximal speed is known. This is related to other work on uncertain trajectories, such as that of Section 3.5.

For moving regions, how data can be obtained depends on the application and kind of data. For natural phenomena (e.g., the shrinking of the Amazon rain forest), the original data will most likely have the form of a time series of satellite images. These can be converted to polygonal (vector-based) descriptions. Tøssebro and Güting, 2001, address the problem of interpolating a moving region from two adjacent observations and hence describe how to compute a region unit in the terminology of Section 4.3. A Java-based software package implementing the algorithm of Tøssebro and Güting, 2001, is available (Tøssebro, 2005).

A collection of links to data sets with real data, assembled partially within the CHOROCHRONOS project, can be found at Pfoser and Rodriguez, 2005.

8.2 Generating Test Data

Since real data are not so easy to obtain, from the beginning of moving objects database research, several groups have developed generators for test data. The main target initially was the testing of index structures. Theodoridis et al., 1999, provide a generator called *GSTD* for moving point data and region data in the form of rectangles. Various distributions can be used and parameters for the generation can be set when attempting to model an application-specific behavior of the moving objects.

Saglio and Moreira, 2001, take a simulation approach, offering the *Oporto* generator. Shoals of fish move in the sea close to some harbors, and fishing ships leave their harbors, go toward the fish, spend some time fishing, and then return to the harbor. Shoals of fish are attracted by plankton areas, and ships try to avoid storm areas. The main idea is to obtain a realistic scenario with natural and consistent movements of moving points and moving regions.

Vehicles often move along spatial networks. A very popular generator for network-based moving objects is provided by Brinkhoff, 2002, simulating car traffic in the city of Oldenburg, Germany. Many aspects of movements in networks are considered in order to be realistic. For example, cars follow the shortest paths from their start position to a target position and get slowed down when too many objects are crowded on the same edge of the network.

Complex time-evolving regions can be generated with *G-TERD* (Tzouramanis et al., 2002). A region is modeled by a set of overlapping rectangles. The result is a sequence of color images. These could be transformed to polygons and then to moving regions, as discussed in the previous section.

All these generators are available for download on the Web (GSTD, 2005; Oporto, 2005; Brinkhoff, 2005; G-TERD 2005).

8.3 Movement in Networks

A fairly obvious observation is that moving point objects in many cases do not move freely in the 2D plane but rather within spatially embedded networks (on roads, highways—even airplanes normally follow fixed routes). It makes a lot of sense to include spatial networks in a data model and query language for moving objects, as well as query processing. We can then represent movements relative to the network rather than to the 2D space. For example, instead of describing the position of a car by geographic coordinates, we can describe it as being at kilometer 170.34 on a particular highway. This has several advantages (Güting et al., 2005):

- It is easier to formulate queries about relationships between the moving object and the network, since the network is a known concept within the database, as opposed to being represented only implicitly.
- Such queries can be evaluated much more efficiently. For example, to check which part of a particular highway has been traversed by a given vehicle, in the model with free movement a complex and time-consuming comparison between the geometries of the object and of the highway has to be performed. In the network-based model, simple comparisons between edge identifiers are sufficient.
- The representation of moving objects becomes much more compact as geometries are factored out and represented not in moving objects but once and for all with the network. For example, in the standard model a vehicle moving with constant speed along a road needs a piece of representation with every bend of the road. In the network-based model, a single piece of representation (a unit in the terminology of Section 4.3) suffices as long as the speed does not change.
- The smaller representation also improves the indexing of trajectories, since less entries are needed.

Modeling and querying moving objects in networks is addressed in Vazirgiannis and Wolfson, 2001, and in Güting et al., 2005. Vazirgiannis and Wolfson, 2001, model a network as an undirected graph where nodes correspond to street crossings and edges are city road blocks. Moving objects are still represented by geometric polylines. A few extensions of SQL are provided (e.g., to allow restrictions by distance or travel time along the network).

Güting et al., 2005, extend the approach with abstract data types presented in Chapter 4 to networks. The data model is extended by a data type `network`, and data types `gpoint` and `gline` are introduced to represent positions and regions[1] within a network, respectively. For example, the part of a road network covered by a fog area can be represented as a `gline` value. These data types are included in the type system of Section 4.2 so that also data types *moving*(`gpoint`) and *moving*(`gline`) are available. Hence, we can represent static and moving network positions and regions. In a highway network, examples of the four types are gas stations, construction areas, cars, and traffic jams, respectively. Many of the query operations of Section 4.2 are applicable and further operations for networks are provided.

Data modeling for moving objects in networks is also discussed in Jensen et al., 2003b; Hage et al., 2003. They describe as a case study the data model used by the Danish road directory and a Danish company. The emphasis here is to explain that real road networks are quite complex and that simple directed graph models are not sufficient. The case study suggests using several interrelated representations called the kilometer post representation, the link node representation, the geographical representation, and the segment representation. All representations are expressed in terms of relational tables.

A more formalized model incorporating some of these ideas is presented in Speicys et al., 2003. They propose to use two network models together, one targeted at a precise geometric description and the other representing the graph or connectivity structure. An algorithm is given to derive the second structure from the first. Their modeling approach is aimed mainly at supporting location-based services applications; hence, there is only a concept of currently moving objects issuing queries relative to the network, not on modeling complete trajectories relative to the network.

Earlier work on handling spatially embedded networks in data modeling and query processing includes Güting, 1994b; Shekhar and Liu, 1997; Huang et al., 1997. A recent article focusing on query processing for spatial networks is Papadias et al., 2003. They compare Euclidean and network-based evaluation of several types of queries, such as nearest neighbor, range query, closest pairs, and distance join.

Several groups have studied network-based indexing of moving objects (Frentzos, 2003; Pfoser and Jensen, 2003; Almeida and Güting, 2005.

Query processing algorithms for certain types of queries for moving objects in networks are adressed in Jensen et al., 2003a; Shahabi et al., 2003; Gupta et al., 2004.

The test data generator for network-based moving objects (Brinkhoff, 2002) was already mentioned; it is an important tool to study the implementation of such models, especially indexing techniques. An experience with collecting real data and an algorithm for matching measured positions with a map of the network is described in Civilis et al., 2004.

[1] A region in a spatially embedded network corresponds geometrically to a `line` value; therefore, the type is called `gline`.

8.4 Query Processing for Continuous/Location-Based Queries

The concept of continuous queries has already come up in Chapter 3 with the MOST model. Some recent work has studied algorithms for special types of continuous queries for moving objects. In fact, there has been a lot of work in this area, of which we can mention only a few examples.

Perhaps the first reference on continuous queries in a general database context is Terry et al., 1992. Continuous queries on data streams have been a very popular research issue in the last years (Chen et al., 2000; Madden et al., 2002).

Several authors have addressed dynamic variants of the nearest neighbor problem. Zheng and Lee, 2001, support queries for the nearest neighbor of a moving query point by constructing the Voronoi diagram and storing its cells (Voronoi regions) in an R-tree. Assuming linear movement of the query point, the result also includes an estimate as to how long it will be valid and which will be the next nearest neighbor.

Song and Roussopoulos, 2001, consider the problem of maintaining the k nearest neighbors for a moving query point efficiently—for example, to keep track of the five nearest gas stations for a car moving along a highway. They adapt earlier branch-and-bound techniques for finding the k nearest neighbors of a static query point.

Benetis et al., 2002, develop techniques to answer nearest neighbor queries not only for moving query but also for moving data points and *reverse nearest neighbor queries*. A reverse nearest neighbor query returns the objects that have a query object as their closest object. Here, results are given as a sequence of pairs <nearest neighbor, validity time interval>. All these publications assume constant velocities of the involved objects and offer predictions of the near future. Results may become invalid with updates to the database, as discussed in Chapter 3.

A more general study of time-dependent spatial queries is offered by Tao and Papadias, 2003. They consider two kinds of queries that they call *time-parameterized* and *continuous*. A time-parameterized query returns an answer with respect to the current time together with an expiration time and a reason for expiration. A continuous query returns pairs of the form *<result, time interval>*, as in the previous paragraph. The article studies query processing for moving data objects, moving query objects, and both, for the most common types of queries, such as window queries, nearest neighbor, and spatial join.

Zhang et al., 2003b, consider the problem of determining the *validity region* for moving nearest neighbor and window queries on static point data sets, that is, the region in space within which the result will remain valid. An advantage compared with some of the previously mentioned methods is that the assumption of linear movement (or constant velocity) can be dropped; the result remains valid as long as the query point remains within the validity region, regardless of how many location/speed updates occur.

Mokbel et al., 2004, consider a set of moving query objects and a set of moving data objects. Query processing is performed as a join between the two, providing shared execution for the queries. Additions and removals to/from the result set are computed incrementally. The idea of shared execution is borrowed from stream processing projects such as NiagaraCQ (Chen et al., 2000) or PSoup (Chandrasekaran and Franklin, 2002).

Further work on evaluating continuous queries on moving objects is discussed in Lazaridis et al., 2002; Gedik and Liu, 2004.

8.5 Aggregation and Selectivity Estimation

Another subfield of research within moving objects databases considers the problem of computing precisely or estimating the *numbers* of moving objects within certain areas in space and time—hence, of computing *aggregates*. Aggregate information is interesting for several reasons: First, in many applications (e.g., in traffic control) the individual moving objects are not of interest, but their numbers are. A related aspect is that keeping information about individuals may even violate privacy rights. The second major motivation is the use for selectivity estimation for various types of queries. In most cases the result of the aggregate computation is not precise but an estimation.

As discussed previously, this work can be divided into two groups:

- Considering aggregation on history of movement
- Computing aggregate values for near-future predictive queries

In the first group, Papadias et al., 2002, develop a data warehouse approach for indexing moving object data. They assume the raw data are given as a set of regions in space (e.g., sections of a road or cell areas in mobile communication systems), together with the sets of objects falling into each region at every timestamp. They provide several multi-tree structures combining R-trees and B-trees. The goal is to support OLAP-like queries on spatio-temporal data. A follow-up article by Tao et al., 2004, solves a remaining problem with the approach of Papadias et al., 2002, the distinct counting problem. The problem is that an object remaining within the same region for several timestamps will be counted several times in a query aggregating over a time interval. They reuse a technique for approximate counting called *sketches*.

The articles by Zhang et al. (2003a) and Sun et al. (2004) consider maintaining aggregate information on moving object data coming in large volumes in the form of data streams, for example, from tracking large numbers of vehicles in road networks. Zhang et al., 2003a, develop a general framework to maintain temporal aggregations at different levels of granularity; older data are aggregated at a coarser level and more recent data at a finer level of granularity. The framework can then be applied to spatio-temporal aggregation. Sun et al., 2004, develop techniques to maintain a histogram structure under a large update load. They also keep track of previous versions of histogram buckets to be able to answer queries about the past. Finally, they also offer a stochastic approach for predictions into the future based on observations from the present and the recent past. Note that in contrast to the work discussed next, this prediction does not rely on linear movement assumptions for the involved objects.

The second category of work considers predictive queries in the style of Chapter 3; hence, we have a collection of moving data objects and/or moving query objects. All these works assume linear movement; hence, the predictions will only be valid for a limited time horizon. This horizon may be different for various kinds of applications (e.g., hours for ships, minutes for air traffic control); for cars in road networks such predictions may be meaningless (Tao et al., 2003c).

The first article addressing this kind of problem was by Choi and Chung, 2002. They consider selectivity estimation for window queries for an instant of time in the near future—for example: Retrieve all airplanes that will be within a query rectangle 10 minutes from now. They reuse the *MinSkew* histogram structure (Acharya et al., 1999) for spatial selectivity estimation and introduce velocity-bounded bucket regions, similar to the TPR-tree of Section 7.3. This article is restricted to moving data points and static window queries.

The article by Tao et al., 2003b, improves and generalizes this work in several ways. They also consider window query selectivity estimation, as well as cases of static and moving data objects, static and moving queries, and objects that may be points or rectangles. They also drop an assumption of uniform velocities made in Choi and Chung, 2002, and the technique used there of combining one-dimensional projections to obtain a result in two dimensions, which leads to an overestimation of the result size. The histograms used here split buckets not only by location but also by velocity, which leads to a large reduction of the estimation error.

A still more general version of the problem is studied in Tao et al., 2003c, who consider, in addition to window queries, join queries and nearest neighbor queries. A join query retrieves all pairs of objects from two data sets that will come within distance d of each other within a future time interval. A nearest neighbor query retrieves the objects that will come closest to the query object within such a time interval. The goal is to provide selectivity estimation for window and join queries, and an estimation of the distance for nearest neighbor queries. In the article, probabilistic cost models are derived; additionally histogram structures are proposed and evaluated.

A thorough experimental comparison of several estimation techniques for such predictive queries is given in Hadjieleftheriou et al., 2003. They also present a new technique based on using the duality transform described in Section 7.3.3 and another one that assumes that a secondary index structure on the moving objects is available.

Further work on aggregation over moving objects is discussed in Revesz and Chen, 2003; Chen and Revesz, 2004. Revesz and Chen, 2003, consider several types of dominance queries over moving points such as: Given a set of moving points S and a moving query point q, determine the number of points from S that will be dominated by q at time instant t. In contrast to the other work mentioned, the techniques developed here return exact results. Chen and Revesz, 2004, consider the query type: Find the maximum number of points that will be simultaneously within a query rectangle within a future time interval. They provide a solution for a one-dimensional version of this problem.

Solutions to Exercises in the Text

Chapter 1

Solution 1.1

1. How many people live within 10 kilometers from the river Rhine? (Cities are modeled as points; hence, if the point is within that distance we count the whole population.)

   Obviously, we need to be able to measure the distance between a point and a line, so we need an operation:

   distance: *points* × *line* → *real*

   This will return the minimal distance between any of the points in the first argument and the second argument line. The query is:

```
SELECT SUM(c.pop)
FROM rivers AS r, cities AS c
WHERE r.name = 'Rhine' and distance(c.location, r.route) < 10
```

2. With which of its neighbor countries does Germany have the longest common border?

   We use an operation:

   common_border: *region* × *region* → *line*

which returns the intersection of two *region* boundaries. The query is:

```
LET border_lengths =
SELECT t.name AS name, length(common_border(s.area, t.area))
  AS length
FROM states AS s, states AS t
WHERE s.name = 'Germany' AND s.area adjacent t.area;

SELECT name, length
FROM border_lengths
WHERE length =
  SELECT MAX(length)
  FROM border_lengths
```

3. Find the locations of all bridges of highways crossing rivers. Return them as a relation with the name of the highway, the name of the river, and the location.

   We introduce a predicate:

   intersects: *line* × *line* → *bool*

   The query is:

```
SELECT r.name, h.name, intersection(r.route, h.route)
FROM rivers AS r, highways AS h
WHERE r.route intersects h.route
```

Solution 1.2

Table S.1 Model by Segev.

Name	*Location*	*Time*
Mr. Jones	Edinburgh, Grand Hotel	5
Mr. Jones	Edinburgh, Traveler's Inn	8
Mr. Jones	Aviemore, Golf Hotel	15
Mr. Jones	Home	17
Anne	Home	5
Anne	Brighton, Linda	7
Anne	Home	12
Anne	Parents	16

Table S.2 Model by Sarda.

Name	*Location*	*Time*
Mr. Jones	Edinburgh, Grand Hotel	[5–7]
Mr. Jones	Edinburgh, Traveler's Inn	[8–14]
Mr. Jones	Aviemore, Golf Hotel	[15–16]
Mr. Jones	Home	[17–∞]
Anne	Home	[5–6]
Anne	Brighton, Linda	[7–11]
Anne	Home	[12–15]
Anne	Parents	[16–∞]

Table S.3 HRDM.

Name	*Location*
5 → Mr. Jones	5 → Edinburgh, Grand Hotel
. . .	. . .
	7 → Edinburgh, Grand Hotel
	8 → Edinburgh, Traveler's Inn
	. . .
	14 → Edinburgh, Traveler's Inn
	15 → Aviemore, Golf Hotel
	16 → Aviemore, Golf Hotel
	17 → Home
	. . .
5 → Anne	5 → Home
. . .	6 → Home
	7 → Brighton, Linda
	. . .
	11 → Brighton, Linda
	12 → Home
	. . .
	15 → Home
	16 → Parents
	. . .

Solution 1.3

We also show all intermediate steps to make it easier to follow.

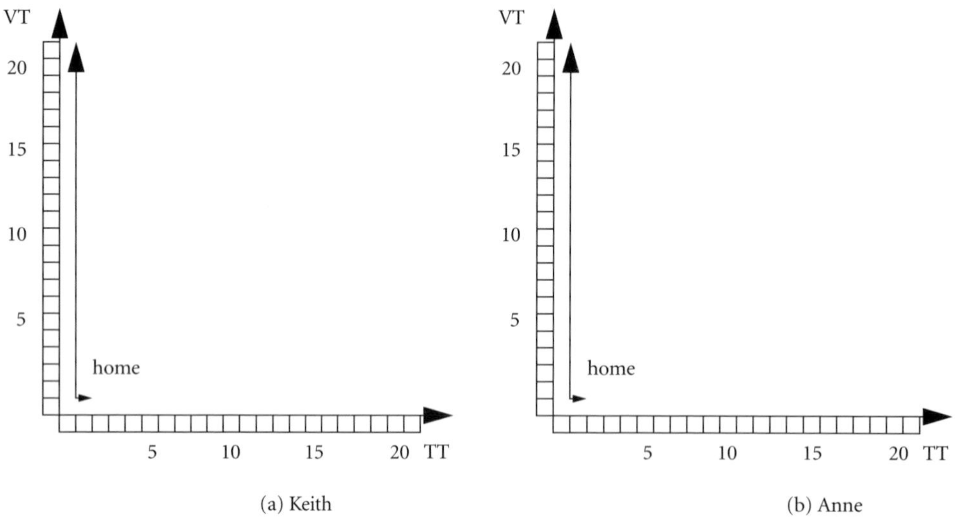

Figure S.1 Jennifer's knowledge, December 1.

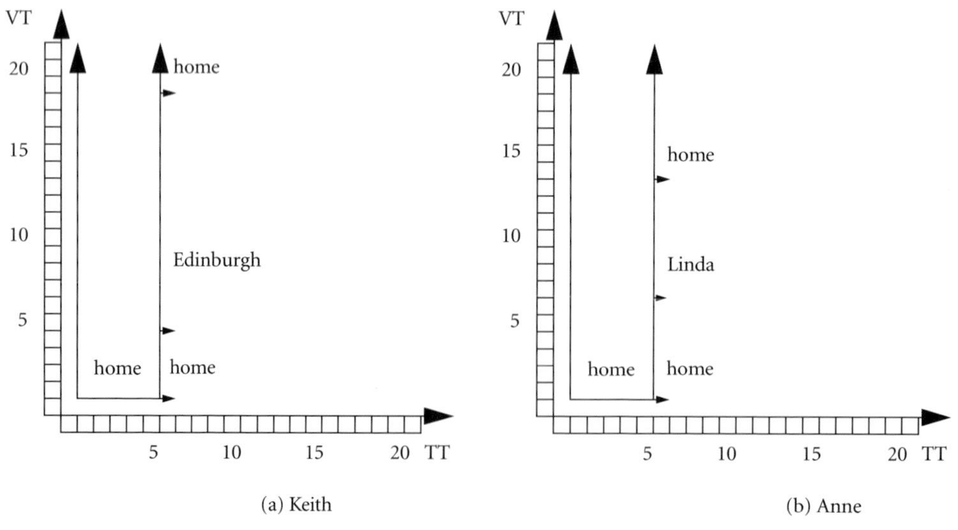

Figure S.2 Jennifer's knowledge, December 6.

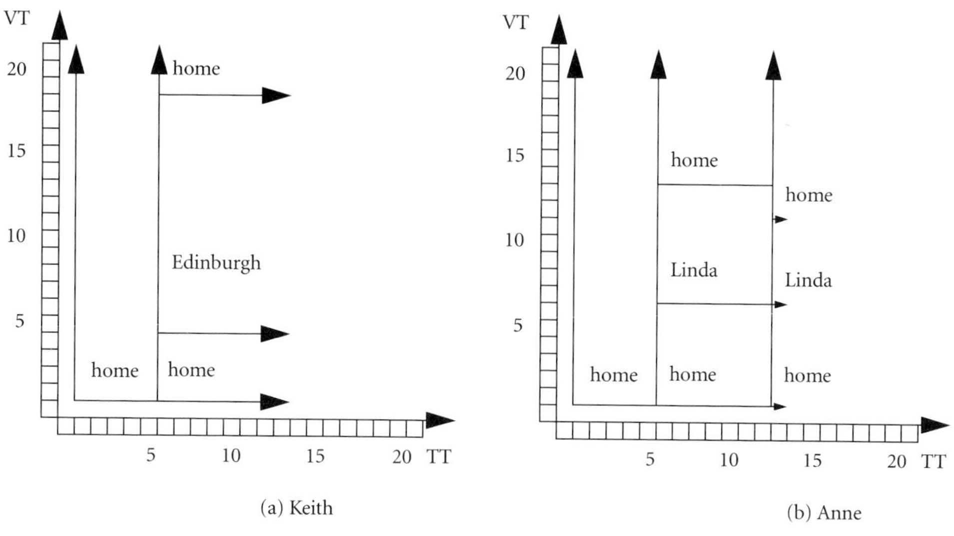

Figure S.3 Jennifer's knowledge, December 13.

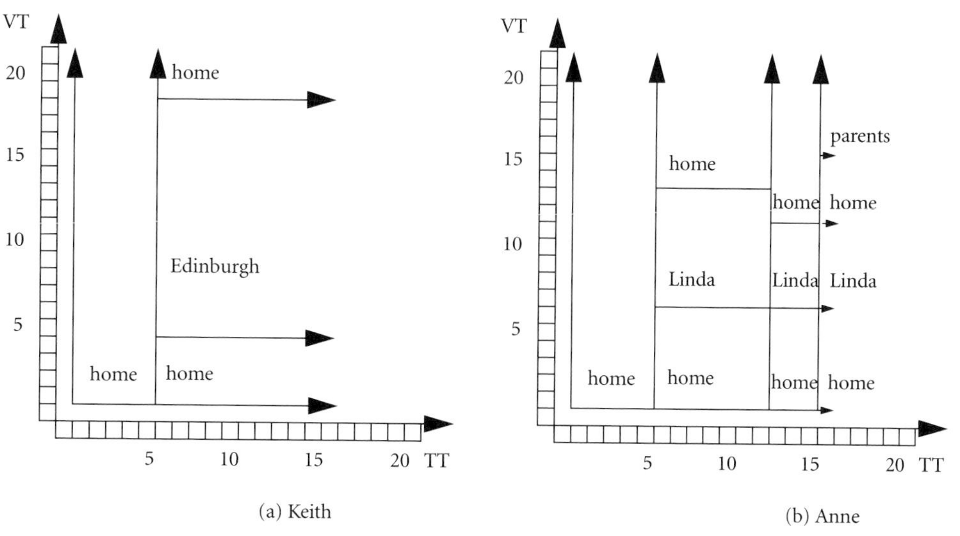

Figure S.4 Jennifer's knowledge, December 16.

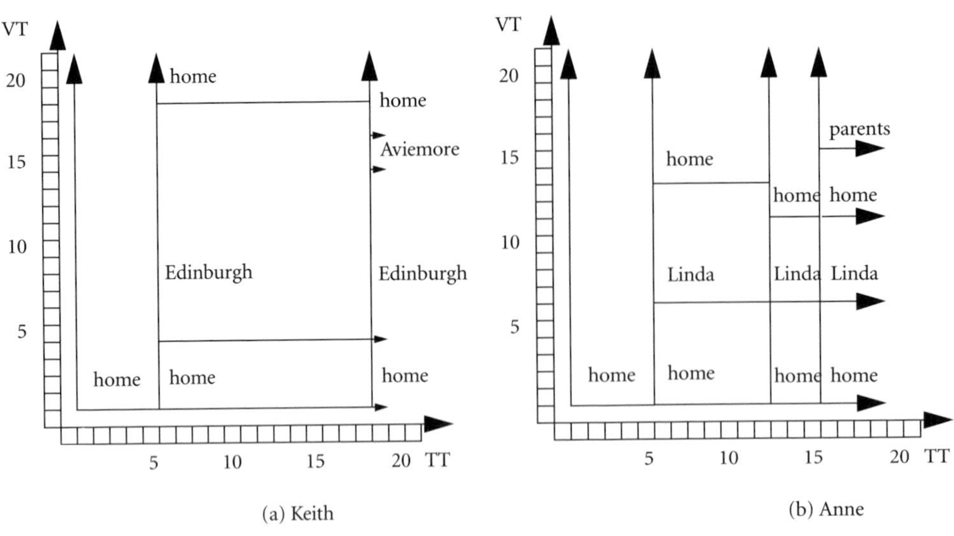

Figure S.5 Jennifer's knowledge, December 19.

Chapter 2

Solution 2.1

The "discrete" nature of this approach becomes visible in Definition 2.8, which defines an ST-simplex as an ordered pair (S, T), where S is a simplex and T is a BTE. In other words, a specific spatial configuration S exists and is *constant* over a given range T of transaction and valid times. There is no change within the duration of T.

Solution 2.2

1. When was a parcel owned by a specific person not a developed real estate?

   We introduce an operation:

   `T-difference`: $BTE \times BTE \rightarrow BTE$

   which returns the temporal difference of two *BTE* values. The query is:

```
SELECT parcel-id, owner,
  T-difference(T-project(area), T-project(building))
    AS undeveloped-area
FROM parcels
```

2. When was the school (as the first building) constructed on parcel 4?

   We use an operation:

   min: *BTE* $\rightarrow$ *BTE*

   which, according to some order on the Cartesian product of periods of a BTE, returns the single-valued, minimum BTE of a *BTE* value. The query is:

```
SELECT min(T-project(building))
FROM parcels
WHERE parcel-id = 4
```

Solution 2.3

The same task utilizing the snapshot model requires the following steps:

1. Find the map with the right timestamp in the map sequence.
2. Create a difference map between that map and the preceding map. This difference map represents the "deltas"—that is, it contains the new values in all cells whose values have changed from the preceding map and zero or null in all cells whose values have not changed. During this computation, for each cell check if its contents match the given value.

This algorithm necessarily requires $n = n_x \cdot n_y$ cell-by-cell comparisons between two adjacent snapshots, where n is the total number of cells. This means that the entire task is performed in $O(n)$ time for a complete snapshot image.

Solution 2.4

The algorithms for queries 1 and 3 are similar to the algorithm for query 2. The algorithm for query 1 outputs all locations of components of the event found for time t_i. The worst time complexity is $O(n_e + c_e \cdot k_c)$, respectively, $O((\log n_e) + c_e \cdot k_c)$. The algorithm for query 3 in addition yields the new values of the changed cells. Analogously, the algorithms for queries 4 and 6 are slight variations of query 5 with the worst time complexity $O((\log n_e) + n_f \cdot c_e \cdot k_c)$.

Query 8 asks for a lookup operation and can be answered in time $O(n_e + c_e \cdot k_c)$, respectively, $O((\log n_e) + c_e \cdot k_c)$. If the right event has been found, we check all its corresponding components for location (x, y). Similarly, query 9 does the same for a time interval and has the time complexity $O((\log n_e) + n_f \cdot c_e \cdot k_c)$. The algorithm for query 10 is even more exhaustive. In the worst case, we have to check all n_e events in the event list and for each event all maximum c_e components for location (x, y). Hence, the worst time complexity is $O(n_e \cdot c_e \cdot k_c)$.

Chapter 3

Solution 3.1

$$g \textbf{ until\_within\_c } h \equiv [t \leftarrow Time]\ (g \textbf{ until } (h \wedge Time \leq t + c))$$

$$g \textbf{ until\_after\_c } h \equiv [t \leftarrow Time]\ (g \textbf{ until } (h \wedge Time \geq t + c))$$

Solution 3.2

For reasons of simplicity, we ignore ρ, which is the same for all tuples, and we only consider time intervals. Further, based on the fact that we have a discrete model of time (clock ticks), we make the following assumptions:

1. Only closed time intervals are considered—that is, we allow intervals $[t, t]$, which model time instants as degenerate time intervals, and we transform intervals of the kind $[t_1, t_2)$ to $[t_1, t_2 - 1]$ for $t_1 < t_2$ and intervals of the kind $(t_1, t_2]$ to $[t_1 + 1, t_2]$ for $t_1 < t_2$ and intervals of the form (t_1, t_2) to $[t_1 + 1, t_2 - 1]$ for $t_1 + 1 < t_2$.
2. An order is defined on closed time intervals through:

$$[t_1, t_2] < [t_3, t_4] \quad \Leftrightarrow \quad t_1 < t_3 \quad \vee \ (t_1 = t_3 \wedge t_2 < t_4)$$

In the first step of the algorithm, all n time intervals are sorted according to the order under assumption 2. This takes time $O(n \log n)$. In the second step, the resulting sequence, let us say $\langle [t_{1,1}, t_{1,2}], [t_{2,1}, t_{2,2}], ..., [t_{n,1}, t_{n,2}] \rangle$, is traversed in $O(n)$ time, and overlapping and consecutive intervals are merged appropriately, as follows:

```
result := ⟨⟩;
i := 2;
start := t_{1,1};
end := t_{1,2};
while i ≤ n do
   if t_{i,1} > end + 1 then
      result := result ∘ ⟨[start, end]⟩;
      start := t_{i,1};
      end := t_{i,2};
      i := i + 1
   elsif t_{i,2} > end then
      end := t_{i,2};
      i := i + 1
   else
      i := i + 1
```

endif
endwhile;
result := *result* ∘ ⟨[*start*, *end*]⟩;

Note that the interval pairs [3, 6] and [4, 8], [3, 6] and [6, 8], [3, 6] and [7, 8] are all merged to the interval [3, 8]. The run-time complexity for the whole algorithm is O(n log n).

Solution 3.3

$h \equiv f$ **until_after_c** g

This is illustrated in Figure S.6.

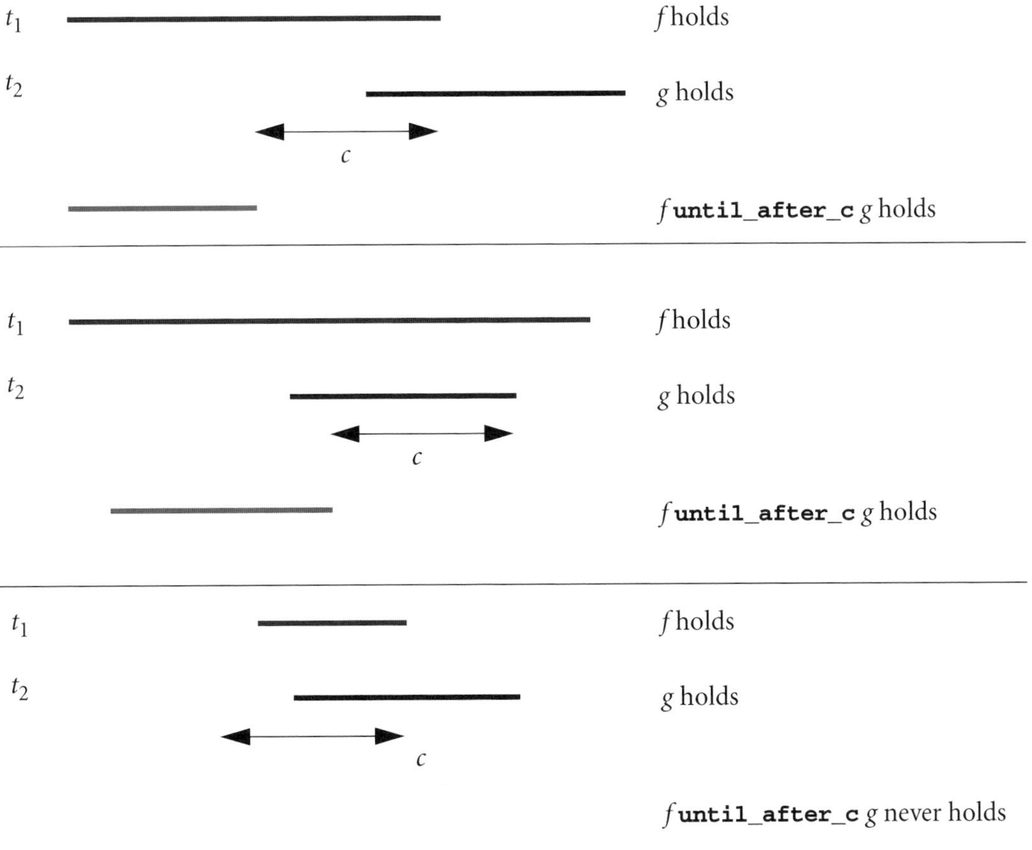

Figure S.6 Time intervals for f `until_after_c` g.

Recall the semantics for this case: f **until_after_c** g asserts that there is a future time after at least c time units from now such that g holds, and until then f will be continuously satisfied.

Let t_1, t_2 be matching pairs of tuples from R_f and R_g with overlapping time intervals. Let $e = \min\{t_1.u, t_2.u\}$. If $t_1.l \leq e - c$, then f **until_after_c** g holds in the interval $[t_1.l, e - c]$. Extend to chains as before.

Solution 3.4

First, we rewrite the query to express **eventually_within_30** by an operator for which evaluation is defined:

```
RETRIEVE t
FROM trucks t
WHERE true until_within_30 (dist(t, T_City) <= 20)
```

We then evaluate bottom-up subformulas, computing the corresponding relations.

```
dist(t, T_City) <= 20
```

This is the base case, an atomic predicate. From Figure 3.4 we can read the distances that need to be traversed by the respective trucks until the predicate becomes true and until it becomes false again. For example, for T12 these distances are 100 and 140 kilometers, respectively. This is summarized in Table S.4.

Table S.4 Distances and speeds of trucks.

Truck	*Distance true [km]*	*Distance false [km]*	*Speed [km/h]*	*Minutes needed for 10 kms*
T12	100	140	60	10
T42	130	170	100	6
T70	140	180	120	5

Table S.5 Result relation R_2 for predicate `dist(t, T_City) <= 20.`

t	*l*	*u*
T12	100	140
T42	78	102
T70	70	90

Table S.6 Result relation R_1 for predicate `true`.

l	u
0	T_{max}

Table S.7 Result relation R_2 for predicate `true until_within_30 (dist(t, T_City) <= 20).`

t	l	u
T12	10	140
T42	0	102
T70	0	90

From this we can easily compute the first result relation (Table S.5). Time units are in minutes.

Next, we compute a relation to represent the predicate *true*. This is a degenerate base case, since no variable attributes are involved. The time interval "forever" is represented as $[0, T_{max}]$. Hence, we obtain a relation shown in Table S.6.

Next, we have to apply the algorithm to evaluate **`until_within_30`** for the two argument relations R_1 and R_2. The single tuple in R_1 matches each tuple in R_2. For each pair of matching tuples we compute the maximum of $t_1.l$ and $t_2.l - 90$ and use it as the lower bound of the time interval of the result tuple. The result relation is shown in Table S.7.

This is the result relation for the continuous query. For the instantaneous query evaluated at time 0 the result is the set of trucks {T42, T70}. For the continuous query, the result changes over time. For example, at time 20 the result is {T12, T42, T70}, at time 100 it is {T12, T42}, and at time 200 it is $\varnothing$.

Solution 3.5

In this case the information costs are:

$$COST_I([t_1, t_2[) = C_1 + 0.5a(t_2 - t_1)^2 + C_2K(1 + 1/2 + 1/3 + \ldots + 1/(t_2 - t_1))$$

The deviation at time t_2 is $a(t_2 - t_1)$, and the threshold at that time is $K/(t_2 - t_1)$. Since the deviation reaches the threshold at time t_2, both values are equal. Therefore, $K = a(t_2 - t_1)^2$ and $\sqrt{K/a} = t_2 - t_1$. If we divide $COST_I([t_1, t_2[)$ by $t_2 - t_1$ in order to obtain the information cost per time unit, and if we substitute K for $a(t_2 - t_1)^2$ and $\sqrt{K/a}$ for $t_2 - t_1$ in the resulting equation, we obtain $f(K)$.

Solution 3.6

For computing the first threshold *loc.uncertainty*, we first determine $a_1 = 2I_1/t_1^2 = 2 \cdot 1/4^2 = 0.125$. Then we obtain:

$$loc.uncertainty = \sqrt{(2a_1C_1)/(2C_2 + 1)} = \sqrt{(2 \cdot 0.125 \cdot 8)/(2 \cdot 1 + 1)} = 0.82.$$

For computing the second threshold *loc.uncertainty*, we first determine $a_2 = 2I_2/t_2^2 = 2 \cdot 1.5/10^2 = 0.03$. Then we obtain:

$$loc.uncertainty = \sqrt{(2a_2C_1)/(2C_2 + 1)} = \sqrt{(2 \cdot 0.03 \cdot 8)/(2 \cdot 1 + 1)} = 0.4.$$

Solution 3.7

For the first minute the threshold is equal to the deviation selected at the beginning—that is, it is equal to $th_1 = 0.5$. During the second time unit the threshold is $th_1/2 = 0.25$.

The new value th_2 for *loc.uncertainty* is computed as follows: First, we determine the slope a_1 of the deviation estimator as $a_1 = 2 \cdot 0.5/2^2 = 0.25$. Then, the new value for *loc.uncertainty* is the solution of the equation $\ln(K) = d_1/K - d_2$ with $d_1 = 2C_1/C_2$ and $d_2 = 1/C_2 + 4 - \ln(a_1)$. This leads to $\ln(K) = 16/K - 1 - 4 + \ln(0.25) = 16/K - 6.39$. By using the Newton-Raphson method we obtain $K = th_2 = 2.226$.

The threshold five minutes later is $th_2/5 = 2.226/5 = 0.445$. The slope a_2 of the deviation estimator is $a_2 = 2 \cdot 1.2/5^2 = 0.096$. This leads to $\ln(K) = 16/K - 1 - 4 + \ln(0.096) = 16/K - 7.343$. The new value of *loc.uncertainty* is 1.992.

Solution 3.8

Let (x, y, t) be a point in the segment trajectory volume between t_i and t_{i+1}. Then, according to Definition 3.13, this point must belong to some possible motion curve between t_i and t_{i+1}. In that case, by Definition 3.12, we know that it must lie inside or on the boundary of the uncertainty area at time t. According to Definition 3.11, the uncertainty area is specified as a circle, with radius r centered at the expected location at time t. With the given velocity components, the expected location at time t is precisely the point $(x_i + v_{x_i} \cdot t, y_i + v_{y_i} \cdot t)$. Consequently, point (x, y, t) must satisfy the two inequalities.

Conversely, if the point (x, y, t) satisfies the two inequalities, by Definition 3.11 it is within the uncertainty area of $(x_i + v_{x_i} \cdot t, y_i + v_{y_i} \cdot t, t)$. Hence, by Definition 3.12, it belongs to some possible motion curve at time t, and by Definition 3.13 it is inside or on the boundary of the segment trajectory volume.

Chapter 4

Solution 4.1

The horizontal lines separate the three groups of operations from Table 4.6.

Table S.8 Binary predicates.

Operation	Signature		
=, ≠	$\pi \times \pi$	$\rightarrow$ *bool*	
	$\sigma_1 \times \sigma_2$	$\rightarrow$ *bool*	
intersects	$\sigma_1 \times \sigma_2$	$\rightarrow$ *bool*	
inside	$\pi \times \sigma$	$\rightarrow$ *bool*	
	$\sigma_1 \times \sigma_2$	$\rightarrow$ *bool*	
<, ≤, ≥, >	$\pi \times \pi$	$\rightarrow$ *bool*	[1D]
before	$\sigma_1 \times \sigma_2$	$\rightarrow$ *bool*	[1D]
	$\pi \otimes \sigma$	$\rightarrow$ *bool*	[1D]
touches, **attached**, **overlaps**	$\sigma_1 \times \sigma_2$	$\rightarrow$ *bool*	
on_border, **in_interior**	$\pi \times \sigma$	$\rightarrow$ *bool*	

Solution 4.2

Table S.9 Semantics of set operations.

	Operation	Signature	Semantics
1.	**intersection**	$\pi \times \pi \rightarrow \pi$	if $u = v$ then u else $\perp$
2.	**intersection**	$\pi \times \sigma \rightarrow \pi$	if $u \in V$ then u else $\perp$
3.	**minus**	$\sigma \times \pi \rightarrow \sigma$	if $is1D(U)$ then $U \backslash \{v\}$ else $\rho(U \backslash \{v\})$
4.	**minus**	$\sigma \times \sigma \rightarrow \sigma$ [1D]	$U \backslash V$
5.	**minus**	$\sigma \times \sigma \rightarrow \sigma$ [2D]	$\rho(U \backslash V)$
6.	**union**	$\sigma \times \sigma \rightarrow \sigma$ [2D]	$U \cup V$

Solution 4.3

1. Show the locations of all volcanoes. (Return the result as a `points` value. Hint: It will be necessary to construct an intermediate table.)

```
LET volcanoes =
  SELECT locations(eruptions) AS place FROM volcano;
ELEMENT(SELECT union(place) FROM volcanoes)
```

After the first step of the query we have a table:

```
volcanoes(place: points)
```

The second step then aggregates over all *place* fields in that table.

2. Were there any eruptions in Italy in the seventeenth century? (Return the names of the volcanoes involved, if any.)

```
LET Italy = ...
LET Century17 = period(year(1600), year(1699));
SELECT name FROM volcano WHERE passes(eruptions, Italy) AND
  present(eruptions, Century17)
```

3. How many times did Etna erupt?

```
LET Etna =
  ELEMENT(SELECT eruptions FROM volcano
  WHERE name = 'Etna');
no_components(deftime(Etna))
```

Solution 4.4

initial(f) = **atinstant**(f, **min**(**deftime**(f))) (**final** similar)
present(f, p) = **not**(**isempty**(**deftime**(**atperiods**(f, p)))) (for a `periods` value p)
atmin(f) = **at**(f, **min**(**rangevalues**(f))) (**atmax** similar)
passes(f, v) = **not**(**isempty**(**deftime**(**at**(f, v))))

Solution 4.5

```
LET always = FUN (mb: mbool) min(rangevalues(mb))
LET sometimes = FUN (mb: mbool) max(rangevalues(mb))
LET never = FUN (mb: mbool) max(rangevalues(mb)) = false
```

Other ways to formulate this exist—for example:

```
LET always = FUN (mb: mbool) not(passes(mb, false))
LET sometimes = FUN (mb: mbool) passes(mb, true)
LET never = FUN (mb: mbool) not(passes(mb, true))
```

Solution 4.6

```
LET closest = FUN (mp: mpoint, p: point)
  atinstant(mp, inst(initial(atmin(distance(mp, p)))));

LET LH078 = ... ;
LET TheEiffelTower = ...;
inst(closest(LH078, TheEiffelTower))
```

Solution 4.7

$$\psi(R_1, R_2) = size(R_1 \backslash R_2) + size(R_2 \backslash R_1)$$

Clearly, this measure of dissimilarity is 0 if the two regions are equal and approaches 0 when the two regions get more and more similar in shape and position.

Solution 4.8

1. What was the largest extent ever of the Roman empire? Return the extent as a number, the time period, and the region of the maximal extent.

```
LET TheRomanEmpire = ELEMENT(
  SELECT area FROM historic_states
  WHERE name = 'Roman Empire');

LET maxarea = atmax(area(TheRomanEmpire));
LET starttime = start(deftime(maxarea));
```

The extent is:

```
size(val(atinstant(TheRomanEmpire, starttime)))
```

The time period is:

```
deftime(maxarea)
```

The region is:

```
val(atinstant(TheRomanEmpire, starttime))
```

2. On which occasions did any two states merge? Return the time when it happened, the names and regions before the merge, and the name and region after the merge.

```
LET hstates = historic_states decompose[area, unit];
```

We now have a relation with schema:

```
hstates (name: string, area: mregion, unit: mregion)
```

Since areas of states change in discrete steps, at each such change a discontinuity occurs. Hence, each unit represents a period of time when the region was static. To answer the query, we need to find three units of which two represent the separate states before the merge and the third represents the state after the merge.

```
SELECT inst(initial(h3.unit) AS time,
  h1.name AS state1, val(final(h1.unit)) AS region1,
  h2.name AS state2, val(final(h2.unit)) AS region2,
  h3.name AS newstate, val(initial(h3.unit)) AS newregion
FROM hstates AS h1, hstates AS h2, hstates AS h2
WHERE inst(final(h1.unit)) = inst(initial(h3.unit))
  AND inst(final(h2.unit)) = inst(initial(h3.unit))
  AND val(initial(h3.unit)) = union(final(h1.unit),
    final(h2.unit))
```

3. List all names of the city now called Istanbul.

```
SELECT rangevalues(name)
FROM historic_cities
WHERE inside('Istanbul', rangevalues(name))
```

4. Which states contained Istanbul? For each state, list the names the city had during the respective period.

   To answer only the first question we can simply say:

```
SELECT s.name
FROM historic_cities AS c, historic_states AS s
WHERE inside(c.pos, traversed(s.area))
```

To answer the question in more detail, as requested, we need to work again with the decomposition of states into continuous units, as in part 2. This is necessary since Istanbul might have belonged to a particular state during several distinct time intervals (if the area containing it belonged to some other state for an intermediate time period).

```
LET hstates = historic_states decompose[area, unit];
```

Furthermore, to be able to manipulate the various names of Istanbul separately, we also need to decompose the historic cities with respect to the names. It suffices to do this for Istanbul.

```
LET IstanbulRel =
  SELECT * FROM historic_cities
  WHERE inside('Istanbul', rangevalues(name));
LET Istanbul = IstanbulRel decompose[name, unit_name];
```

Hence, now we have a relation:

```
Istanbul (name: mstring, pos: point, unit_name: mstring)
```

where each *unit_name* contains only a single string value.

The query can now be formulated as:

```
SELECT DISTINCT s.name,
  val(initial(i.unit_name)) AS IstanbulName
FROM hstates AS s, Istanbul AS i
WHERE inside(i.pos, traversed(s.unit))
```

Solution 4.9

Let $s = (u, v) \in Seg$, $t \in Seg$.

$points(s) = \{w \in Point \mid w = u + \alpha(v - u), \alpha \in [0, 1]\}$
$endpoints(s) = \{u, v\}$
$interior(s) = points(s) \backslash endpoints(s)$
$p\text{-}intersect(s, t) \Leftrightarrow interior(s) \cap interior(t) \neq \emptyset$
$touch(s, t) \Leftrightarrow endpoints(s) \cap interior(t) \neq \emptyset \vee endpoints(t) \cap interior(s) \neq \emptyset$

Solution 4.10

Let P and Q be two `points` values consisting of a finite set of points each. We can distinguish the following five cases:

$equal(P, Q) \quad := \quad P = Q$
$disjoint(P, Q) \quad := \quad P \cap Q = \emptyset$

$$\begin{array}{lcl} inside(P, Q) & := & P \subset Q \\ contains(P, Q) & := & P \supset Q \\ overlap(P, Q) & := & P \cap Q \neq \varnothing \wedge P \backslash Q \neq \varnothing \wedge Q \backslash P \neq \varnothing \end{array}$$

Solution 4.11

The implication can be shown as follows:

$$\begin{array}{lcl} \forall_{\cup} p(S_1, S_2) & \Leftrightarrow & \forall t \in dom(S_1) \cup dom(S_2) : p(S_1(t), S_2(t)) \\ & \Rightarrow & \forall t \in dom(S_1) : p(S_1(t), S_2(t)) \\ & \Leftrightarrow & \forall_{\pi_1} p(S_1, S_2) \end{array}$$

Solution 4.12

We could define the "directed" spatio-temporal predicates as follows:

$$\begin{array}{lcl} Meets & := & \forall_{\pi_1} meet \\ MetBy & := & \forall_{\pi_2} meet \\ Overlaps & := & \forall_{\pi_1} overlap \\ OverlappedBy & := & \forall_{\pi_2} overlap \end{array}$$

Solution 4.13

This can be proved as follows:

$$\begin{array}{lcl} (P|_I)|_{I'}(S_1, S_2) & = & P|_I(S_{1|I'}, S_{2|I'}) \\ & = & P((S_{1|I'})|_I, (S_{2|I'})|_I) \\ & = & P(S_{1|I' \cap I}, S_{2|I' \cap I}) \\ & = & P|_{I \cap I'}(S_1, S_2) \end{array}$$

Solution 4.14

Consider two spatio-temporal objects S_1 and S_2, for which P **until** p **then** Q holds. By definition of P **until** p **then** Q there must be a time point t such that (i) $p(S_1(t), S_2(t))$, (ii) $P_{<t}(S_1, S_2)$, and (iii) $Q_{>t}(S_1, S_2)$ are true. From (i) and (ii) follows that P **until** p holds for S_1 and S_2, and from (i) and (iii) follows that p **then** Q holds for S_1 and S_2.

Solution 4.15

The Lemma can be shown as follows:

$$\begin{array}{lcl} \mathtt{True} \rhd p \rhd \mathtt{True} & = & \mathtt{True}\ \mathbf{until}\ p\ \mathbf{then}\ \mathtt{True} \\ & = & \lambda(S_1, S_2).\exists t : p(S_1(t), S_2(t)) \wedge \mathtt{True}_{<t}(S_1, S_2) \wedge \mathtt{True}_{>t}(S_1, S_2) \\ & = & \lambda(S_1, S_2).\exists t : p(S_1(t), S_2(t)) \\ & = & \exists p \end{array}$$

Solution 4.16

We show the equivalence as follows:

$$\begin{aligned}\lambda(S_1, S_2).P(S_1, S_2) \wedge Q(S_1, S_2) &= \lambda(S_1, S_2).\neg(\neg P(S_1, S_2) \vee \neg Q(S_1, S_2)) \\ &= \sim(\lambda(S_1, S_2).\neg P(S_1, S_2) \vee \neg Q(S_1, S_2)) \\ &= \sim(\lambda(S_1, S_2).\neg P(S_1, S_2) \mid \lambda(S_1, S_2).\neg Q(S_1, S_2)) \\ &= \sim(\sim P \mid \sim Q)\end{aligned}$$

Solution 4.17

Cases 1 and 2 follow directly from Definition 4.39, since an alternative of spatio-temporal predicates is reduced to $\vee$ and since **`True`** (**`False`**) yields always true (false) for two objects. Equations 3 and 4 just rephrase Lemma 4.4 in sequencing syntax. Case 5 follows immediately from Definition 4.38, since, for example, **`False`** $\rhd p \rhd P$ requires the existence of a time point t so that **`False`**$_{<t}$ is true. However, this is not possible (see also 7). Equations 6 and 7 hold, because **`True`** (**`False`**) yields true (false) irrespective of the domains of the spatio-temporal objects, which are the only parts affected by constriction.

Solution 4.18

Both results follow immediately from Definition 4.66 together with the fact that the corresponding property holds for logical or.

Solution 4.19

For case 1 we have: $\sim P \,\&\, \sim Q = \sim(\sim(\sim P) \mid \sim(\sim Q))$ by Definition 4.43. By Lemma 4.10 this is equal to $\sim(P \mid Q)$. In case 2 we know from Definition 4.43 that $\sim(P \,\&\, Q) = \sim(\sim(\sim P \mid \sim Q))$. By Lemma 4.10 this is equal to $\sim P \mid \sim Q$.

Chapter 5

Solution 5.1

1. The lexicographic order on points is usually defined as follows: Let $p, q \in P$. Then:

$$p <_P q \Leftrightarrow p.x < q.x \vee (p.x = q.x \wedge p.y < q.y).$$

2. The interesting situations for halfsegments are those where two halfsegments share a common end point. Let $h_1, h_2 \in H$ be two distinct halfsegments with a common end point p (an overlapping of h_1 and h_2 is excluded by the assump-

tions of the ROSE algebra). Further, let α be the enclosed angle of h_1 and h_2 such that $0° \leq \alpha < 180°$. Then, we can define a predicate *rot* as follows:

$$rot(h_1, h_2) = true \quad \Leftrightarrow \quad h_1 \text{ can be rotated around } p \text{ through } \alpha \text{ to overlap } h_2 \text{ in counterclockwise direction}$$

Finally, we need the obvious equality on points. Let $p, q \in P$. Then:

$$p =_P q \Leftrightarrow p.x = q.x \wedge p.y = q.y.$$

We can now define a complete order relation "$<_H$" on halfsegments that is basically the (x, y)-lexicographic order by dominating points. For two halfsegments $h_1 = (s_1, d_1)$ and $h_2 = (s_2, d_2)$ with $s_1, s_2 \in P \times P$ and $d_1, d_2 \in \{left, right\}$, we can define (for example):

$$\begin{aligned} h_1 <_H h_2 \quad \Leftrightarrow \quad & dp(h_1) <_P dp(h_2) \vee \\ & (dp(h_1) =_P dp(h_2) \wedge ((d_1 = right \wedge d_2 = left) \vee \\ & \qquad (d_1 = d_2 \wedge rot(h_1, h_2)))) \end{aligned}$$

3. Let us consider the following spatial configuration:

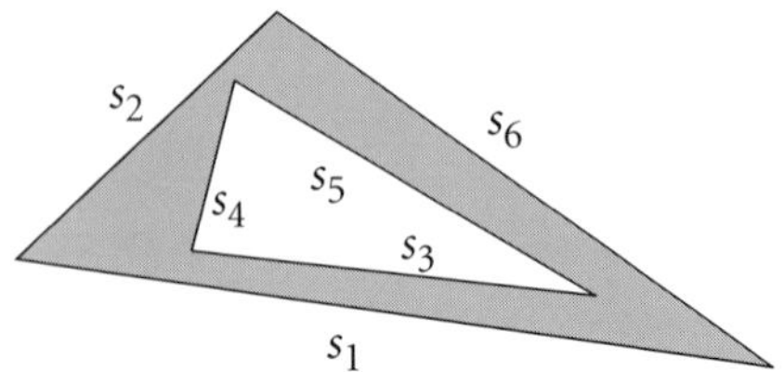

Let $h_i^l = (s_i, left)$ and $h_i^r = (s_i, right)$ denote the left and right halfsegments belonging to the segments s_i for $1 \leq i \leq 6$. Let *IA* (for "inside above") be a flag indicating that the interior of the region is located above or left of the corresponding segment s_i. Then, the spatial configuration can be described by the following halfsegment sequence in which each halfsegment is extended by a set containing the flag *IA* or not:

$$\langle (h_1^l, \{IA\}), (h_2^l, \varnothing), (h_3^l, \varnothing), (h_4^l, \{IA\}), (h_4^r, \{IA\}), (h_5^l, \{IA\}),$$
$$(h_2^r, \varnothing), (h_6^l, \varnothing), (h_5^r, \{IA\}), (h_3^r, \varnothing), (h_6^r, \varnothing), (h_1^r, \{IA\})\rangle$$

Solution 5.2

The function **mdirection**(v, t) can be computed as follows:

$$\textbf{mdirection}(v, t) = \arcsin \frac{y(t_1) - y(t_0)}{\sqrt{(x(t_1) - x(t_0))^2 + (y(t_1) - y(t_0))^2}}$$

Hence, **mdirection**(v, t) is a constant.

Solution 5.3

The algorithm can be formulated as follows:

Algorithm *upoint_inside_uregion(up, ur)*

Input: A *upoint* unit *up* and a *uregion* unit *ur*

Output: A set of moving boolean units, as a value of *mapping(const(bool))*, representing when the point of *up* was inside the region of *ur* during *i*.

Method:

let $up = (i, p)$ and $ur = (i, F)$;
if projection bounding boxes (*object_pbb*) of p and F do not intersect **then**
  return $\varnothing$
else
  determine all intersections between p and msegments occurring in
    (the cycles of faces of) F. Each intersection is represented as a pair
    $(t, action)$ where t is the time instant of the intersection, and
    $action \in \{enter, leave\}$;
  sort intersections by time, resulting in a list $\langle(t_1, a_1), \ldots, (t_k, a_k)\rangle$ if there are
    k intersections;
    /* Note that actions in this list must be alternating, i.e., $a_k \neq a_{k+1}$ */
  let $t_0 = s$ and $t_{k+1} = e$;
  if $k = 0$ **then**
    if p at instant s is inside F at instant s **then**
      return $\{((s, e, true, true), true)\}$
    else
      return $\{((s, e, true, true), false)\}$
    endif
  else
    if $a_1 = leave$ **then**
      return $\{((t_j, t_{j+1}, true, true), true) \mid j \in \{0, \ldots, k\}, j \text{ is even}\}$
        $\cup \{((t_j, t_{j+1}, false, false), false) \mid j \in \{0, \ldots, k\}, j \text{ is odd}\}$
    else

```
            return {((t_j, t_{j+1}, true, true), true) | j ∈ {0, ..., k}, j is odd}
                   ∪ {((t_j, t_{j+1}, false, false), false) | j ∈ {0, ..., k}, j is even}
         endif
      endif
   endif
end.
```

The *action* can be determined if we store with each msegment (trapezium or triangle in 3D) a *face normal vector* indicating on which side the interior of the `uregion` unit is.

Solution 5.4

The function **center**(ur, t) can be computed as follows:

$$\mathbf{center}(ur, t) = \frac{\mathbf{center}(ur, t_1) - \mathbf{center}(ur, t_0)}{t_1 - t_0} \cdot (t - t_0) + \mathbf{center}(ur, t_0)$$

Hence, **center**(ur, t) is a linear function in t.

Chapter 6

Solution 6.1

The simplified relation is shown in Figure S.7. Each symbolic tuple corresponds to one of the three intersection segments in Figure 6.7(a).

$-x$	$+2y$	$=$	4
$3x$	$-y$	$\geq$	2
x	$+3y$	$\leq$	14
$2x$	$+3y$	$=$	20
x		$\leq$	7
x	$-y$	$\geq$	2
x	$-y$	$=$	5
x		$\geq$	7
$3x$	$+2y$	$\leq$	31

Figure S.7 Simplified symbolic relation for $l \cap r$.

Solution 6.2

So we have a symbolic tuple:

$2x$	$+3y$	$+5z$	$\leq$	30
		x	$\geq$	0
		y	$\geq$	1
		z	$\geq$	2

Isolating variable z yields:

$$z \geq 2$$
$$z \leq -2/5x - 3/5y + 6$$

These two are combined in step 2 into a single constraint:

$$2 \leq -2/5x - 3/5y + 6$$

which evaluates to

$$2x + 3y \leq -4$$

Hence, the tuple resulting from the projection is:

$2x$	$+3y$	$\leq$	-4
	x	$\geq$	0
	y	$\geq$	1

Solution 6.3

The proof is by induction on the number of vertices of the polygon. Clearly, the statement holds for a polygon with three vertices. Now consider a polygon P with $n > 3$ vertices and select a diagonal. It splits P into two polygons P_1 and P_2 with k and m vertices, respectively. Because the two vertices of the diagonal are counted twice in the two separate polygons we have:

$$n = k + m - 2$$

Since both k and m are smaller than n, due to the induction hypothesis we know that:

$$P_1 \text{ has } k-2 \text{ triangles and } k-3 \text{ diagonals}$$

$$P_2 \text{ has } m-2 \text{ triangles and } m-3 \text{ diagonals}$$

Combining P_1 and P_2 into P we find that P has:

$$k-2+m-2 = (k+m-2)-2 = n-2 \text{ triangles}$$

$$k-3+m-3+1 = (k+m-2)-3 = n-3 \text{ diagonals}$$

Chapter 7

Solution 7.1

Since MBBs are allowed to overlap, the illustration can only correspond to an R-tree (or an R*-tree). We obtain the following R-tree:

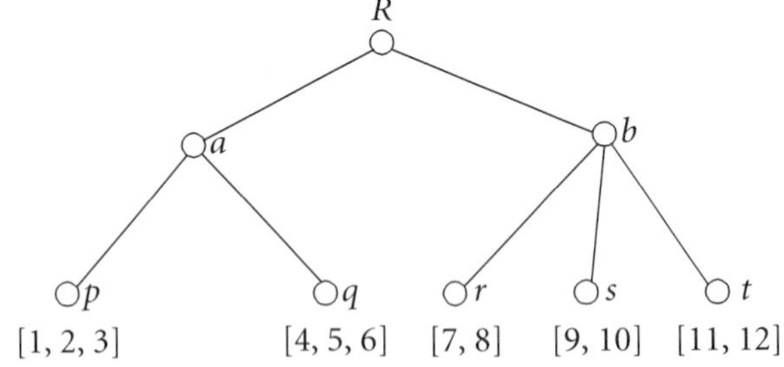

The search starts at root R and continues with MBB a, which intersects the query rectangle qr. Therefore, its children p and q have to be checked, too. Both MBBs intersect qr, so their children have to be explored, too. But none of p's children intersects intersect qr, whereas two of q's children, MBBs 4 and 5, intersect qr. Due to recursion we reach MBB b, which also overlaps with qr. From b's children r, s, and t only r and s overlap with qr, so only their children have to be investigated. It turns out that only r's son MBB 7 and s's son MBB 9 intersect qr.

Solution 7.2

A logical choice for s^* is the union of the duals of all points of s. Since the set of points on s is infinite, we obtain an infinite set of lines. All points on s are collinear, so that all dual lines pass through one point. The union of these dual lines forms a *double wedge*, which is bounded by the duals of the end points p and q of s. The lines dual to the end points of s define two double wedges, a left-right wedge and a top-bottom wedge; s^* is the left-right wedge.The following figure shows the dual of a segment s:

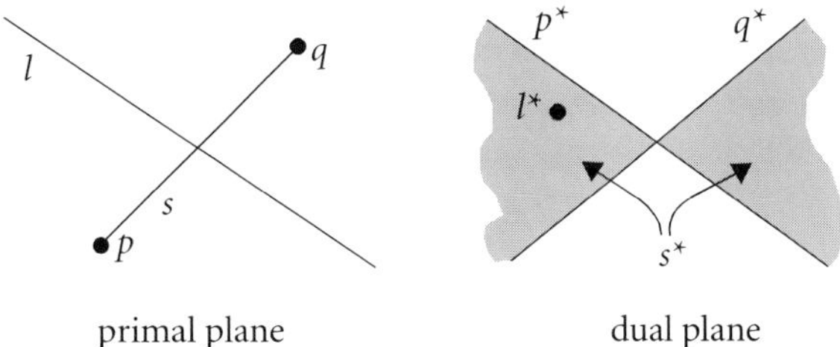

Further, the figure shows a line l intersecting s, whose dual l^* lies in s^*. This is a logical consequence of the order preserving property of the dual transform: any line l^* that intersects s must have either p or q above it and the other point below it, so that the dual l^* of such a line is located in s^*.

Solution 7.3

The size r of the simplicial partition is its number of triangles. Hence, $r = 7$. The simplicial partition is balanced. Following the "chain" of rectangles beginning with the upper left triangle, we obtain $|S_1| = 8$, $|S_2| = 9$, $|S_3| = 9$, $|S_4| = 6$, $|S_5| = 11$, $|S_6| = 6$, and $|S_7| = 7$. With $N = 56$ we see that for all $1 \leq i \leq r$ holds that $|S_i| \leq 2N/r = 16$. The crossing number is equal to 5, since we can find only lines that intersect at most five triangles.

Solution 7.4

The first level of the partition tree includes the root node. The second level incorporates nodes for the seven triangles. Since Δ_3 lies completely in the strip bounded by the lines f and l, all its points are selected. Since Δ_5, Δ_6, and Δ_7 are completely outside the strip, their point sets are not selected. Only the triangles Δ_1, Δ_2, and Δ_4, which intersect l, have to be recursively visited and checked.

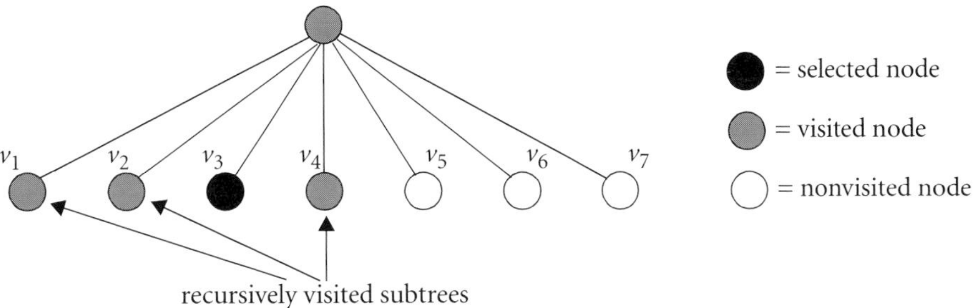

Solution 7.5

An example of a three-dimensional curve that does not represent the trajectory of a moving point is given in the following figure.

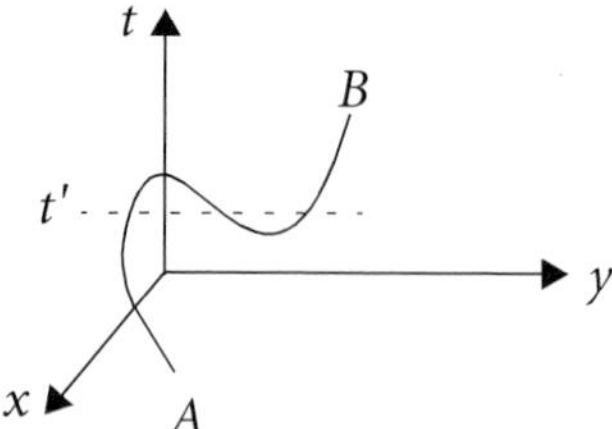

We see that the temporal interpretation of the three-dimensional curve from *A* to *B* means that the moving point moves "back into the past," which is impossible. Time instant t' is associated with three locations but there can be at most one location where the moving point has been at time t'. In other words, there is a functional relationship between time and space (`mpoint` = `time` → `point`).

Solution 7.6

1. The velocity vector $v(t)$ is the derivative of the position. That is:

$$v(t) = \frac{dp(t)}{dt} = \left(\frac{dx(t)}{dt}, \frac{dy(t)}{dt}\right)$$

For a linear function p the velocity vector $v = (v_1, v_2)$ is the slope of the function, v_1 is the speed of the moving point along the x-axis, and v_2 is the speed along the y-axis. For a polynomial function of degree n we obtain as the derivative a polynomial function of degree $n - 1$.

2. The velocity vector can be specified by stating the speed v_{xy} (i.e., the magnitude of the velocity vector) and its direction as an angle α. We obtain

$$v_{xy} = \sqrt{v_1^2 + v_2^2} \text{ and } \alpha = \operatorname{atan}\frac{v_2}{v_1}.$$

Solution 7.7

Let $v > 0$. The constraints $v \geq v_{min}$ and $v \leq v_{max}$ are given by the problem statement. Based on the assumption that $a \leq y_{2q}$, a line with intercept a can intersect the query rectangle if the slope has values (see Figure 7.17):

$$\tan(\varphi_1) \leq v \leq \tan(\varphi_2) \Rightarrow \frac{y_{1q} - a}{t_{2q}} \leq v \leq \frac{y_{2q} - a}{t_{1q}}$$

From these inequalities we obtain the two other constraints, similarly for $v < 0$.

Solution 7.8

In our spatio-temporal setting, an MBB is a three-dimensional cube, and four different 3D segments can be approximated by such a cube.

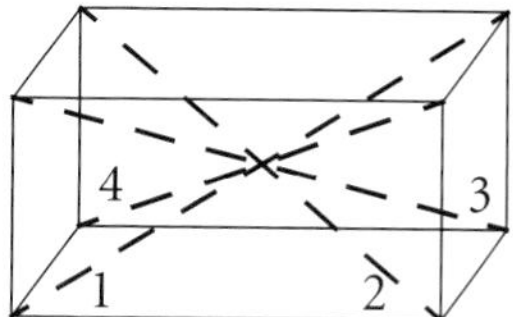

Solution 7.9

The algorithm *Insert* is as follows:

algorithm *Insert*(*node*, *elem*)
    node' := *FindNode*(*node*, *elem*);
    if *node*' $\neq$ *nil* **then**
        if *node*' has space **then** insert new segment *elem*
        else create new leaf node for new segment *elem*
        endif
    else create new leaf node for new segment *elem*
    endif
end.

The algorithm *FindNode* is the same as for the STR-tree.

Bibliography

Note: For the cited Web sites, the year means that the site was accessible in that year, not that it has been originally created or last modified in that year. The latter information is not always available or meaningful. We have generally assigned the year 2005 for Web sites.

Abraham, T., and Roddick, J. F. (1999). "Survey of Spatio-Temporal Databases." *GeoInformatica* 3: 61–99.

Acharya, S.; Poosala, V.; and Ramaswamy, S. (1999). "Selectivity Estimation in Spatial Databases." In: *Proceedings of the ACM SIGMOD Conference on Management of Data.*

Agarwal P. K.; Arge, L.; and Erickson, J. (2003). "Indexing Moving Points." *Journal of Computer and System Sciences* 66: 207–243.

Almeida, V. T. de, and Güting, R. H. (2005). "Indexing the Trajectories of Moving Objects in Networks." *GeoInformatica* 9(1): 33–60.

Arge, L.; Samoladas, V.; and Vitter, J. S. (1999). "On Two-Dimensional Indexability and Optimal Range Search Indexing." In: *Proceedings of the Eighteenth Symposium on Principles of Database Systems (PODS).*

Armstrong, M. A. (1983). *Basic Topology.* Berlin: Springer-Verlag.

Basch, J.; Guibas L.; and Zhang, L. (1997). "Proximity Problems on Moving Points." In: *Proceedings of the Fifteenth Annual ACM Symposium on Computational Geometry.*

Beckmann, N.; Kriegel, H. P.; Schneider, R.; and Seeger, B. (1990). "The R^*-Tree: An Efficient and Robust Access Method for Points and Rectangles." In: *Proceedings of the ACM SIGMOD Conference on Management of Data.*

Behr, T., and Schneider, M. (2001). "Topological Relationships of Complex Points and Complex Regions." In: *Proceedings of the Twentieth International Conference on Conceptual Modeling (ER).*

Belussi, A.; Bertino, E.; and Catania, B. (1997). "Manipulating Spatial Data in Constraint Databases." In: *Proceedings of the Fifth International Symposium on Large Spatial Databases (SSD).*

Benetis, R.; Jensen, C. S.; Karciauskas, G.; and Saltenis, S. (2002). "Nearest Neighbor and Reverse Nearest Neighbor Queries for Moving Objects." In: *Proceedings of the International Database Engineering and Applications Symposium (IDEAS).*

Bentley, J. L., and Ottmann T. (1979). "Algorithms for Reporting and Counting Geometric Intersections." *IEEE Transactions on Computers* C-28: 643–647.

Bhargava, G., and Gadia, S. K. (1993). "Relational Database Systems with Zero Information Loss." *IEEE Transactions on Knowledge and Data Engineering* 5(1): 76–87.

Brinkhoff, T. (2002). "A Framework for Generating Network-Based Moving Objects." *GeoInformatica* 6(2): 153–180.

Brinkhoff, T. (2005). "Network-Based Generator of Moving Objects." Available at: http://www.fh-oow.de/institute/iapg/personen/brinkhoff/generator/.

Chandrasekaran, S., and Franklin, M. J. (2002). "Streaming Queries over Streaming Data." In: *Proceedings of the International Conference on Very Larga Databases (VLDB).*

Chazelle, B. (1991). "Triangulating a Simple Polygon in Linear Time." *Discrete & Computational Geometry* 6: 485–524.

Chen, J.; DeWitt, D. J.; Tian, F.; and Wang, Y. (2000). "NiagaraCQ: A Scalable Continuous Query System for Internet Databases." In: *Proceedings of the ACM SIGMOD Conference on Management of Data.*

Chen, Y., and Revesz, P. (2004). "Max-Count Aggregation Estimation for Moving Points." In: *Proceedings of the Eleventh International Symposium on Temporal Representation and Reasoning (TIME).*

Cheng, R.; Kalashnikov, D. V.; and Prabhakar, S. (2004). "Querying Imprecise Data in Moving Object Environments." *IEEE Transactions on Knowledge and Data Engineering* 16(9): 1112–1127.

Choi, Y. J., and Chung, C. W. (2002). "Selectivity Estimation for Spatio-Temporal Queries to Moving Objects." In: *Proceedings of the ACM SIGMOD Conference on Management of Data.*

Chomicki, J., and Revesz, P. (1997). "Constraint-Based Interoperability of Spatio-Temporal Databases." In: *Proceedings of the Fifth International Symposium on Large Spatial Databases (SSD).*

Chomicki, J., and Revesz, P. (1999). "A Geometric Framework for Specifying Spatiotemporal Objects." In: *Proceedings of the Sixth International Workshop on Temporal Representation and Reasoning (TIME).*

Civilis, A.; Jensen, C. S.; Nenortaite, J.; and Pakalnis, S. (2004). "Efficient Tracking of Moving Objects with Precision Guarantees." In: *Proceedings of the First Ann. International Conference on Mobile and Ubiquitous Systems: Networking and Services (MobiQuitous).*

Clifford, J., and Croker, A. (1987). "The Historical Relational Data Model (HRDM) and Algebra Based on Lifespans." In: *Proceedings of the International Conference on Data Engineering (ICDE).*

Cotelo Lema, J. A.; Forlizzi, L.; Güting, R. H.; Nardelli, E.; and Schneider, M. (2003). "Algorithms for Moving Object Databases." *The Computer Journal* 46(6): 680–712.

Croom, F. H. (1978). *Basic Concepts of Algebraic Topology.* Berlin: Springer-Verlag.

de Berg, M.; van Krefeld, M.; Overmars, M.; and Schwarzkopf, O. (2000). *Computational Geometry: Algorithms and Applications.* Berlin: Springer-Verlag.

Djafri, N.; Fernandes, A. A. A.; Paton, N. W.; and Griffiths, T. (2002). "Spatio-Temporal Evolution: Querying Patterns of Change in Databases." In: *Proceedings of the Tenth ACM International Symposium on Advances in Geographic Information Systems (ACM-GIS).*

Egenhofer, M. J. (1989). "A Formal Definition of Binary Topological Relationships." In: *Proceedings of the Third International Conference on Foundations of Data Organization and Algorithms (FODO).*

Egenhofer, M. J. (1991). "Reasoning about Binary Topological Relations." In: *Proceedings of the Second International Symposium on Advances in Spatial Databases (SSD).*

Egenhofer, M. J., and Franzosa, R. D. (1991). "Point-Set Topological Spatial Relations." *International Journal on Geographical Information Systems* 5(2): 161–174.

Egenhofer, M. J., and Herring, J. (1990). "A Mathematical Framework for the Definition of Topological Relationships." In: *Proceedings of the Fourth International Symposium on Spatial Data Handling (SDH).*

Egenhofer, M. J.; Frank, A.; and Jackson, J. P. (1989). "A Topological Data Model for Spatial Databases." In: *Proceedings of the First International Symposium on the Design and Implementation of Large Spatial Databases (SSD).*

Elmasri, R., and Navathe, S. B. (2003). *Fundamentals of Database Systems.* 4th ed. Reading, MA: Addison-Wesley.

Erwig, M., and Schneider, M. (1999a). "Developments in Spatio-Temporal Query Languages." In: *Proceedings of the IEEE International Workshop on Spatio-Temporal Data Models and Languages (STDML).*

Erwig, M., and Schneider, M. (1999b). "The Honeycomb Model of Spatio-Temporal Partitions." In: *Proceedings of the International Workshop on Spatio-Temporal Database Management (STDBM).*

Erwig, M., and Schneider, M. (2000). "Query-By-Trace: Visual Predicate Specification in Spatio-Temporal Databases." In: *Proceedings of the Fifth IFIP 2.6 Working Conference on Visual Database Systems (VDB).*

Erwig, M., and Schneider, M. (2002). "Spatio-Temporal Predicates." *IEEE Transactions on Knowledge and Data Engineering* 14(4): 881–901.

Erwig, M., and Schneider, M. (2003). "A Visual Language for the Evolution of Spatial Relationships and its Translation into a Spatio-Temporal Calculus." *Journal of Visual Languages and Computing* 14(2): 181–211.

Erwig, M.; Güting, R. H.; Schneider, M.; and Vazirgiannis, M. (1999). "Spatio-Temporal Data Types: An Approach to Modeling and Querying Moving Objects in Databases." *GeoInformatica* 3: 265–291.

Forlizzi, L.; Güting, R. H.; Nardelli, E.; and Schneider, M. (2000). "A Data Model and Data Structures for Moving Objects Databases." In: *Proceedings of the ACM SIGMOD Conference on Management of Data.*

Frank, A. U., and Kuhn, W. (1986). "Cell Graphs: A Provably Correct Method for the Storage of Geometry." In: *Proceedings of the Third International Symposium on Spatial Data Handling (SDH).*

Frentzos, R. (2003). "Indexing Moving Objects on Fixed Networks." In: *Proceedings of the Eighth International Symposium on Spatial and Temporal Databases (SSTD).*

Garcia-Molina, H.; Ullman, J. D.; and Widom, J. (2002). *Database Systems: The Complete Book.* Upper Saddle River, NJ: Prentice-Hall.

Garey, M. R.; Johnson, D. S.; Preparata, F. P.; and Tarjan, R. J. (1978). "Triangulating a Simple Polygon." *Information Processing Letters* 7(4): 175–180.

Gedik, B., and Liu, L. (2004). "MobiEyes: Distributed Processing of Continuously Moving Queries on Moving Objects in a Mobile System." In: *Proceedings of the Ninth International Conference on Extending Database Technology (EDBT).*

Griffiths, T.; Fernandes, A. A. A.; Djafri, N.; and Paton, N. W. (2001a). "A Query Calculus for Spatio-Temporal Object Databases." In: *Proceedings of the Eighth International Symposium on Temporal Representation and Reasoning (TIME).*

Griffiths, T.; Fernandes, A. A. A.; Paton, N. W.; Mason, K. T.; Huang, B.; and Worboys, M. (2001b). "Tripod: A Comprehensive Model for Spatial and Aspatial Historical Objects." In: *Proceedings of the Twentieth International Conference on Conceptual Modeling (ER).*

Grumbach, S.; Rigaux, P.; and Segoufin, L. (1998). "The DEDALE System for Complex Spatial Queries." In: *Proceedings of the ACM SIGMOD Conference on Management of Data.*

Grumbach, S.; Rigaux, P.; and Segoufin, L. (2000). "Manipulating Interpolated Data is Easier than You Thought." In: *Proceedings of the Twenty-Sixth International Conference on Very Large Databases (VLDB).*

Grumbach, S.; Rigaux, P.; and Segoufin, L. (2001). "Spatio-Temporal Data Handling with Constraints." *GeoInformatica* 5: 95–115.

Grumbach, S.; Rigaux, P.; Scholl, M.; and Segoufin, L. (1997). "DEDALE, A Spatial Constraint Database." In: *Proceedings of the International Workshop on Database Programming Languages (DBPL).*

GSTD (2005). "Benchmarking Spatio-Temporal Databases: the GSTD Tool." Available at: http://db.cs.ualberta.ca:8080/gstd/index.html.

G-TERD (2005). "G-TERD: Generator for Time-Evolving Regional Data." Available at: http://delab.csd.auth.gr/stdbs/g-terd.html.

Gupta, S.; Kopparty, S.; and Ravishankar, C. (2004). "Roads, Codes, and Spatiotemporal Queries." In: *Proceedings of the Twenty-Third Symposium on Principles of Database Systems (PODS).*

Güting, R. H. ((1994a). "An Introduction to Spatial Database Systems." *VLDB Journal* 4(3): 357–399.

Güting, R. H. (1994b). "GraphDB: Modeling and Querying Graphs in Databases." In: *Proceedings of the Twentieth International Conference on Very Large Databases (VLDB).*

Güting, R. H., and Schneider, M. (1995). "Realm-Based Spatial Data Types: The ROSE Algebra." *VLDB Journal* 4: 100–143.

Güting, R. H.; Almeida, V. T. de; and Ding, Z. (2005). "Modeling and Querying Moving Objects in Networks." *VLDB Journal*: in press.

Güting, R. H.; Böhlen, M. H.; Erwig, M.; Jensen, C. S.; Lorentzos, N. A.; Schneider, M.; and Vazirgiannis, M. (2000). "A Foundation for Representing and Querying Moving Objects in Databases." *ACM Transactions on Database Systems* 25: 1–42.

Güting, R. H.; de Ridder, T.; and Schneider, M. (1995). "Implementation of the ROSE Algebra: Efficient Algorithms for Realm-Based Spatial Data Types." In: *Proceedings of the Fourth International Symposium on Large Spatial Databases (SSD).*

Guttman A. (1984). "R-Tree: A Dynamic Index Structure for Spatial Searching." In: *Proceedings of the ACM SIGMOD Conference on Management of Data.*

Hadjieleftheriou, M.; Kollios, G.; and Tsotras, V. J. (2003). "Performance Evaluation of Spatio-Temporal Selectivity Estimation Techniques." In: *Proceedings of the Fifteenth International Conference on Scientific and Statistical Database Management (SSDBM).*

Hadjieleftheriou, M.; Kollios, G.; Tsotras, V. J.; and Gunopulos, D. (2002). "Efficient Indexing of Spatiotemporal Objects." In: *Proceedings of the International Conference on Extending Database Technology (EDBT).*

Hadjieleftheriou, M.; Kollios, G.; Tsotras, V. J.; and Gunopulos, D. (2005). "Indexing Spatio-Temporal Archives." *VLDB Journal*: in press.

Hage, C.; Jensen, C. S.; Pedersen, T. B.; Speicys, L.; and Timko, I. (2003). "Integrated Data Management for Mobile Services in the Real World." In: *Proceedings of the Twenty-Ninth International Conference on Very Large Databases (VLDB).*

Hertel, S., and Mehlhorn, K. (1983). "Fast Triangulation of Simple Polygons." In: *Proceedings of the International Conference on Fundamentals of Computation Theory (FCT).*

Huang, Y. W.; Jing, N.; and Rundensteiner, E. A. (1997). "Integrated Query Processing Strategies for Spatial Path Queries." In: *Proceedings of the Thirteenth International Conference on Data Engineering (ICDE).*

Jensen, C. S.; Kolar, J.; Pedersen, T. B.; and Timko, I. (2003a). "Nearest Neighbor Queries in Road Networks." In: *Proceedings of the Eleventh International Symposium on Advances in Geographic Information Systems (ACM-GIS).*

Jensen, C. S.; Lin, D.; and Ooi, B. C. (2004). "Query and Update Efficient B^+-Tree Based Indexing of Moving Objects." In: *Proceedings of the International Conference on Very Large Databases* (*VLDB*).

Jensen, C. S.; Pedersen, T. B.; Speicys, L.; and Timko, I. (2003b). "Data Modeling for Mobile Services in the Real World." In: *Proceedings of the Eighth International Symposium on Spatial and Temporal Databases (SSTD).*

Kanellakis, P. C.; Kuper, G. M.; and Revesz, P. Z. (1990). "Constraint Query Languages." In: *Proceedings of the Ninth Symposium on Principles of Database Systems (PODS).*

Kanellakis, P. C.; Kuper, G. M.; and Revesz, P. Z. (1995). "Constraint Query Languages." *Journal of Computer and System Sciences* 51(1): 26–52.

Keil, J. M. (1985). "Decomposing a Polygon into Simpler Components." *SIAM Journal of Computing* 14(4): 799–817.

Kifer, M.; Bernstein, A.; and Lewis, P. M. (2005). *Database Systems: An Application-Oriented Approach. Introductory Version.* 2nd ed. Boston: Addison-Wesley.

Kollios, G.; Gunopulos, D.; and Tsotras, V. J. (1999). "On Indexing Mobile Objects." In: *Proceedings of the Eighteenth Symposium on Principles of Database Systems (PODS).*

Kollios, G.; Gunopulos, D.; Tsotras, V. J.; and Papadopoulos, D. (2005). "Indexing Mobile Objects Using Dual Transformations." *VLDB Journal* 14(2): 238–256.

Kollios, G.; Tsotras, V. J.; Gunopulos, D.; Delis, A.; and Hadjieleftheriou, M. (2001). "Indexing Animated Objects Using Spatiotemporal Access Methods." *IEEE Transactions on Knowledge and Data Engineering* 13(5): 758–777.

Kothuri, R.; Godfrind, A.; and Beinat, E. (2004). *Pro Oracle Spatial: An Essential Guide to Developing Spatially-Enabled Business Applications.* Berkeley, CA: Apress L. P.

Koubarakis, M.; Sellis, T. K.; Frank, A. U.; Grumbach, S.; Güting, R. H.; Jensen, C. S.; Lorentzos, N. A.; Manolopoulos, Y.; Nardelli, E.; Pernici, B.; Schek, H.-J.; Scholl, M.; Theodoulidis, B.; and Tryfona, N.; eds. (2003). *Spatio-Temporal Databases: The CHOROCHRONOS Approach. Lecture Notes in Computer Science 2520.* Berlin: Springer-Verlag.

Kuper, G.; Libkin, L.; and Paredaens, J.; eds. (2000). *Constraint Databases.* Berlin: Springer-Verlag.

Laurini, R., and Thompson, D. (1992). *Fundamentals of Spatial Information Systems.* London: Academic Press.

Lazaridis, I.; Porkaew, K.; and Mehrotra, S. (2002). "Dynamic Queries over Mobile Objects." In: *Proceedings of the Eighth International Conference on Extending Database Technology (EDBT).*

Lee, D. T., and Preparata, F. P. (1977). "Location of a Point in a Planar Subdivision and its Applications." *SIAM Journal of Computing* 6(3): 594–606.

Madden, S.; Shah, M.; Hellerstein, J.; and Raman, V. (2002). "Continuously Adaptive Continuous Queries over Streams." In: *Proceedings of the ACM SIGMOD Conference on Management of Data.*

Matousek, J. (1992). "Efficient Partition Trees." In: *Proceedings of the ACM Symposium on Applied Computing (SAC).*

McCreight, E. M. (1985). "Priority Search Trees." *SIAM Journal of Computing* 14: 257–276.

Mehlhorn, K. (1984). *Multi-dimensional Searching and Computational Geometry.* Berlin: Springer-Verlag.

Mokbel, M. F.; Ghanem, T. M.; and Aref, W. G. (2003). "Spatio-Temporal Access Methods." *Bulletin of the TC on Data Engineering* 26(2): 40–49.

Mokbel, M. F.; Xiong, X.; and Aref, W. G. (2004). "SINA: Scalable Incremental Processing of Continuous Queries in Spatio-Temporal Databases." In: *Proceedings of the ACM SIGMOD Conference on Management of Data.*

Mokhtar, H.; Su, J.; and Ibarra, O. (2002). "On Moving Object Queries." In: *Proceedings of the Twenty-First Symposium on Principles of Database Systems (PODS).*

Mokhtar, H., and Su, J. (2004). "Universal Trajectory Queries for Moving Objects Databases." In: *Proceedings of the IEEE International Conference on Mobile Data Management (MDM).*

Nascimento, M. A., and Silva, J. R. O. (1998). "Towards Historical R-Trees." *Proceedings of the ACM Symposium on Applied Computing (SAC).*

Onofrio, A. de, and Pourabbas, E. (2003). "Modelling Temporal Thematic Map Contents." *SIGMOD Record* 32(2): 34–41.

Oporto (2005). "Oporto: A Realistic Scenario Generator for Moving Objects." Available at: http://www.infres.enst.fr/~saglio/etudes/oporto/.

Overmars M. H. (1983). *The Design of Dynamic Data Structures.* Berlin: Springer-Verlag.

Özsoyoglu, G., and Snodgrass, R. T. (1995). "Temporal and Real-Time Databases: A Survey." *IEEE Transactions on Knowledge and Data Engineering* 7(4): 513–532.

Papadias, D.; Tao, Y.; Kalnis, P.; and Zhang, J. (2002). "Indexing Spatio-Temporal Data Warehouses." In: *Proceedings of the Eighteenth International Conference on Data Engineering (ICDE).*

Papadias, D.; Zhang, J.; Mamoulis, N.; and Tao, Y. (2003). "Query Processing in Spatial Network Databases." In: *Proceedings of the Twenty-Ninth Conference on Very Large Databases (VLDB).*

Patel, J. M.; Chen, Y.; and Chakka, V. P. (2004). "STRIPES: An Efficient Index for Predicted Trajectories." In: *Proceedings of the ACM SIGMOD Conference on Management of Data.*

Peuquet, D. (2001). "Making Space for Time: Issues in Space-Time Data Representation." *GeoInformatica* 5: 11–32.

Peuquet, D., and Duan, N. (1995). "An Event-Based Spatiotemporal Data Model (ESTDM) for Temporal Analysis of Geographic Data." *International Journal of Geographical Information Systems* 9(1): 7–24.

Pfoser, D., and Rodriguez, M. (2005). "Spatio-Temporal Data Sets." Available at: http://dke.cti.gr/people/pfoser/data.html.

Pfoser, D., and Jensen, C. S. (1999). "Capturing the Uncertainty of Moving-Object Representations." In: *Proceedings of the Sixth International Symposium on Spatial Databases (SSD).*

Pfoser, D., and Jensen, C. S. (2003). "Indexing of Network Constrained Moving Objects." In: *Proceedings of the Eleventh International Symposium on Advances in Geographic Information Systems (ACM-GIS).*

Pfoser, D.; Jensen, C. S.; and Theodoridis, Y. (2000). "Novel Approaches in Query Processing for Moving Object Trajectories." In: *Proceedings of the Twenty-Sixth International Conference on Very Large Databases (VLDB).*

Preparata, F. P., and Shamos, M. I. (1991). *Computational Geometry: An Introduction.* New York: Springer-Verlag.

Revesz, P., and Chen, Y. (2003). "Efficient Aggregation over Moving Objects." In: *Proceedings of the Tenth International Symposium on Temporal Representation and Reasoning and the Fourth International Conference on Temporal Logic (TIME-ICTL).*

Revesz, P. (2002). *Introduction to Constraint Databases.* New York: Springer-Verlag.

Rigaux, P.; Scholl, M.; Segoufin, L.; and Grumbach, S. (2003). "Building a Constraint-Based Spatial Database System: Model, Languages, and Implementation." *Information Systems* 28(6): 563–595.

Rigaux, P.; Scholl, M.; and Voisard, A. (2002). *Spatial Databases: With Application to GIS.* San Francisco: Morgan Kaufmann Publishers.

Roth, J. "Data Collection." In: Schiller, J., and Voisard, A.; eds. (2004). *Location-Based Services.* San Francisco: Morgan Kaufmann Publishers.

Saglio, J. M., and Moreira, J. (2001). "Oporto: A Realistic Scenario Generator for Moving Objects." *GeoInformatica* 5: 71–93.

Saltenis, S.; Jensen, C. S.; Leutenegger, S. T.; and Lopez, M. A. (2000). "Indexing the Positions of Continuously Moving Objects." In: *Proceedings of the ACM SIGMOD Conference on Management of Data.*

Samet, H. (1990). *The Design and Analysis of Spatial Data Structures.* Reading, MA: Addison-Wesley.

Sarda, N. (1990). "Extensions to SQL for Historical Databases." *IEEE Transactions on Knowledge and Data Engineering* 2(2): 220–230.

Schiller, J., and Voisard, A. (2004). *Location-Based Services.* San Francisco: Morgan Kaufmann Publishers.

Schrijver, A. (1986). *Theory of Linear and Integer Programming.* Chichester, England: John Wiley & Sons.

Segev, A., and Shoshani, A. (1987). "Logical Modeling of Temporal Data." In: *Proceedings of the ACM SIGMOD Conference on Management of Data.*

Sellis, T.; Roussopoulos, N.; and Faloutsos, C. (1987). "The R^+-Tree: A Dynamic Index for Multi-Dimensional Objects." In: *Proceedings of the International Conference on Very Large Databases (VLDB).*

Shahabi, C.; Kolahdouzan, M. R.; and Sharifzadeh, M. (2003). "A Road Network Embedding Technique for K-Nearest Neighbor Search in Moving Object Databases." *GeoInformatica* 7(3): 255–273.

Shamos, M. I., and Hoey, D. (1976). "Geometric Intersection Problems." In: *Proceedings of the Seventeenth Annual IEEE Symposium on Foundations of Computer Science (FOCS).*

Shekhar, S., and Chawla, S. (2003). *Spatial Databases: A Tour.* Upper Saddle River, NJ: Prentice Hall.

Shekhar, S., and Liu, D. R. (1997). "CCAM: A Connectivity-Clustered Access Method for Networks and Network Computations." *IEEE Transactions on Knowledge and Data Engineering* 9(1): 102–119.

Sistla, A. P., and Wolfson, O. (1995). "Temporal Triggers in Active Databases." *IEEE Transactions on Knowledge and Data Engineering* 7(3): 471–486.

Sistla, A. P.; Wolfson, O.; Chamberlain, S.; and Dao, S. (1997). "Modeling and Querying Moving Objects." In: *Proceedings of the Thirteenth International Conference on Data Engineering (ICDE).*

Sistla, A. P.; Wolfson, O.; Chamberlain, S.; and Dao, S. (1998). "Querying the Uncertain Position of Moving Objects." In: Etzion, O.; Jajodia, S.; and Sripada, S.; eds. *Temporal Databases—Research and Practice.* Berlin: Springer-Verlag.

Snodgrass, R. T., and Ahn, I. (1986) "Temporal Databases." *IEEE Computer* 19(9): 35–42.

Snodgrass, R. T., ed. (1995). *The TSQL2 Temporal Query Language.* Boston: Kluwer Academic Publishers.

Song, Z., and Roussopoulos, N. (2001). "K-Nearest Neighbor Search for Moving Query Point." In: *Proceedings of the Seventh International Symposium on Spatial and Temporal Databases (SSTD).*

Speicys, L.; Jensen, C. S.; and Kligys, A. (2003). "Computational Data Modeling for Network-Constrained Moving Objects." In: *Proceedings of the Eleventh ACM Symposium on Advances in Geographic Information Systems (ACM-GIS).*

Su, J.; Xu, H.; and Ibarra, O. (2001). "Moving Objects: Logical Relationships and Queries." In: *Proceedings of the Seventh International Symposium on Spatial and Temporal Databases (SSTD).*

Sun, J.; Papadias, D.; Tao, Y.; and Liu, B. (2004). "Querying about the Past, the Present and the Future in Spatio-Temporal Databases." In: *Proceedings of the Twentieth International Conference on Data Engineering (ICDE).*

Tansel, A. U.; Clifford, J.; Gadia, S.; Jajodia, S.; Segev, A.; and Snodgrass, R. T.; eds. (1993). *Temporal Databases: Theory, Design, and Implementation.* Redwood City, CA: Benjamin/Cummings.

Tao, Y., and Papadias, D. (2001). "MV3R-Tree: A Spatio-Temporal Access Method for Timestamp and Interval Queries." In: *Proceedings of the International Conference on Very Large Databases (VLDB).*

Tao, Y., and Papadias, D. (2003). "Spatial Queries in Dynamic Environments." *ACM Transactions on Database Systems* 28(2): 101–139.

Tao, Y.; Kollios, G.; Considine, J.; Li, F.; and Papadias, D. (2004). "Spatio-Temporal Aggregation Using Sketches." In: *Proceedings of the Twentieth International Conference on Data Engineering (ICDE).*

Tao, Y.; Papadias, D.; and Sun, J. (2003a). "The TPR*-Tree: An Optimized Spatio-Temporal Access Method for Predictive Queries." In: *Proceedings of the International Conference on Very Large Databases (VLDB).*

Tao, Y.; Sun, J.; and Papadias, D. (2003b). "Selectivity Estimation for Predictive Spatio-Temporal Queries." In: *Proceedings of the Nineteenth International Conference on Data Engineering (ICDE).*

Tao, Y.; Sun, J.; and Papadias, D. (2003c). "Analysis of Predictive Spatio-Temporal Queries." *ACM Transactions on Database Systems* 28(4): 295–336.

Terry, D. B.; Goldberg, D.; Nichols, D.; and Oki, B. M. (1992). "Continuous Queries over Append-Only Databases." In: *Proceedings of the ACM SIGMOD Conference on Management of Data.*

Theodoridis, Y.; Sellis, T.; Papadopoulos, A.; and Manolopoulos, Y. (1998). "Specifications for Efficient Indexing in Spatiotemporal Databases." In: *Proceedings of the Tenth International Conference on Scientific and Statistical Database Management (SSDBM).*

Theodoridis, Y.; Silva, J. R. O.; and Nascimento, M. A. (1999). "On the Generation of Spatiotemporal Datasets." In: *Proceedings of the Sixth International Symposium on Spatial Databases (SSD).*

Theodoridis, Y.; Vazirgiannis, M.; and Sellis, T. (1996). "Spatio-Temporal Indexing for Large Multimedia Applications." In: *Proceedings of the Third IEEE Conference on Multimedia Computing and Systems (ICMCS).*

Tøssebro, E. (2002). "Representing Uncertainty in Spatial and Spatiotemporal Databases." Ph.D. diss., Norwegian University of Science and Technology, Department of Computer and Information Science, Trondheim, Norway.

Tøssebro, E. (2005). "Snapshot Interpolator: A System for Constructing Moving Region Representations from Observations." Available at: http://www.informatik.fernuni-hagen.de/import/pi4/tossebro/preface.html.

Tøssebro, E., and Nygård, M. (2002). "Uncertainty in Spatiotemporal Databases." In: *Proceedings of the Second International Conference on Advances in Information Systems (ADVIS).*

Tøssebro, E., and Nygård, M. (2003). "A Medium Complexity Discrete Model for Uncertain Spatial Data." In: *Proceedings of the Seventh International Database Engineering and Applications Symposium (IDEAS).*

Tøssebro, E., and Güting, R. H. (2001). "Creating Representations for Continuously Moving Regions from Observations." In: *Proceedings of the Seventh International Symposium on Spatial and Temporal Databases (SSTD).*

Trajcevski, G.; Wolfson, O.; Hinrichs K.; and Chamberlain, S. (2004). "Managing Uncertainty in Moving Objects Databases." *ACM Transactions on Database Systems* 29(3): 463–507.

Trajcevski, G.; Wolfson, O.; Zhang, F.; and Chamberlain, S. (2002). "The Geometry of Uncertainty in Moving Objects Databases." In: *Proceedings of the Eighth International Conference on Extending Database Technology (EDBT).*

Tzouramanis, T.; Vassilakopoulos, M.; and Manolopoulos, Y. (2002). "On the Generation of Time-Evolving Regional Data." *GeoInformatica* 6: 207–231.

Vandeurzen, L. (1999). "Logic-Based Query Languages for the Linear Constraint Database Model." Ph.D. diss., University of Limburg, Belgium.

Vandeurzen, L.; Gyssens, M.; and Van Gucht, D. (1995). "On the Desirability and Limitations of Linear Spatial Database Models." In: *Proceedings of the Fourth International Symposium on Large Spatial Databases (SSD).*

Vandeurzen, L.; Gyssens, M.; and Van Gucht, D. (2001). "On the Expressiveness of Linear-Constraint Query Languages for Spatial Databases." *Theoretical Computer Science* 254(1-2): 423–463.

Vazirgiannis, M., and Wolfson, O. (2001). "A Spatiotemporal Model and Language for Moving Objects on Road Networks." In: *Proceedings of the Seventh International Symposium on Spatial and Temporal Databases (SSTD).*

Wolfson, O.; Cao, H.; Lin, H.; Trajcevski, G.; Zhang, F.; and Rishe, N. (2002). "Management of Dynamic Location Information in DOMINO." In: *Proceedings of the Eighth International Conference on Extending Database Technology (EDBT).*

Wolfson, O.; Chamberlain, S.; Dao, S.; Jiang, L.; and Mendez, G. (1998a). "Cost and Imprecision in Modeling the Position of Moving Objects." In: *Proceedings of the Fourteenth International Conference on Data Engineering (ICDE).*

Wolfson, O.; Sistla, A. P.; Chamberlain, S.; and Yesha, Y. (1999a). "Updating and Querying Databases that Track Mobile Units." *Distributed and Parallel Databases* 7: 257–287.

Wolfson, O.; Sistla, A. P.; Xu, B.; Zhou, J.; and Chamberlain, S. (1999b). "DOMINO: Databases for Moving Objects Tracking." In: *Proceedings of the ACM SIGMOD Conference on Management of Data.*

Wolfson, O.; Xu, B.; and Chamberlain, S. (2000). "Location Prediction and Queries for Tracking Moving Objects." In: *Proceedings of the Sixteenth International Conference on Data Engineering (ICDE).*

Wolfson, O.; Xu, B.; Chamberlain, S.; and Jiang, L. (1998b). "Moving Objects Databases: Issues and Solutions." In: *Proceedings of the Tenth International Conference on Scientific and Statistical Database Management (SSDBM).*

Worboys, M. F. (1994). "A Unified Model for Spatial and Temporal Information." *The Computer Journal* 37(1): 26–34.

Worboys, M. F., and Duckham, M. (2004). *GIS: A Computing Perspective.* 2nd ed. Boca Raton, FL: CRC Press.

Xu, X.; Han, J.; and Lu, W. (1990). "RT-tree: An Improved R-tree Index Structure for Spatiotemporal Databases." In: *Proceedings of the Fourth International Symposium on Spatial Data Handling (SDH).*

Zaniolo, C.; Ceri, S.; Faloutsos, C.; Snodgrass, R. T.; Subrahmanian, V. S.; and Zicari, R. (1997). *Advanced Database Systems.* San Francisco: Morgan Kaufmann Publishers.

Zhang, D.; Gunopulos, D.; Tsotras, V. J.; and Seeger, B. (2003a). "Temporal and Spatio-Temporal Aggregations over Data Streams Using Multiple Time Granularities." *Information Systems* 28(1-2): 61–84.

Zhang, J.; Zhu, M.; Papadias, D.; Tao, Y.; and Lee, D. L. (2003b). "Location-Based Spatial Queries." In: *Proceedings of the ACM SIGMOD Conference on Management of Data.*

Zheng, B., and Lee, D. L. (2001). "Semantic Caching in Location-Dependent Query Processing." In: *Proceedings of the Seventh International Symposium on Spatial and Temporal Databases (SSTD).*

Citation Index

A
Abraham and Roddick, 1999 55
Acharya et al., 1999 327
Agarwal et al., 2003 319
Almeida and Güting, 2005 320, 324
Arge et al., 1999 319
Armstrong, 1983 54

B
Basch et al., 1997 319
Beckmann et al., 1990 319
Behr and Schneider, 2001 185
Belussi et al., 1997 260
Benetis et al., 2002 325
Bentley and Ottmann, 1979 216
Bhargava and Gadia, 1993 30
Brinkhoff, 2002 322, 324
Brinkhoff, 2005 323

C
Chandrasekaran and Franklin, 2002 326
Chazelle, 1991 260
Chen and Revesz, 2004 328
Chen et al., 2000 325, 326
Cheng et al., 2004 98
Choi and Chung, 2002 327
Chomicki and Revesz, 1997 260
Chomicki and Revesz, 1999 260
Civilis et al., 2004 97, 324
Clifford and Croker, 1987 30
Cotelo Lema et al., 2003 127, 145, 185, 216
Croom, 1978 54

D
de Berg et al., 2000 216, 319
Djafri et al., 2002 185

E
Egenhofer and Franzosa, 1991 185
Egenhofer and Herring, 1990 185
Egenhofer et al., 1989 54, 185
Egenhofer, 1989 55
Egenhofer, 1991 55
Elmasri and Navathe, 2003 30
Erwig and Schneider, 1999a 185
Erwig and Schneider, 1999b 185
Erwig and Schneider, 2000 185
Erwig and Schneider, 2002 185
Erwig and Schneider, 2003 185
Erwig et al., 1999 30, 184

F
Forlizzi et al., 2000 145, 184, 185, 216
Frank and Kuhn, 1986 54
Frentzos, 2003 320, 324

G

Garcia-Molina et al., 2002 30
Garey et al., 1978 216, 260
Gedik and Liu, 2004 326
Griffiths et al., 2001a 185
Griffiths et al., 2001b 185
Grumbach et al., 1997 259, 260
Grumbach et al., 1998 259
Grumbach et al., 2000 259
Grumbach et al., 2001 259
GSTD, 2005 323
G-TERD, 2005 323
Gupta et al., 2004 324
Güting and Schneider, 1995 30
Güting et al., 1995 30, 216
Güting et al., 2000 112, 117, 127, 184, 185
Güting et al., 2005 185, 323, 324
Güting, 1994a 30
Güting, 1994b 324
Guttman, 1984 319

H

Hadjieleftheriou et al., 2002 320
Hadjieleftheriou et al., 2003 327
Hadjieleftheriou et al., 2005 320
Hage et al., 2003 324
Huang et al., 1997 324

J

Jensen et al., 2003a 324
Jensen et al., 2003b 324
Jensen et al., 2004 319

K

Kanellakis et al., 1990 259, 260
Kanellakis et al., 1995 259, 260
Keil, 1985 260
Kifer et al., 2005 30
Kollios et al., 1999 319
Kollios et al., 2001 319
Kollios et al., 2005 319
Kothuri et al., 2004 30
Koubarakis et al., 2003 30
Kuper et al., 2000 259

L

Laurini and Thompson, 1992 30
Lazaridis et al., 2002 326
Lee and Preparata, 1977 260

M

Madden et al., 2002 325
Matousek, 1992 319
McCreight, 1985 319
Mehlhorn, 1984 260
Mokbel et al., 2003 320
Mokbel et al., 2004 326
Mokhtar and Su, 2004 98
Mokhtar et al., 2002 260

N

Nascimento and Silva, 1998 319

O

Onofrio and Pourrabas, 2003 185
Oporto, 2005 323
Overmars, 1983 319
Özsoyoglu and Snodgrass, 1995 30

P

Papadias et al., 2002 326
Papadias et al., 2003 324
Patel et al., 2004 319
Peuquet and Duan, 1995 55
Peuquet, 2001 55
Pfoser and Jensen, 1999 98, 322
Pfoser and Jensen, 2003 320, 324
Pfoser and Rodriguez, 2005 322
Pfoser et al., 2000 319
Preparata and Shamos, 1991 216

R

Revesz and Chen, 2003 328
Revesz, 2002 259
Rigaux et al., 2002 30, 216, 259, 319
Rigaux et al., 2003 259, 260
Roth, 2004 321

S
Saglio and Moreira, 2001 322
Saltenis et al., 2000 319
Samet, 1990 274
Sarda, 1990 30
Schiller and Voisard, 2004 31
Schrijver, 1986 260
Segev and Shoshani, 1987 30
Sellis et al., 1987 319
Shahabi et al., 2003 324
Shekhar and Chawla, 2003 30, 216, 319
Shekhar and Liu, 1997 324
Sistla and Wolfson, 1995 97
Sistla et al., 1997 97
Sistla et al., 1998 97
Snodgrass 1995 30
Snodgrass and Ahn, 1986 30
Snodgrass, 1995 30
Song and Roussopoulos, 2001 325
Speicys et al., 2003 324
Su et al., 2001 260
Sun et al., 2004 326, 327

T
Tansel et al., 1993 30
Tao and Papadias, 2001 319
Tao and Papadias, 2003 325
Tao et al., 2003a 319
Tao et al., 2003b 327
Tao et al., 2003c 327
Tao et al., 2004 326
Terry et al., 1992 325
Theodoridis et al., 1996 319
Theodoridis et al., 1998 319
Theodoridis et al., 1999 322
Tøssebro and Güting, 2001 185, 322
Tøssebro and Nygård, 2002 185
Tøssebro and Nygård, 2003 185
Tøssebro, 2002 185
Tøssebro, 2005 322
Trajcevski et al., 2002 98
Trajcevski et al., 2004 98
Tzouramanis et al., 2002 322

V
Vandeurzen et al., 1995 260
Vandeurzen et al., 2001 260
Vandeurzen, 1999 260
Vazirgiannis and Wolfson, 2001 323

W
Wolfson et al., 1998a 97
Wolfson et al., 1998b 30, 97
Wolfson et al., 1999a 97
Wolfson et al., 1999b 98
Wolfson et al., 2000 98
Wolfson et al., 2002 98
Worboys and Duckham, 2004 30
Worboys, 1994 54

X
Xu et al., 1990 319

Z
Zaniolo et al., 1997 13, 30
Zhang et al., 2003a 326
Zhang et al., 2003b 325
Zheng and Lee, 2001 325

Index

A

Absolute time 11
Abstract data types
  approach 99–105
  language embedding 104–5
  See also Data types
Abstract model 105–36
  data types 106–8
  data types definition 108–13
  definitions 102
  discrete model vs. 102–4
  infinite relations 218–25
  operations on nontemporal types 114–21
  operations overview 113–14
  temporal types correspondence 138
  type system 136
  See also Discrete model
Access rights management 3
Adaptive dead-reckoning policy 82
Aggregate functions 105
Aggregation 119–20
  computation 326
  defined 119
  lifted operations 210
  operations 119
  temporal 151, 156–57
  unlifted mode 210
Algebraic topology 36
Algebra operations
  difference 255–57
  implementation 254–57
  intersection 254
  join 254
  product 254
  projection 255
  selection 254
  union 254
Algorithms
  combined search 315
  lifted operation 204–15
  normalization 250, 253
  operations on temporal data types 192–204
  plane sweep 196
  query processing 51–53, 324
  spatio-temporal operation 91–95
  spatio-temporal predicate 91–95
  split 291
  temporal data type operation 192–204
  traversed 198
`And` operation 215
`Area` operation 211
Assignments
  defined 8, 104
  variable 69
`Atinstant` operation 197
`Atmax` operation 202
`Atmin` operation 202
Atomic constraints 225, 228
`Atperiods` operation 198
Attributes 76
  data types 187

- dynamic 58, 60

Attributes *(cont'd.)*
- static 60
- value timestamps 14

B

Base types 106, 108–9
- discrete model 137
- operations for 121
- temporal units for 144

Basic spatio-temporal predicates 157–59
Bhargava's data model 17
Bitemporal conceptual data model (BCDM) 18
Bitemporal databases 11
Bitemporal elements (BTEs) 35–36
- defined 36
- example 36
- graphical representation 35, 36

Bitemporal relations 12, 13
Bitemporal space 16
Boolean operations 215
Bounded time space 10
Bounding boxes 9
- load-time 287
- minimum (MBBs) 262, 263–64, 265, 276
- moving, intersection 289
- update-time 287

C

Candidate sets 92
Cartridge 9
Catalog structures 270–71
- defined 270
- dynamic 271
- illustrated 271

Cell decomposition 256, 257
`Center` operation 210
Change
- continuous 23
- of direction 127
- discrete 23, 33
- rate of 126–28, 202–4

Closure 105–6
Coalescing 20
Combinatorial topology 36
Combinator relationships 161
Combined queries 312–13, 314
Components 48
Compositions 163
- as associative operation 164
- constriction 160
- derived 162
- distributivity 166
- temporal 161, 163

Consistency 106
Constraint database approach 217–57
- abstract model 218–25
- constraint model 239–57
- discrete model 225–38
- main ideas 217

Constraint relations 218, 225–38
- defined 225
- linear 230
- relational algebra 230–38
- representation 239

Constraints
- atomic 225, 228
- conjunction of 226
- half-plane 226
- linear 228
- model implementation 239–57
- polynomial 228
- representation 229
- representation of spatial data types 227
- spatial modeling with 225–29

Constriction composition 160
Continuity 134, 135
Continuous changes 23
Continuous movement 159
Continuous queries 58, 62, 63, 71
Continuous time 11
Convex polygons
- building from triangulation 248–50
- intersecting 251
- *See also* Polygons

Cost
- derivation function 78

information 80
uncertainty 79
update 79
Cycles
defined 141
edge-disjoint 141
edge-inside 141
infinite 175
quasi 175

D

Data
blade 9
capture 321–22
independence 2
loading 240–50, 275
protection 2
test, generating 322–23
Database management systems (DBMSs) 1–3
classical 3
component registration interfaces 9
data model 2
defined 1
functions 2–3
implementation 3–4
query and data manipulation language 2
three-level architecture 2
Databases
bitemporal 11
dynamics 275
historical 11
history 61–62
image 4
roles 1–2
rollback 11
snapshot 11
spatial 3–9
state 62
temporal 9–21
Data models
BCDM 18
Bhargava's 17
extending 12–19
HRDM 14–15
linear constraint 229–30
Sarda 15
temporal, classification 14
Data structures 187–92
as attribute data types 187
general requirements 187–88
kinetic 303
nontemporal data types 188–90
partition tree 267–70
quadtree 274
strategy 188
temporal data types 190–92
unit function 190
Data types
abstract 99–105
abstract model 106–13
attribute 187
auxiliary 188
base 106, 108–9
formal definition of 108–13
range 112
spatial 107, 109–11
temporal 112–13
time 107, 111–12
See also specific data types
`Date` data type 11
Dead-reckoning polices 82–84
adaptive 82
cost-based optimization 80–81
defined 77
disconnection detection 83
speed 82
Deftime index 191, 193, 205
`Deftime` operation 195
De Morgan's law 170
Dense time 10–11
`Derivable` operation 203, 213
Derivation
cost function 78
defined 59
moving objects 78
`Derivative` operation 103, 127, 203
Derived combinators 168

Derived compositions 162
Derived values 8, 105
Development graphs
  defined 174
Development graphs *(cont'd.)*
  moving point 175
  moving region 175
  paths 175
  point/point 184
  point/region 174
  two moving regions 176
Development paths 175
Developments
  concise syntax for 162–65
  factorization 171–72
  normal form 166
  "normalized" mode 164
  query, in STQL 177–80
  querying 180
  "raw" mode 164
  specifying 159
  on two moving regions 180
Difference operation 43, 44, 255–57
Direction
  change of 127
  function 121
  operation 214
Disconnection detection dead-reckoning policy 83
Discrete changes 23, 33
Discrete model 136–50
  abstract model vs. 102–4
  definitions 102
  nontemporal types 139–43
  overview 136–39
  temporal types 143–50
  temporal types correspondence 138
  type system 137
  See also Abstract model
Discrete time
  defined 10
  domain 48
Disjunction 227
Disk page capacity 263
Distance function 121, 212
Double negation 169
Dual data transformation approach 292–99
  almost optimal solution 294–95
  average time improvement 295–98
  indexing in two dimensions 298–99
  lower bounds 293–94
  time-space representation 292–93
Duality 266–67
  defined 266
  transform 266, 267
  use 267
Dynamic attributes
  defined 58
  MOST 60
  values 58
  See also Attributes

E

Event-based approach 48–53
  model 48–50
  query processing algorithms 51–53
Event relations 19
Events
  list 49
  location, set of 25
  region 26
  region, set of 26
  in space and time 24
  temporal ordering 49
Exact match queries 261
Existential expansion 165
Extender 9
External partition trees 267–70
External priority search trees 271–72
External range trees 272–74
  defined 272
  kinetic 301–3
  three-sided range queries 272–73
  update 274
  use 273

F

Faces 111

defined 141
edge-disjoint 142
moving 149

Filter(s) 194–95
defined 194
step 195

Final operation 199

First-cycle-in-face 191

Flat relations 218–23

Formulas 65, 66
conjunctive 71
evaluating 72
satisfaction 69–70
subformulas 72
well-formed 68, 72
See also FTL

FTL 64–77
conjunctive formulas 71
defined 57, 64
formulas 65, 66
formulas satisfaction 69–70
implementation 67
instantaneous queries 65
query evaluation 71–77
query examples 64–66
semantics 68–71
symbols 66–67
symbols definition 68–69
syntax 66–68
variable assignment 69
well-formed formulas 68

Future database history 62

G

Genericity 106

Geographic information systems (GIS) 4

Geometrically independent 36–37

Geometric index structures 261

Global Positioning System (GPS) 78

Global rebuilding 271

GSTD generator 322

H

Halfsegments 188
left 189
lexicographical sort 198
right 189

Historical relational data model (HRDM) 14–15

Historical time 11

Histories of movement 99–180
abstract model 105–36
approach based on abstract data types 99–105
discrete model 136–50
spatio-temporal predicates/developments 150–80

Hough-X transform 292, 296

Hough-Y transform 295, 298

I

Image databases 4

Indexed sequential access method (ISAM) 261

Indexing trajectories 306–16
preservation 306
query processing 312–16
STR-tree 306, 307–10
TB-tree 306, 310–12

Index rebuilding 282

Index structures 261
geometric 261
spatio-temporal 261–62
temporal 261

Infinite relations 218–25

Infinite time space 10

Information cost 80

Initial operation 199

Inside operation 209

Instantaneous queries 62, 63
defined 63
FTL 65, 71

Instantiations 72, 74

Instant predicates 160, 161

Instant type 11, 111–12

Integrity constraints 3

Interior cusps 243

Intersection
computing, of set of half-planes 251–52

constraint relations 234–36
convex polygons 251
evaluation method 234
operation 43, 44, 208, 210
sectors 256
symbolic relations 236
`Interval` data type 11
Intervals
construction 128
Intervals *(cont'd.)*
disjoint, finite set 142
load-time bounding 287
ordered lists 199
unit 143
update-time bounding 287

J

Join queries 279

K

Kernel algebra 128
Kinds 108
Kinetic B-trees 301
external, time-responsive indexing with 304–6
time-responsive indexing with 303–4
Kinetic external range trees 301–3
K-simplex
boundary 38–39
C 37–38
oriented 38
spanned 37

L

Lifted operation algorithms 204–15
aggregation 210
Boolean 215
distance and direction 212–14
numeric properties 211–12
predicates 205–8
set operations 208–10
Lifting 132
defined 113, 129
operations to time-dependent operations 128–32
temporally, topological predicates 155
Linear constraints 228
data model 229–30
form 229
formulas 229
relation 230
representation 239
See also Constraints
Lines
defined 4–5, 5
moving 147
segments 140
symbolic relations 233, 234
`Line` type 6, 7, 109–10, 111, 139–40
Load-time bounding intervals/boxes 287
Location management 57–59
derivation 59
dynamic attributes 58
perspective 21–22
problem 58
Locations
database 77
events, set of 25
operation 196
stepwise constant 25
valid for time period 24
Location update policies 77
dead-reckoning 82–84
defined 82
Location updates 77–84
background 77–78
cost-based optimization 80–81
dead-reckoning policies 82–84
information cost model 78–80

M

Many-sorted algebra 102
Maximal chains 74
Mdirection operation 204
Minimum bounding boxes (MBBs) 262, 263, 264, 265

defined 262
of moving point 276
overlapping 263–64
R+-tree 264–65
R*-tree 264
spatial objects indexed by 263
Minimum bounding rectangles (MBRs) 9, 262
Minimum bounding volumes (MBVs) 92
Minus operation 209
Monotone polygons 241–48
decomposing into 241–45
defined 241
with diagonals added 246
numbering edges of 244
triangulating 245–48
See also Polygons
MOST 59–64
assumptions 59–60
database histories 61–62
defined 57
dynamic attributes 60
implementation 67
object position representation 61
queries 62–64
Time object 60
Motion vectors 22, 58
Movement indexing 281–306
dual data transformation approach 292–99
general strategies 282
kinetic B-trees 301
kinetic external range trees 301–3
time-oblivious, with multilevel partition trees 299–300
time-responsive 303–6
TPR-tree 283–92
See also Spatio-temporal indexing
Moving arguments 194
Moving faces 149
Moving objects 21–29
approximations of 275–76
databases 1
data modeling for 324
derivation 78
indexing requirements 274–81
location management perspective 21–22
location updates 77–84
querying, with uncertainty 88–91
questions 23
spatio-temporal data perspective 22–23
temporal/spatial projection 278
uncertainty of trajectory 84–95
Moving points
defined 23
development graph 175
MBB of 276
projection of 196
questions 24
See also Points
Moving queries 284
Moving reals 100, 101
Moving regions
defined 23
development graph 175
questions 25
Moving segments 147, 148
Multilevel partition trees 299, 300
Multistep queries 8, 104
Multiversion kinetic B-trees 281

N

Navigational queries 312
Nearest-neighbor queries 279
Negation
double 169
predicate 166–67
Nested relations 223–25
Networks
defined 5, 6
movement in 323–24
Next-cycle-in-face 191
No_components operation 211
Nontemporal types
abstract model 114–21
aggregation 119–20
auxiliary 188
classification 114

- data structures 188–90
- discrete model 139–43
- distance and direction 121
- notations for signatures 115–16
- numeric operations 120–21
- operations for base types 121
- operations on 114–21
- predicates 116–17
- set operations 117–19

Normal form 240
Normalization
- algorithm 250, 253
- of symbolic tuples 250–53

Not operation 215
Numeric properties 211–12

O

Objects
- collections, spatially related 4
- modeling 4
- motion plan 85
- moving 21–29
- point 59
- polygon 59
- position representation 61
- reflection 167
- sets, operations on 133–36
- spatio-bitemporal 33–47

Operations
- aggregation 119–20
- algebra, implementation 254–57
- base types 121
- Boolean 215
- defining 105
- derivative 127
- generic 115
- interval construction 128
- lifted 204–15
- lifting 128–32
- on nontemporal types 114–1121
- overview 113–14
- relational algebra 231
- set 117–19, 208–10
- sets of objects 133–36
- symbolic relations 231
- temporal types 121–23
- time constants 125
- when 132–33
- *See also specific operations*

Oriented *k*-simplex 38
Or operation 215

P

Partitions
- defined 5
- illustrated 5
- simpicial 267–68

Partition trees 267–70, 294
- building 268–69
- defined 267
- external 267–70
- multilevel 299, 300
- partial rebuilding 269
- primary 300

Passes operation 202
Past database history 62
Perimeter operation 211
Period data type 11
Period predicates 160, 161
Periods data type 11
Persistent queries 62, 63–64
Plane sweep algorithm 196
Point objects 59
Points
- as constraint tuple 240
- defined 4
- definition 140
- development graph 174
- illustrated 5
- interaction with 124–26
- moving 23
- units 145

Point sets
- defined 113
- interaction with 124–26

Points type 6, 7, 109, 111
Polygon chains 241, 242
Polygons 59

- convex 248–50
- decomposing, into monotone polygons 241–45
- monotone 241–48
- remaining 245
- simple 242

Polylines representation 241

Polynomial constraints 228

Predicates 116–17
- binary 117
- compound 179
- constriction 160
- disjoint 152
- inside 152
- instant 160, 161
- lifted operations 205–8
- meet 152
- negation 166–67
- period 160, 161
- reflection 168
- sequencing syntax 162
- spatial 177
- spatio-temporal 88, 89, 90, 91, 150–80
- topological 151, 152–55
- unary 116

Present operation 199–200

Projections 122–24
- constraint relations 237–38
- to domain/range 195–97
- implementation 255
- moving point 196
- region unit 197

Q

Quadratic polynomials 212

Quadtrees 274

Quantification ordering 157

Quasi-cycles 175

Queries
- combined 312–13, 314
- continuous 58, 62, 63, 71
- exact match 261
- formulating 8
- FTL 64–66, 71–77
- instantaneous 62, 63, 65, 71
- join 279
- MOST 62–64
- moving 284
- moving objects, with uncertainty 88–91
- multistep 8, 104
- navigational 312
- nearest-neighbor 279
- orthogonal range 295
- persistent 62, 63–64
- range 261
- reverse nearest neighbor 325
- with SDT operations 7
- selection 278
- semantics 62
- sequential access 261
- spatial-temporal database 46–48
- spatio-temporal development 180
- timeslice 284
- topological 312, 313
- trajectory-based 312
- window 284, 292

Query algebra 46

Query languages
- relational 230
- spatio-temporal 176
- visual 176

Query optimizer 2

Query prism 92

Query processing algorithms 51–53, 324
- run-time complexity 51, 52, 53
- variation 52, 53

R

Radio frequency identification (RFID) transponders 321–22

Range queries 261

Range types 112

Rangevalues operation 193, 195

Rate of change 126–28

Refinement partitions 194

Reflection 167–68
- object 167–68
- predicate 168

propagation 170–71
Regions
border 173
cusp 243
defined 5
development graph 174
events 26
holes 5
moving 23, 173
semantics definition 142
stepwise constant 26
symbolic relations 233, 235
unit 148, 149
valid for time period 26
validity 325
`Region` type 6, 7, 110, 111, 141–42
Relational algebra
for constraint relations 230–38
intersection 234–36
operations 231
Relational algebra *(cont'd.)*
projection 237–38
selection 232–34
Relations
bitemporal 12, 13
constraint 218, 225–38
event 19
flat 218–23
infinite 218–25
linear constraint 229
nested 223–25
representation of 239
snapshot 12
state 19
symbolic 227, 230
transaction-time 13
TSQL2 19
valid-time 12
Relative time 11
Reverse nearest neighbor queries 325
Rollback databases 11
Root record 188
R-tree family 262–66
R+-tree 264–66
R*-tree 264
R-trees 262–64

S

Sarda data model 15
Segment uncertainty zone 87
`SELECT` clause 48
Selection
constraint relations 232–34
implementation 254
queries 278
Selection queries 278
Selectivity estimation 326–28
Sequences
development language of 163
of spatio-temporal predicates 159–62
Sequential access 261
Set operations 117–19
availability 117
lifted 208–10
list of 118
Sets
numeric properties 120–21
object, operations on 133–36
point 113, 124–26
Signatures
groups 117
notation for 115–16
type systems 108
Simplex range searching 293–94
Simplicial complexes 36
Simplicial partitions 267–68
Sketches 326
Sliced representation 149–50, 190
Snapshot databases 11
Spatial access methods (SAMs) 261
Spatial databases 3–9
collection of objects 5
data types 6–8
goal 3
implementation strategy 9
modeling concepts 4–6
queries with 7
single objects 4–5

study motivation 4
Spatial data types (SDTs) 6–8, 107, 109–11
constraint representation of 227
defined 6
`line` 6, 7, 109–10, 111
`points` 6, 7, 109, 111
`region` 6, 7, 110, 111
temporal databases with 26–27
temporal units for 144–49
See also Data types
Spatial objects
collection 263
R-tree representation 263
topological predicates for 152–54
See also Objects
Spatial predicates 177
Spatial selection operation 44
Spatio-bitemporal objects 33–47
application scenario 33–35
bitemporal elements 35–36
defined 39
modeled as simplicial complexes 36–39
See also Objects
Spatio-bitemporal ß-product 42
Spatio-temporal access methods (STAMs) 274
construction of 276
efficient design 275
evaluation of 281
past, survey 279–81
Spatio-temporal conjunction 168
Spatio-temporal data
classification 23–26
events in space and time 24
locations for time period 24
moving entities 25
moving entities with extent 26
region events in space and time 26
regions valid for time period 26
set of location events 25
set of region events 26
stepwise constant locations 25
stepwise constant regions 26
view 23
Spatio-temporal databases
management systems (STDBMS) 275
past 33–47
querying 46–48
Spatio-temporal data perspective 22–23
Spatio-temporal data types 27–29
`mpoint` 27, 28, 99
`mregion` 27, 28, 99
operations 28
Spatio-temporal grouping 180
Spatio-temporal implication 168, 173
Spatio-temporal indexing 261–316
current and near-future movement 281–306
geometric preliminaries 262–74
moving objects requirements 274–81
multidimensional space 262–66
trajectories 306–16
in two dimensions 298–99
Spatio-temporal index structures 261–62
approximations of moving objects 275–76
change timestamp granularity 278
construction 277–78
database dynamics 275
data set supported 275
data types/data sets supported 277
fully-dynamic 277
growing 277
insert/split operations 278
loading of data 275
pack/purge operations 278
peculiarity of time dimension 276
query processing 278–79
query support 276–77
specification criteria 277–79
specifics 274–77
valid vs. transaction time 275
Spatio-temporal joins 150
Spatio-temporal objects 33–47
application scenario 33–35
bitemporal elements 35–36
operations 41–45
querying 46–48
See also Objects
Spatio-temporal operations. *See* Operations

Spatio-temporal predicates 88, 89, 150–80
algebra 165–72
algorithms for 91–95
basic 157–59
canonical collection 174–76
defined 88
definitions 89
disjoint 158
examples 90
integrating 178
motivation 151–52
nature of 151
relationships among 91
sequences of 159–62
temporal aggregation 156–57
temporal composition 151
See also Predicates
Spatio-Temporal R-tree (STR-tree) 306, 307–10
defined 307
preservation parameter 308
Spatio-Temporal R-tree (STR-tree) *(cont'd.)*
spatial closeness 307
trajectory preservation 307
Spatio-temporal selections 150
Speed dead-reckoning policy 82
Speed operation 204
State relations 19
ST-comparable 45
ST-complexes 41, 43
difference 43–44
equality 41
integrated into relational setting 46
spatial selection 44–45
use of 46
ST-minimum 45
ST-ß-product 43
ST-simplex 40–41
C 40
defined 40
example 40
set 43
Subattributes 60, 61
Symbolic relations 227, 230
complement, computing 231
line 233, 234
operations 231
region 233, 235
representation of 239–40
storage 240
subrelations 239
See also Relations
Symbolic tuples 227, 228, 230, 238, 250–53

T

Temporal aggregation 151, 156–57
Temporal alternative 165–66
Temporal composition 161, 163, 165
Temporal databases 9–21
coalescing 20
data model extension 12–19
defined 11
goal 10
with spatial data types 26–27
time dimensions 11–12
time domain 10–11
TSQL2 19–21
Temporal data type operation algorithms 192–204
common considerations 192–95
filtering approach 194–95
interaction with domain/range 197–202
notations 192–93
projection to domain/range 195–97
rate of change 202–4
refinement partitions 194
subset selection 192
Temporal index structures 261
Temporal ordering 49
Temporal selection operation 45
Temporal types 112–13
abstract model 121–33
data structures 190–92
defined 114
discrete model 143–50
interaction with point/point sets 124–26

operations on 121–33
project to domain and range 122–24
rate of change 126–28
sliced representation 149–50
units for base types 144
units for spatial types 144–49
unit types 143
Temporal uncertainty 85
Test data generators 324
Time
absolute 11
bounded model 18
complexity 200
constants, construction 125
continuous 11
data types 11
dense 10–11
dimensions 11–12, 13
discrete 10
domain 10–11
intervals 73–74, 75
managing 9–10
relative 11
space 10
transaction 11
type 111–12
valid 11
values 49
`Time` data type 11
Time-oblivious indexing 299–300
Time-parameterized bounding box 286
Time-parameterized R-tree (TPR-tree) 281, 283–92
defined 283
deletions 292
indexing 283
insertion 291
problem description 283–84
problem parameters 285–86
querying 287–90
query types 284–85
reference position 283
split algorithm 291
structure 286–87
tree organization heuristics 290–91
Time-responsive indexing 303–6
with multiversion external kinetic range trees 304–6
with multiversion kinetic B-trees 303–4
Timeslice queries 284
`Timestamp` data type 11
Timestamps
attribute value 14
change granularity 278
period 14
type used 13
Topological distance 154
Topological predicates 151, 152–55
defined 151
illustrated 153
for spatial objects 152–54
temporally lifting 155
Topological queries 312, 313
Trajectories 293
concept 84
expected location 85
indexing 306–16
model 85
motion curve 87
partial, extraction 314
as polyline 85
segment volume 86
uncertainty 57, 84–95
uncertainty concepts 86–88
volume 87
Trajectory-based queries 312
Trajectory-Bundle tree (TB-tree) 306, 310–12
combined search algorithm 315
defined 310
insertion into 311
linked lists 316
structure 311
structure illustration 312
trajectory bundle 310
`Trajectory` operation 196
Transaction time 11, 13

Traversed operation 197, 222
Triangulation 245–50
  building convex polygons from 248–50
  monotone polygon 245–48
TSQL2 19–21
  capabilities 19–21
  defined 19
  relations 19
Turn operation 204
Type constructors 108
Type systems
  abstract model 136
  defined 106
  discrete model 137
  as signature 108
  See also Data types
Type variables 115

U

Uncertainty
  cost 79
  cost function 79
  querying moving objects with 88–91
Uncertainty *(cont'd.)*
  segment zone 87
  temporal 85
  threshold 86
  of trajectory 84–95
  zone 94
Union operation 43, 44, 254
Unit projection bounding box 191
Unit(s)
  for base types 144
  defined 143
  for discretely changing types 190
  functions 143, 191
  interval 143
  point 145
  refinement partitions 194
  region 148, 149
  for spatial types 144–49
  types 143
Update cost 79
Update-time bounding intervals/boxes 287

V

Valid time 11
  dimensions 12
  relations 12
Variable assignment 69
Velocity operation 204
Visual query language 176

W

Well-formed formulas 68, 72
When operation 132–33
WHERE clause 46, 47
Window queries 284, 292

About the Authors

Ralf Hartmut Güting has been a full professor in Computer Science at the University of Hagen, Germany, since 1989. He received his Diploma and Dr. rer. nat. degrees from the University of Dortmund in 1980 and 1983, respectively, and became a professor at that university in 1987. From 1981 until 1984 his main research area was Computational Geometry. After a one-year stay at the IBM Almaden Research Center in 1985, extensible and spatial database systems became his major research interests; more recently, also spatio-temporal or moving objects databases. He is an associate editor of the *ACM Transactions on Database Systems* and an editor of *GeoInformatica*. He is also chairing the steering committee of the SSTD series of conferences (International Symposium on Spatial and Temporal Databases).

Markus Schneider has been an Assistant Professor in the Department of Computer and Information Science and Engineering (CISE) at the University of Florida and a member of the Database Systems Research and Development Center since 2002. He received his Diploma degree in Computer Science from the University of Dortmund, Germany, in 1990. In 1995, he received his Doctoral degree (Dr. rer. nat.) in Computer Science from the University of Hagen, Germany. After that, until 2001, he held a postdoctoral position at the University of Hagen. He is on the editorial board of *GeoInformatica*. His research interests are spatial and spatio-temporal databases, moving objects databases, fuzzy databases, and biological databases.